Impact of Disruptive Technologies on the Socio-Economic Development of Emerging Countries

Fredrick Japhet Mtenzi
Institute for Educational Development, The Aga Khan University, Tanzania

George S. Oreku
The Open University of Tanzania, Tanzania

Dennis M. Lupiana
Institute of Finance Management, Tanzania

IGI Global
PUBLISHER of TIMELY KNOWLEDGE

A volume in the Advances in Human and Social Aspects of Technology (AHSAT) Book Series

Published in the United States of America by
IGI Global
Information Science Reference (an imprint of IGI Global)
701 E. Chocolate Avenue
Hershey PA, USA 17033
Tel: 717-533-8845
Fax: 717-533-8661
E-mail: cust@igi-global.com
Web site: http://www.igi-global.com

Library of Congress Cataloging-in-Publication Data

Names: Mtenzi, Fredrick, editor. | Oreku, George S., editor. | Lupiana, Dennis M., editor.
Title: Impact of disruptive technologies on the socio-economic development of emerging countries / Fredrick Mtenzi, George Oreku, and Dennis Lupiana, editors.
Description: Hershey, PA : Information Science Reference, [2023] | "The first edition of the "Mobile Technologies and Socio-Economic Development in Emerging Nations" was published in 2018 ... this book which is a second edition of the book we published in 2018 ..."--Introduction. | Includes bibliographical references and index. | Summary: "This book researches the design, development and usage of digital solutions that have impact in addressing societal problems in emerging economies, specifically addressing current developments, innovations, laws and legislation, research and analysis on the usage of digital solutions worldwide"-- Provided by publisher.
Identifiers: LCCN 2022039870 (print) | LCCN 2022039871 (ebook) | ISBN 9781668468739 (hardcover) | ISBN 9781668468746 (paperback) | ISBN 9781668468753 (ebook)
Subjects: LCSH: Information technology--Economic aspects--Developing countries. | Information technology--Social aspects--Developing countries. | Disruptive technologies--Developing countries. | Economic development--Developing countries. | Social planning--Developing countries.
Classification: LCC HC59.72.I55 I495 2023 (print) | LCC HC59.72.I55 (ebook) | DDC 303.48/33091724--dc23/eng/20220923
LC record available at https://lccn.loc.gov/2022039870
LC ebook record available at https://lccn.loc.gov/2022039871

This book is published in the IGI Global book series Advances in Human and Social Aspects of Technology (AHSAT) (ISSN: 2328-1316; eISSN: 2328-1324)

British Cataloguing in Publication Data
A Cataloguing in Publication record for this book is available from the British Library.

Advances in Human and Social Aspects of Technology (AHSAT) Book Series

Mehdi Khosrow-Pour, D.B.A.
Information Resources Management Association, USA

ISSN:2328-1316
EISSN:2328-1324

Mission

In recent years, the societal impact of technology has been noted as we become increasingly more connected and are presented with more digital tools and devices. With the popularity of digital devices such as cell phones and tablets, it is crucial to consider the implications of our digital dependence and the presence of technology in our everyday lives.

The **Advances in Human and Social Aspects of Technology (AHSAT) Book Series** seeks to explore the ways in which society and human beings have been affected by technology and how the technological revolution has changed the way we conduct our lives as well as our behavior. The AHSAT book series aims to publish the most cutting-edge research on human behavior and interaction with technology and the ways in which the digital age is changing society.

Coverage

- Philosophy of technology
- Cyber Behavior
- Technology Dependence
- Technology and Social Change
- Cyber Bullying
- Technoself
- Computer-Mediated Communication
- End-User Computing
- Activism and ICTs
- Technology Adoption

IGI Global is currently accepting manuscripts for publication within this series. To submit a proposal for a volume in this series, please contact our Acquisition Editors at Acquisitions@igi-global.com or visit: http://www.igi-global.com/publish/.

The Advances in Human and Social Aspects of Technology (AHSAT) Book Series (ISSN 2328-1316) is published by IGI Global, 701 E. Chocolate Avenue, Hershey, PA 17033-1240, USA, www.igi-global.com. This series is composed of titles available for purchase individually; each title is edited to be contextually exclusive from any other title within the series. For pricing and ordering information please visit http://www.igi-global.com/book-series/advances-human-social-aspects-technology/37145. Postmaster: Send all address changes to above address.

Titles in this Series

For a list of additional titles in this series, please visit: www.igi-global.com/book-series

Exergaming Intervention for Children, Adolescents, and Elderly People
Shahnawaz Khan (Bahrain Polytechnic, Bahrain) Thirunavukkarasu Kannapiran (S2 Integrators, USA) Arunachalam Muthiah (Karnavati University, India) and Sharad Shetty (Karnavati University, India)
Information Science Reference • ©2023 • 278pp • H/C (ISBN: 9781668463208) • US $215.00

Handbook of Research on Andragogical Leadership and Technology in a Modern World
Viktor Wang (California State University, San Bernardino, USA)
Information Science Reference • ©2023 • 474pp • H/C (ISBN: 9781668478325) • US $270.00

ICT as a Driver of Women's Social and Economic Empowerment
Pankaj Dhaundiyal (CHRIST University (Deemed), India) and Sana Moid (Amity University, India)
Information Science Reference • ©2023 • 306pp • H/C (ISBN: 9781668461181) • US $215.00

Handbook of Research on Digitalization Solutions for Social and Economic Needs
Richard Pettinger (University College London, UK) Brij B. Gupta (Asia University, Taiwan) Alexandru Roja (West University of Timisoara, Romania) and Diana Cozmiuc (West University of Timisoara, Romania)
Engineering Science Reference • ©2023 • 387pp • H/C (ISBN: 9781668441022) • US $380.00

Digital Psychology's Impact on Business and Society
Muhammad Anshari (Universiti Brunei Darussalam, Brunei) Abdur Razzaq (Universitas Islam Negeri Raden Fatah Palembang, Indonesia) Mia Fithriyah (Indonesia Open University, Indonesia) and Akmal Nasri Kamal (Universiti Brunei Darussalam, Brunei)
Information Science Reference • ©2023 • 330pp • H/C (ISBN: 9781668461082) • US $270.00

Frugal Innovation and Social Transitions in the Digital Era
Muhammad Nawaz Tunio (Mohammad Ali Jinnah University, Karachi, Pakistan) and Atia Bano Memon (University of Sindh, Badin Campus, Pakistan)
Information Science Reference • ©2023 • 208pp • H/C (ISBN: 9781668454176) • US $250.00

Handbook of Research on Implementing Digital Reality and Interactive Technologies to Achieve Society 5.0
Francesca Maria Ugliotti (Politecnico di Torino, Italy) and Anna Osello (Politecnico di Torino, Italy)
Information Science Reference • ©2022 • 731pp • H/C (ISBN: 9781668448540) • US $295.00

Exploring Ethical Problems in Today's Technological World
Tamara Phillips Fudge (Purdue University Global, USA)

IGI Global
PUBLISHER of TIMELY KNOWLEDGE

701 East Chocolate Avenue, Hershey, PA 17033, USA
Tel: 717-533-8845 x100 • Fax: 717-533-8661
E-Mail: cust@igi-global.com • www.igi-global.com

Table of Contents

Detailed Table of Contents

The growth of computer science, robotics, and artificial intelligence (AI) worldwide has been considered a catalyst for developments in several sectors including health, education, trade, and telecommunication. AI is now dominating every aspect of life, and it is not surprising that it has entered into several domains that are subject to negligence or negligence equivalents, including medical misconduct, data security, investment advice, and financial advice. This novel development has brought serious legal discussions about liability in the law of negligence. The language of liability in the law of negligence has put much weight on personhood. These and other reasons invite a critical discussion on the development of new jurisprudence in the law of negligence.

There is limited literature on the application of digital technology applications for disease surveillance in Tanzania. This chapter reviewed digital application technologies, existing challenges, and future perspectives in Tanzania. The data collection process involved searching for peer reviewed articles from databases such as Web of Science, Google Scholar, Scopus, and PubMed. Stakeholder consultation was also conducted through interviews of healthcare officials who were directly involved in disease surveillance process in Tanzania. Findings from this chapter showed that digital public health data in Tanzania is mainly collected through the HMIS monthly reports from IDSR. The main challenges affecting implementation of digital surveillance are poor internet, unreliable power supply, lack of integration between the existing and newly developed digital technologies, limited financial resources, and inadequate ICT personnel. The government of Tanzania should improve e-health apps funding and reporting of mobile health interventions for infectious diseases and NCDs using the WHO mERA checklist.

Healthcare services are dependent on health information systems (HIS), which enable health data collection and storage with improved management of healthcare service provision. However, several data security weaknesses in HIS have been identified by various studies in Tanzania. The majority are on data and information exchange leading to breaches of system security. In order to reduce security threats and accomplish security objectives (i.e., confidentiality, integrity, availability), disruptive technologies like blockchain must be used to address security breaches, attacks, and vulnerabilities of HISs. In this chapter, a problem-solving technique with digital innovative solutions for addressing real-world problems was used to arrive at the problem's solution. This chapter then shows how the data security weakness of HISs can be improved using the hyper-ledger blockchain. The system was virtually integrated with an existing HIS. Data storage security was attained through private data collection to meet security goals.

This chapter identifies climate-smart agriculture (CSA) practices and their impact on smallholder farmers in six African countries. Various CSA practices are discussed. Observations show that farmers who adopted CSA practices obtained positive results in terms of adaptability to climate change and productivity. Furthermore, internet of things (IoT)-enabled smart agricultural systems are explored. Observations indicate that IoT-based agricultural systems enable efficient utilization of farm inputs such as fertilizer, pesticides, herbicides, and water. Also, using IoT systems, it is possible to provide customized, location-specific, and easily understood climate data for smallholder farmers to facilitate decision making and planning of CSA practices. Therefore, this chapter has presented recommendations for the adoption of IoT-enabled CSA in African countries. IoT-enabled agricultural systems are recommended for a country like Senegal where climate data is considered an agricultural input and also for Tanzania where IoT devices such as UAVs are considered to be useful agricultural tools.

Innovative digital payment systems (DPS) are a crucial solution for greater financial inclusion assisting low-income households in overcoming poverty using lower-cost methods for managing their finances. The advancement in internet communication technologies and the arrival of e-commerce and e-business simulated digital payment systems providesvarious electronic payment options such as payment cards, mobile payments, mobile wallets, electronic cash, and contactless payment methods. This chapter discusses the current state of the art in digital payment systems in emerging markets. Also, it analyzes the advantages of DPS in emerging economies, challenges in emerging economies, the economic impact of DPS in emerging economies, cyber security issues in DPS, and the future of the DPS in emerging economies.

Digital technologies like smartphones, social media, the internet, software applications, websites, and e-books are redefining the educational landscape, which was accentuated amid the COVID-19 pandemic. This chapter discussed the impact of digital technologies in enabling academic institutions to perform their noble responsibilities in delivering instructions virtually during the lockdown. The effects of using these technologies and the challenges encountered by developing countries in migrating to the digital environment amid the lockdown with particular reference to the educational ecosystem in Nigeria was the focal point in the chapter. Striking among these challenges is the issue of compatibility, the high cost of internet data, inadequate digital literacy skill, and environmental distraction. Thus, it was recommended that administrators of academic institutions and regulatory bodies such as the National Universities Commission (NUC) must provide lecturers and students at all levels with adequate training to ensure operational productivity in the use of digital technologies and resources.

The experience of the COVID-19 pandemic has revealed a need for the educational sector in Africa to adopt innovative ways for assessment by leveraging technology with the increasing number of student enrollments at all levels of education. A systematic approach is also required to circumvent the challenges faced by developing countries transdisciplinary. Transdisciplinarity is still evolving and has been proved to be a viable tool for engagement, societal impact, new partnerships, fresh ideas, reality checks, new capacities, and systemic thinking leading to new career possibilities. This study conducted a documentary analysis of standardised examination administration in Africa and proposed a framework for action adopting a transdisciplinary approach to research for problem-solving. The study used a qualitative approach for collecting and analysing data from reports and documents supported by empirical findings from existing literature. The study created a framework for action through which the gains of the transdisciplinary approach can be translated to practice.

The chapter is on ICT skills training for the deaf to enhance employability prospects to improve social-economic development. Deaf employment is a global issue. ICT skills training might reduce the challenge. Little is known about ICT skills training for the deaf. The author interviewed 5 parents and 15 ICT skills training for the deaf graduates at the Open University of Tanzania. Data were collected using an interview guide with support from an experienced sign language interpreter. Findings indicated that ICT skills training increased participation in learning, employment, networking, and social inclusion. However, they faced challenges related to community perception, resources availability, affordability, connectivity, funding, and availability of ICT skills training opportunities that met their special learning needs. Based on the results, people with disabilities have to learn ICT skills that meet their unique special needs to reduce the negative effects of the impact of disruptive technologies and employability in the 4th Industrial Revolution.

In the COVID-19 pandemic crisis, educational institutions had to be temporarily shut down by their respective governments around the world in order to contain the spread of the virus. The pandemic globally engendered new ways of teaching and learning amidst the restrictions. Schools in emerging countries are mostly dependent on the traditional face-to-face method of teaching and learning and barely had any substantial experience in virtual education prior to the outbreak. Moreover, many countries lack adequate infrastructure for ICTs and internet usage. Nonetheless, these countries also adopted various digital technologies for virtual teaching and learning. This chapter discusses digital technologies and resources for learning in emerging countries under lockdown and proposes a research model for evaluating their impact amidst the effects of the digital divide.

Digital payments are increasingly becoming popular worldwide, especially in underdeveloped and developing countries, despite the challenges these countries face regarding required infrastructure and digital literacy. Digital payments have emerged as an important tool for governments to distribute the funds for social welfare schemes to their citizens directly in their accounts with zero corruption and delays. Socio-financial inclusion of society's deprived and marginalized section is another advantage of digital payments. Having access to transaction accounts, credit, savings products, and insurance helps the poor raise their incomes and become more resilient. Paperless and cashless transactions are a huge advantage of digital payments. This chapter aims to discuss the impacts of digital payments on the socio-economic factors in emerging markets and developing economies. In addition, it highlights the solution and recommendations for policymakers.

Tanzania's small-scale dairy industry faces similar challenges to those of other developing nations whereby insufficient infrastructure, outdated technology, and low productivity are serious problems

Preface

Global emergencies, such as the COVID-19 pandemic and environmental concerns, have challenged the readiness of societies and forced them to operate in more innovative ways. In response, the world has witnessed new technologies emerge and researchers continually finding better solutions to cope with these situations. It is crucial that these innovations are investigated so that we may better the world during times of crisis.

Our society has, of course, seen earlier times of significant transformation, spurred by inventions like the steam engine, railroad, telephone, and car. But never before have we seen technology develop so quickly (tripling in power every decade), change the boundaries of place and time, and transform the ways in which we interact, learn, and think.

In response, institutions of all stripes are struggling to modify their plans and operations. The fast development of digital technology is providing both new possibilities and difficulties for our society. Governments and businesses are restructuring to increase production, raise standards, and save costs. Whole sectors have undergone restructuring to better suit the demands of the digital era. It is hardly overstating things to suggest that information technology is profoundly altering how individuals interact with knowledge.

The *Impact of Disruptive Technologies on the Socio-Economic Development of Emerging Countries* provides relevant case studies, innovative disruptive applications, and the latest empirical research findings in the digital technology space. Additionally, it provides accounts of the design, development, and usage of digital solutions that have an impact on addressing societal problems in emerging economies. Covering topics such as e-social work, social media addiction, and adaptive testing, this premier reference source is an essential resource for government officials, entrepreneurs, politicians, business leaders, students and educators of higher education, sociologists, librarians, researchers, and academicians.

The review and selection procedure of the submitted chapter was performed carefully, with each manuscript being reviewed by at least three reviewers through a double-blind peer-review process. After reviewing, only 13 full chapters out of total 43 chapters submitted were accepted, giving an acceptance rate of about 30%. The accepted chapters covered the topics in adaptive testing, e-social work, educational assessment, ERP-based systems, learning resources, perception of social workers, public health surveillance, social media addiction, social media usage, socio-economic challenge, sustainable development.

Through extensive and annotated practical examples and easy-to-understand and easy-to-follow, this book explains the status of the current research enterprise, emerging trends affecting the world, and issues central to its future. An overview of the global challenges and describes long-term trends in responses from academia, policy makers, researchers and human resources. This new book will be useful in stimulating policy discussions especially among individuals and organizations that fund or perform academic research.

There are 13 separate chapters in the table of contents which have been covered thorough. In-depth analyses of the chapters are from major scientific research documents, including ICT applications, scientific research papers, literature reviews, review articles, and technology applications. The book may be used as a research manual for researchers, undergraduate and graduate students, a science writing classes, or companion text for advanced technology courses with a writing-intensive component, or for student-published work because of its extensive treatment of many means of communication. Each chapter also offers thorough discussion of composition, style, and writing mechanics which several are applicable to real-world instances.

Throughout examples that explain key text components and concepts provided, typical mistakes and examples were followed by successful corrections. Each book's chapter-by-chapter descriptions brought to life the book "Impact of Disruptive Technologies on the Socio-Economic Development of Emerging Countries" by these annotated examples.

Chapter 1: Impact of Disruptive Technologies on the Socio-Economic Development of Emerging Countries – Artificial Intelligence and Legal Liability in Tanzania

The growth of Computer science, robotics, and Artificial Intelligence (AI) worldwide has been considered a catalyst for developments in several sectors including health, education, trade, and telecommunication. AI is now dominating every aspect of life and is not surprising that it has entered into several domains that are subject to negligence or negligence equivalents, including medical misconduct, data security, investment advice, and financial advice. This novel development has brought serious legal discussions about liability in the law of negligence. The language of liability in the law of negligence has put much weight on personhood. These and other reasons invite a critical discussion on the development of new jurisprudence in the law of negligence.

Chapter 2: Application of Digital Technologies to Enhance Public Health Surveillance in Tanzania – Current Status, Challenges, and Future Perspective

There is limited literature on application of digital technology applications for disease surveillance in Tanzania. This chapter reviewed digital application technologies, existing challenges and future perspectives in Tanzania. The data collection process involved searching for peer reviewed articles from databases such as Web of Science, Google Scholar, Scopus, and PubMed. Stakeholder consultation was also conducted through interviews of healthcare officials who were directly involved in disease surveillance process in Tanzania. Findings from this chapter showed that, digital public health data in Tanzania is mainly collected through the HMIS monthly reports from IDSR. The main challenges affecting implementation of digital surveillance are poor internet, unreliable power supply, lack of integration between the existing and newly developed digital technologies, limited financial resources and inadequate ICT personnel. The government of Tanzania should improve e-health apps funding and reporting of mobile health interventions for infectious and NCDs using the WHO mERA checklist.

Chapter 3: Blockchain-Based Health Information Systems to Improve Data Security

Healthcare services are dependent on health information system (HIS), which has enabled health data collection and storage, with improved management of healthcare service provision. However, several data security weaknesses in the HIS have been identified by various studies in Tanzania. The majority are on data and information exchange leading to breaches of system security. In order to reduce security threats and accomplish security objectives (i.e., Confidentiality, Integrity, Availability), disruptive technologies like blockchain must be used to address security breaches, attacks, and vulnerabilities of HISs. In this chapter, a problem-solving-oriented technique with digital innovative solutions for addressing real-world problems was used to arrive at the problem's solution. This chapter then shows how the data security weakness of HISs can be improved using the Hyper-ledger blockchain. The system was virtually integrated with an existing HIS. Data storage security was attained through private data collection to meet security goals.

Chapter 4: Climate-Smart Agriculture and Internet of Things Systems for Agricultural Production Efficiency in African Countries

This chapter identifies climate-smart agriculture (CSA) practices and their impact on smallholder farmers in six African countries. Various CSA practices are discussed. Observations show that farmers who adopted CSA practices obtained positive results in terms of adaptability to climate change and productivity. Furthermore, Internet of Things (IoT)-enabled smart agricultural systems are explored. Observations indicate that IoT-based agricultural systems enable efficient utilization of farm inputs such as fertilizer, pesticides, herbicides, and water. Also, using IoT systems, it is possible to provide customized, location-specific, and easily understood climate data for smallholder farmers to facilitate decision making and planning of CSA practices. Therefore, this chapter has presented recommendations for the adoption of IoT-enabled CSA in African countries. IoT-enabled agricultural systems are recommended for a country like Senegal where climate data is considered an agricultural input. Also, for Tanzania where IoT devices such as UAVs are considered to be useful agricultural tools.

Chapter 5: Digital Payments Systems for Emerging Economies – Case of Tanzania

Innovative digital Payment Systems (DPS) are a crucial solution for greater financial inclusion assisting low-income households in overcoming poverty using lower-cost methods for managing their finances. The advancement in Internet communication technologies and the arrival of e-commerce and e-business simulated digital payment systems by providing various electronic payment options such as payment cards, mobile payments, mobile wallets, electronic cash, and contactless payment methods. This chapter discusses the current state of the art in digital payment systems in emerging markets. Also, it analyzes the advantages of DPS in emerging economies, challenges in emerging economies, the Economic impact of DPS in emerging economies, cyber security issues in DPS, and the future of the DPS in emerging economies.

Chapter 6: Digital Technologies and Resources for Learning Under Lockdown

Digital technologies like smartphones, social media, the Internet, software applications, websites, and e-books are redefining the educational landscape which was accentuated amid the Covid-19 pandemic. This chapter discussed the impact of digital technologies in enabling academic institutions to perform their noble responsibilities in delivering instructions virtually during the lockdown. The effects of using these technologies and the challenges encountered by developing countries in migrating to the digital environment amid the lockdown with particular reference to the educational ecosystem in Nigeria was focal in the chapter. Striking among these challenges is the issue of compatibility, the high cost of Internet data, inadequate digital literacy skill, and environmental distraction. Thus, it was recommended that Administrators of academic institutions and regulatory bodies such as the National Universities Commission (NUC) must provide lecturers and students at all levels with adequate training to ensure operational productivity in the use of digital technologies and resources.

Chapter 7: Digitising Standardised Educational Assessment in Africa Using Computerised Adaptive Testing – Transdiciplinary Framework for Action

The experience of the COVID-19 Pandemic has revealed a need for the educational sector in Africa to adopt innovative ways for assessment by leveraging technology with the increasing number of student enrollments at all levels of education. A systematic approach is also required to circumvent the challenges faced by developing countries transdisciplinary. Transdisciplinary is still evolving and has been proved to be a viable tool for engagement, societal impact, new partnerships, fresh ideas, reality checks, new capacities and systemic thinking leading to new career possibilities. This study conducted a documentary analysis of standardized examination administration in Africa and proposed a framework for action adopting a transdisciplinary approach to research for problem-solving. The study used a qualitative approach for collecting and analyzing data from reports and documents supported by empirical findings from existing literature. The study created a framework for action through which the gains of the transdisciplinary approach can be translated to practice.

Chapter 8: ICT Skills Training for the Deaf to Enhance Employment Prospects

The chapter is on ICT skills training for the deaf to enhance employability prospects to improve social-economic development. Deaf employment is a global issue. ICT skills training might reduce the challenge. Little is known about ICT skills training for the deaf. The author interviewed 5 parents and 15 ICT skills training for the deaf graduates at the Open University of Tanzania. Data were collected using an interview guide with support from an experienced sign language interpreter. Findings indicated that ICT skills training increased participation in learning, employment, networking, and social inclusion. However, they faced challenges related to community perception, resources availability, affordability, connectivity, funding and availability of ICT skills training opportunities that met their special learning needs. Based on the results, people with disabilities have to learn ICT skills that meet their unique special needs to reduce the negative effects of the impact of disruptive technologies and employability in the 4th Industrial Revolution.

Chapter 9: Impact of Disruptive Technologies on the Socioeconomic Development of Emerging Countries – Digital Tech and Resources for Learning Under Lockdown

In the Covid-19 pandemic crisis, educational institutions had to be temporarily shut down by their respective governments around the world in order to contain the spread of the virus. The pandemic globally engendered new ways of teaching and learning amidst the restrictions. Schools in emerging countries are mostly dependent on the traditional face-to-face method of teaching and learning and barely had any substantial experience in virtual education prior to the outbreak. Moreover, many of such countries lack adequate infrastructure for ICTs and Internet usage. Nonetheless, these countries also adopted various digital technologies for virtual teaching and learning. This chapter discusses digital technologies and resources for learning in emerging countries under lockdown and proposes a research model for evaluating their impact amidst effects of the digital divide.

Chapter 10: Impacts of Digital Payments on Socio-Economic Factors in Emerging Markets and Developing Economies

Digital payments are increasingly becoming popular worldwide, especially in underdeveloped and developing countries, despite the challenges these countries face regarding required infrastructure and digital literacy. Digital payments have emerged as an important tool for governments to distribute the funds for social welfare schemes to their citizens directly in their accounts with zero corruption and delays. Socio-financial inclusion of society's deprived and marginalized section is another advantage of digital payments. Having access to transaction accounts, credit, savings products, and insurance helps the poor raise their incomes and become more resilient. Paperless and cashless transactions are a huge advantage of digital payments. This chapter aims to discuss the impacts of digital payments on the socio-economic factors in emerging markets and developing economies. In addition, it highlights the solution and recommendations for policymakers.

Chapter 11: Leveraging Machine Learning Techniques to Improve Learning and Recommendations Within Dairy Farms – Towards High Milk Yields for Small-Scale Farmers

Tanzania's small-scale dairy industry faces similar challenges to those of other developing nations whereby, insufficient infrastructure, outdated technology, and low productivity are serious problems for higher milk yield. Tanzania urgently needs to adopt cutting-edge solutions in order to boost dairy performance. With 3500 households' secondary data and 202 households' primary data from 8 villages throughout the Kilimanjaro and Arusha regions, this chapter demonstrates the use of Machine Learning (ML) techniques to derive homogeneous production clusters and recommendations for more milk yield among dairy farmers. The likelihood for higher milk yield is demonstrated for various clusters with the use of support, confidence and lift values of association rules analysis. Finally, the production clusters and recommendations are deployed through a mobile application. Recommendations for future improvement are suggested especially on further deployment of learning recommendations and development of a platform-independent mobile solution.

Chapter 12: Someone Like Us – Anthropomorphism in the Consumer Behavior in the Scope of Emerging Countries

This study analyzes the development of anthropomorphism research in consumer behavior over the last three decades, with a particular focus on emerging countries. A dataset of 475 articles was collected from the Web of Science database, using the keywords "anthropomorph*" and "consum*". The study includes graphics related to annual scientific production, corresponding author's country, most cited countries, most relevant sources, word cloud, word tree, trend topics, and thematic map, revealing the visualization technique. The meta-analysis aims to create a comprehensive framework for articles on anthropomorphism in consumer behavior published in the last thirty years, with a specific focus on emerging countries. The study will examine the anthropomorphism studies carried out in these countries separately and make suggestions for anthropomorphism applications that can be applied in consumer behavior in emerging countries, comparing the general findings to those from emerging countries.

Chapter 13: Digitalization of the Tanzania's Tourism Industry – A Marketing Perspective

In Tanzania the tourism industry is one of the main contributors to the economy. Despite the steady increase in tourists after the COVID-19 pandemic, the industry's performance is low compared to the unique and abundant tourism resources with which the country is endowed. Tanzania is ranked 1st in Africa and 12th worldwide on the quality of its nature-based resources and 32nd in Africa on its cultural resources. Yet the country holds 5th place in Sub-Saharan Africa. This is due to several factors, and the low integration of digital solutions is one of them. In order to improve the performance, the chapter identifies areas in the customer journey that can benefit from digitalization and proposes relevant interventions. The challenges include underutilization of user-generated content, limited internet access, the dominance of traditional marketing practices, inadequate planning services, and limited access to local businesses. The proposed interventions include the development of an interactive web portal and e-tourism stickers and the inclusion of planning features in a tourism portal.

We thank the reviewers for their time and valuable comments during the reviewing process. The high-quality book would not have been possible without their expertise and dedication. The reviewing process timetable was ambitious, and the reviewers' efforts to submit their reports within the reviewing period were greatly appreciated. Their comments were instructive for us in selecting the chapters.

We hope that readers find the book exciting, and that the chapters collected in this volume offer inspiration and open new research windows.

Fredrick Japhet Mtenzi
The Aga Khan University, Tanzania

George S. Oreku
The Open University of Tanzania, Tanzania

Dennis M. Lupiana
Institute of Finance Management, Tanzania

Chapter 1
Impact of Disruptive Technologies on the Socio-Economic Development of Emerging Countries:
Artificial Intelligence and Legal Liability in Tanzania

Abdallah Mrindoko Ally
The Open University of Tanzania, Tanzania

ABSTRACT

The growth of computer science, robotics, and artificial intelligence (AI) worldwide has been considered a catalyst for developments in several sectors including health, education, trade, and telecommunication. AI is now dominating every aspect of life, and it is not surprising that it has entered into several domains that are subject to negligence or negligence equivalents, including medical misconduct, data security, investment advice, and financial advice. This novel development has brought serious legal discussions about liability in the law of negligence. The language of liability in the law of negligence has put much weight on personhood. These and other reasons invite a critical discussion on the development of new jurisprudence in the law of negligence.

INTRODUCTION

The technological development in Information and Communication Technologies (ICTs) which is taking place globally, is bringing fabulous innovations and applications in the Information Age. The emerging technologies such as the Internet of Things (IoT), Cloud Computing (CC), Big Data Analytics (BDA), Artificial Intelligence (AI) and Robotics and Machine Learning (ML) are improving efficiencies in industries, minimize infrastructure investments and deploy solutions rapidly and securely (Rotolo & Martin,

DOI: 10.4018/978-1-6684-6873-9.ch001

2015). The United Republic of Tanzania (URT) has recognised the importance of Science, Technology and Innovations in driving viable industrialization for human development. This is in line with the National and International Agenda; the National Development Vision 2025 and long term perspective plan (LTPP) and African Union Agenda 2063 and Science Technology and Innovation Strategy for Africa 2024 (NSTI policy, 2022). The URT has continued in formulating and implementing strategic policies that require Science Technology and Innovation (STI) as inputs for their implementation. In the course of its effort, it has benefited from the end results of disruptive technologies such as cloud computing, biotechnology, AI and robotics (NSTI policy, 2022). The URT government has shown commitment in digitising several of its operations for greater efficiency. It has also developed an e-government strategy and set up an implementing institution (GSMA, 2023). According to Oxford Insights in its 'Government AI Readiness Index 2021,' governments across the continent are turning to AI to improve their public services and gain strategic economic advantages. Tanzania has a score of 32.69 out of 100, just above Sub-Saharan Africa's average but still low compared to countries globally.

The prospective socio-economic benefits of these innovations and applications are great, and are currently being harnessed in various sectors such as education, health, fintech and agriculture. According to Sukums et al. (2023) in their paper entitled "the use of artificial intelligence-based innovations in the health sector in Tanzania: A scoping review", shows a growing interest in adopting these emerging technologies in health services but at a relatively low pace. The Ministry of Health is currently drafting an AI policy framework and is eager to understand how emerging technologies can help the advancement of this sector. The innovation hubs and accelerator programmes such as Tanzania AI Lab, AI Commons and Sahara Ventures are supporting the development of the ecosystem (GSMA, 2023). Since the efforts of adopting AI and Robotics are so fragmented, Tanzania must move on from a departmental approach and implement a National AI strategy.

OVERVIEW OF ARTIFICIAL INTELLIGENCE (AI)

Although AI represents one of the major technologies of our time, there is no common or accepted definition of Artificial Intelligence (AI). Some define AI loosely as a computerized system that exhibits behavior that is commonly thought of as requiring intelligence. Others define AI as a system capable of sensibly solving complex problems or taking appropriate actions (Dempsey, 2020).

In 1955, John McCarthy, the founding father of the discipline of AI, termed the process as, that of making a machine work in such ways that would be called intelligent if a human were so behaving (Shahul Ikram & Zul Kepli, 2018). In 2018, a book issued by Microsoft defined AI as "a set of technologies that enable computers to perceive, learn, reason and assist in decision-making to solve problems in ways that are similar to what people do (Dempsey, 2020). AI denotes the computer-generated intelligence in machines that enables them to imitate, mimic and act like humans. Developers of AI believe that human behaviour can be precisely categorised and simulated by intelligent machines that have been programmed to behave so. The achievement of this is the development of the intelligent robot, Sophia (Agunbiade, 2019).

The widespread and increase in popularity of AI have captured all circles of human life such as business, education, health, and industry. The introduction of social media applications with Artificial Intelligence (AI) based algorithms as well as Facebook, Twitter, Instagram, and WhatsApp has revolutionised the way people interact with each other, for better or worse (Ikram, 2018).

AI is applied in science for analyzing large amounts of data for the decision-making process. In the field of medicine, AI is applied in designing treatment plans for patients (Manne & Kanthet, 2021). AI by analyzing data from previous patients, can provide superior strategies for treating patients and monitoring treatment plans. With the help of medical images like CT scans, MRI, X-rays, and Ultrasound, AI can recognize signs of disease more accurately and rapidly. It helps patients, with fast identification of disease accurately and more precise treatment choices (Manne & Kanthet, 2021). In the business Industry, the applications of AI range from detecting trends in data to mitigate market risks, enhancing customer service through virtual personal assistants, or even analyzing millions of documents across a company's servers to find compliance failures (Palanivelu & Vasanthi, 2020).

In Tanzania, the AI technology is growing and has been adopted in different activities. Among the innovations in the country is the Agrobot platform that uses Artificial Intelligence (AI) to help farmers get proper information and advice regarding fertilizers, tools, medicine, and diseases through a chatbot or a normal SMS message. The platform aims to solve the problem of access to accurate and timely information on diseases, fertilizers, tools and to increase productivity and efficiency in the farming process (Sahara Ventures, 2019, p. 4). Another AI powered platform in the country is e-Shangazi, which is a knowledge sharing platform that educates, informs and advice youths on Sexual Reproductive Health Rights (SRHr). The e-Shangazi came as a solution to solve the problem of access to quality, age appropriate and timely SRHr information to young people(Sahara Ventures, 2019, p. 4).

While the growth of AI in business, science, education, etc., brings such significant progress, there are serious legal issues accompanied with such developments that need special attention to avoid future problems. The existing laws in liabilities, criminal law, employment, contracts, etc. have not spared room for AI and therefore courts will encounter challenges in applying traditional rules to AI. It is therefore the aim of this paper to examine the legal challenges associated with the development of Artificial Agents and robotics in various fields to disclose the existing gaps and bridge them.

THE LEGAL AND REGULATORY FRAMEWORK FOR ICT AND INNOVATION IN TANZANIA

Artificial Intelligence and Robotics growth that is witnessed worldwide and in Tanzania, escalate several legal challenges for the traditional legal system. The legal system in Tanzania has its genesis in the British Legal system and legal reforms to incorporate technological developments such as Artificial agents, dispute settlement, digital rights, and e-payments are at an infant stage. Most of the laws in Tanzania were designed to facilitate paper-based transactions and to address conventional world issues. Despite the legislative developments that have been made in the country to address technological developments, most of the laws that were enacted since the British colonial regime are still in force and therefore inefficient to address cyber world issues including disruptive technologies.

The country's commitment to ICT and innovation is recognized in various legal and policy instruments such as National ICT Policy 2016 (NICTP 2016) which is a result of the revision of the National ICT Policy (NICTP) 2003. The NICTP 2003 has provided a National framework for ICTs to contribute effectively towards achieving national development goals and transform Tanzania into a knowledge-based society through the application of ICT. The National Science Technology and Innovation Policy (NSTI), 2022 also acknowledges the importance of Science Technology and Innovation in solving the Societal challenges and enhancing socioeconomic development.

The government has also made reformist development in the area of the legal framework through amendments to the Evidence Act, 1967 which introduced the legal provisions that allow and recognize the admissibility of electronic evidence through the amendments of Evidence Act No. 15 of 2007, Act No. 3 of 2011 and other amendments. Further, the Government enacted the Electronic and Postal Communications Act No. 3 of 2010 and the Universal Communications Service Access Act. No. 11 of 2006 the Cybercrime Act No. 14 of 2015 and the Electronic Transactions Act No. 13 of 2015 to address emerging technologies challenges.

In 2015 Tanzania launched the National Payment System Act, 2015, and its Regulations. The primary objective was to modernise the country's payment system to internationally acceptable best practices by decreasing risks and increasing the convenience, affordability, and timeliness of the systems. The Act and its Regulations were enacted, to harmonise the growth of mobile money services in the country. However, with all these efforts the laws have not offered a specific space to address liability issues for AI and robotics. Besides, the specific sectoral laws establishing the Institutions dealing with Science, Technology and Innovations have also not addressed AI and robotics liability issues. The COSTECH Act, No.7 of 1986, The National Institute for Medical Research Act of 1979, Tanzania Industrial Research and Development Act No.5 of 1979 and the Centre for Agricultural Mechanisation and Rural Technology Act, No.19 of 1981 are still silent in addressing AI and robotics.

LEGAL LIABILITIES

Legal liability is the obligation a person has under the law for the injuries or losses they inflict upon others. Legal liability is the obligation of a party imposed by a court for its actions or inactions, and for which the courts will award pecuniary damages to redress the injury. A legal wrong is either a violation of a person's rights or the failure to perform a legal duty for a party (White & Chopra, 2014). Legal liability can be assessed from the three categories of legal wrongs; crime, breach of contract and Tort. Legal liability for a crime occurs when a person intentionally inflicts injury, rob, rape, kill or takes something from another. Breach of contract is an act of dishonoring the terms of the contract to satisfy a contract that the parties agreed to.

A tort is defined as a legal term describing an act where one person causes damage, injury, or harm to another person. It is a civil wrong that causes a claimant to suffer loss or harm, resulting in legal liability for the person who commits the tortious act (McBride & Bagshaw, 2018). The violation may result from intentional actions, a breach of duty as in negligence, or due to a violation of statutes. Under most tort laws, the injury suffered by the plaintiff does not have to be physical. A person who commits a tort may be required to pay damages for other types of harm, including emotional distress or a violation of personal rights. Patients may recover compensatory and punitive damages from physicians, health care organizations, pharmaceutical companies, and medical device manufacturers if they are injured as a result of the party's failure to meet judicially accepted standards (Sullivan & Schweikart, 2019). This position is not new in Tanzanian context, in the case of Michael Mwamiko v. Angetile Mwanjela Civil case No.7 of 1999 (HC) DSM (unreported), the landlord was held liable for failure to observe a duty of care for making sure that the toilets were for use by his tenants. In this case the tenant lost his wife and his mother in law as a result of using the defective premises of a toilet.

While developments in AI and robotics are growing very fast, the laws dealing with legal liabilities including the tort of negligence are still yesterday and liabilities are still imposed on a person who is recognized by the law or has some form of legal personality. The reason here is that the tort of negligence was created for humans and other entities, such as companies, vested with legal personality. But with AI, this definition remains redundant on the face except for Sophia, the intelligent robot created by Hanson Robotics which was given citizenship by Saudi Arabia in 2017 (Agunbiade, 2019).

Tort Liability for Artificial Agents

Applying the doctrine of tort liability schemes to AI and robotics brings several legal challenges as the law is built on legal doctrines that focus on human conduct as opposed to machines. Even if the advancements in ICT have gone so far in creating robots and AI that has full autonomy but that autonomy does not give them personhood. The autonomy of robots is purely technical and makes them take decisions based on algorithms. Therefore, it is not the same as a human (Rossum, 2018).

Since AI and robots are now exercising self-control in varying degrees the question of ascertaining liability, both civil and criminal, concerning harm or loss resulting from any of their activities, becomes essential. While the operation of AI is not regulated by specific legislation, we have to deal with the issue of liability for damages caused by the actions of AI. Legal norms provide that the damages caused by unlawful actions of others must be compensated. Legal norms provide that the damage is to be compensated by the offender or a person who is responsible for the actions of the offender. Given these legal regulations and the fact that AI is not the subject of law yet, a question arises: who is required to assume liability and compensate for damages caused by the actions of AI? (Sirbikyte et al., 2015). Because no specific legal regimes currently define or regulate the operation of modern AI, courts dealing with these questions must attempt to solve liability issues by applying general laws often drafted years before the advent of this technology.

AI is constantly developing and keeps shocking us with unexpected achievements. In this context, it is difficult to draft any kind of legislation specifically governing it, including covering liability issues, as such legislation would need to be both universal and constantly amended to remain effective. Although natural persons and legal persons have been the vital players.

of liability issues in our legal system, this should not limit us to open up a window for the development of new jurisprudence. Large and small businesses, private organizations and government organizations are entitled to carry out all kinds of acts as legal entities and can be held responsible for the things they do (Corrales, 2018).

The thinking of prosecuting and punish animals and lifeless things was traditionally common in the middle ages. Then inanimate things such as stones, beams, pieces of iron, etc. and animals that had caused the death of a man were put on trial at the prytaneum (Corrales, 2018). In considering whether an autonomously functioning Artificial Intelligent entity or robot must have a certain legal liability or not, several issues at this modern time should be considered including social and economic necessities, cultural values and legal acceptance by other actors.

For this reason, it appears reasonable to start an analysis of AI liability by relying on existing general legal principles to both find elementary answers and identify their shortcomings. We may then assess how laws can be developed to bridge the existing legal gaps. Amongst the potential liability regimes that may be the most directly applicable in the context of AI-related tort claims are general tort liability and product liability (Benhamou & Ferland, 2020).

The Contractual Liability of Software Agents

Advancement in ICT technology has brought in place the term Software Agent which can conclude transactions autonomously without the involvement of the business owner. The powers that have been bestowed to the software agents have brought a legal discussion about the validity and enforcement of the contracts (Almajid, 2010).

The term *agent* in ICT represents a broad cluster of technologies and a large research program within artificial intelligence, all concerned with relatively autonomous information processing systems. Agents might be defined as "a piece of software that acts on behalf of its user and tries to meet certain objectives or complete the assigned responsibilities without any direct input or direct supervision from its user (White & Chopra, 2011).

In governmental settings, decision-making is often delegated to systems that, with varying degrees of autonomy, terminate or renew welfare benefits. In this regard, the powers that have been vested to software agents have positive and negative implications and therefore the question of liability is imperative. In contractual liability, the question of legal capacity is imperative in determining the validity and enforceability of the contract. Even if intelligent agents somehow achieved the status of the person in law, it is not clear that every such device would be capable of entering into a contract. As stated by Cheshire and Fifoot:

If all of the elements of a contract exist between two parties, the agreement may nevertheless lack legal effect if one or both of the parties cannot contract. (Starke, Seddon, & Ellinghaus, 1992, p. 545)

Section 10 of the law of contract Act, Cap.345 offers the same position with regards to validity of the contract. The Act provides that "all agreements are contracts if they are made by the free consent of parties competent to contract, for a lawful consideration and with a lawful object, and are not hereby expressly declared to be void." Section 11 of the Act in subsection 1 and 2 clarifies the importance of competence of the parties for the lawfulness of the contract. The section explains that:

Every person is competent to contract who is of the age of majority according to the law to which he is subject, and who is of sound mind, and is not disqualified from contracting by any law to which he is subject. An agreement by a person who is not hereby declared to be competent to contract is void.

In other words, before giving legal effect to their agreements, the common law legal position is that all contracting parties should be capable of demonstrating a certain degree of intellectual capacity.

The traditional view of a contract includes not only an exchange of promises but also a mutual concordance between the parties as to the nature and scope of the rights and obligations that coincide with that exchange of promises. That is, the parties must be said to have formed an agreement with each other. The metaphor which has taken hold throughout the common law to describe this phenomenon is the idea of a consensus ad idem which means a meeting of the minds. In sum, when one considers the fact that intelligent agents are not legal persons, that they cannot contract, and that they are incapable of reaching a consensus ad idem, it is unclear whether the transactions generated by intelligent agents will be considered binding in law. For this reason and others, lawmakers in most jurisdictions are proposing legislation aimed at curing these doctrinal defects.

Although opinions differ regarding their degree of autonomy, the consensus is in agreement that using electronic agents to draw up contracts, with little or no human involvement, can create legal problems (Almajid, 2010). When it comes to the legal status of a software agent, the notion of agency is important. Agency in a legal sense is the relationship between the principal and the agent, based on authority, or the power conferred on the agent to constitute legal relations between the principal and a third party (De Miglio et al. 2002). The same position is also considered from an economic perspective in which "agency" is defined as any relationship in which one person engages another to perform service under circumstances that involve delegating some discretion over decision-making to the service-performer (White & Chopra, 2011). To create a principal-agent relationship under agency law, the consent of both parties is necessary. In a principal-computer-agent relationship, the concept of the computer consenting is absurd as the powers are delegated to a machine and not a human being.

The application of Principal-agency relationship is also applied under the doctrine of vicarious liability in establishing liabilities. Vicarious liability refers to legal responsibility that a supervisory party bears for the actionable conduct of a subordinate or associate (such as an employee) based on the relationship between the two parties. Vicarious liability is guided by a Latin maxim, *qui facit per alium facit perse,* i.e., *he who does something through another is deemed to have done it himself.* The maxim establishes a principle that resembles the law of agency or the principle of an undisclosed principal. However, the two doctrines of vicarious liability and the law of agency differ on the aspect of authority. Whereas, in agency, the principal is liable for acts that have been specifically authorized. Under vicarious liability, the master is liable for the wrongful acts of his servant committed during the course of employment.

Vicarious liability regimes could be the most appropriate way to ensure compensation, in particular for autonomous technologies, which makes the principal for auxiliary's action. This interpretation is based on the way AI's actions are interpreted in the field of contracts, where strict liability rules apply to a machine's actions and bind the person on whose behalf it acts, regardless of whether these actions were planned or envisaged, and complies with the general rule that the principal of a tool is responsible for the results obtained by the use of that tool since the tool has no independent volition of its own.

Under agency law, the agent may be liable for his acts. However, as computers are not capable under the law, they may not be considered liable for their acts. Establishing liability for damages caused by AI used to be rather straightforward when only one or few stakeholders are involved, or when the AI could only take a limited range of pre-defined decisions under specific parameters defined by a human programmer. However, AI usually involves several stakeholders and components (e.g., sensors and hardware, software and applications, data itself and data services, connectivity features), which makes it difficult to allocate liability between all stakeholders (Benhamou & Ferland, 2020).

In Tanzania, electronic contracts are regulated by the Electronic Transaction Act, 2015. This Act provides for the legal recognition of electronic transactions, e-Government services, the use of Information and Communication Technologies in collection of evidence, admissibility of electronic evidence, to provide for the facilitation of use of secure electronic signatures; and to provide for other related matters. The law has neither addressed legal liabilities of AI nor explaining essential elements for the validity of contracts. Section 21 of the Act in sub sections 1 and 2 has just offered a general provision about recognition of electronic contracts. The section explains as follows:

For avoidance of doubt, a contract may be formed electronically unless otherwise agreed by the parties. Where an electronic record is used in the formation of a contract, that contract shall not be denied validity or enforceability on the ground that an electronic record was used for that purpose.

The wordings of section 21(1) about the parties of the contract is not very clear regarding their status. It is not very clear as to whether the term parties extend their meanings to AI.

Criminal Liability

For an act to be punished in terms of criminal law, the existence of fundamental elements are necessary. The fundamental principle of crime is that a wrongful act (actus Reus) is to be combined with a wrongful intention (mens rea) to construe criminal liability. The maxim *"actus non facit reum nisi mens sit rea"* embodies this principle that an act does not make one guilty unless the mind is also legally blameworthy. Actus Reus represents the physical aspect of crime in the juristic concept, while the mens rea constitutes the mental aspect of crime, which must be criminal and concurrent to actus Reus (Ghuman, 2018). However, one of the most troublesome questions that criminal law is currently facing is the criminal liability of legal persons, AI and robots. Should criminal penalties be solely imposed upon an individual or should a legal person be subjected to those penalties and, being so, in what way would that occur? (Freitas, 2014).

Currently, Robots are performing a wide range of Activities in different sectors i.e. production and manufacturing in multi-national companies, medical treatment and defense activities. While performing these activities, the Robots commit severe wrongs including death. In the year 1981, an engineer who was performing maintenance work on the robot at Kawasaki Heavy Industries Plant was killed by the robot. While performing the maintenance work, he was under the presumption that he has turned off the robot but as he entered the prohibited area of the manufacturing line, the robot identified him as an obstacle in the manufacturing process and immediately threw him out with its powerful hydraulic arms and he died (Tripathi & Saxena, 2020). This case open up a discussion on the development of new jurisprudence to legislature as well judiciary in order to determine who will be liable for the murder of the engineer.

The construction of SOPHIA robot is another area of discussion in legal jurisprudence. She is the first social humanoid robot who has been granted citizenship in Saudi Arabia. Sophia robot is one evidence of the progress of Artificial Intelligence that is increasingly developing along with the times. Sophia is not only designed to do certain jobs but also gets citizenship status from a country. The question is whether Sophia has rights and obligations as other citizens in that country? Every citizen has a responsibility if there is an unlawful action that results in a criminal act. What will happen if Sophia robot does a criminal act that must go with a punishment? (Rizki Habibulah, 2020).

There are several questions that invite legal discussion in this aspect. What if Sophia commits any criminal wrong during the course of the activity? Who will be responsible for that action? Is it Mr. David Hanson, the creator of Sophia or Sophia herself as she has been given a legal citizen of a country? These difficulty questions cannot be left to vanish in the air.

The criminal liability of legal persons appears to be not only essential for suitable and adequate response of criminal law to an increasingly complex human society, but it also meets the requirements imposed by various international bodies such as the European Union, the Council of Europe, and the United Nations, which require States to adopt the necessary legislative measures to sanction legal persons for acts that constitute certain offenses (Freitas, 2014).

However, the existence of the two essential elements of criminal liability brings several challenges of vesting criminal liability to legal entities. Some authors, including most German authors, defend that legal entities are not able to act for themselves. Only natural or physical persons may carry out criminally relevant behaviors. And as such, criminal responsibility cannot fall on a legal entity, but rather on the individual (Correia 2010). It is morally and ethically impossible to judge legal entities for not acting lawfully since liability for an unlawful action demands the existence of an agent that has a free and conscious will and chooses to break the law in a supposition he/she could and should have acted differently (Castro & Sousa, 1985, p. 114).

In this aspect the liability can only be equated to a natural person with the ability to think and act unlawful. Therefore, the conclusion should be obvious about the lack of ontological unfitness to be blamed, legal entities cannot be held criminally accountable (Dias, 2012, p. 196). Accordingly, only the individuals that have committed the relevant criminal acts on behalf of legal entities or in their interest can suffer criminal sanctions, and not the legal entities themselves (Freitas, 2014).

The legal position of Tanzania is also the same in determining criminal liability of an accused person. For an accused person to be guilty of an offence the two elements must be proved, these elements are 'actus reus' to mean there must be an act or omission forbidden by law and 'men rea' to mean evil intention. In determining the legal responsibility for the offenses of murder and Manslaughter Section 195 and 196 of the Penal code of Tanzania, Cap. 16 has vested the liability to a person. Although section 5 of the Act has not been very precisely in defining the term person, the wordings of the term as it has been applied in the Act implies a natural person or a legal person. Since AI and robotics are neither natural nor legal persons, it is quiet difficulty to determine their criminal liabilities.

Product Liability

Products liability refers to the liability of any or all parties along the chain of manufacture of any product for damage caused by that product. This includes the manufacturer of parts, an assembling manufacturer, the wholesaler, and the retail store owner. When a person is injured by a defective product that is unreasonably dangerous or unsafe, the injured person may have a claim or cause of action against the company that designed, manufactured, sold, distributed, leased, or furnished the product (Dempsey, 2014).

Most countries have laws establishing civil liability for negligent or unreasonable behavior that causes damage and for addressing the harms caused by defective products. A product liability claim generally cites multiple theories of liability, the typical theories are negligence, strict liability, misrepresentation, and breach of warranty. Courts commonly utilize either negligence or strict liability except when analyzing the theories of misrepresentation and express warranty under contract law (Wardel, 2022).

The most famous case for product liability is the case of Donoghue v Stevenson [1932] AC 562 in which the Court created the modern concept of negligence, by setting out general principles whereby one person would owe a duty of care to another person. The position of this case is that the duty of care is extended to another person. However, as companies are increasingly integrating AI and robots into their products and systems the likelihood for AI and robots to cause injury and property damage continues to grow.

There has been extensive litigation against manufacturers by workers injured on the job by robots, over the safety of surgical robots, over autopilot systems in airplanes, and the software already embedded in automobiles. By and large, the courts have applied traditional concepts to conceptualize liability and apportion it among machines, their makers, and users (Wardel, 2022).

Application of the product liability concept is more challenging when the product at issue incorporates more fully autonomous AI technology. It is unclear how the law should assign liability for AI that learns and makes the decision on its own and whether analytical elements like the foreseeability and substantially unchanged standards that underpin the traditional tort framework remain workable in an AI- driven world.

The case of Nilson v General motors LLC, illustrates some challenges on how product liability claims may evolve as AI technology develops. In this case, a motorcyclist claimed that he was injured by an autonomous AI. Although a backup driver was present in the autonomous vehicle the driver was not operating.

Product liability and consumer protection issues are still at an infant stage in Tanzania. There are no specific legislation dealing with product liability governing manufacturers' duties to consumers. Courts in Tanzania generally rely on precedent and principles of common law to guide them in making decisions. Consumer Protection rights are generally stretched from the Constitution of the United Republic of Tanzania, 1977 under article, 11, 14 and 18. Other legislation that deal with consumer protection include the Fair Competition Act, 2003, The Merchandise Marks Act, 1963, The Weights and Measures Act, 1982, The Standards Act, 1975 (now the Standards Act, 2009) and The Tanzania Food, Drugs and Cosmetics Act, 2003.

The available laws do not seem adequate to address unique features of e-commerce regime and the complexity of the unique issues that have been brought by AI and robotics.

Professional Liability

Professional liability law governs legal proceedings brought by patients and clients who have suffered as a result of the negligent actions of professionals. A negligence claim can be brought against any type of professional whose careless actions have harmed the plaintiff. Professionals can be held liable to various parties. The first that comes to mind is the client because there is normally a contractual relationship between professionals and their clients (Zech, 2021). However, there are many other individuals to whom a professional may be liable depending on whether or not the professional owed them a duty of care and whether a breach of that duty was the proximate cause of the loss and not too remote. This rule was adopted in Tanzania in the case of *Francis Ngaire v National Insurance Corporation (N.I.C' (1972) HCD 134 in which the professional was held liable for acting negligently.* In the case of Theodoclina Alphaxad v Medical Officer in Charge of Nkinga Hospital [1992] TLR 235. Nkinga hospital was held liable for causing the amputation of the minor's hand due to the negligence of the doctor on duty.

In professional liability, there are generally three main elements that should be considered in assessing whether an act of a person is negligent. The existence of a duty of care, a breach of such duty, and harm caused to the victim. Each of these elements has been extensively directed to a natural person. As AI and robots are now widely applied in the health sector, in forecasting, as autonomous drivers, and in other areas where traditional professionals were operating, the serious question to be debated in the courts is how the three traditional tort negligence questions can be addressed. The AI known as Hanover is being trained to memorize all the papers related to cancer so that it can predict which combination of drugs will be most suitable for each patient. AI has also been found to be as good as doctors in detecting skin cancer with accuracy. Autonomous robots (powered by AI) have also been known to successfully perform surgeries, with as much accuracy as humans (Agunbiade, 2019).

In this scenario, the powers of professional, natural being has been vested to a robot. The duty element can somehow easily be tackled as it can be assumed that, as a matter of policy, the manufacturers, distributors, operators, and even users of AI-based robots have a general duty of care toward potential victims of the robots. The challenge becomes greater with the breach element (Twaig, 2020). This happen when the act was conducted by AI in the absence of professional doctor or medical practitioner. Under such a condition, who will be liable?

The effects of the liability rules described above depend on clear causation. Only where one or more individuals causing the damage can be determined, liability rules can affect their behavior. If a person is liable who cannot influence the risk, or, if a person who can influence the risk cannot be determined, liability rules fail (Twaig, 2020).

PERSONHOOD FOR ARTIFICIAL INTELLIGENCE AND ROBOTICS

According to Kurki and Pietrzykowski (2017), the notion of the person (*persona*) was introduced for the first time in Roman law. It was a technical term which denoted a bundle of rights. A human, in accordance with *unus homo sustinet plures personas*, could be many persons. The technical legal meaning of being a legal person is in a simplified version: "a subject of legal rights and duties." The idea of legal personhood involves the status of an entity as a person before the law, leading to recognition of certain rights and obligations under the law. Accordingly, a legal person has the duty to obey the law, while enjoying the benefit of protections to rights and privileges accorded to a legal person (Corrales et al., 2018).

The concept of legal personality or personhood is stretchy and dynamic concept. It depends on what is reasoned acceptable within a certain society. If animals are accepted to have a certain status in that society and culture, they can have a legal status going beyond that of a mere object. If a company has legal personhood because it is socially and economically desirable, why should it not be acceptable and even desirable to give a robot a certain legal status and to have a new kind of personhood (Corrales et al., 2018).

There are varying theories in this area of legal personality leading to different opinion about legal status of AI and robots. For instance, the fact that corporations have legal personalities does not necessarily mean that AI entities should be granted legal personality or the same legal capacity. There are varying reasons for the rejection of granting personhood to AI, based on the reason that the acceptance would undermine the meaning of being a person and it will reduce the exclusivity personhood to humans. This exclusivity has been represented by religious texts such as the Bible. "Man is separate from nature and is created in God's own image". This hierarchy sets humans above "things," be it animals, property, or the environment (Corrales et al., 2018).

In considering this thinking, the legal challenge about liability of AI and robots will be on the concept of personhood. The most basic concept in legal liability is that the law deals with the behavior of people and liability could only be accredited to a person demonstrating the capability to act as a purposive agent. As the liability for most, intentional torts and negligence is directed to the actors for their acts or conduct, tort law holds persons liable for wrongful acts or omissions.

Since AI and robots are not human it seems almost impossible to attribute any concept of personhood or agency to them. If this is the case, the immediate result is that AI-based robots cannot currently be directly liable for their actions and conduct, even those that inflict harm (Twaig, 2020).

Legal entities, such as corporate bodies, have human owners or representatives who can possibly display their actions. In contrast, AI and robots function autonomously rather than through human beings. Therefore, the concept 'legal personality' suggested for electronic agents resembles the predicate conferred to human, rather than non-human, beings. Legal personality, in this sense, is based on the moral agency that is generally regarded as having cognition, autonomy, intention, free will, etc. (Almajid, 2010).

Typically, a legal person can sue and be sued, to hold property in her or its name, and enter in to contracts. Legal persons also enjoy various immunities and protections in courts of law such as the right to life and liberty. Such a statement is not typically found at a single location in a particular legal system's code of legislation, but rather describes the way the term *person* functions within that legal system and agrees with the way the law commonly views those subject to it (White & Chopra, 2011). Another view about personhood and its exclusivity to a natural being is that self-consciousness is usually a unique characteristic of human conduct rather than other objects. If these arguments are followed to their conclusion, then AI and robots are not concise entities and, therefore, not human (Almajid, 2010).

CONCLUSION AND RECOMMENDATIONS

Artificial intelligence and other emerging digital technologies, such as block chain, robotics, the Internet of Things (IoT), and biotechnology have the potential to transform our societies and advance our economies. However, their wider application must come with sufficient policy and legal framework to minimize the risk of harm these technologies may cause. It has been recognised that most of the laws that are still in place were designed without considering the rapid development of ICT. It is a fact that the adoption of AI and robots challenge traditional legal concepts and therefore there is a need of developing new laws that will address the challenges that can be caused by the utilization of AI and robots. While the application of AI is now applied in health and autonomous vehicles, criminal liability is still vested in human beings. Section 195 and 196 of the Penal code vests criminal liabilities to human beings. Section 195 of the penal code state that:

Any person who by an unlawful act or omission causes the death of another person is guilty of the felony termed "manslaughter."

Section 196 of the penal code proceed to maintain the same position and it states as follows:

Any person who of malice aforethought causes the death of another person by an unlawful act or omission is guilty of murder.

Section 2(1) of the road traffic Act, 1973 has also not been activated to address the generation of autonomous motor vehicles. The section defines a driver concerning a motor vehicle or any other vehicle, as a person who drives or attempts to drive or is in charge of the vehicle and includes an instructor of a learner driver. The definitions indicates that liabilities have been vested to natural persons and not to machines. Since liability issues have not been settled at these early stages and granting personhood to AI is not yet settled there is a need of doing the following in order to address key issues for proper development of legislations.

1. There is a need of conducting a research in order to determine the scope of its definition and the risks associated with its utilization. Due to the complexity of the term AI, the notion of an AI system should be more clearly defined to ensure legal certainty, given that the determination of what an 'AI system' constitutes is essential for the allocation of legal responsibilities.

2. There is a need of conducting conferences and seminars for Academicians, government officials, researchers, key technology companies and other stake holders in order to gain common understanding of the importance and risks associated with this technology.
3. Tanzania can also borrow the experience of European Union approach to Artificial Intelligence and other industrialised Nations such as Japan, USA etc. in addressing AI and robotics related issues. The European Union has launched several initiatives aimed at developing a comprehensive AI strategy, including its regulation. The key documents in this regard are the General Data Protection Regulation (GDPR), the European Parliament's Resolution of February 2017 on Civil Laws for Robotics, and the Ethics guidelines for trustworthy AI produced by the European Commission's High-Level Expert Group on Artificial Intelligence (AI HLEG), a final version of which was presented in April 2019. Although we are sailing in different direction, the experience of European Union in cyber related issues has offered positive benefits in the development of cyber –crime legislations for various Nations in the world.

REFERENCES

Agunbiade, A. (2019). *Artificial Intelligence and Law: A Nigerian Perspective*. LAP LAMBERT Academic Publishing.

Almajid, W. M. (2010). Can Electronic Agents Be Granted Legal Personality under Islamic Law? A Conceptual Rethink Is Imperative. *Arab Law Quarterly*, *24*(4), 393–416. doi:10.1163/157302510X526733

Almajid, W. M. (2010). Can Electronic Agents Be Granted Legal Personality under Islamic Law? A Conceptual Rethink Is Imperative. *Arab Law Quarterly*, *24*(4), 393–416. doi:10.1163/157302510X526733

Benhamou, Y., & Ferland, J. (2020). *Artificial intelligence & damages: assessing liability and calculating the damages. Academic Press.*

Corrales, M. (2018). Robotics, AI and the Future of Law, Perspectives in Law, Business and Innovation. Springer Nature Singapore Pte Ltd.

Dempsey, J. X. (2020). *Artificial Intelligence: An Introduction to the Legal, Policy and Ethical Issues.* Berkeley Center for Law & Technology.

Dempsey, P. S. (2014). *The law of products liability*. McGill University.

Freitas, P.M. (2014). *Criminal Liability of Autonomous Agents: From the unthinkable to the plausible.* Academic Press.

Ghuman, A. (2018). Elements of Crime. *International Journal of Law Management & Humanities, 1*(4).

GSMA. (2023). *Tanzania's Digitalisation Journey: Opportunities for value creation*. GSMA.

Ikram, N. H. S., & Kepli, M. Y. (2018). Establishing legal rights and liabilities for Artificial Intelligence. IIUM Law Journal, 26(1).

Manne, R., & Kanthet, S. C. (2021). *Application of Artificial Intelligence in Healthcare: Chances and Challenges*. Current Journal of Applied Science and Technology.

McBride, N. J., & Bagshaw, R. (2018). *Tort Law* (6th ed.). Pearson Education Limited.

MoEST. (2022). *The National Science, Technology and Innovation Policy, 2022*. Academic Press.

Opitz, P. (2019). *Civil Liability and Autonomous Robotic Machines: Approaches in the EU and US*. TTLF Working Papers No. 43.

Palanivelu, V.R., & Vasanthi, B. (2020). Article. *International Journal of Advanced Science and Technology, 29*(4).

Pietrzykowski, T., & Kurki, V. A. J. (2017). *Legal Personhood: Animals, Artificial Intelligence and the Unborn*. Springer International Publishing AG.

Rizki Habibulah, R. (2020). *The Criminal Liability of Artificial Intelligence: Is It Plausible to Hitherto Indonesian Criminal System?* Academic Press.

Rossum, C. V. (2018). *Liability of robots: Legal responsibility in cases of errors or malfunctioning, LLM Paper*. Ghent University.

Sahara Ventures. (2019). *Artificial Intelligence in Tanzania, What's happening? Latest Information on Artificial Intelligence Startups and projects in Tanzania*. Author.

Shahul Ikram, N. A. H., & Zul Kepli, M.Y. (2018). Establishing Legal Rights and Liabilities for Artificial. IIUM Law Journal, 26(1).

Sirbikyte, G. (2015). Liability for damages caused by artificial intelligence. *Computer Law & Security Review*.

Sukums, F., Mzurikwao, D., Sabas, D., Chaula, R., Mbuke, J., Kabika, T., Kaswija, J., Ngowi, B., Noll, J., Winkler, A. S., & Andersson, S. W. (2023). The use of artificial intelligence-based innovations in the health sector in Tanzania: A scoping review. *Health Policy and Technology*, *12*(1), 100728. doi:10.1016/j.hlpt.2023.100728

Sullivan, H. R., & Schweikart, S. J. (2019). Are Current Tort Liability Doctrines Adequate for Addressing Injury Caused by AI? *AMA Journal of Ethics*, *21*(2). PMID:30794126

Tripathi, P., & Saxena, P. (2020). Are robots criminally liable? *International Journal of Creative Research Thoughts, 8*(12).

Twaig, O. (2020). *Whose robot is it anyway? Liability for artificial-intelligence-based robots. Academic Press.*

Wardel, I.A. (2022). Product Liability Applied to Automated Decisions, Law school student scholarship. Seton Hall University.

White, L.F., & Chopra, S. (2014). *A Legal Theory for Autonomous Artificial Agents*. The University of Michigan Press.

Zech, H. (2021). *Liability for AI: Public policy considerations.* ERA Forum.

Chapter 2
Application of Digital Technologies to Enhance Public Health Surveillance in Tanzania:
Current Status, Challenges, and Future Perspective

Elingarami Sauli
Nelson Mandela African Institution of Science and Technology, Tanzania

Grantina Modern
Nelson Mandela African Institution of Science and Technology, Tanzania

Ummul-khair Mustafa
Nelson Mandela African Institution of Science and Technology, Tanzania

ABSTRACT

There is limited literature on the application of digital technology applications for disease surveillance in Tanzania. This chapter reviewed digital application technologies, existing challenges, and future perspectives in Tanzania. The data collection process involved searching for peer reviewed articles from databases such as Web of Science, Google Scholar, Scopus, and PubMed. Stakeholder consultation was also conducted through interviews of healthcare officials who were directly involved in disease surveillance process in Tanzania. Findings from this chapter showed that digital public health data in Tanzania is mainly collected through the HMIS monthly reports from IDSR. The main challenges affecting implementation of digital surveillance are poor internet, unreliable power supply, lack of integration between the existing and newly developed digital technologies, limited financial resources, and inadequate ICT personnel. The government of Tanzania should improve e-health apps funding and reporting of mobile health interventions for infectious diseases and NCDs using the WHO mERA checklist.

DOI: 10.4018/978-1-6684-6873-9.ch002

BACKGROUND

Public health surveillance is important towards prevention and control of infectious/emerging disease, and involves the systematic collection, analysis, interpretation and use of data by various players in the health system to enhance human health (World Health Organization, 2018). Public health disease surveillance helps to provide early warning to the public on emergency/re-emergence of diseases of national and global threat. Surveillance also assists individual nations and global health authorities to monitor the trends of endemic and pandemic diseases, and evaluate the impacts of implemented intervention. Disease surveillance also assist in monitoring the progress made towards elimination and eradication of priority diseases (World Health Organization, 2018). Disease surveillance can be either active or passive, which is generally less expensive and involves use of data reported by health providers to the higher authorities as part of their routine activities. Passive surveillance will be the main focus of this proposed book chapter. The World Health Organization (WHO) recommends integrating digital health (e-health) technologies in disease surveillance process (WHO, n.d.-a). The term digital health refers to the use of mobile devices; mobile phones, tablet computers and personal digital assistants, as well as other information and communication technologies, Internet of things, artificial intelligence, big data and robotics, for health-related purposes (*GSMA_MobileEconomy2021_3 (1)*, 2021).

The application of e-health technologies in disease surveillance has several benefits, including; assisting timely disease detection, investigation and response to outbreaks, fast data sharing across actors, safe storage and easy access of data, minimization of errors caused by manual data entry and results into quality data, cost effectiveness and can automatically produce alerts and reports (WHO, n.d.-b). In addition, the e-health digital applications can improve timeliness and completeness of the reports which are important element of the successful surveillance system (Kastner et al., 2021).

In Tanzania, digital health technology has also gained huge recognition and digital technologies and applications are used to facilitate patient registration, diagnosis and treatment, payment of hospital bills and revenue collection, keeping of pharmacy records, provision of health education, monitoring of patients progress and promoting treatment adherence, management of human resources and collection and storage of health information (GSMA Intelligence, 2014).

There are two platforms used for obtaining surveillance data, such as integrated disease surveillance and response system and routine health management information system (HMIS), (Francois, 2021). The disease surveillance is basically conducted by following the World Health Organization Africa region (WHO/AFRO) Integrated Disease Surveillance and Response guideline of 2011. In this guideline, the WHO emphasizes on continuous surveillance and response to 34 priority diseases, conditions or events, which by their nature require special reporting and response mechanisms compared to other diseases (WHO, n.d.-b). Following the adaptation of this guideline, Tanzania included 34 priority diseases, conditions or events in its public health surveillance process, and they are classified into epidemic prone diseases, diseases targeted for elimination or eradication, diseases of public health importance, non-communicable diseases and public health emergencies of international concern (Force, 2016).

Inclusion of e-health technology in the disease surveillance process has been advocated by the Tanzanian Ministry of Health in several guidelines including; United Republic of Tanzania Digital Health Strategy 2019-2024, Tanzania national eHealth strategy June, 2013-July, 2018, and Tanzania digital health investment roadmap 2017-2023. Moreover, numerous articles have been published regarding disease surveillance and application of e-health applications in Tanzania. However, the available information still remains exceedingly disperse. This book chapter can thus assist in reviewing and updating the public and researchers on available of e-health digital technology applications for disease/public health surveillance in Tanzania.

One of the challenges facing the currently used digital surveillance system in Tanzania is the use of tedious paper-based data entry process in the HMIS registers. Surveillance under HMIS is also affected by insufficient data collection and reporting documents; registers, tally sheet and report forms, incomplete data, poor adherence to the coding procedures, data cooking habit at the both outpatient and inpatient sections and unreliable quality checking mechanisms (Susan F Rumisha et al., 2020). Also, data verification is time consuming, especially for districts with many healthcare facilities, and they can spend the whole day in the verification exercise. Other challenging factors include use of multiple reporting tools for surveillance in the country, which cause data inconsistence, for example data collected through the government centralized HMIS and disease-specific programs from non-governmental private stakeholders do not reflect one another and are causing challenges in monitoring and evaluation of public health information. Also, lack of ICT infrastructures; computers, enough human resource capacity, unreliable power supply and internet connection are hindering adoption of more sophisticated digital surveillance tools in the country (Van Schalkwyk, 2018).

MAIN OBJECTIVE OF THE CHAPTER

The main objective of this book chapter is to give an overview on e-health technology applications for disease surveillance in Tanzania and their current gaps and challenges that need to be addressed.

METHODOLOGY

The information collection strategy for this chapter was guided by the formative methodological framework for scoping reviews (Tricco et al., 2018) which included desktop searching for papers in English from the databases in the past 10 years, such as PubMed, Medline, Web of Science, Scopus, Google scholar, government websites, and official documentation, such as Tanzania's e-Health strategic plans and policies.

The data collection process was conducted to review the disease surveillance systems in Tanzania and application of digital technology for surveillance of infectious and non-infectious disease activities in the country, focusing on World Health Organization Africa region (WHO/AFRO) Integrated Disease Surveillance and Response (IDSR) guideline (WHO Regional Office for Africa, 2019). Other information sources included publications or documents related to surveillance of non-communicable diseases (NCDs) reported on digital health technologies. Further screening process was conducted by reading the entire downloaded documents until suitable documents which reflected the objective set for this chapter were obtained.

RESULTS

In summary, 30 publications and 5 public documents, and other related documents were found to contain the needed information on infectious and non-infectious disease digital surveillance in Tanzania.

Infectious Disease Surveillance in Tanzania

Infectious disease surveillance is conducted mainly under passive disease surveillance approach in Tanzania (Nkowane, 2019) through two platforms used for obtaining infectious disease data, such as integrated disease surveillance and response system (IDSR) and routine health management information system (HMIS), (Nkowane, 2019; Rutatola et al., 2018; Van Schalkwyk & Silaa, 2018). The IDSR is conducted by following the WHO/AFRO Integrated Disease Surveillance and Response guideline of 2011 (Nkowane, 2019; Saleh, Kitau, Konradsen, Mboera, & Schiøler, 2021), which emphasizes on continuous surveillance and response to priority diseases (WHO Regional Office for Africa, 2019). Following the adaptation of this guideline, Tanzania include 34 priority diseases, conditions or events in its IDSR process and they are classified as epidemic prone diseases, diseases targeted for elimination or eradication, diseases of public health importance, NCDs and public health emergencies of international concern (Maternal and Child Survival Program [MCSP], 2019; Mwamnyange et al., 2021; Nkowane, 2019).

Implementation of the IDSR involves several actors, including community health workers (CHWs), Health facilities, district health authorities, regional health authorities, the ministry of health and the WHO (Nkowane, 2019; WHO Regional Office for Africa, 2019). Successful IDSR has following eight core functions; case identification, reporting, investigation and confirmation, analysis and interpretation of data, preparedness and response actions, as well as feedback provision and monitoring and evaluations (Nkowane, 2019; WHO Regional Office for Africa, 2019). The Tanzania health system is decentralized in nature, where by planning and implementation of health services, including surveillance operations, is conducted by local government councils (Silaa & Van Schalkwyk, 2018; MCSP, 2019; Nkowane, 2019).

Detection and Reporting of Infectious Diseases in Tanzania

Healthcare workers in healthcare facilities and community health workers (CHWs) are responsible for disease detection and reporting in Tanzania (Nkowane, 2019; WHO Regional Office for Africa, 2019). The healthcare facilities workers use standard case definition to identify priority disease conditions and events while simplified case definitions are used at the community level (WHO Regional Office for Africa, 2019). It was found that, community- based surveillance (CBS) is not operational in Tanzania and CHWs play little role in detection and reporting of infectious diseases (MCSP, 2019; Mboera et al., 2021; Nkowane, 2019; Sindato et al., 2021). The case identification and reporting activities are therefore limited to healthcare facilities in Tanzania, through nurses and clinicians (Nkowane, 2019).

Data reporting from the facilities to the next level is conducted through mobile phone application called electronic integrated disease surveillance and response system (eIDSR)(MCSP, 2019; Nkowane, 2019), which was developed in 2013 (Ministry of Health and Social Welfare, 2013). This system is used for reporting of IDSR diseases in Tanzania (MCSP, 2019; Nkowane, 2019). The reporting modality is through unstructured Supplementary Service Data (USSD) (Joachim et al., 2018; Nkowane, 2019; Rutatola et al., 2018). The eIDSR is linked to electronic national health management information system (DHIS2), which allows data analysis and use by district, regional and Ministry of Health officers (Joachimet al., 2018). The interviewed medical professionals reported that, immediate reportable diseases, conditions and events captured through the eIDSR included; emerging and re -emerging infectious diseases, neglected tropical diseases, hemorrhagic fevers, diarrhea, acute malnutrition, upper respiratory diseases and malaria.

Monthly reports for infectious diseases are collected through the HMIS (Nkowane, 2019), where every health facility is provided with 18 HMIS documents for reporting different healthcare services.

Important HMIS documents for surveillance include; outpatient department (OPD) and inpatient department (IPD) documents (MoHCDGEC, 2017). Each HMIS document has three subdocuments; a register, tally sheet and a monthly summary form (MoHCDGEC, 2017). The monthly summary forms generated at the healthcare facilities by medical personnel are used to inform the district health authorities on the community health status through the HMIS database (MoHCDGEC, 2017).

Under the HMIS, reporting from healthcare facilities to district is predominantly paper-based, where by monthly summary forms are submitted physically to the office of the district medical officer (Silaa & Van Schalkwyk, 2018; MoHCDGEC, 2017), who then verifies all received monthly reports and upon his approval, the district HMIS focal person enters the data into the DHIS2 (MoHCDGEC, 2017) using computers or smart phones.

District health information system 2 (DHIS2) is the national web-based modular platform used for data collection, data management and data analysis in Tanzania. It allows visualization of the reported data in terms of graphs, maps and dashboards by health authorities from the district to national level (Kumalija, 2017; Sukums et al., 2021). The DHIS2 system receives data from the HMIS, eIDSR, and vertical disease specific programs, such as national malaria control program (NMCP), national AIDS control program (NACP) and national tuberculosis and leprosy program (TBLP) (Kumalija, 2017; MoHCDGEC, 2017). DHIS2 allows multiple users who are assigned to different tasks to simultaneously access the system (MoHCDGEC, 2017). For the part of infectious disease surveillance data, the DHIS2 sends alert to the district, regional, and national epidemiologist immediately when an outbreak is suspected, and this is done in forms of emails and text messages for follow-up purposes (Rutatola et al., 2018; Joachim et al., 2018).

Strength of the Existing Infectious Disease Surveillance System in Tanzania

The use of eIDSR is reported to have improved timeliness and completeness of the reports and consequently early detection and response to outbreaks in Tanzania (Joachim et al., 2018). The eIDSR is also reported to be simple and user friendly, allowing mobile phone data reporting irrespective of internet connectivity. It also can send quick alert and notifications to surveillance officers for timely action (Joachim et al., 2018). Use of computerized DHIS2 for reporting of monthly HMIS data at regional and national levels has facilitated achievement of high rates of data completeness, reaching up to 98% in Tanzania. The national data reporting completeness statistics showed that only three districts recorded data completeness rates below 90% in 2018 (MOHCDGEC, 2019).

DISCUSSION

This chapter provides an overview on current status of disease surveillance in Tanzania. It also summarizes available literature on current and previous digital technology applications used for management of both infectious and NCDs in Tanzania.

WHO emphasizes on implementation of community-based disease surveillance (WHO Regional Office for Africa, 2019), which helps to capture data from individuals that do not attend healthcare facilities due to unavailability or lack of access (Guerra et al., 2019), hence minimizing timely detection and response to outbreak prone diseases. It was herein found that, data obtained from the healthcare facilities and sent to the central government is collected through monthly HMIS reports in Tanzania. It was also found that, the digital technologies, such as mobile phones, tablets and computers are employed to enhance disease surveillance process in Tanzania. It was further found that, the majority of healthcare facilities rely on paper-based submission of monthly reports to the district level HMIS. The paper based surveillance was previously found to be ineffective data sharing method in Tanzania (Mghamba et al., 2008; Rumisha et al., 2020), making it a drawback that may delay timely decision making, and thus epidemiological investigations and timely response to disease outbreaks. Moreover, the government of Tanzania has made remarkable efforts in transforming the paper-based to digital-based reporting system. For example, the reporting of weekly notifiable diseases under the IDSR was found to be completely digitalized, and data reports were sent to higher authorities by use of the eIDSR mobile-based application. The government of Tanzania is also taking more initiatives to implement e-technologies to enhance collection and analysis of weekly reports, for example, direct transmission of weekly data to the electronic national health management information system data base (DHIS2). The use of both eIDSR and DHIS2 for reporting of IDSR diseases have contributed to timeliness and completeness of reports, consequently facilitating timely decision and response to epidemic events (Rumisha et al., 2007). Other examples from other parts of Africa show that, the use of digital technology in disease surveillance is increasing. For example, 33 out of 47 African countries were using electronic tools for reporting of diseases in 2017, and they had good performance in terms of timeliness and completeness of reporting (Fall et al., 2019). Similar to Tanzania, other African countries are also currently using the DHIS2 in disease surveillance process (Kiberu et al., 2014; Martin et al., 2020; Njeru et al., 2020; Reynolds et al., 2022).

Non-governmental organizations and individual healthcare stakeholders have also shown interest and efforts to bring digital health technology applications in disease surveillance in Tanzania. This was proven by availability of many privately-owned digital health tools currently implemented or previously piloted for helping disease surveillance in different parts of Tanzania. However, many of these e-health applications are not yet connected to the national disease surveillance system, and some are just in their trial stage. Moreover, implementation of both eIDSR and DHIS2 digital health systems in Tanzania was found to be hindered by many factors, including unreliable network and internet connections, unreliable power supply and lack of digital devices, including computers at the healthcare facilities. Access to digital infrastructures is also still low in the country, for example, only half of Tanzanians had access to internet in 2020 (Statista, 2021).

eHealth is defined as cost-effective and secure use of information and communication technology (ICT) in support of health and health-related fields, including healthcare services, health surveillance, health literature, health education, knowledge, and research. This definition introduces a range of services, such as electronic health records, to ensure continuity of patient care across time, mobile health services (mHealth), telehealth, health research, consumer health informatics to support individuals in health decision making, and e-learning by health workers. eHealth can be used as a means of ensuring provision of correct health information in a timely manner, where it is needed and to whom it is needed, in a secure, electronic form for the purpose of improving the quality and efficiency of healthcare delivery and prevention programs. Examples of ICT applications for health include; electronic health records showing patients' health histories, mobile apps designed to raise awareness about non-communicable diseases (NCDs) and internet connected devices, such as those used by doctors to monitor patients' blood glucose levels (Aerts, 2018).

Non communicable diseases (NCDs) account for approximately 70% of deaths worldwide, of which three-quarters occur in low- and middle-income countries (LMICs) (WHO, 2018). Funding for tackling NCDs is low in low- and middle-income countries (LMICs) like Tanzania compared to other diseases and preventive measures (WHO, 2018). Investing in digital health to strengthen entire health systems can therefore accelerate efforts to combat NCDs. Ultimately, digital health can allow the LMICs to move from disease silos in healthcare to integrated, resilient health systems. NCDs, such as cardiovascular disease, cancer, diabetes and respiratory diseases caused 41 million deaths in 2016, accounting for 71% of deaths globally (WHO, 2018). Approximately 15 million people between the ages of 30 and 69 years die annually from NCDs, during their prime working years. Moreover, over 85% of these deaths occur in LMICs (Broadband Commission, 2018), which often have health systems that are better suited to delivering acute care for urgent medical conditions (WHO, 2018). However, funding for tackling NCDs is especially donor funded and lags behind the funding earmarked for communicable diseases, such as HIV/AIDS or tuberculosis. Even though NCDs cause 56.2% of disability-adjusted life-years (DALYs), defined by the WHO as "loss of 'healthy' life" year in LMICs, only 2.2% of development assistance for health (DAH) in 2017 was allocated to NCDs. By contrast, the HIV/AIDS was responsible for 2.5% of DALYs in LMICs but received 24.2% of the year's health related development assistance (WHO, 2016b; Seattle, 2018).

Some digital technologies, such as mHealth, have been widely adopted over the past few years in managing and monitoring NCDs. In the case of mHealth tools, the already broad range of lifestyle and wellness apps are currently being complemented by new digital therapeutics that have a measurable impact on diseases' progression and can often be used on mobile phones to monitor NCDs. Digital therapeutics are technologies that can complement or even replace traditional clinical treatments. As of mid-2018, 120 countries, including Tanzania, have developed strategies in the digital health, telehealth or eHealth fields (Abdellatif et al., 2007). In some cases, these strategies have been successfully implemented at the national level as primary healthcare initiatives addressing NCDs (URT, 2019; Ministry of Health and Social Welfare, 2013).

Mobile health (mHealth) has been hailed as a potential gamechanger for NCDs management, especially in LMICs. Individual studies illustrate barriers to implementation and scale-up of mHealth technology, but an overview of implementation issues for NCDs mHealth interventions in LMICs is lacking. This chapter explored mHealth implementation issues from two ways, namely; information in published papers and field-based knowledge from people working in this field. A two-stage web-based survey on implementation barriers was thus performed within infectious and NCDs research networks in Tanzania and through online platforms on mHealth targeting researchers and implementors as herein reported. The m-Health technology has great potential to empower patients, health workers and health system managers through applications, such as self-monitoring devices, electronic information systems and mobile services, for follow-up of interventions and community support. mHealth tools can improve the performance of health workers through provision of online guidelines and referral services. They also help retain patients in care through reminders and self-management of information and monitoring tools (Seattle, 2018).

Many m-Health projects in Tanzania remain stuck at pilot stages and there is limited evidence on their effectiveness, cost, and uptake in NCDs management settings (WHO, 2016b). Individual studies have been focusing on implementation barriers. However, very few publications provide detailed description of m-Health implementation process, implementation barriers and how they are addressed. The mHealth evidence reporting and assessment (mERA) checklist was therefore developed in response to the observed need for increased clarity in reporting and describing mHealth interventions, especially in LMICs like Tanzania. According to the Tanzania Digital Health 2019-2024 Strategy, several initiatives have been executed as regards to e-health, including installation of a local area network and national ICT backbone network in health facilities and institutions, existence of eHealth governance and leadership at the national level, strengthening and scaling up of the District Health Information System software version 2, implementation of planning and reporting system in all councils, implementation of the electronic Logistics Management Information System countrywide, national rollout of an electronic Integrated Diseases Surveillance and Response System (eIDSR), implementation of an electronic Health Facility Registry, and implementation of the National Sanitation Management Information System.

Other eHealth initiatives in Tanzania include the following: Hospital Management Information Systems (HMIS), disease-specific information systems, such as Care and Treatment Clinic databases versions 2 and 3 for HIV and AIDS, a management information system for neglected tropical diseases, electronic Tuberculosis and Leprosy registers, and malaria MISs, telemedicine infrastructure and services, a vaccine information management system, the Tanzania Immunization Registry, a mobile health (mHealth) platform for enhancing health education, information, and communication (e.g., reporting and client feedback), and National Health Insurance Fund e-solutions.

An in-depth overview on implementation issues for infectious diseases and NCDs mHealth interventions in Tanzania is still lacking. In view of this, this chapter has produced evidence in mHealth tools and their implementation in Tanzania.

CONCLUSION

This chapter has reported the status of digital disease surveillance in Tanzania. It was also found that, the surveillance data are obtained through routine reports of weekly IDSR diseases and HMIS monthly reports. Disease data are mainly collected from healthcare facilities while community-based data still remains weak. Both manual paper-based, as well as digital technologies, are employed in sharing of both infectious and NCDs data to the higher-level health authorities. Apart from nationally implemented digital technologies, disease specific programs also use digital technologies to enhance the surveillance process. The main challenges affecting implementation of digital surveillance technologies in Tanzania are unreliable infrastructure, such as poor internet, unreliable power supply, as well as lack of integration between the existing and newly developed digital technologies. The following challenges of existing infectious and NCDs surveillance in Tanzania:

Implementation of the eIDSR was in this chapter found to have following specific challenges:

- It does not accommodate all infectious and zoonotic diseases.
- It captures aggregated numerical data only, which are insufficient for epidemiological analysis.
- The USSD format is insufficient for reporting many cases, and it also has timeouts when there is delayed user action.
- It does not capture community based data, and its implementation is donor dependent (Joachim et al., 2018; Nkowane, 2019; Rutatola et al., 2018).
- The entry into the eIDSR was also found to be tedious, because each disease is reported independently, and separate logins are required for reporting each disease.
- Only registered mobile phone numbers can be used, thus the focal person has to send data even when they are on leave, so when the registered person leaves the health facility, reports may also be absent for several weeks.

- Absence of community-based disease surveillance is also minimizing efficiency of disease surveillance process in Tanzania. The community based disease surveillance is not routinely done, and is generally weak (MCSP, 2019) and not operational in urban areas (Mboera et al., 2021). The paper-based data entry process in the HMIS registers and DHIS2 is tedious (Kumalija, 2017). The disease reporting under the HMIS is also affected by insufficient data collection and reporting documents, registers, tally sheet and report forms, incomplete data, poor adherence to the coding procedures, data cooking habit at the outpatient (OPD) and in-patient (IPD) and unreliable quality checking mechanisms (Silaa & Van Schalkwyk, 2018; Rumisha et al., 2020). Data verification under the HMIS is also time consuming, especially for districts with many healthcare facilities.
- The other challenging factors for implementation of digital disease surveillance in Tanzania include; use of multiple reporting tools for surveillance, which cause data inconsistence. For example, data collected through the IDSR, HMIS and disease-specific programs do not reflect one another, which causes challenges during monitoring and evaluation of e- health information (Kumalija, 2017; Nkowane, 2019). Lack of ICT infrastructures; computers, human resource capacity, unreliable power sources and internet connection also hinder adoption of more sophisticated digital disease surveillance tools (Silaa & Van Schalkwyk, 2018; MOHCDGEC, 2019b).
- Many m-Health interventions in Tanzania use low-cost software and devices with limited capacity that do not allow linkage with NCDs routine data or patient records with fragmented delivery and increased workload.
- Healthcare education given via a mobile device requires adaptation of the content to the delivery channel. Health education on NCDs and inclusion of motivations techniques is an area in development in Tanzania, and is still very limited in many health care settings. Although there are many apps for smartphones, quality varies and they are not always relevant for people (Kim & So, 2018).
- The mentioned technical barriers are related to the network providers and operating systems, the hardware and software and linking of different digital systems. Only a few projects have managed to link their project software with existing HMIS or to electronic medical records.
- The mentioned health care services barriers to e-health technology deployment in Tanzania are related to the lack of resources, access to care and integration of m-Health interventions into infectious diseases and NCDs health care processes, including resistance of health professionals to change. The lack of technical possibilities to link digital systems with each other leads to interventions set up in a fragmented fashion, which in turn increases the workload for health workers.
- Some respondents mentioned that, continuing education and feedback maintained their commitment while other respondents mentioned that discussions with health authorities on the need for upgrading public health facilities, and through partnering with other health care providers, pharmacies and community organizations, served as a means to expose the unmet need for NCDs interventions, and could therefore contribute to a change process to increase resources for NCDs management.
- A number of challenges also affected implementation of the Tanzania Digital Health 2019-2024 Strategy. These include inadequate ICT infrastructure, unreliable electric power supply, limited financial resources, inadequate ICT personnel, inadequate digital literacy amongst health workers and managers, and resistance to the adoption of eHealth solutions, as well as existence of multiple fragmented electronic health information systems that were not interoperable or not well aligned with the workflow in the health sector.

- Moreover, there is also an unclear governance structure and weak coordination and engagement of stakeholders in the e-Health strategic implementation for both infectious diseases and NCDs at different levels of the health system.

RECOMMENDATIONS FOR SUCCESSFUL IMPLEMENTATION OF M-HEALTH TECHNOLOGY APPLICATIONS IN INFECTIOUS AND NON-COMMUNICABLE DISEASE SURVEILLANCE IN TANZANIA

- Authors from this chapter recommend the government of Tanzania and the rest of stakeholders to come up with digital technologies that would completely replace the paper-based registration of patients, collection of disease data and reporting of HMIS data in Tanzania.
- The chapter authors also recommend to the government of Tanzania and the rest of stakeholders to take measures to improve network and internet connections and increase healthcare facilities' access to reliable power sources, to facilitate implementation of digital surveillance in the country. The government of Tanzania and digital technologies developers, including university students and researchers, should take measures to ensure scale up of current and previous digital technologies that have demonstrated positive impacts on surveillance, and to ensure these available technologies are integrated with the national health management systems, as well as other digital systems that are used in in the country.
- Moreover, the government should take the lead in coordinating funding for digital health platforms, which can be done through applying for increased donor and development banks funding, to step up funding of core health IT systems.
- Policymakers, donors, private companies and other digital health stakeholders should also use the tools described in this chapter to foster sustainable digital health surveillance solutions that will properly address specific needs of patients with infectious and NCDs.
- As budgets are often constrained, e-Health technology end users should be protected against financial hardship through possible use of an insurance structure.

FUTURE PERCEPTIVE FOR E-HEALTH TECHNOLOGY DEPLOYMENT IN TANZANIA

Sustainability of e-health solutions for infectious and NCDs management in Tanzania should be regarded as having the following key aspects in the future:

- Digital health solutions should be implemented in a way that will integrate easily with existing clinical processes and workflows, including the health system's general structure and challenges, as well as associated needs. Other national technology systems, such as a citizens' ID program or health information and monitoring system should also be included in the e-Health solutions.
- Digital health solutions should be made in such a way that they are able to reach all targeted users at both national and regional levels in Tanzania. The digital solutions should be simple to use in existing digital infrastructure.

- National-level leadership is vital in Tanzania, for ensuring the sustainability of digital health solutions, as they can drive plans forward throughout the solution's lifecycle. Good governance techniques will in turn allow the government to coordinate various infectious and NCDs digital solutions being implemented.
- There should be a digital health strategy that supports transformation of infectious and NCDs management, which should include; assessment of health needs of a country and consider how digital health solutions can address them. The strategy should also use established frameworks for maturity assessment, such as the questionnaire additional toolkits, such as the Health Information Systems Interoperability Maturity Toolkit (USAID, 2019). The strategy should also define a vision and roadmap that will feature clear and measurable milestones.
- The e-Health interventions for infectious and NCDs should be aligned with stakeholders from both within and outside the government. Deploying a national digital health strategy is a complex and costly undertaking, so joint work from various ministries or government bodies is essential. The digital health stakeholders should be empowered to connect with other stakeholders within the government, especially with the Ministry of Health, Ministry of Communication and e-government agency, as well as those external to the government such as donors, the private sector and NGOs from health, ICT and adjacent sectors (e.g., banking, food), including them in government based working groups.
- An intersectoral governance system should be established with an action-oriented taskforce that advocates, advises, builds the capacity and monitors digital health initiatives for infectious and NCDs' monitoring in the country.
- The government of Tanzania should consider setting up an investment fund for digital health interventions and attract other sources of funding that can complement MoH resources, including establishing a robust monitoring and evaluation framework that draws on existing frameworks, such as the WHO's Guidance on Monitoring and Evaluating Digital Health Interventions (World Health Organization, 2016).
- The government of Tanzania should collaborate with universities and other learning organizations to define digital health skills required, identify gaps in the current educational offer, promote the creation or upgrade of training opportunities for different user segments, such as prospective college students and researchers. A human resource plan should also include interaction with end users and monitoring for software maintenance and digital health information management, and for evaluation cycles with feedback from users, to ensure relevance and quality on the longer term. This information is relevant for decisions on scaling-up of mHealth technologies in the domain of infectious and NCDs in Tanzania.
- The government of Tanzania should improve the completeness of reporting of mobile health (mHealth) interventions for infectious and NCDS using the WHO mHealth evidence reporting and assessment (mERA) checklist (Agarwal et al., 2016).

Table 1. Summary of digital systems currently and previously implemented to facilitate infectious disease surveillance in Tanzania

Digital System	Function	Status	Source
Eidsr	Sending Immediate and weekly report of infectious diseases	Currently used throughout the country	(Joachim et al., 2018)
DHIS2	Collection, collation, analysis and dissemination of health data	Currently used throughout the country	(MoHCDGEC, 2017)
GoTHoMIS	Can facilitate generation of HMIS monthly reports and outbreak reports	Rolling out Continues throughout the country	(PO-RALG, 2017)
MEED and Coconut Surveillance	Weekly notification of malaria cases and Active malaria surveillance at households' level/ reactive case detection	Currently used throughout Zanzibar	(Ministry of health and social welfare Zanzibar, 2016)
AfyaData	Community based Surveillance of animal, human and zoonotic diseases	Currently used in six districts (Kilosa, Malinyi, Ulanga, Ngara, Ngorongoro and Wete)	(Fondation Pierre Fabre, 2019)
IBCM	Integrated surveillance of rabies through one health approach and specifically implementation of integrated bite case management approach	Currently still in pilot phase in all district of Mara, Morogoro Mtwara and Lindi, region, two districts in Arusha (Karatuand Ngorongoro) and threedistricts in Zanzibar (Wete, Chakechake, Mkoani and Micheweni.	(Lushasi et al., 2020)
Mobile phone-based surveillance system for rabies	Integrated surveillance of rabies through one health approach	Currently not in use. Implementation ended on pilot phase and was replaced by IBCM app	(Mtema, 2013)
Community- based disease surveillance system (ComD- STM)	Passive an active malaria surveillance and drug resistant	Currently not in use. Implementation ended on pilot phase in Tanga	(Francis et al., 2017)
Smartphone-based reporting application	Routine reporting of weekly and monthly infectious diseases	Currently not in use. Implementation ended on validation and testing phase	(Pascoe, 2016)
Mobile application for collecting Integrated Disease Surveillance and Response data	Reporting of weekly IDSR diseases	Adopted as eIDSR system used for IDSR reporting in Tanzania	(Pascoe, Lungo, Kaasbøll, & Koleleni, 2012)
Mobile technologies for disease surveillance in humans and animals	Community health reports for both human and animal related events, weekly and monthly reports for human diseases as well as animal surveillance.	Improved to AfyaData application used to enhance CBS of humans and animal diseases.	(Mwabukusi, Karimuribo, Rweyemamu, & Beda, 2014)

Table 2. Examples of e-health programs and applications demonstrating impact in NCDs prevention and management globally

Programs	Solutions	Impact
WellDoc – BlueStar Diabetes Management App (Krohn, Metcalf, & Salber, 2017) (Wellcom.com, 2018) (United States)	Diabetes management – Mobile prescription therapy system for diabetes that provides users with access to real-time individualized coaching, educational tools, medication regimen support and health records that can be shared with providers to inform clinical decision-making.	1.2% or greater decline of HbA1c levels in users compared to patients undergoing usual care D 58% reduction in emergency room visits D Average saving of US$254 to US$271 per user per month.
Discovery – Vitality Health App (Patel et al., 2010) (Patel et al., 2010) (South Africa and other countries)	Reduce risk factors – App-based activity tracking and rewards program used by insurance companies to incentivize members to lead healthier lifestyles. Users can earn rewards ranging from reduced premiums to gift cards and discounted flights by meeting activity goals and making healthy food choices	Admission rates to the hospital were 7.4% lower for cardiovascular diseases, 13.2% lower for cancers, and 20.7% lower for endocrine and metabolic diseases D Deployed by five of world's leading insurers D 6 million individual users
Be He@lthy, Be Mobile (BHBM) – India mTobacco Cessation (WHO, 2016a) (IQVIA Institute, 2017) (India)	Smoking cessation – As the world's largest mobile-based smoking cessation program, India's tobacco Cessation is helping people quit tobacco use through interactive support delivered by mobile phones.	7.2% six-months quit rate D 2.1M+ users enrolled as of Aug 2017
Novartis Foundation – Ghana Telemedicine (Ghana) (Foundation, 2016)	Telemedicine – The Ghana Telemedicine program connects community health workers with specialists via a 24-hour teleconsultation center.	Reached 6 million patients D 31% unnecessary referrals avoided through teleconsultation ($31 USD saved per avoided referral), as more than half of all teleconsultations could be resolved directly by phone
Carlos Slim Foundation – CASALUD (Gallardo-Rincón et al., 2021) (Deloitte, 2016) (GSMA, 2019) (Mexico)	NCD prevention and disease management program – Proactive prevention of NCD risk factors using MIDOTM and disease management through SIC (an NCD information system). In addition, mobile technologies are used to provide online training to health professionals and community workers, monitor the supply of medicines and lab tests and empower patients.	Implementation as a national policy, with outreach to +12,000 primary care clinics. D 1M+ individuals screened with MIDO D 1.8M+ patients with daily updates in the NCDs Integrated Dashboard D Increased A1c testing in diabetic patients throughout participating clinics in Mexico from 10% in 2014 to 54.8% in 2018
AccuHealth (Intel, 2018)(Chile)	NCD risk prediction – Wearable sensors linked to a smart monitoring device that connects to the AccuHealth virtual hospital remote monitoring center. Data mining and predictive modeling anticipate any health deterioration that would require an ER visit or hospitalization.	Monitored over 15,000 patients D 42% decrease in emergency room visits.
AxisMed (GSMA Intelligence, 2017) (Brazil)	Remote monitoring solution – Tracking and transmission of biometric data with personal device (e.g., blood glucose levels and blood pressure) from chronic patients to medical professionals who oversee their treatment plans.	Over 80% of patients monitored have adhered to their treatment plan D Reduced hospital emergency ward visits by two-thirds

REFERENCES

Abdellatif, A., Bagian, J. P., Barajas, E. R., Cohen, M., Cousins, D., Denham, C. R., Essinger, K., Gegelashvili, G., Glenister, H., Hoffman, C., Horvath, D., Khoja, T., Klazinga, N., Lee, C. E., Letlape, T. K., Lilja, B., Manasse, H. R. Jr, Massoud, M. R., Wilson, R. M. L., ... Youngson, R. (2007). Communication During Patient Hand-Overs. *Joint Commission Journal on Quality and Patient Safety*, *33*(7), 439–442. doi:10.1016/S1553-7250(07)33128-0

Aerts, A. (2018). *The Novartis Foundation*. Academic Press.

Agarwal, S., LeFevre, A. E., Lee, J., L'engle, K., Mehl, G., Sinha, C., & Labrique, A. (2016). Guidelines for reporting of health interventions using mobile phones: Mobile health (mHealth) evidence reporting and assessment (mERA) checklist. *BMJ (Clinical Research Ed.)*, 352. doi:10.1136/bmj.i1174 PMID:26988021

And, R. S. (2018). *Mapping Hyperlocal Health Data Flows:The Case of Kyela District, Tanzania*. Dar es Salaam: DataZetu.

Broadband Commission. (2018). *Working Group on Digital Health*. Retrieved from https://broadbandcommission.org/Documents/publications/DigitalHealthReport2018.pdf

Deloitte. (2016). *High-value health care - Innovative approaches to global challenges*. Retrieved from https://www2.deloitte.com/content/dam/Deloitte/global/Documents/Life-Sciences-Health-Care/gx-lshc-high-value-health-care.pdf

Fall, I. S., Rajatonirina, S., Yahaya, A. A., Zabulon, Y., Nsubuga, P., Nanyunja, M., … Talisuna, A. O. (2019). *Integrated Disease Surveillance and Response (IDSR) strategy : Current status, challenges and perspectives for the future in Africa*. doi:10.1136/bmjgh-2019-001427

Fondation Pierre Fabre. (2019). *Field survey report AfyaData Project : Promoting Proper Management of Zoonotic Diseases through e-based One Health Training of Frontline Health Worker Global South eHealth Observatory*. Author.

Force, M. H. T. (2016). *Maternal and Child Survival Program (MCSP)*. Retrieved from https://www.mhtf.org/organization/maternal-and-child-survival-program-mcsp/

Foundation, N. (2016). *Ghana Telemedicine: Digital Health Ghana*. Retrieved from https://www.novartisfoundation.org/past-programs/digital-health/ghana-telemedicine

Francis, F., Ishengoma, D. S., Mmbando, B. P., Rutta, A. S. M., Malecela, M. N., Mayala, B., Lemnge, M. M., & Michael, E. (2017). Deployment and use of mobile phone technology for real - time reporting of fever cases and malaria treatment failure in areas of declining malaria transmission in Muheza district north - eastern Tanzania. *Malaria Journal*, *16*(308), 1–14. doi:10.118612936-017-1956-z PMID:28764792

Francois. (2021). *Mapping health data flows and use in rural Tanzania*. Retrieved from https://medium.com/data-zetu/learning-about-hyperlocal-data-f78084136cf

Gallardo-Rincón, H., Montoya, A., Saucedo-Martínez, R., Mújica-Rosales, R., Suárez-Idueta, L., Martínez-Juárez, L. A., Razo, C., Lozano, R., & Tapia-Conyer, R. (2021). Integrated Measurement for Early Detection (MIDO) as a digital strategy for timely assessment of non-communicable disease profiles and factors associated with unawareness and control: A retrospective observational study in primary healthcare facilities in Mexico. *BMJ Open*, *11*(9), e049836. doi:10.1136/bmjopen-2021-049836 PMID:34475175

GSMA. (2019). *CASALUD: A suite of digital health services for the prevention and management of NCDs. Delivered in partnership with the Mexico Ministry of Health and Carlos Slim Foundation.* Retrieved from www.gsma.com/mobilefordevelopment/

GSMA_MobileEconomy2021_3 (1). (2021).

Guerra, J., Acharya, P., & Barnadas, C. (2019). Community-based surveillance : A scoping review. *PLoS One*, 1–25. https://doi.org/https://doi.org/ 10.1371/journal.pone.0215278 PMID:30978224

Intel. (2018). *Intel and Partners Come Together to Solve Healthcare*. Retrieved from https://newsroom.intel.com/editorials/intel-partners-come-together-solve-healthcare/

Intelligence, G. S. M. A. (2014). *GSMA: Digital inclusion Report*. Retrieved from https://www.ncbi.nlm.nih.gov/pubmed/19547787

Intelligence, G. S. M. A. (2017). *Scaling digital health in developing markets*. Retrieved from https://www.gsmaintelligence.com/research/?file=c581aa43bdb7b7d236bb937698c2d6fd&download

IQVIA Institute. (2017). *The Growing Value of Digital Health*. Retrieved from https://www.iqvia.com/insights/the-iqvia-institute/reports/the-growing-value-of-digital-health

JJoachim, Yassin, Cosmas, & Darcy. (2018). Electronic Integrated Disease Surveillance and Response eIDSR implementation in Tanzania. In *Electronic Integrated Disease Surveillance and Response eIDSR implementation in Tanzania: The 5th Annual Global Digital Health Forum.* Ministry of Health Community Development Gender, Elderly and Children. doi:10.13140/RG.2.2.24365.03049

Kastner, M., Makarski, J., Hayden, L., Hamid, J. S., Holroyd-Leduc, J., Twohig, M., ... Sklar, B. (2021). Effectiveness of an eHealth self-management tool for older adults with multimorbidity (KeepWell): Protocol for a hybrid effectiveness–implementation randomised controlled trial. *BMJ Open*, *11*(2), e048350. doi:10.1136/bmjopen-2020-048350 PMID:33597147

Kiberu, V. M., Matovu, J. K. B., Makumbi, F., Kyozira, C., Mukooyo, E., & Wanyenze, R. K. (2014). Strengthening district-based health reporting through the district health management information software system : The Ugandan experience. *BMC Medical Informatics and Decision Making*, *14*(40), 1–9. doi:10.1186/1472-6947-14-40 PMID:24886567

Kim, S., & So, J. (2018). How message fatigue toward health messages leads to ineffective persuasive outcomes: Examining the mediating roles of reactance and inattention. *Journal of Health Communication*, *23*(1), 109–116. doi:10.1080/10810730.2017.1414900 PMID:29272208

Krohn, R., Metcalf, D., & Salber, P. (2017). *Connected health: improving care, safety, and efficiency with wearables and IoT solution*. Productivity Press.

Kumalija, C. J. (2017). *The United Republic of Tanzania*. Academic Press.

Lushasi, K., Steenson, R., Bernard, J., Changalucha, J. J., Govella, N. J., Haydon, D. T., Hoffu, H., Lankester, F., Magoti, F., Mpolya, E. A., Mtema, Z., Nonga, H., & Hampson, K. (2020). One Health in Practice: Using Integrated Bite Case Management to Increase Detection of Rabid Animals in Tanzania. *Frontiers in Public Health*, *8*(February), 1–10. doi:10.3389/fpubh.2020.00013 PMID:32117850

Martin, D. W., Sloan, M. L., Gleason, B. L., Wit, L. De, Vandi, M. A., Kargbo, D. K., … Singh, T. (2020). Implementing Nationwide Facility-based Lessons Learned. *Health Security, 18*(S1), 1–9. doi:10.1089/hs.2019.0081

Maternal and Child Survival Program. (2019). *Disease Surveillance MCSP Tanzania Program Brief.* Author.

Mboera, L. E. G., Sindato, C., Mremi, I. R., Rumisha, S. F., George, J., Ngolongolo, R., Misinzo, G., Karimuribo, E. D., Rweyemamu, M. M., Haider, N., Hamid, M. A., & Kock, R. (2021). Socio-Ecological Systems Analysis and Health System Readiness in Responding to Dengue Epidemics in Ilala and Kinondoni Districts, Tanzania. *Frontiers in Tropical Diseases*, *2*(September), 1–11. doi:10.3389/fitd.2021.738758

Mghamba, J., Mboera, L., Krekamoo, W., Senkoro, K., Rumisha, S., Shayo, E., & Mmbuji, P. (2008). Challenges of implementing an Integrated Disease Surveillance and Response strategy using the current Health Management Information System in Tanzania. *Tanzania Health Research Bulletin*, *6*(2), 57–63. doi:10.4314/thrb.v6i2.14243

Ministry of Health and Social Welfare. (2013). *Tanzania eHealth Strategy. Tanzania National eHealth Strategy June, 2013 – July, 2018.* Author.

Ministry of Health and Social Welfare Zanzibar. (2016). *National Guidelines for Malaria Surveillance and Response in Zanzibar*. Ministry of Health and Social Welfare Zanzibar.

MoHCDGEC. (2017). *DHIS 2 Functions and data use for health information system*. MOHCDGEC.

MOHCDGEC. (2019). Data systems, data generation and data use, Technical report. Ministry of Health, Community Development, Gender, Elderly and Children. *Mid Term Review of the Health Sector Strategic Plan*, *4*, 2015–2020.

Mwabukusi, M., Karimuribo, E. D., Rweyemamu, M. M., & Beda, E. (2014). Mobile technologies for disease surveillance in humans and animals. *The Onderstepoort Journal of Veterinary Research*, *81*(2), 1–5. doi:10.4102/ojvr.v81i2.737 PMID:25005126

Mwamnyange, M., Luhanga, E., & Thodge, S. R. (2021). Big Data Analytics Framework for Childhood Infectious Disease Surveillance and Response System using Modified MapReduce Algorithm A Case Study of Tanzania. *International Journal of Advanced Computer Science and Applications*, *12*(3), 373–385. doi:10.14569/IJACSA.2021.0120345

Njeru, I., Kareko, D., Kisangau, N., Langat, D., Liku, N., Owiso, G., Dolan, S., Rabinowitz, P., Macharia, D., Ekechi, C., & Widdowson, M. (2020). Use of technology for public health surveillance reporting : Opportunities, challenges and lessons learnt from Kenya. *BMC Public Health*, *20*(1101), 1–11. doi:10.118612889-020-09222-2 PMID:32660509

Nkowane, B. M. (2019). *Streamlining and Strengthening the Disease Surveillance System in Tanzania, Disease Surveillance System Review, Asset Mapping, Gap Analysis, and Proposal of Strategies for Streamlining and Strengthening Disease Surveillance.* Maternal and Child Survival Program.

Nsubuga, P., Eseko, N., Wuhib, T., Ndayimirije, N., Chungong, S., & McNabb, S. (2002). Structure and performance of infectious disease surveillance and response, United Republic of Tanzania, 1998. *Bulletin of the World Health Organization, 80*(3), 196–203. PMID:11984605

Pascoe, L. (2016). *Electronic information capturing, processing and reporting of routine health data using smartphone-based application.* The Nelson Mandela African Institution of Science and Technology NM-AIST.

Pascoe, L., Lungo, J., Kaasbøll, J., & Koleleni, I. (2012). Collecting Integrated Disease Surveillance and Response Data through Mobile Phones. *IST-Africa*, 1–6.

Patel, D. N., Lambert, E. V., da Silva, R., Greyling, M., Nossel, C., Noach, A., Derman, W., & Gaziano, T. (2010). The association between medical costs and participation in the vitality health promotion program among 948,974 members of a South African health insurance company. *American Journal of Health Promotion, 24*(3), 199–204. doi:10.4278/090217-QUAN-68R2.1 PMID:20073387

President's Office – Regional Administration and Local Government. (2017). *Government of Tanzania-Hospital Management Information System (GoT-HOMIS version 3.0) User Manual v1.* President's Office – Regional Administration and Local Government.

Reynolds, E. (2022). Implementation of DHIS2 for Disease Surveillance in Guinea : 2015 – 2020. *Frontiers in Public Health, 9*, 2015–2020. doi:10.3389/fpubh.2021.761196

Rumisha, S. F., Lyimo, E. P., Mremi, I. R., Tungu, P. K., Mwingira, V. S., Mbata, D., Malekia, S. E., Joachim, C., & Mboera, L. E. G. (2020). Data quality of the routine health management information system at the primary healthcare facility and district levels in Tanzania. *BMC Medical Informatics and Decision Making, 20*(1), 1–22. doi:10.118612911-020-01366-w PMID:33334323

Rumisha, S. F., Mboera, L. E., Senkoro, K. P., Gueye, D., & Mmbuji, P. K. (2007). Monitoring and evaluation of integrated disease surveillance and response in selected districts in Tanzania. *Tanzania Health Research Bulletin, 9*(1), 1–11. doi:10.4314/thrb.v9i1.14285 PMID:17547094

Rutatola, E. P., Yonah, Z. O., Nyambo, D. G., Mchau, G. J., & Musabila, A. K. (2018). A Framework for Timely and More Informative Epidemic Diseases Surveillance: The Case of Tanzania. *Journal of Health Informatics in Developing Countries, 12*(2).

Saleh, F., Kitau, J., Konradsen, F., Mboera, L. E. G., & Schiøler, K. L. (2021). Assessment of the core and support functions of the integrated disease surveillance and response system in Zanzibar, Tanzania. *BMC Public Health, 21*(1), 1–12. doi:10.118612889-021-10758-0 PMID:33865347

Seattle, W. A. (2018). *Financing global health 2017: funding universal health coverage and the unfinished HIV.* AIDS Agenda.

Sindato, C., Mboera, L. E. G., Beda, E., Mwabukusi, M., & Karimuribo, E. D. (2021). Community health workers and disease surveillance in Tanzania: Promoting the use of mobile technologies in detecting and reporting health events. *Health Security*, *19*(1), 116–129. doi:10.1089/hs.2019.0096 PMID:33217238

Statista. (2021). *Tanzania voice telecom and internet penetration 2020*. Statista.

Sukums, F., Simba, D., Kumalija, C., Asiimwe, S., Pothepragada, S., & Githendu, P. (2021). Avoiding pitfalls: Key insights and lessons learnt from customizing and rolling out a national web-based system in Tanzania. *The Electronic Journal on Information Systems in Developing Countries*, *87*(6), 1–16. doi:10.1002/isd2.12193

Tricco, A. C., Lillie, E., Zarin, W., O'Brien, K. K., Colquhoun, H., Levac, D., Moher, D., Peters, M. D. J., Horsley, T., Weeks, L., Hempel, S., Akl, E. A., Chang, C., McGowan, J., Stewart, L., Hartling, L., Aldcroft, A., Wilson, M. G., Garritty, C., ... Straus, S. E. (2018). PRISMA extension for scoping reviews (PRISMA-ScR): Checklist and explanation. *Annals of Internal Medicine*, *169*(7), 467–473. doi:10.7326/M18-0850 PMID:30178033

URT. (2019). *Digital health strategy: July 2019-June 2024*. URT.

USAID. (2019). *Health Information Systems Interoperability Maturity Toolkit*. USAID.

Van Schalkwyk, F. (2018). *Connecting Flows and Places: Making data Useful to Hyperlocal Communities in Tanzania*. Retrieved from https://www.academia.edu/38423614/Connecting_Flows_and_Places_Making_Data_Useful_to_Hyperlocal_Communities_in_Tanzania

van Schalkwyk, F. S. R. W. (2018). Connecting Flows and Places. Dar es Salaam: DataZetu.

Wellcom.com. (2018). *WellDoc Validates Potential of Its Digital Therapeutic, BlueStar®, to Significantly Reduce Healthcare Costs*. Author.

WHO. (2016a). *Framework on integrated people-centred health services. Report by the Secretariat. World Health Organization.*

WHO. (2016b). *Global Health Estimates*. Retrieved from https://www.who.int/data/gho/data/themes/mortality-and-global-health-estimates

WHO. (2018). *Non Communicable Diseases*. Retrieved from https://www.who.int/news-room/fact-sheets/detail/noncommunicable-diseases

WHO. (n.d.-a). Retrieved from https://www.afro.who.int/

WHO. (n.d.-b). Retrieved from https://www.afro.who.int

WHO Regional Office for Africa. (2019). *Integrated Disease Surveillance and Response Technical Guidelines, Booklet One: Introduction Section*. WHO Regional Office for Africa.

World Health Organization. (2016). *Monitoring and evaluating digital health interventions. A practical guide to conducting research and assessment*. WHO. Retrieved from https://www.who.int/reproductive-health/publications/mhealth/digital-health-interventions/en/%0Ahttp://www.who.int/reproductivehealth/publications/mhealth/digital-health-interventions/en/

World Health Organization. (2018). *WHO Water, Sanitation and Hygiene strategy 2018-2025*. World Health Organization. Retrieved from https://apps.who.int/iris/bitstream/handle/10665/274273/WHO-CED-PHE-WSH-18.03-eng.pdf

Zacharia, J. M. (2013). *Integrated Disease Surveillance and Response Systems in Resource - Limited Settings* [Doctoral thesis]. University of Glasgow.

KEY TERMS AND DEFINITIONS

District Health Management Information System (DHIS2): Is the national web-based modular platform used for data collection, data management and data analysis in Tanzania.

E-Health: Defined as cost-effective and secure use of information and communication technology (ICT) in support of health and health-related fields, including healthcare services, health surveillance, health literature, health education, knowledge, and research.

Electronic Integrated Disease Surveillance and Response System (eIDSR): This is a mobile-based application that is used to send digital reports to higher authorities from the integrated disease surveillance and response system (IDSR).

Health Management Information System (HMIS): This is a digital platform used for obtaining surveillance data that is collected from manual monthly reports from healthcare facilities in Tanzania.

Mobile Health (mHealth): Involves use of self-monitoring devices, electronic information systems and mobile services for follow-up of interventions and community support.

Unstructured Supplementary Service Data (USSD): This is a global System for Mobile Communications (GSM) protocol that is used to send text messages.

Chapter 3
Blockchain-Based Health Information Systems to Improve Data Security

Richard W. Mnyawi
Mwenge Catholic University, Tanzania

Devotha G. Nyambo
Nelson Mandela African Institution of Science and Technology, Tanzania

ABSTRACT

Healthcare services are dependent on health information systems (HIS), which enable health data collection and storage with improved management of healthcare service provision. However, several data security weaknesses in HIS have been identified by various studies in Tanzania. The majority are on data and information exchange leading to breaches of system security. In order to reduce security threats and accomplish security objectives (i.e., confidentiality, integrity, availability), disruptive technologies like blockchain must be used to address security breaches, attacks, and vulnerabilities of HISs. In this chapter, a problem-solving technique with digital innovative solutions for addressing real-world problems was used to arrive at the problem's solution. This chapter then shows how the data security weakness of HISs can be improved using the hyper-ledger blockchain. The system was virtually integrated with an existing HIS. Data storage security was attained through private data collection to meet security goals.

INTRODUCTION

Health Information System (HIS) plays a vital role in health care service delivery, control, and management. The system has facilitated quality service delivery with the provision of health data collection, and storage, increased revenue collection, improved health care facilities management, and lessened their control. This has greatly increased the adoption of HIS due to improved productivity, quality, and efficiency of health services.

DOI: 10.4018/978-1-6684-6873-9.ch003

However, HIS are facing a lot of challenges such as security threats, attacks, information tampering, unauthorized data access, identity tracking and theft and many other security vulnerabilities. All these have threatened the integrity, confidentiality, and availability (CIA triad) of HISs (Chuma & Ngoepe, 2021). These security issues of HISs can be tackled through integration of HIS with blockchain technology to mitigate security threats, hence achieving system security goals (Javed et al., 2020).

Several studies conducted in Tanzania reveals the challenges of the existing HISs. Among them are security challenges in information and data sharing (Kajirunga & Kalegele, 2015; Kombe, 2020; Nehemiah, 2014). (Kombe, Dida, & Sam, 2018; Mtebe & Nakaka, 2018; Mtey & Dida, 2019). Mtey & Dida (2019) indicated that this has resulted in a breach of transparency, accountability, integrity, and privacy of patients' data. These challenges are based on centralized HIS architecture, which is also known as client-server network environment encouraging all clients of respective HIS to access data from central storage.

Centralized data sources have limitations including loss of data in case of a natural disaster but more significantly, creating a target for malicious attack (Kombe et al., 2018). Data security challenges become difficult to handle due to either the centralized nature or third-party management of HIS (Kombe et al., 2018; Mahore, Aggarwal, Andola, & Venkatesan, 2019; Nagasubramanian et al., 2020). Therefore; security breaches, attacks, and vulnerabilities of HISs can be addressed through integration of HIS with secured technologies such as blockchain.

The Use of Blockchain-Based HIS

Blockchain technology is an immutable digital public ledger with a distributed database secured by means of cryptography. Information is stored in blocks of data structures with data encryption. The blocks contain time stamp which shows transaction occurrence time, in a distributed consensus (H. Wang & Zhang, 2019). Blockchain key security characteristic features are decentralization, immutability, privacy, verifiability, transparency and auditability (Sun et al., 2019). These led to its gradual adoption for innovative solution to information system security challenges (Sun et al., 2019; Tsoulias, Palaiokrassas, Fragkos, Litke, & Varvarigou, 2020; H. Wang & Zhang, 2019).

Blockchain technology is a disruptive trending technology with remarkable impacts on information systems' security improvements. The technology can be integrated with HISs to leverage its security capabilities. The integration of blockchain technology with HIS leads to the security improvement of information sharing and exchange in a decentralized peer-to-peer network environment. The use of this technology leads to the assured HIS's data privacy, availability and controlled access to HIS's data (Khatoon, 2020). Integration of HIS's with blockchain technology has led to improved information sharing and data exchange security due to data immutability, transparency, and decentralization. Much consideration of the technology is on its integrity verification and decentralized environment of blockchain. A decentralized peer-to-peer network environment has facilitated information exchange without a central authority. This has addressed problems of data storage security for centralized HISs (Khatoon, 2020; H. Wang & Zhang, 2019).

Rationale of the Chapter

The chapter aims at describing how HISs can be integrated with the blockchain technology to improve HIS security and data privacy. The integration will lead decentralized per-to-peer network environment resulting to a secured blockchain-based HIS which is not only fault tolerant but also resistant to data modification. This creates a trusted relationship among the system users in the network and removes third-party data management. The blockchain-based HIS will be resilient and ensures data security and protection of system's data.

Chapter Objectives

The main objective of this chapter to demonstrate how data security can be improved in a shared decentralized peer-to-peer network environment. This is shown through the development of a blockchain-based Health Information System (HIS). Specifically, data security characteristics of blockchain technology are explored in view of the main data security challenges of HIS in Tanzania. Then, a blockchain-based HIS is developed and validated to demonstrate improvement on security of data during transmission and at storage.

LITERATURE REVIEW

Zheng, Mukkamala, Vatrapu, and Ordieres-Mere (2018) analyzed challenges of health data sharing and storage security due to centralized architecture. In this study, a conceptual design was designed for individual data sharing using blockchain technology aided by cloud storage. The main goal was to securely own, control and share health data. Ethereum was used as the design framework in which cloud storage was integrated to the data sharing system to provide off chain storage. Off-chain storage technique was used due to the large data set. Encryption mechanisms were applied to ensure security, privacy, integrity and non-repudiation of the data.

It was also discussed by Shahnaz, Qamar, and Khalid (2019) on the implementation of technology in electronic health records (EHR). The framework came with the provision of storage security through access rules. All technology issues related to scalability, interoperability, and information asymmetry and data security risks were addressed. System scalability mainly referred to the big data challenge and how this challenge was solved through the use of off-chain storage of electronic health data. Information asymmetry in health systems refers to data centralization in which hospitals have access to patients' records. Only one part, healthcare controls information making it difficult for a patient to access his records. Interoperability focused on how different health systems can communicate in a given system setting. Data breaches described how hospitals became a point of cyberattacks hence requiring a secured platform. Suggested solution to these challenges was the use of blockchain, an Ethereum platform which is secure, transparent with data integrity of patients' records.

A framework for health data sharing by (Akkaoui, Hei, and Cheng (2020)) used blockchain technology for privacy and security of health data sharing. The framework handled data generated from patients using IoT devices and body sensors. Blockchain technology was adopted for privacy and security in data sharing. Both off-chain and on-chain techniques were implemented to avoid security challenges, but off-chain was purposely used for storage of data sets.

The review of related studies indicates that, most of the studies focused on the use of Ethereum blockchain platform to address data security weakness. The literature is also based on data storage without considering the security of the system and data as well. The storage is based on on-chain and off-chain storage. On-chain storage has space limitations as this occupies much of space since each node has to store same copy of data. Off-chain storage has not only unanswered security concerns but also cost of storage. It requires cloud storage which needs renting to several service providers to avoid single point of failure.

The purpose of this book chapter is to show how data security weakness of HISs can be improved using Hyperledger blockchain platform. The system was developed and virtually integrated with HIS. Data storage security were taken care through private data collection to meet security goals.

Integration of HIS With Blockchain

HIS was integrated with hyperledger which is a permissioned blockchain platform (Figure 1). This platform is also referred to as a private blockchains. The private blockchain is a restricted network with identity management intended for the protection of private data. It is the blockchain network with the privacy of information and confidentiality whereby, only involved entities in information sharing and data exchange can see transactions (Rennock, Cohn, & Butcher, 2018).

Figure 1. Integration of HIS with blockchain

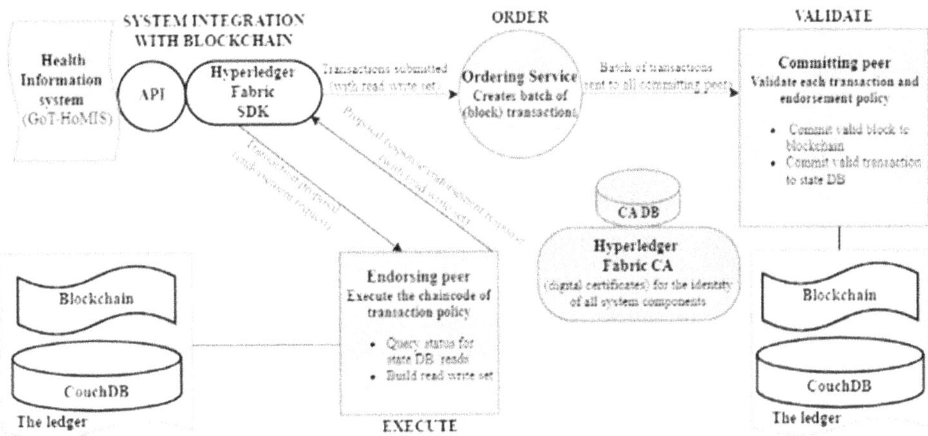

The developed blockchain based HIS is an integrated system components in its architectural design, namely HIS (system integration with blockchain); transaction execution (EXECUTE); ordering service (ORDERER); and transaction validation (VALIDATE). The first part of the proposed system integrates HIS with blockchain through an application program interface (API). The API facilitates the translation of data from HIS to the blockchain. For this case, Government of Tanzania Hospital Management Information System (GoT-HoMIS) is selected as an example used HIS. Hyperledger Fabric SDK initiates the transaction processing cycle from endorsing peer to ordering peer and finalizes with validating peer for committing valid data to the ledger.

METHODOLOGY

This chapter uses Design Science Research (DSR) methodology. It is a problem-solving oriented technique with digital innovative solutions for addressing real world problems in system designing. DSR has iterative procedures seeking to bring relationship between problem and solution. The chapter will use prototyping software process model. The model reflects the research design of the study which has an iterative process allowing refinement of a developed prototype model. The prototype is evaluated and refined to reflect system requirements. The actual system is developed based on a final working prototype which complies with system requirements.

System Development and Environmental Setting

The developed blockchain based HIS was configured in a virtual data sharing environment. The system used Ubuntu operating system 20.04.2.0, i7-9700 3.00 GHz CPU, 24 GB of RAM, and secondary storage of 1 TB installed in VirtualBox. The system was developed using Hyperledger Fabric v2.3.2. Several application packages were installed as prerequisites to set up a development environment. These prerequisites include installation of tools such as; Curl version 7.68.0, Docker version 20.10.2, Docker-compose 1.29.1, node.js V10.19.0, npm 6.14.4 and python 2.7.18. JavaScript was used for the development of the smart contract. The study used Visual Studio Code version 1.55.2 for writing and editing codes.

FINDINGS

Data Security Characteristics of Blockchain Technology

A blockchain is composed of chain of blocks resulted from transactions recorded over a time (Kombe et al., 2018). One block is created after another forming a chain. Each block contains individual block details recorded as a hash. Hash is a unique value contained in every created block with the information of each respective block. The blocks of data are encrypted using hashes and digital signatures with respective encryption algorithms making blockchain secure. Any change to the hash value of any of the block in the chain will lead to the disconnection of all other blocks to the chain due to incorrect hash value in the chain.

Figure 2 shows the connected chain of blocks, where each block has its own hash and the hash of the previous block. The last block created points to the previous block respectively. Genesis block is the first block created and it does not point to any previous block.

Figure 2. Security attributes of blockchain

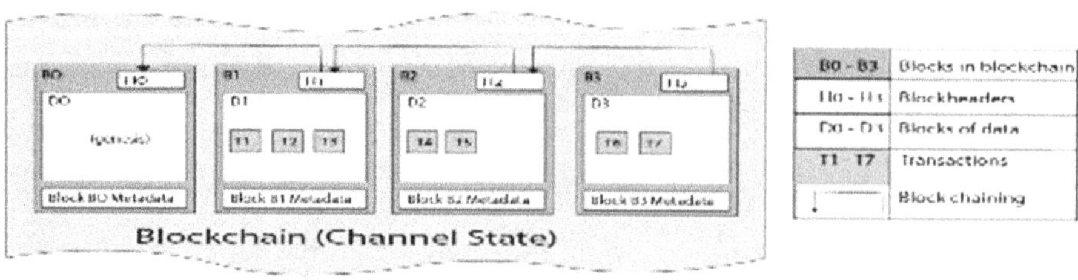

Hyperledger blockchain platform is a permissioned blockchain in which, its information flows in the execute-order-validate fashion (Figure 3). Its structural security design consists of peers, orderers, and clients. The structural security design creates data security environment and information sharing with managed identities provided by Fabric Certificate Authority. Data security characteristic feature is demonstrated through information processing cycle of the permissioned hyperledger fabric.

Figure 3. Security characteristics of hyperledger blockchain

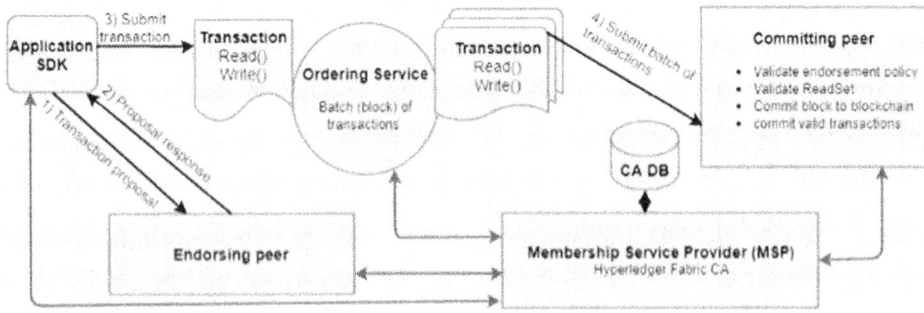

Information processing starts from transaction proposal from a client to endorsing peer. Transaction proposal is endorsed and submitted back to the client as a proposal response. All transaction details of the proposal response are gathered and sent to the ordering node. The ordering node collects, order batches of transactions, and sends them to committing peer for execution. A block of data is generated from the logical ordered batch of transactions, which are then validated, and then committed to the blockchain for storage (Javaid, Hu, & Brebner, 2019; Manevich, Barger, & Tock, 2018; Nguyen, Jourjon, Potop-Butucaru, & Thai, 2019).

Data security properties of blockchain lead to its trust due to its uniqueness of the network design, storage structure, cryptographic mechanisms, and consensus protocol (Sun et al., 2019). Improved data security and information sharing is due to its characteristic features such as: data immutability, decentralization, consensus mechanism, digital signature, and fault tolerance.

1. Data Immutability

Data immutability is one of the data security characteristic feature of blockchain which prevents data modification. The chaining of blockchain blocks hardens hacking and tampering of systems' data. Blockchain makes data immutable to changes making blockchain information system permanent, hence preserving data integrity (ah Khan, Jadhav, Bharadwaj, Rooj, & Shiravale, 2020; Paik, Xu, Bandara, Lee, & Lo, 2019; Sousa, Bessani, & Vukolic, 2018).

Therefore, loss of data integrity is prevented since no any data modification is allowed once the block of data is created. Therefore, validated records will be irreversible and they cannot be modified either by editing, changing or deletion (Zhuang et al., 2020). Blockchain technology resists any intentional or unintentional tampering of data. The information is generated and stored in form of a linked lists of the chain making it difficult to be tampered. Tampering is controlled through secured transactions using hash functions and digital signatures (Idrees, Nowostawski, Jameel, & Mourya, 2021).

Blockchain assures integrity of data through storage of time-stamped information in data blocks. Transactions are contained in the blocks, and each block is connected to form a chain. Every block has a unique hash value created through principles of cryptography to ensure data integrity. Connection of data blocks is through hash values forming a linked list. Each block is connected to another block by a hash of the previous block to form a chain (Idrees et al., 2021).

2. Digital Signature

Digital signature refers to the process confirming the originality of information shared between the communicating parties through encryption and decryption of data. During data transaction endorsement, endorsement request is signed by the sender of the data and validated by the receiver. Valid information matching endorsements are executed, and committed for storage.

Digital signature is applied during processing of transactions and creation of blocks so as to prove the identity of the message owner, and that data has not been modified. Public key serves as a user identity to be used for signature verification. This establishes validity of the data, and data integrity can be verified through private key. Private key generates the signature of the document and the public key verifies the identity of the signature (Idrees et al., 2021). These are cryptographic algorithms which helps to prove the authenticity of the information.

These cryptographic mechanisms creates system accountability by eliminating impersonation and forging of data. This is made possible since each system component is identified through its identity and it is easy to track who did what during data processing and storage (Saad *et al.*, 2019).

3. System Component Identity

Hyperledger fabric is a private blockchain that provides data and network security through authentication of entities to a blockchain network (Ismail & Materwala, 2019; Nguyen *et al.*, 2019). Each system component in the network is given its identity through membership service provider (MSP). MSP contains Hyperledger Fabric Certificate Authority which is responsible for giving identities to all system objects in the network.

Object identities are secured through private key and a public certificate (Saad et al., 2019; Sankar, Sindhu, & Sethumadhavan, 2017). These identities mitigates the challenge of object impersonation techniques which tampers with trusted source credentials. Hyperledger Fabric mitigates the risk through generation of unique X.509 digital certificates to all its network members.

4. Confidentiality and Privacy

Confidentiality and privacy is maintained through encryption algorithms during endorsement of a transaction. Generated transactions and smart contracts are hidden to unauthorized entities leading to high level confidentiality and privacy to system components (Sankar et al., 2017).

5. Data Integrity

Hyperledger Fabric uses endorsement policies to ensures integrity of the information system is not compromised. (Nguyen et al., 2019). The policy ensures secured storage of system data thus preventing tampering of system data. This simplifies the process of detecting any changes to system data (ah Khan et al., 2020). Proposed transaction will be endorsed only if the endorsement responses matches the endorsement policy to protect data from malicious activity (Javaid et al., 2019).

6. Data Verification

Hyperledger blockchain has ordering service component which facilitates the approval of blocks to be added to the chain (C. Wang & Chu, 2020). Data is verified through communication between the endorser and committing peers (Ismail & Materwala, 2019). The orderer component checks if all cryptographic details of the policy match. If the details of the policy are correct, the orderer sends the data for storage (Saad et al., 2019). Data verification by odering node helps to avoid the additon of malicious data to the system. All system nodes will confirm that they have correct information for secured storage.

7. Data Validation Through Consensus Mechanisms

Data validation is another data characteristic feature of Hyperledger through consensus mechanism. Consensus between nodes in the network helps decision making during transaction validation (Sankar et al., 2017). It is the mutual agreement between nodes in the network to decide whether a transaction is accepted and be added to the chain (Zhuang et al., 2020). The process of creating network blocks and addition of these blocks to the network is validated by all nodes. This makes blockchain to maintain network data through consensus mechanisms of all participating network members (Idrees et al., 2021).

8. Decentralization

Decentralization is a security feature of blockchain ensuring consistent data across the network. It is an innovated distributed peer-to-peer technology with no single authority. The technology removes a single point of administration of a client server and create a decentralized system. The network has several nodes sharing the same copy of data contained in a digital ledger without central authority (Idrees et al., 2021).

9. Fault Tolerance

Blockchain database storage technology is highly fault tolerant. In case one of the nodes is down, there will be other nodes available to run the blockchain (Tsoulias et al., 2020). The technology uses a peer-to-peer or P2P network architecture which does not require access to a centralized database, instead all participating nodes in the network can connect with each other (Tsoulias et al., 2020). There is no "master" that controls all nodes. Each peer is equal to each other in how they access the blockchain without requiring an administrator access.

Data Security Challenges of HISs in Tanzania

The study found three main categories of security challenges which create vulnerabilities to HISs. These security challenges are; network based (malicious IPs), malicious software, and web based vulnerabilities (Team, 2019-2021).

1. Network Based Security Challenges

Network based security challenges refers to system challenges which leads to network attacks through malicious IPs and commonly used user credentials (usernames and passwords).

2. Malicious Software-Based Security Challenges

Malicious software attacks includes Trojan horses, backdoors, and Ransomware causing downtimes in the system.

3. Web-Based Security Challenges

HISs are web based information systems. Web based information system share their data through centralized mode of communication. Centralized mode of communication is the information sharing between the client and the server. This information sharing depends on the central authority with centralized data storage. Centralized client-server architectural nature of HIS has exposed health systems' data to security threats, attacks, and vulnerabilities. During authentication process of a client to the server to access data, there is a high risk of system vulnerability (Parmar, Roy, Bhattacharyya, Bandyopadhyay, & Kim, 2017).

Architectural nature of web based HIS creates a specific point of attack as well as a target for malicious execution of systems' data. Since the system is centralized, there is only one point of system failure hence affecting the whole system. System architecture creates vulnerabilities to system attacks, where sensitive data can be accessed and easily manipulated. This threatens the Confidentiality, Integrity, and Availability (CIA triad) of health data (Chuma & Ngoepe, 2021). The following are some examples web based security challenges; spoof attacks, replay attacks, non-repudiation, among others.

a. Spoof Attacks

This is an impersonation technique for tampering with trusted credentials. Authorized user communication within the network is redirected to a malicious source. This security challenge leads to system vulnerability and attack to HIS. Spoof attacks is used in combination with other attacks such as IP address spoofing, together with SYN flood attacks. This vulnerability leads to health information system attack through opened connection.

b. Replay Attacks/Man-in-the-Middle

This is an attack which interferes communication between two communicating parties. The attacker eavesdrops the network with the intention of fraudulently intercepting the communication. After intercepting the communication, the hacker gain access to data transmission and can retransmit them as if it is from an authenticated source. HIS will be subjected to this attack and visualize this attack as a normal and authenticated communication. Data transmission will be delayed and its integrity can even be tampered and then resent to the receiver.

c. Repudiation

HIS are subjected to this attack through denial of one part involved in the communication. It is not possible to prove that the message was sent by particular entity during communication between two parties. There is no accountability between entities since data exchange can be forged and impersonated hence lacking accountability.

Other Security Challenges of HISs

Database back up is another data security challenge of HISs. For example, backup of GoT-HoMIS is a daily activity. The backed data are stored in a safe place for retrieval in case of any event leading to loss of data. The backup is sent to PO-RALG ICT department after every week (Office, 2021). This is a tedious job of addressing data security and obsolete technology for data backup.

Proposed Solution Architecture of Blockchain-Based HIS

1. System Requirement Specifications

The system developed is based on system requirements with the focus of eliminating the challenges of HISs. Table 1 gives the summary of requirements for the proposed blockchain-based system.

Table 1. System requirements

S/N	Item	System Requirement
1	User identity	Blockchain based-HIS should be able to identify all system users with their credentials to authentic system usage and its resources.
2	Integrity of data	Blockchain based-HIS should ensure data integrity to avoid modification of data.
3	System privacy	Blockchain based-HIS should maintain confidentiality of data to prevent unauthorized disclosure.
4	System verification	Blockchain based-HIS should be able to do data verification to avoid addition of malicious data to HIS database.
5	System validation	Blockchain based-HIS should be able to validate data which will be shared among blockchain members.
6	System audit	Blockchain based-HIS should have audit mechanisms to view the history of system transactions to hold system users accountable of their actions.
7	Data backup	Blockchain based-HIS should do an automated data backup throughout the blockchain network.

2. System Development

Figure 4 shows the proposed blockchain-based system. The proposed blockchain-based system is a Hyperledger fabric with the composition of the main two parts, CouchDB database and a hash of the stored data in the database. This system has one channel with two organizations; the actual private data and a hash of the data. The private state database stores data of the actual private state. These holds key

Figure 4. Blockchain-based system components

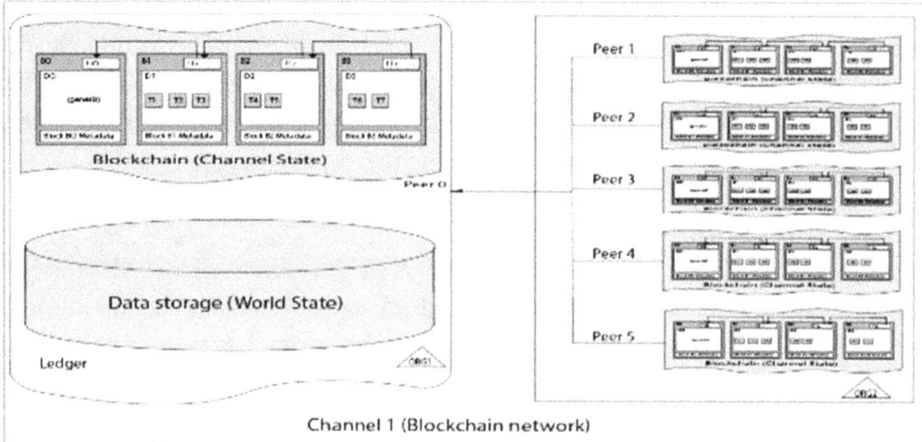

values pair of ledger states which can be accessed through smart contracts. Every node on the blockchain network contains the hash of stored data in a private stse. This makes a proof of transactions carried out in a data sharing in a decentralized environment. The proposed system has two organizations. Organization one serves the server, with the blockchain and a private state while organization two has several nodes with blockchain only.

Health information system was virtually integrated with the blockchain system, through API to enable system functionality for data storage security (Figure 5). System records are submitted to API for data translation. Transfer of data from HIS to blockchain network is attained through integration of modules. Data conversion can either be from MySQL relational database to CouchDB key-value database system. Converted records in the key-value database are sent to Fabric SDK for chaincode execution. Data is transferred from HIS in structured query language format to blockchain system, no structured query language format and vice versa. After chaincode processing, data is stored in private state data collection in the ledger. The hashes of a private state are stored in a channel state for data integrity verification.

Figure 5. Proposed system components
Source: Mnyawi et al. (2022)

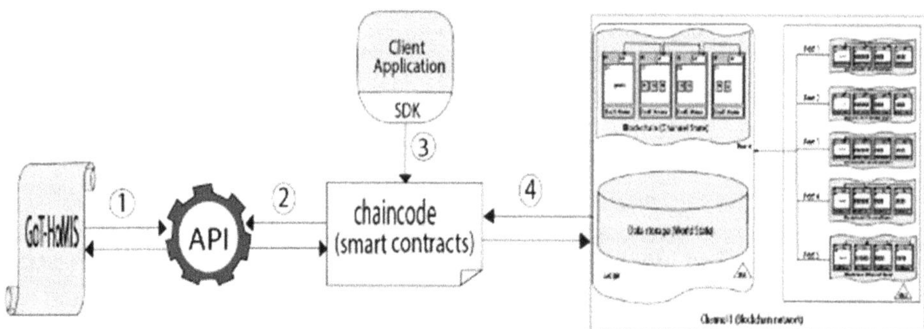

Validation of the Developed Blockchain-Based HIS

Validation process of the developed system is based on proposed system requirements which aimed at improving HIS's data storage security. Validation process followed smart contract executions and it was carefully monitored to conform the expected system outputs. System operation was successfully observed during execution of smart contracts. Figures 6-11 provide detailed clarification of the system execution.

Figure 6 shows an invocation command of a smart contract *(./net-pln.sh invoke equipment MSD 2000.07 Wheelchair MSD)* which was executed for the creation of a blockchain data. This is the screenshot which shows the command used to start creation of blocks of data.

Figure 6. Invoking of smart contract

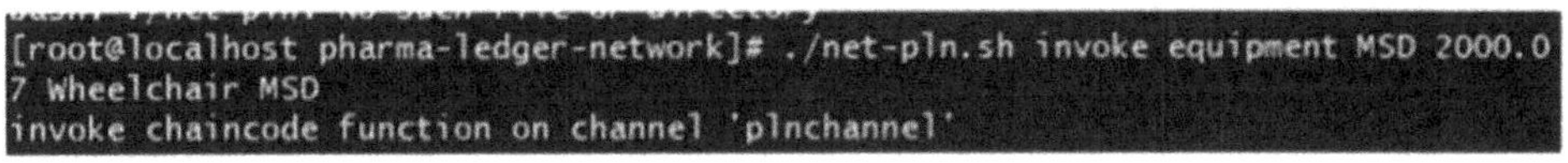

Figure 7 shows the results of a successfully invoked smart contract for creation of a blockchain data. It is a screenshot which shows the details of specific peers involved in smart contract execution. This gives detailed description of a smart contract execution and starting point for creation of a block of data with block details.

Figure 7. Results of a smart contract

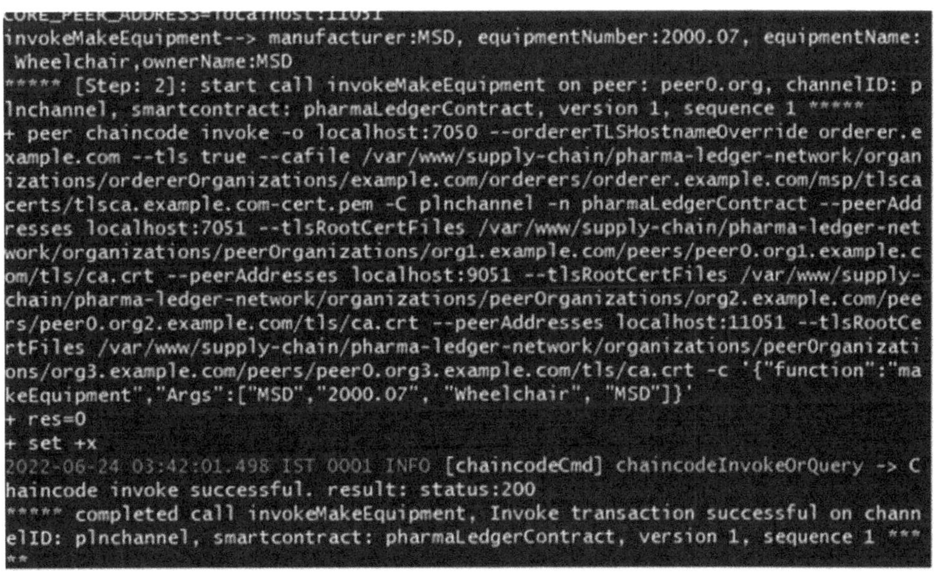

Figure 8 shows procedural stages of a smart contract execution. The screenshot illustrate the smart contract details with security features encrypted within. The contract has security features which are shared to all nodes involved in the execution of this contract.

Figure 8. Stages of smart contract execution

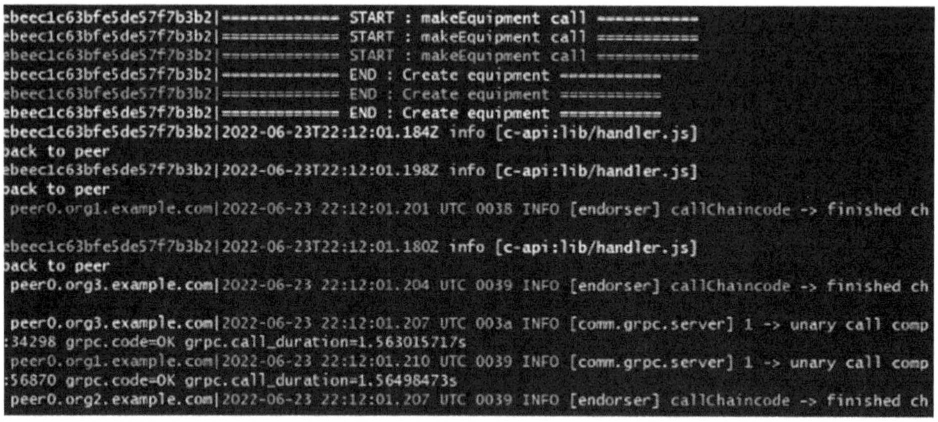

Figure 9 shows series of steps on how a block of data is created and added to the ledger. The screenshot shows all the stages of block creation. This starts from transaction proposal which is the request sent to the peer in the network for endorsement. The proposal is endorsed by the endorsing peer, and endorsed transactions are submitted to orderer. The orderer submits the batch of transactions to committing peer for validation and storage to a blockchain. This screenshot shows what happens as illustrated in Figure 9.

Figure 9. Execution of a smart contract from endorser to committer

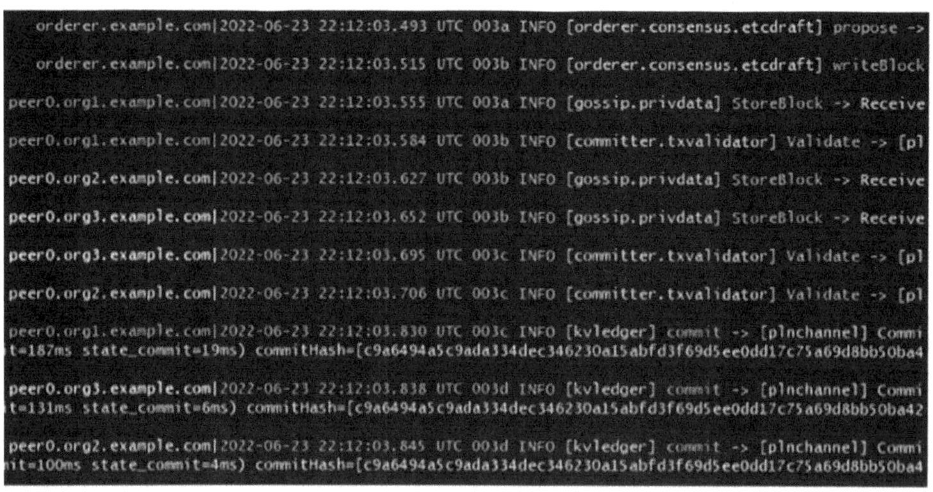

Figure 10 shows smart contract command *(./net-pln.sh invoke queryHistory 2000.07)* that queries the history of data transactions with key value 2000.07. The query will display all transactions which were carried for that particular data item.

Figure 10. Invoked smart contract to show the history transactions

```
[root@localhost pharma-ledger-network]# ./net-pln.sh invoke queryHistory 2000.07
invoke chaincode function on channel 'plnchannel'
```

Figure 11 shows the query history of a transaction, to prove that the system is auditable. The figure shows an example of requested query history of data with key value 2000.07. The smart contract invoked *(./net-pln.sh invoke queryHistory 2000.07)* with the results displayed to show the history executed transactions.

Figure 11. Query history results of the transactions

```
63bfe5de57f7b3b2|getting history for key: 2000.07
63bfe5de57f7b3b2|[
63bfe5de57f7b3b2|  {
63bfe5de57f7b3b2|    equipmentNumber: '2000.07',
63bfe5de57f7b3b2|    manufacturer: 'MSD',
63bfe5de57f7b3b2|    equipmentName: 'Wheelchair',
63bfe5de57f7b3b2|    ownerName: 'MnyawiPharmacy',
63bfe5de57f7b3b2|    previousOwnerType: 'WHOLESALER',
63bfe5de57f7b3b2|    currentOwnerType: 'PHARMACY',
63bfe5de57f7b3b2|    createDateTime: 'Thu Jun 23 2022 22:12:00 GMT+0000 (Coordinated Universal

63bfe5de57f7b3b2|    lastUpdated: 'Fri Jun 24 2022 08:58:35 GMT+0000 (Coordinated Universal Ti

63bfe5de57f7b3b2|  },
63bfe5de57f7b3b2|  {
63bfe5de57f7b3b2|    equipmentNumber: '2000.07',
63bfe5de57f7b3b2|    manufacturer: 'MSD',
63bfe5de57f7b3b2|    equipmentName: 'Wheelchair',
63bfe5de57f7b3b2|    ownerName: 'XYDistributers',
63bfe5de57f7b3b2|    previousOwnerType: 'MANUFACTURER',
63bfe5de57f7b3b2|    currentOwnerType: 'WHOLESALER',
63bfe5de57f7b3b2|    createDateTime: 'Thu Jun 23 2022 22:12:00 GMT+0000 (Coordinated Universal

63bfe5de57f7b3b2|    lastUpdated: 'Fri Jun 24 2022 08:54:14 GMT+0000 (Coordinated Universal Ti

63bfe5de57f7b3b2|  },
63bfe5de57f7b3b2|  {
63bfe5de57f7b3b2|    equipmentNumber: '2000.07',
63bfe5de57f7b3b2|    manufacturer: 'MSD',
63bfe5de57f7b3b2|    equipmentName: 'Wheelchair',
63bfe5de57f7b3b2|    ownerName: 'MSD',
63bfe5de57f7b3b2|    previousOwnerType: 'MANUFACTURER',
63bfe5de57f7b3b2|    currentOwnerType: 'MANUFACTURER',
63bfe5de57f7b3b2|    createDateTime: 'Thu Jun 23 2022 22:12:00 GMT+0000 (Coordinated Universal

63bfe5de57f7b3b2|    lastUpdated: 'Thu Jun 23 2022 22:12:00 GMT+0000 (Coordinated Universal Ti

63bfe5de57f7b3b2|  }
63bfe5de57f7b3b2|]
```

Validation of the system was done according to the following requirements; user identity, data integrity, system privacy, system verification, system validation, system audit, and data backup.

1. User Identity

All system components were cryptographically identified. Their identities were secured using private key and a public certificate. Certificate Authority (CA) is used as a proof to all members and their identities. Their identities are created using digital certificates giving the authenticity of the entity in a network.

2. Data Integrity

Data integrity is preserved through chaining of data blocks. It is not possible to tamper with stored data. Integrity of data is preserved through data verification of stored database of the entire system. In case a block is tampered, a hash of the tampered block will change including other hashes of the connecting blocks. This invalidates chaining of the blocks since the tampered block does not contain the correct hash of the previous data block. Successful tampering of data will require simultaneous attack to the whole network and alter data at once, and this is not possible (Paik et al., 2019).

3. System Privacy

System privacy is maintained through privacy of smart contracts. Smart contracts are concealed to unauthorized system nodes. This is enabled through endorsement policy which helps to ensure confidential smart contract through encryption algorithms. Implementation of encryption algorithms is through the use of hashes and digital signatures. This is based on asymmetric key encryption hence creating system confidentiality.

4. System Verification

Data verification is maintained through endorsing and committing nodes of the system. The order issuer will verify all information contained in the endorsement policy, if there is mismatch of the policy details, the database will not be updated. If the policy will be correct, the order issuer will send all data to all nodes for storage.

5. System Validation

Developed system aimed at every system component to share data their data. At the same time, before updating the ledger, data verification should be done to ensure incorrect data is not added to the network. The system is also required to ensure that existing data is not erased. The nodes should agree on whether the new block can be shared in the database by determining its validity and eligibility. Endorsement of transactions enable data validation process through chaincode execution. Transactions will be endorsed if the policy contains valid data.

6. System Audit

The system is able to track events through digital signature mechanism. This happens as the ledger is created through addition of data blocks to the ledger through transaction endorsement. Since the system manages user identity, it is possible for the system to be audited for the user behavior leading to user accountability. System users will not be able to deny their actions since their actions cannot be forged.

7. Data Backup

Developed system is a blockchain-based which is a decentralized peer to peer architecture. The system has an automated data backup management in which every node in a network has the same copy of data. Data sharing and exchange is enabled without central control. This creates system availability and fault tolerance as well.

System Performance

The new system was developed using Hyperledger fabric. The system was carefully evaluated against Ethereum system to compare systems' throughput and their latency. Developed system has high throughput compared to Ethereum. This is because Hyperledger has low consumption of computation power compared to Ethereum. Fabric uses execute-order-validate, signature-based transaction processing, while Ethereum uses execute-validate model which has complex mathematical computations leading to high consumption of computing resources. Fabric system has low latency compared to Ethereum. Figure 12 shows comparisons of system performance as indicated.

Figure 12. System performance (hyperledger fabric vs. Ethereum)

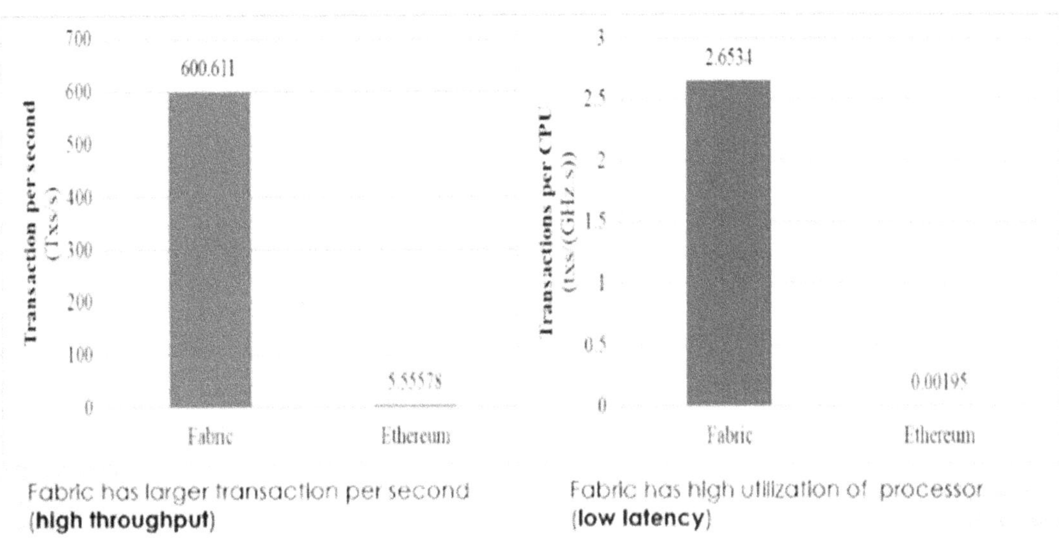

DISCUSSION

This book chapter aimed to describe the development of a blockchain-based system, virtually integrated HIS for improvement of data storage security. The system was developed which addressed data security challenges of HIS which are within its architecture. System performance was taken care through the use of signature-based architecture for transaction execution. The system leveraged security characteristics of blockchain technology to address data security weaknesses of HIS. These security features of immutability, decentralization, verifiability, privacy, and auditability of the technology lead to attainment of HIS security goals of confidentiality, integrity, and availability (CIA triad).

Architectural design of the developed system deployed private data storage with signature-based model of transactions. System design considered proposed security system requirements, of which they were used for system validation. System validation was carried out through various system testing for system verification and validation. System design used uses execute-order-validate with faster consensus protocol compared to Ethereum. This resulted to high performance system due to its higher throughput and low latency.

CONCLUSION AND RECOMMENDATIONS

This book chapter was based on identifying data security challenges of HISs in Tanzania as well as identifying blockchain data security characteristics. The findings of this chapter show vividly that blockchain data security characteristics can be integrated with HIS to address data security challenges of HISs. System storage architecture provides data privacy and confidentiality. Confidentiality is highly demonstrated during execution of chaincodes for data storage leading to data privacy. Private data collection methodology addresses the challenge of big data and redundancy since the nodes are decentralized with blockchain only.

Health care industry in collaboration with other research scholars of HIS, should use these findings which will enable them to come up with secured health information systems. This will help to them develop health systems which guarantee security of shared and stored data of the HISs.

REFERENCES

ah Khan, S., Jadhav, A., et Bharadwaj, I., Rooj, M., & Shiravale, S. (2020). *Blockchain and the Identity based Encryption Scheme for High Data Security*. Paper presented at the 2020 Fourth International Conference on Computing Methodologies and Communication (ICCMC).

Akkaoui, R., Hei, X., & Cheng, W. (2020). EdgeMediChain: A Hybrid Edge Blockchain-Based Framework for Health Data Exchange. *IEEE Access : Practical Innovations, Open Solutions*, *8*, 113467–113486. doi:10.1109/ACCESS.2020.3003575

Chuma, K. G., & Ngoepe, M. (2021). Security of electronic personal health information in a public hospital in South Africa. *Information Security Journal: A Global Perspective*, 1-17.

Idrees, S. M., Nowostawski, M., Jameel, R., & Mourya, A. K. (2021). Security aspects of blockchain technology intended for industrial applications. *Electronics (Basel), 10*(8), 951. doi:10.3390/electronics10080951

Ismail, L., & Materwala, H. (2019). A review of blockchain architecture and consensus protocols: Use cases, challenges, and solutions. *Symmetry, 11*(10), 1198. doi:10.3390ym11101198

Javaid, H., Hu, C., & Brebner, G. (2019). *Optimizing validation phase of hyperledger fabric*. Paper presented at the 2019 IEEE 27th International Symposium on Modeling, Analysis, and Simulation of Computer and Telecommunication Systems (MASCOTS). 10.1109/MASCOTS.2019.00038

Javed, M. U., Rehman, M., Javaid, N., Aldegheishem, A., Alrajeh, N., & Tahir, M. (2020). Blockchain-based secure data storage for distributed vehicular networks. *Applied Sciences (Basel, Switzerland), 10*(6), 2011. doi:10.3390/app10062011

Kajirunga, A., & Kalegele, K. (2015). *Analysis of activities and operations in the current E-Health landscape in Tanzania: focus on interoperability and collaboration*. arXiv preprint arXiv:1507.00176.

Khatoon, A. (2020). A blockchain-based smart contract system for healthcare management. *Electronics (Basel), 9*(1), 94. doi:10.3390/electronics9010094

Kombe, C. (2020). *A secure and interoperable blockchain-based information sharing system for healthcare providers in developing countries*. NM-AIST.

Kombe, C., Dida, M., & Sam, A. (2018). *A review on healthcare information systems and consensus protocols in blockchain technology*. Academic Press.

Mahore, V., Aggarwal, P., Andola, N., & Venkatesan, S. (2019). *Secure and Privacy Focused Electronic Health Record Management System using Permissioned Blockchain*. Paper presented at the 2019 IEEE Conference on Information and Communication Technology. 10.1109/CICT48419.2019.9066204

Manevich, Y., Barger, A., & Tock, Y. (2018). Service discovery for hyperledger fabric. *Proceedings of the 12th ACM International Conference on Distributed and Event-Based Systems*. 10.1145/3210284.3219766

Mnyawi, R., Kombe, C., Sam, A., & Nyambo, D. (2022). Blockchain-based Data Storage Security Architecture for e-Health Care Systems: A Case of Government of Tanzania Hospital Management Information System. *IJCSNS, 22*(3), 364.

Mtebe, J., & Nakaka, R. (2018). Assessing electronic medical record system implementation at Kilimanjaro Christian Medical Center. Academic Press.

Mtey, M., & Dida, M. (2019). *Towards interoperable e-Health system in Tanzania: analysis and evaluation of the current security trends and big data sharing dynamics*. Academic Press.

Nagasubramanian, G., Sakthivel, R. K., Patan, R., Gandomi, A. H., Sankayya, M., & Balusamy, B. (2020). Securing e-health records using keyless signature infrastructure blockchain technology in the cloud. *Neural Computing & Applications, 32*(3), 639–647. doi:10.100700521-018-3915-1

Nehemiah, L. (2014). *Towards EHR interoperability in Tanzania hospitals: issues, challenges and opportunities.* arXiv preprint arXiv:1410.2205.

Nguyen, T. S. L., Jourjon, G., Potop-Butucaru, M., & Thai, K. L. (2019). *Impact of network delays on Hyperledger Fabric*. Paper presented at the IEEE INFOCOM 2019-IEEE Conference on Computer Communications Workshops (INFOCOM WKSHPS). 10.1109/INFCOMW.2019.8845168

Office, N. A. (2021). *Ripoti ya mdhibiti na mkaguzi mkuu wa hesabu za serikali kwa mwaka wa fedha 2019/2020*. The National Audit Office.

Paik, H.-Y., Xu, X., Bandara, H. D., Lee, S. U., & Lo, S. K. (2019). Analysis of Data Management in Blockchain-Based Systems: From Architecture to Governance. *IEEE Access : Practical Innovations, Open Solutions*, *7*, 186091–186107. doi:10.1109/ACCESS.2019.2961404

Parmar, R. R., Roy, S., Bhattacharyya, D., Bandyopadhyay, S. K., & Kim, T.-H. (2017). Large-scale encryption in the Hadoop environment: Challenges and solutions. *IEEE Access : Practical Innovations, Open Solutions*, *5*, 7156–7163. doi:10.1109/ACCESS.2017.2700228

Rennock, M. J., Cohn, A., & Butcher, J. R. (2018). Blockchain technology and regulatory investigations. *Practical Law Litigation*, 35-44.

Saad, M., Spaulding, J., Njilla, L., Kamhoua, C., Shetty, S., Nyang, D., & Mohaisen, A. (2019). *Exploring the attack surface of blockchain: A systematic overview*. arXiv preprint arXiv:1904.03487.

Sankar, L. S., Sindhu, M., & Sethumadhavan, M. (2017). *Survey of consensus protocols on blockchain applications*. Paper presented at the 2017 4th International Conference on Advanced Computing and Communication Systems (ICACCS). 10.1109/ICACCS.2017.8014672

Shahnaz, A., Qamar, U., & Khalid, A. (2019). Using blockchain for electronic health records. *IEEE Access : Practical Innovations, Open Solutions*, *7*, 147782–147795. doi:10.1109/ACCESS.2019.2946373

Sousa, J., Bessani, A., & Vukolic, M. (2018). *A byzantine fault-tolerant ordering service for the hyperledger fabric blockchain platform*. Paper presented at the 2018 48th annual IEEE/IFIP international conference on dependable systems and networks (DSN). 10.1109/DSN.2018.00018

Sun, Y., Zhang, L., Feng, G., Yang, B., Cao, B., & Imran, M. A. (2019). Blockchain-enabled wireless Internet of Things: Performance analysis and optimal communication node deployment. *IEEE Internet of Things Journal*, *6*(3), 5791–5802. doi:10.1109/JIOT.2019.2905743

Team, T. C. E. R. (2019-2021). *Tanzania Computer Emergency Response Team-Honeypots weekly report*. Dar-es-Salaam: Tanzania Communication Regulatory Authority.

Tsoulias, K., Palaiokrassas, G., Fragkos, G., Litke, A., & Varvarigou, T. A. (2020). A Graph Model Based Blockchain Implementation for Increasing Performance and Security in Decentralized Ledger Systems. *IEEE Access : Practical Innovations, Open Solutions*, *8*, 130952–130965. doi:10.1109/ACCESS.2020.3006383

Wang, C., & Chu, X. (2020). *Performance characterization and bottleneck analysis of hyperledger fabric*. Paper presented at the 2020 IEEE 40th International Conference on Distributed Computing Systems (ICDCS). 10.1109/ICDCS47774.2020.00165

Wang, H., & Zhang, J. (2019). Blockchain Based Data Integrity Verification for Large-Scale IoT Data. *IEEE Access : Practical Innovations, Open Solutions*, *7*, 164996–165006. doi:10.1109/ACCESS.2019.2952635

Zheng, X., Mukkamala, R. R., Vatrapu, R., & Ordieres-Mere, J. (2018). *Blockchain-based personal health data sharing system using cloud storage.* Paper presented at the 2018 IEEE 20th International Conference on e-Health Networking, Applications and Services (Healthcom). 10.1109/HealthCom.2018.8531125

Zhuang, Y., Sheets, L. R., Chen, Y.-W., Shae, Z.-Y., Tsai, J. J., & Shyu, C.-R. (2020). A patient-centric health information exchange framework using blockchain technology. *IEEE Journal of Biomedical and Health Informatics*, *24*(8), 2169–2176. doi:10.1109/JBHI.2020.2993072 PMID:32396110

KEY TERMS AND DEFINITIONS

Application Programming Interface: This is software developed and deployed to allow two or more applications to exchange data and information.

Availability: An act of ensuring that in information system and its related data is made available to the authorized users.

Blockchain: This is a shared database that promotes data storage in form of blocks. Each data block is stored in all the nodes in the network.

Centralized System Architecture: This is a conceptual layout of an information system where there all users are connected to a central system that stores all data and information of the network.

Confidentiality: An act of preserving authorized access and disclosure of data and information with the main goal of protecting subjects' privacy and proprietary information.

Data Security: Refers to all the processes employed to protect digital information and ensure Confidentiality, Integrity, and Availability of such information is guaranteed to authorized users only.

De-Centralized System Architecture: This is a conceptual layout of an information system where several peer-to-peer user groups are formed and there is a local server for each user group to store all data and information relevant to the user group.

Health Information System: This is a collection of multiple hardware peripherals and software that is dedicated to the collection, processing, storage, and dissemination of health-related information.

Information System: This is a collection of multiple hardware peripherals and software that collects data, process, store, and disseminate information.

Integrity: An act of preserving a system and its data from unauthorized modification; In other terms, data that is transferred across a network should reach its recipient as it was sent.

Natural Disaster: This is an impact that results from natural hazards and results in community harm and/or destruction.

Software Process Model: This is a logical abstraction of a software development process that defines various phases of the development of an information system.

System Architecture: This is a technical layout defining the structure, behavior, and views of an information system.

Transaction: This is a unit of work or query that is executed in a database management system against a database.

Chapter 4
Climate-Smart Agriculture and Internet of Things Systems for Agricultural Production Efficiency in African Countries

Lilian C. Mutalemwa
The Open University of Tanzania, Tanzania

ABSTRACT

This chapter identifies climate-smart agriculture (CSA) practices and their impact on smallholder farmers in six African countries. Various CSA practices are discussed. Observations show that farmers who adopted CSA practices obtained positive results in terms of adaptability to climate change and productivity. Furthermore, internet of things (IoT)-enabled smart agricultural systems are explored. Observations indicate that IoT-based agricultural systems enable efficient utilization of farm inputs such as fertilizer, pesticides, herbicides, and water. Also, using IoT systems, it is possible to provide customized, location-specific, and easily understood climate data for smallholder farmers to facilitate decision making and planning of CSA practices. Therefore, this chapter has presented recommendations for the adoption of IoT-enabled CSA in African countries. IoT-enabled agricultural systems are recommended for a country like Senegal where climate data is considered an agricultural input and also for Tanzania where IoT devices such as UAVs are considered to be useful agricultural tools.

INTRODUCTION

It is predicted that the population of the world will reach nine billion people by the year 2050. Consequently, the global demand for food continues to increase. However, agricultural production is significantly affected by factors such as urbanization, soil erosion, climate change, and water shortages. Therefore, food security is one of the important goals in the United Nations sustainable development goals for 2030. This chapter addresses the challenge of food insecurity that is caused by climate change. Climate change refers to the increase in greenhouse gas (GHG) emissions such as nitrous oxide (N_2O), carbon dioxide

DOI: 10.4018/978-1-6684-6873-9.ch004

(CO_2), and methane (CH_4) in the atmosphere resulting in irregularity, variability and unpredictability of rainfall, temperature increase, floods, and droughts (Ariom et al., 2022). Climate change causes variations in the intensity and frequency of extreme events such as droughts, which affects the agricultural production. It has been reported that Africa is among the most vulnerable zones across the globe. In Sub-Saharan Africa, climate change will result in reduced production of major cereal crops including maize, sorghum, and millet. It is predicted that by the year 2025, maize, sorghum, and millet yields will fall by 22%, 17%, and 17%, respectively. Furthermore, rain-fed crop yields will decrease by almost 50%. Many studies have indicated the vulnerability of African countries to climate change. For example, it has been projected that by 2050, East Africa will experience warmer temperatures, a 5 to 20% increase in rainfall between December and February, and 5 to 10% less rainfall from June to August (Ariom et al., 2022).

To address these challenges, the food and agriculture organization (FAO) of the United Nations proposed that agriculture practices should evolve and adapt to climate change by introducing the concept of climate-smart agriculture (CSA). CSA provides mechanisms for agricultural systems to support food production under new climatic conditions (Selbonne et al., 2023). CSA practices help to increase the adaptive capacity of farmers and ensure food security. Agricultural production is also increased when farmers use Internet of Things (IoT)-enabled smart agricultural systems. IoT-enabled smart systems help farmers to remotely monitor and report conditions of the field, climate, and crops. This enables efficient management of resources and effective control of farm inputs such as fertilizer, pesticides, and water, resulting in reduced costs and increased productivity. Furthermore, the IoT-enabled systems employ Artificial Intelligence (AI) algorithms to make predictions of the future based on present and past farm conditions so as to make agriculture less susceptible to climate change effects and sustainably produce sufficient food. The objectives of this chapter are to:

- Identify CSA practices and their impact on smallholder farmers in six African countries (Tanzania, Zambia, Nigeria, Benin, Senegal, and Algeria).
- Discuss the use of IoT-enabled smart agricultural systems for efficient utilization of fertilizer, pesticides, herbicides, and water.
- Provide recommendations for the adoption of IoT-enabled CSA in African countries.

BACKGROUND

CSA presents mechanisms for agricultural systems to produce sufficient food and ensure food security under new climatic conditions (Selbonne et al., 2023). Since the establishment of CSA in 2010, African countries have devised policies and frameworks to promote and scale CSA practices. This is because African countries have smallholder farmers who are vulnerable and worst affected by climate change. In 2014, The Malabo Declaration on Accelerated Agricultural Growth and Transformation of Africa's Agriculture for Shared Prosperity and Improved Livelihoods prioritized developing resilient agriculture as a development agenda (Kirina et al., 2022). During the summit, Vision 25 × 25 was launched with the target of at least 25 million farm households practicing CSA by 2025. Climate Change Policies in African countries provide frameworks that prioritize the adaptation and mainstreams climate change into development plans (Kirina et al., 2022). Furthermore, individual countries have devised CSA strategies to promote effective investments in CSA.

CSA has three main objectives: sustainably improve the production efficiencies of agricultural systems to increase the income of farmers, ensure food security, and enable agricultural systems to adapt to climate change; reduce or eliminate the GHG emissions of agricultural systems; enhance the carbon sequestration capacities (Zhao et al., 2023). The study in Nciizah & Wakindiki (2015) highlighted some of the necessary practices to achieve CSA. The practices include soil management practices that regulates carbon in the soil, controls GHG emissions, and increase production. Also, the practices that improve the natural resource base. Soil management practices such as direct seeding under reduced-tillage, crop diversification through rotations, improved soil cover protection through the use of cover crops, soil fertility management through the use of fertilizers, and mulch.

The study in Qureshi et al. (2022) presented a relation hierarchical model that classified the various operations of CSA as shown in Figure 1. The operations for soil smart, water smart, carbon smart, livestock smart, and knowledge smart were described. Soil smart involves mechanisms to develop an optimized environment for the crops to grow by ensuring availability of water, nutrients, and oxygen. Water smart improves water management in rain-fed and various irrigated agricultural systems. Carbon smart promotes practices that reduce GHG emissions from agricultural practices. Livestock smart focuses of useful practices to improve farm animal management and production. Knowledge smart employs technologies to keep famers informed and aware of mechanisms that promote resilience and reduce risks. The practices shown in Figure 1 are described in Table 1.

Figure 1. Climate-smart agriculture practices

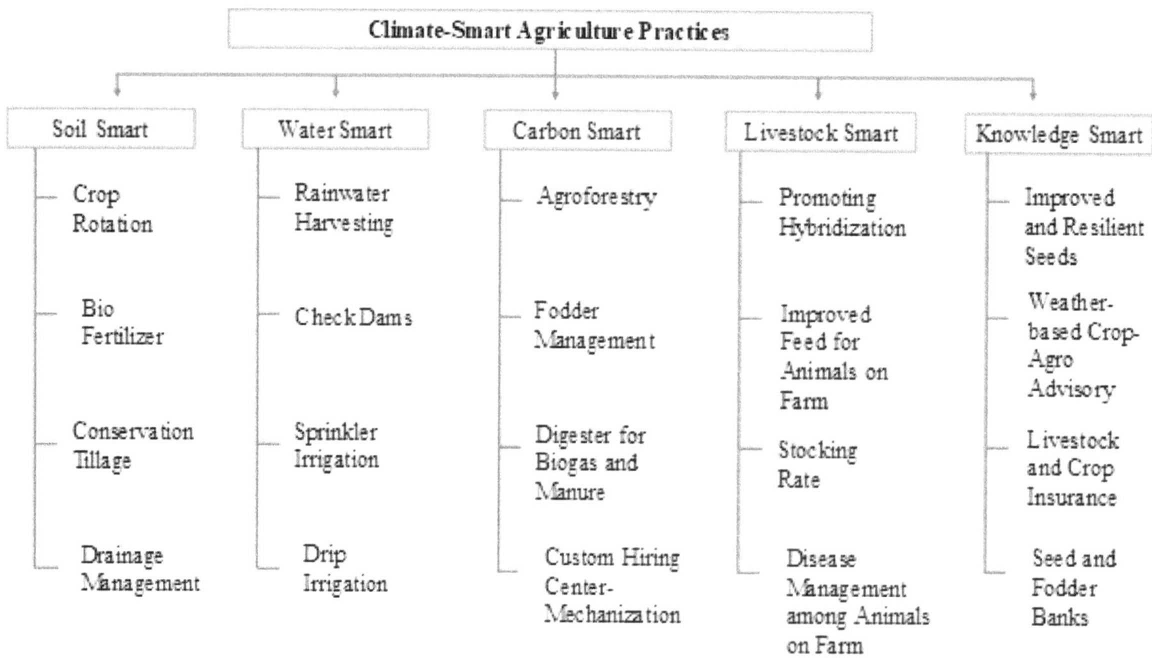

Studies have shown that CSA practices are able to provide satisfactory outcomes in developing countries (Mizik, 2021). Six CSA sites have been established in East Africa (Lushoto in Tanzania, Rakai and Hoima in Uganda, Borana in Ethiopia, Wote and Nyando in Kenya) while five are in West Africa

Table 1. Description of climate-smart agriculture practices

Practice	Description
Crop Rotation	Technique of growing a series of different types of crops in the same agricultural field in a sequence to improve nutrient efficiency and control diseases.
Bio fertilizers	Substances that contain microorganisms. The substances are added to the soil in order to improve the soil fertility and biodiversity.
Conservation Tillage	Technique of soil cultivation that leaves sufficient crop residue to cover the soil surface to reduce soil degradation while maintaining ecosystem stability.
Drainage Management	A technique where an outlet from a conventional drainage system is controlled by a water control structure. It aims to promote irrigation water efficiencies.
Drip Irrigation	Method of applying water that reduces usage of water by minimizing the rate of evaporation and reduces leaching.
Sprinkler Irrigation	Method of applying water in a controlled manner similar to natural rainfall. It aims to reduce water loss.
Rainwater Harvesting	Method of collecting and storing rain water for further use.
Check Dams	Small and sometimes temporary dam constructed across a waterway to improve moisture and reduce erosion activities.
Agroforestry	A practice where crops are integrated with trees and shrubs to provide various environmental and financial benefits.
Fodder Management	Dried livestock feed to maintain healthy productive animals.
Digester for Biogas and manure	Decomposition of organic matter under controlled conditions. It has potential to counteract the GHG emission due to the cultivation of crops.
Custom Hiring Centre-Mechanization	Supplying farm equipment to smallholder farmers at subsidized rates on hire. Aims to reduce the cost of cultivation.
Improved Feed for Animals on Farm	Animal feeding strategies that lower methane emissions by changing the composition of feed.
Livestock Hybridization	Cross-breeding different species to produce animals that adapt to different extreme conditions.
Stocking Rate Management	Manage the number of animals in a farm to ensure no soil erosion or water pollution.
Disease Management among Animals	Improved animal husbandry practices to control animal diseases in the farm and reduce losses.
Livestock and Crop Insurance	Protection against accidents and unexpected events that may affect livestock and crops. It helps farmers to overcome uncertainties and financial risk.
Improved and Resilient Seeds	Seeds that are resilient to drought and unpredictable weather.
Seed and Fodder Banks	Plantings of high-quality fodder species to ensure availability of healthy productive animals. Preserves surplus fodder to help during dry seasons and forage scarcity.
Weather Based Crop Agro Advisory	Farmers make weather sensitive decisions like scheduling when to apply pesticide and fertilizer, when to irrigate, and when to vaccinate animals in order to improve resilience to climate change.

(Fakara in Niger, Yatenga in Burkina Faso, Cinzana in Mali, Kaffrine in Senegal, and Lawra-Jirapa in Ghana) (Okolie et al., 2022). Due to the advancement in technology, there are many new CSA products that employ advanced technologies such as Artificial Intelligence (AI) and IoT (Mizik, 2021). Therefore, developing countries are considering IoT-based agricultural systems as an effective tool to upscale CSA and increase food security (Okolie et al., 2022).

Farmers use IoT-enabled smart systems at various levels and scales of agricultural production. An IoT-enabled agricultural system comprises a network of interconnected intelligent devices. The devices are capable of communicating with each other. Also, the devices are able to generate relevant data about the environment in which they operate. Examples of the devices include sensors, cameras, robots, unmanned aerial vehicles (UAVs), smartphones, computers, and agricultural machinery. For instance, different types of sensors can be used to collect data such as temperature, pressure, humidity, light, and presence. Other IoT devices can be used to monitor and collect data in the form of image and video. Communication networks are used to send and receive data, which is then analyzed by data analysis tools. Therefore, farmers obtain insightful data from the farm. The data is then used to estimate the farm conditions, allowing farmers to take the necessary actions at the right time, quantity, and place (Navarro et al., 2020). Hence, IoT systems enable farmers to use resources more efficiently, increase productivity, and improve food safety. For example, IoT systems allow farmers to effectively control and reduce waste in the application of farm inputs such as fertilizer, pesticides, and water. In addition, through the use of AI, IoT systems have the ability to make timely decisions and perform actions on the environment in order to improve its condition.

CLIMATE-SMART AGRICULTURE PRACTICES IN AFRICAN COUNTRIES AND THEIR IMPACT ON SMALLHOLDER FARMERS

The work in Ariom et al. (2022) presented that many recent studies have indicated the susceptibility of African countries to climate change. For example, it has been predicted that by 2050, East Africa will experience warmer temperatures, a 5 to 20% increase in rainfall between December and February, and 5 to 10% less rainfall from June to August, due to climate change. As a result, crop production will decrease. Furthermore, in West, Central, Eastern and Southern Africa, drought and a rise in mean annual temperature have been noted as factors that cause high risk to rain-fed crop production systems. Therefore, increasing resilient productivity is a central component of 42 African countries' Nationally Determined Contributions that outlines the countries' climate strategies under the Paris Agreement (Kurgat et al., 2020). CSA practices help to increase resilient productivity. Studies show that the determining factors of CSA adoption in smallholder farming systems include the farmers' level of education, revenue, extension services, credit, possession of livestock, experience in agriculture, size of the agricultural field, exposure to information, accessibility to the market, distance to water resources, leadership position, risk orientation of the farmer, gender, land ownership, and family size. Policies to support these factors have great potential to increase the adoption of CSA practices (Abegunde & Obi, 2022; Ariom et al., 2022). Impact of CSA practices in some African countries (Tanzania, Zambia, Algeria, Senegal, Benin, and Nigeria) are presented below.

CSA Practices in Tanzania

As part of the agreement that was reached at the Dakar 2 Summit on Feed Africa: Food Sovereignty and Resilience that took place in Dakar, Senegal, January 25-27, 2023, the Government of Tanzania launched the Food and Agriculture Delivery Council on March 17, 2023. The responsibilities of the council include overseeing the country's food and agriculture delivery compacts' implementation (Said, 2023). The objectives of the council are to increase value and productivity of agricultural production, employment creation, enhanced diversification of products, and strengthened value chains. Techniques to increase productivity of agricultural production focuses mainly on the production of wheat, sunflower, horticulture, beef, and diary. To ensure the project is successful, investments are done to encourage CSA practices such as the use of quality farm inputs (improved seeds and fertilizers), IoT-enabled irrigation systems that deploy UAVs, and crop insurance. Also, land ownership and capacity building of women and youth is emphasized because their contribution in the household economic activities is considerable.

The studies in Jones et al. (2023) and Kurgat et al. (2020) identified some CSA practices in Tanzania. Kurgat et al. (2020) conducted a study in four regions of Tanzania (Iringa, Dodoma, Tabora, and Zanzibar). In the study it was found that 25 to 34% of the households across the four regions had adopted at least one CSA practice (livestock diversity, irrigation, application of chemical fertilizers, or agroforestry). However, the rate of adoption varied by practice and region. Utilization of chemical fertilizers was 34% throughout the regions. Iringa had the highest adoption rate of more than 42% while Dodoma and Zanzibar had use rates of 18%. Irrigation and livestock diversity practices were less popular at 26% overall. Livestock diversity was more popular in Iringa than in Zanzibar and most farmers owned poultry. Overall, only 25% of the farmers practiced crop diversity. Determinants of the CSA adoption were observed to be household size, age, gender, land ownership, and off-farm income. Household size positively influenced livestock diversity. Age of male-headed household negatively influenced the uptake of irrigation while female-headed households were more likely to practice crop diversification, livestock production, and fertilization. Land ownership positively influenced crop diversity and agroforestry, while size of the agricultural field, off-farm income, livestock ownership and holdings encouraged livestock diversity. Government investments in soil management also promoted agroforestry.

The study also found that land ownership and involvement of female in decision making positively influenced the adoption of CSA practices. Farmers who hired farm labor were more willing to use chemical fertilizers but preferred not to irrigate their farms. Age and the need to pay for labor negatively affected the adoption CSA practices for irrigation. This is mainly due to the fact that setting up irrigation facilities is normally costly and labor intensive, especially if the source of water is far from the farm. Overall, the observations in Kurgat et al. (2020) suggested that it would be possible to upscale the adoption of CSA practices in the four regions of Tanzania if land ownership rights and women's involvement in household decision making were improved. The importance of women's empowerment was also highlighted in Okolie et al. (2022). The study in Jones et al. (2023) reviewed the literature on CSA practices in Tanzania. It focused on studied that were done within ten years. Results show that CSA practices have a positive impact on productivity, mixed impacts on resilience, short-term negative impacts on emissions intensity, and highly variable impacts on socio-economic characteristics.

CSA Practices in Zambia

Zambia experiences the effects of climate change, which include drought, extremely high temperatures, seasonal and flash floods, and dry periods. Therefore, several initiatives have focused on promoting CSA practices in Zambia (Ariom et al., 2022). The CSA practices in Zambia were presented in Ariom et al. (2022). The practices are discussed below.

Smallholder farmers in Zambia practice conservation agriculture. Their practices include minimum soil tillage, crop rotation, and continuous soil cover. An investigation on the impact of minimum tillage and crop rotation on maize yields in six districts found that by practicing low tillage and crop rotation, farmers were able to increase maize productivity by 26 to 38% and 21 to 24%, respectively. It has been found that agroforestry increases crop yields and soil fertility in Zambia. Therefore, the indigenous, nitrogen-fixing acacia species of trees locally known as Musangu are commonly used for agroforestry practices in Zambia. CSA practices in the livestock sector in Zambia include the following: (i) micro-level adaptation such as shifts in species, breeds and/or production systems; (ii) policies such as animal breeding policy; and (iii) breeding of animals that have high resistance to drought and heat. Integration of agroforestry into crop–livestock production systems have shown to improve housing and feeding approaches, and enhanced the management of grazing, forages, and animal waste. More than 90% of Zambia's smallholder agriculture is rain-fed, therefore, irrigation is promoted as an appropriate CSA practice during dry periods. Farmers are also encouraged to practice efficient water utilization.

The study in Ariom et al. (2022) presented the impact of CSA practices on smallholder farmers in Zambia. When maize farmers practiced crop rotation, reduced tillage, inorganic fertilizer, legume intercropping, and use of improved seeds, the maize yield significantly increased even during critical weather conditions. As a result, the income of farmers increased. Also, in eastern Zambia, intercropping of maize with cowpea resulted in increased yield. During dry seasons, maize and soybean gross margins were the highest in farms that used zero tillage. A cost-benefit analysis to evaluate the different CSA practices in some African countries including Zambia found that using more than one CSA practices resulted in the highest economic and environmental gains for smallholder farmers (Mizik, 2021). However, Zambia had low CSA adoption rates among smallholder farmers due to limited resources such as funding and agricultural inputs, incompatible land management practices, and some cultural practices (Ariom et al., 2022).

CSA Practices in Algeria

CSA practices in Algeria include water saving, construction of dams and hill reservoirs, anti-drought mechanisms, combating erosion and desertification, protection and rehabilitation of steppe lands, and preservation and extension of forests (Ariom et al., 2022). Some of the CSA innovations in Algeria are presented below.

Algeria has a collaborative project with the Netherlands to devise a practical greenhouse system suitable for the local harsh arid environment. The adaptive greenhouse systems apply the concepts of smart sustainable horticulture, which aims to optimize greenhouse designs to one specific setting. Farmers are using the greenhouse system and it has enabled them to increase the yield. Moreover, the integration of crop and livestock systems, crop diversification, and crop rotation are popular techniques in Algeria because they help farmers to reduce climate vulnerability and increase yield. The green dam project was launched to help protect watersheds against erosion and it has presented positive outcomes. Algeria has also collaborated with other African countries and Greece to devise CSA practices by restoring biodiversity and producing livestock that is resilient to harsh conditions.

To overcome the challenges of drought, farmers in the Algerian Sahara consider CSA practices such as efficient use of water in potato crop production, innovative equipment and precision techniques, smart irrigation, and the production of resilient and climate-smart potato varieties. Studies have shown that resilient and climate-smart potato varieties produced better yields. Studies have also shown that when farmers used underground drip fertigation technique, it was possible to reduce water usage and save more than 50% of the water. In terms of policies, Algeria has developed national policies to encourage investments in CSA. The policies are used to guide various national plans, including the National Agricultural Development Program, the Agricultural and Rural Renewal Policy, and the FILAHA Plan. The use of the policies has resulted in increased agricultural productivity.

CSA practices that utilize the mechanisms of conservation agriculture have also helped farmers to make more profit and improve their finances (Ariom et al., 2022). For example, in the region of Sétif (northeastern Algeria), the practices of no-till and tilled were applied in 28 wheat farms and their output was compared. Observations showed that the no-till mechanisms presented more profit and it needed less labor and fuel. Furthermore, utilization of greenhouses for horticultural production and irrigated agriculture has helped farmers in Algeria to increase their profits. The authors in Ariom et al. (2022) discussed a survey that was done in the city of El Ghrous in Biskra. The survey collected data from 100 farms that specialized in early tomatoes under greenhouses. Results revealed that farmers who used greenhouses achieved a significant increase in profits.

CSA Practices in Senegal

The study in Ariom et al. (2022) reported that a large number of smallholder farmers in Senegal grow millet, maize, sorghum, and rice. However, due to climate change, farmers experiences the challenges of drought, frequent flooding, and reduced harvests. Therefore, Senegal has developed various initiatives to promote the adoption of CSA practices. Some of the CSA practices in Senegal are presented below.

Farmers take efforts to ensure efficient utilization of water. Ongoing practices include the development of anti-salt dikes and storm water retention, practice of micro-irrigation, storage of runoff by micro retention, rainwater harvesting, and integrated management of water resources. Also, utilization of improved weather and climate information services (WCIS) is popular in Senegal. To provide farmers with the necessary skills for effective utilization of WCIS, trainings are conducted. Documented evidence show that through the use of WCIS, smallholder farmers have been able to improve their adaptive capacity to ensure sufficient food production despite the climate variability and extreme weather events. Furthermore, a Participatory Integrated Climate Service for Agriculture (PICSA) has been used to expand the use of WCIS. PISCA is useful to farmers because it helps them to identify CSA practices that are practical in their specific situations and climatic conditions. Observations from studies suggest that PICSA has played an important role in promoting the adoption of CSA practices in Senegal. Due to the use of PISCA, farmers have been encouraged to consider CSA practices such as changing the timing of activities like sowing dates, applying soil and water management practices, diversifying crop varieties, crop insurance, control of fertilizer application, and adjusting seasonal plans according to the available resources.

The study in Ariom et al. (2022) reported the influence of CSA practices on smallholder farmers in Senegal. In the case of forest and cropland regeneration practices, the study reported that an investigation involving 1080 households found that farmer-managed natural regeneration can be used to safeguard farmers when the farmers incur reduced crop yield due to the effects of climate change. The study also presented that farmers who grew multipurpose trees on farmlands were able to achieve a significant increase in their income. For example, a community of 1000 households was able to achieve an increase of about 72,000 USD. Furthermore, the trees provided a source of firewood and fuel. Therefore, the amount of time that women used to collect firewood was reduced from 2.5 to 0.5 hours per day. The practice of re-greening the land was useful in reducing tension between farmers and herders. It was observed that tension between farmers and herders was reduced by 80%. Overall, about 90% of farmers who adopted CSA practices provided positive feedback. The farmers reported an increase of income, food access and diversity and climate resilience. Also, they reported that labor time was reduced. Moreover, the use of WCIS resulted in an increase in farmers' ability to produce quality crops and profits. Ariom et al. (2022)

presented that the use of WCIS for CSA in Senegal resulted in an increase of household income by 10 to 25%. Climate data is now considered an agricultural input in Senegal, together with the fundamental agricultural inputs like seeds, fertilizer, pesticides, and water.

CSA Practices in Benin

It has been predicted that Benin will experience increased drought, late and violent rains, floods and temperature rise (Ariom et al., 2022). Therefore, farmers in Benin practice various CSA techniques. Some of the CSA practices in Benin are presented below as discussed in Ariom et al., (2022).

Maize is cultivated by 85% of the farmers in Benin. The farmers have developed some adaptation techniques to reduce the negative effects of climate change. To ensure crops grow in favorable conditions, farmers adjust the cropping calendar. For example, farmers change the dates for planting and sowing. They also use improved (short-cycle) crop varieties, crop–livestock integration, and agroforestry. During prolonged dry seasons, farmers plant trees to naturally shade crops. Many of the farmers who practice crop–livestock integration make sure they comply with the vaccination recommendations. Also, farmers practice transhumance where herds move to find fresh water and grass. Some farmers practice watering in rivers. In the northern part of Benin, farmers practice techniques such as intercropping, crop rotation, water and soil conservation, field relocation, and altered cropping patterns. Studies have shown that a significant number of farmers in Benin practice agroforestry and perennial plantation. These techniques are considered to be the most beneficial techniques because they have many advantages including soil protection and improvement of biodiversity.

CSA Practices in Nigeria

Due to climate change, Nigeria faces challenges such as droughts, desertification, rising temperature, changing rainfall patterns, and floods. Therefore, farmers adopt various CSA practices to ensure food security. Some of the CSA practices in Nigeria were discussed in Ariom et al., (2022). The CSA practices are presented below.

Soil degradation is a significant challenge in the northeast regions of Nigeria. Due to soil degradation, there is low percentage of soil organic matter and farmers in that region experience reduced crop yields. Therefore, CSA practices are being adopted. Other causes of low crop yield include limited use of fertilizer inputs, and persistent droughts. It has been reported that conservation agriculture has helped to increase agricultural productivity, especially for crops such as maize, sorghum, and millet. Diversified schemes of crop rotation have also presented economic benefits. Mulching is used to provide soil cover. The soil cover has many advantages, which include lower rates of run-off, improved soil moisture retention, and conservation of soil organic matter. Farmers also practice zero or minimum tillage, which has shown great benefits in terms of cost reduction for land preparation.

The use of improved crop varieties has shown positive results among cereal growers in Nigeria. This is because improved crop varieties are more resistant to pest and disease. Also, improved crop varieties have low water requirements and they mature early. To address the challenges caused by excessive rains that cause flooding and soil erosion, farmers use mixed cropping, tied ridging, mulching, and terracing. Mechanisms of water harvesting have also shown to be beneficial because they help to retain moisture for crops such as sorghum and millet. During extended dry periods, farmers practice transhumance where herds move to find fresh water and grass. Furthermore, farmers preserve forage for off-season utilization and they develop feed formulation with alternative feed resources. Farmers normally prefer to grow resistant breeds and maintain a good vaccination routine to ensure good productivity even during extreme weather conditions. Regarding the use of WCIS, it has been reported that when Nigerian farmers have access to WCIS they tend to get more involved in CSA practices. For instance, access to WCIS encourages the farmers to plant early-maturing crops.

The study in Ariom et al. (2022) reported about CSA practices in Nigeria and how they impact smallholder farmers. It presented that the use of improved seed varieties has resulted in increased yield for cereal farmers in Nigeria. When observations were done for three cropping seasons, results showed a better harvest and increased farmers' income when the improved SOSAT millet cultivar was planted as compared to when the local Gwagwa millet was used. Also, intercropping techniques resulted in higher yields. For example, intercropping sorghum and cowpea resulted in 64% increase in the yield. Studies have also found that rice farmers who used a locally crossbred variety and early-planting strategies obtained significantly higher yields. Terracing is a popular technique for soil water conservation in the southwest Nigeria. It has been observed that terraced maize and sorghum farms achieve up to 47% higher yield than non-terraced farms.

INTERNET OF THINGS-ENABLED SMART AGRICULTURAL SYSTEMS FOR EFFICIENT UTILIZATION OF FARM INPUTS

CSA includes the integration of different farming processes and systems as well as efficient utilization of farm inputs (Mizik, 2021). Due to the advancements in technology, many IoT-enabled smart agricultural systems are available to help farmers utilize farm inputs more efficiently. For example, IoT-based smart agricultural systems enable farmers to effectively control the application of fertilizer, pesticides, and water. Various IoT-enabled smart agricultural systems are presented below. The systems provide effective mechanisms to ensure efficient utilization of water, fertilizer, pesticides, fungicides, and herbicides.

IoT Systems for Irrigation

It has been predicted that there will be shortage of water throughout the world by the year 2030 (Khan et al., 2021). In 2013, it was presented at the United Nations Convention to Combat Desertification that around 168 countries in the world experienced shortage of water for irrigation (Khan et al., 2021). Due to the alarming rate of reduction in groundwater levels throughout the world, IoT-enabled intelligent irrigation systems are being devised. Intelligent irrigation systems enable farmers to efficiently use water resources. Efficient use of water resources is a necessary step towards sustainability. The systems use data on ground water levels and rainfall to decide when to irrigate. Systems also monitor the weather to avoid irrigating the land immediately before or after rainfall. Furthermore, the systems enable crop water stress index (CWSI)-based irrigation management. A CWSI-based system attains crop canopy and air temperature measurements. The measurements are processed by intelligent software and used to analyze the farm data. In addition, information from other sources including climate data and satellite imaging are applied to CWSI models to enable water need assessment, and finally specific irrigation index value is produced (Ayaz et al., 2019). For example, the IoT-enabled irrigation system in Kashyap et al. (2021) contains five main components. The components include sensor nodes, anchor nodes and servers, AI algorithms, farmer's device such as smartphone, and water valves/sprinklers. The components of the system work together to help the farmer decide when to irrigate and the right amount of water to apply. The farmer is able to remotely operate the irrigation system by sending commands from his smartphone. Thus, a farmer remotely opens the water sprinkles to allow irrigation of the farm field according to the specific water requirements.

The IoT-enabled irrigation system in Hasan et al. (2021) uses sensors to monitor the humidity, moisture level, temperature, and air quality. Also, it detects rain and forecasts floods or drought. Based on the data that is received from the sensor nodes, the water sprinklers get activated or deactivated automatically to ensure an efficient irrigation process. The system in Cambra et al. (2017) uses a mesh network with UAVs, aerial mapping sensor, and cameras to capture videos that are useful in the monitoring and control of the irrigation process. To make water management smarter and optimize water utilization in Khoa et al. (2019), an IoT system obtains real-time data inputs from sensors that are deployed in a farm field. Then, it sends suggestions for watering schedules to farmer's mobile phone. The system enables the farmer to monitor and prepare a watering plan for the farms by scheduling the date and time effectively. Furthermore, the system is automatic and it switches on the water pump at the right time. In García et al. (2020), it was reported that due to the growing interest in low-cost sensors for smart irrigation systems, low-cost sensors are being developed. The list of low-cost sensors includes leaf water stress monitoring sensors, multi-level soil moisture sensors, water salinity monitoring sensors, and water turbidity sensors. In Bipasha & Tariq (2018), an IoT-based automatic solar water pumping irrigation system was presented for use in developing countries. The system employs a microcontroller which receives data from sensors. The data shows the water level, humidity, temperature, and soil moisture level. The data is used to help the microcontroller decide when to start and stop the water pump motor. Furthermore, user can operate the irrigation system remotely by a simple click on a smartphone.

IoT Systems for Fertilization

Crop health can be affected if the use of fertilizers is not well controlled. Excessive application of fertilizers results in poor crop health and economic losses. It also affects the environment, quality of soil, water, and air. IoT-enabled systems provide exact estimation of the rate of fertilizers to use. For example, in Lavanya et al. (2020), a smart fertilization system based on IoT and AI was developed by designing a Nitrogen-Phosphorus-Potassium (NPK) sensor with light dependent resistor (LDR) and light emitting diodes (LED). The data sensed by the NPK sensor was sent to a cloud server to enable fast retrieval of data and the deficiency of nutrients from the sensed data was detected. A notification message was sent to the farmer to inform about the appropriate amount of fertilizer to be applied and suggestions about the right time to apply.

Fertilization can require site-specific soil nutrient measurements according to various parameters such as type of crop, type of soil, absorption capacity of the soil, fertility type and rate of utilization, product yield, and weather conditions. IoT systems that are based on technologies such as normalized vegetation index (NDVI), geographic information systems (GIS), variable rate technology (VRT), and global positioning systems (GPS) are useful in fertilization processes that require site-specific soil nutrient measurements. NDVI uses satellite images to monitor the status of crop nutrients, which helps in assessing the soil nutrient level and requirement of nutrients in the soil. Also, GIS, VRT, and GPS estimate nutrients in the field which can indicate the need for fertilizer. Hence, farmers use the IoT systems to acquire site-specific soil nutrient requirements and utilize fertilizer more efficiently.

IoT Systems for Pesticide, Fungicide, and Herbicide Control

The effects of climate change such as warmer temperatures and flooding are projected to favor an increase in insect pests and fungi. FAO estimates that the annual agricultural losses that are caused by insects, weeds, and diseases is between 20 and 40% of the total production (Friha et al., 2021). Therefore, it is important to use pesticides, herbicides, insecticides, and fungicides to help reduce crop losses. However, if misused, pesticides, herbicides, insecticides, and fungicides can have harmful effects. It is estimated that, in each year, more than two million tons of pesticides are used globally (Ayaz et al., 2019). Most of these pesticides are harmful to humans, animal health, and the environment. IoT systems that use sensors, robots, and UAVs are a great solution to enable controlled use of chemical or synthetic pesticides. The systems enable real-time monitoring, modelling, and forecasting. In organic farming where it is necessary to minimize the utilization of chemical or synthetic pesticides, weed control robots and UAVs are equipped with sensors, cameras, and image processing methods, and they are able to detect plant row fields for weed detection and mapping. The robots and UAVs detect plants, automatically take pictures, classify the plants, and then destroy the weeds without using any chemicals. In Czymmek et al. (2020); Pérez-Ortiz et al. (2016), UAVs with cameras and image processing methods were used to provide weed coverage maps for weed control.

UAVs and robots are able to precisely control pests when they have access to a remote IoT disease management system and they are equipped with multispectral sensing devices and precision spraying nozzles. For example, in Cambra et al. (2015), an IoT-enabled system empowered with UAV-based video sensing was deployed for precision spraying in a corn field. The components of the system included UAVs, laptop, and a sprayer on a tractor. The system was able to save large amounts of herbicides, reduce the cost spent on fertilizers, and increase the quality of the yield. The UAV and sensor network-based pesticide spraying system in Faiçal et al. (2017) was specifically designed to ensure safer conditions and more precise spraying process even in changing weather such as sudden changes of wind speed and direction. The multi-purpose smart farming robot in Chand et al. (2021) utilized IoT sensors and computer vision to continuously monitor pests. Thereafter, it made smart decisions in terms of pesticide spraying. The robot was autonomous and it made intelligent decisions to ensure efficient utilization of pesticides.

In Arakeri et al. (2017), a remote controlled computer vision-based robotic weed control system was developed to work in onion fields and provide real-time control of weeds. The system identified weeds and selectively sprayed the right amount of herbicide. As a result, efficient use of herbicide was achieved. In Misra et al. (2020), several examples of IoT-enabled agricultural systems were presented including the tractor-propelled weeding machine that used machine vision, control system, and a weeding mechanism. Also, an autonomous mechanical weed controller was presented. The weed controller used a GPS antenna to be self-guided within the field and cameras to distinguish crops such as sugar beet from weed. Furthermore, it used artificial lighting conditions to enable it to work for long hours including night times. Another IoT-enabled weed control machine in Misra et al. (2020) used cameras, computers, and AI to differentiate crops from weeds. The machine was able to effectively control weeds by specifically spraying herbicides on sites where weed was present. Efficient utilization of herbicides was achieved by selectively spraying the right amount of herbicides.

Figure 2 shows an example of IoT-enabled agricultural system empowered with UAV-based video sensing. The system was presented in Ojha et al. (2021). It employs UAVs, an IoT gateway (laptop), and a sprayer mounted on a tractor. The UAVs fly over an agricultural field to capture videos and stream the videos to the laptop. The laptop is equipped with a video processing module that exchanges GPS coor-

Figure 2. An example of IoT-enabled agricultural system with UAV-based video sensing

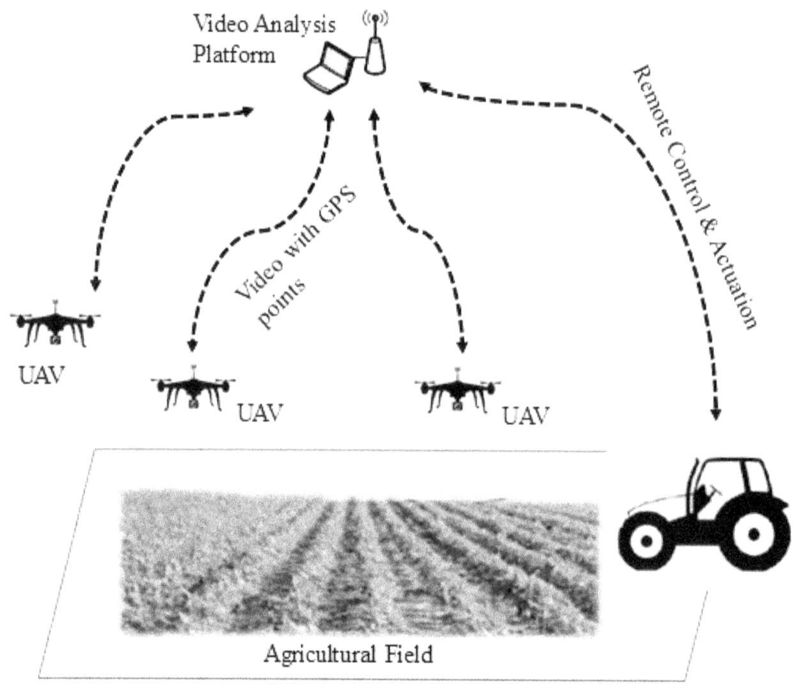

dinates with the UAVs. It is able to analyze the videos and locate weeds in real-time. The information is transmitted to the sprayer on the tractor to spray precisely over the weeds. Thus, the system enables real-time identification of weed and sprays herbicides on the weed with precision in terms of location and amount. As a result, it improved the efficiency in the application of herbicides. Similarly, the IoT system may precisely identify areas that require fertilizer and spray fertilizer with precision in terms of location and amount. The sprayer may also be installed on a UAV. The study in Hanif et al. (2022) presented that a UAV sprayer has greater benefits over a tractor sprayer in terms of mobility. Also, it is 40 times faster than the conventional backpack sprayer. Using UAV sprayers results in a 30 to 40% reduction in pesticides usage. In addition, Hanif et al. (2022) presented that farmers can achieve up to 90% reduction in water usage when using UAV sprayers.

RECOMMENDATIONS

The quality and quantity of crop yield can be affected if farm inputs such as fertilizer, pesticides, and water are used inefficiently. Without the help of digital technologies, it is challenging to always determine the optimal farm inputs. When IoT-based smart agricultural systems are used, they enable real-time data acquisition and analysis to facilitate controlled application of farm inputs. It has been reported by the International Telecommunication Union (ITU) that electricity and Internet connectivity are becoming increasingly available in remote rural areas. This suggests that there is opportunity to implement advanced technologies such as IoT-based smart agricultural systems in remote rural areas. The IoT systems can be used to effectively control the application of farm inputs and ensure efficient use of resources for CSA.

However, before the IoT systems are implemented, numerous aspects of the IoT systems implementation should be examined.

For the IoT systems to be effective, the systems must be highly adaptable and be customizable to local environments. This is important because farmers from different regions have different requirements. IoT systems require reliable connections between devices. Therefore, the network connection and farm infrastructure must be reliable with skilled human resource. When accurate predictions on farm conditions are required, IoT systems should integrate AI and the infrastructure must enable the collection and analysis of data from different sources such as soil, climate, diseases, and pests. Also, the application of deep learning algorithms should be considered because more accurate predictions are made when deep learning algorithms are used.

IoT and AI allow the use of data analytics techniques which have advanced the agricultural practices from input-intensive to knowledge-intensive processes that increases productivity. Therefore, communication of the IoT systems must be secure because agricultural data is valuable to farmers and it can be considered a trade secret. WCIS have shown great potential in helping farmers to adapt to severe climate conditions. IoT devices play a great role in the provision of weather-based crop agro advisory through WCIS. Therefore, availability of affordable IoT devices will help encourage the adoption of weather-based crop agro advisory practices. Furthermore, using IoT systems, it is possible to provide location-specific, tailor made, easily understood WCIS to smallholder farmers to facilitate decision making and planning of CSA practices. This is particularly important in a country like Senegal where climate data is now considered an agricultural input.

Agriculture in Africa is highly dependent on rainfall, making the continent's agricultural system vulnerable to climate change. In countries that experience long periods of drought, IoT-based smart irrigation systems guarantee all-year-round farming and all-year-round productivity. Thus, IoT-based smart irrigation systems reduce the risk of drought and encourage CSA practices such as crop diversification. Studies have shown that UAV-based irrigation systems achieve up to 90% reduction in water usage. Also, UAV-based pesticide application systems achieve a 30 to 40% reduction in pesticides usage. However, the installation cost of these systems can be high. Therefore, smallholder farmers should be provided with financial support. In scenarios where the application of CSA requires investments in advanced technologies (IoT network, sensors, UAVs), limited financial resources could make the adoption impossible. This is particularly important in a country like Tanzania where agricultural UAVs are considered to be useful agricultural tools for CSA. Since 2016, UAVs are being deployed in Tanzania for land mapping in rural areas to help control the conflicts that frequently occur between farmers and cattle herders. The conflicts occur due to the scarcity of land and water resources. Also, the JembeKilimo agritech platform uses UAVs to collect data. The data is then analyzed so as to give insights to farmers in Tanzania and enable the farmers to make informed decisions in agricultural processes. Financial support will enable smallholder farmers to access these technologies and increase agricultural production efficiency.

CONCLUSION

This chapter has identified CSA practices and their impact on smallholder farmers in six African countries (Tanzania, Zambia, Nigeria, Senegal, Benin, and Algeria). CSA practices such as agroforestry, minimum soil tillage, crop rotation, legume intercropping, improved seeds, inorganic fertilizer, crop-livestock integration, use of greenhouses, rainwater harvesting, use of improved WCIS, livestock diversity, changing planting dates and sowing times, planting early-maturing crops, and mulching are discussed. Generally, farmers who adopted these CSA practices observed positive outcomes in terms of adaptability to climate change and productivity. Furthermore, IoT-enabled smart agricultural systems are explored. Observations show that IoT-enabled agricultural systems enable efficient utilization of farm inputs such as fertilizer, pesticides, herbicides, and water. Also, using IoT systems, it is possible to provide customized, location-specific, and easily understood WCIS for smallholder farmers to facilitate decision making and planning of CSA practices. Therefore, this chapter has presented recommendations for the adoption of IoT-enabled CSA in African countries. IoT-enabled agricultural systems are recommended for a country like Senegal where climate data is considered an agricultural input. Also, the systems are important in a country like Tanzania where IoT devices such as UAVs are considered to be useful agricultural tools for CSA.

REFERENCES

Arakeri, M. P., Vijaya Kumar, B. P., Barsaiya, S., & Sairam, H. V. (2017). Computer vision based robotic weed control system for precision agriculture. *2017 International Conference on Advances in Computing, Communications and Informatics (ICACCI)*, 1201–1205. 10.1109/ICACCI.2017.8126005

Ariom, T. O., Dimon, E., Nambeye, E., Diouf, N. S., Adelusi, O. O., & Boudalia, S. (2022). Climate-Smart Agriculture in African Countries: A Review of Strategies and Impacts on Smallholder Farmers. *Sustainability (Basel)*, *14*(18), 11370. doi:10.3390u141811370

Ayaz, M., Ammad-Uddin, M., Sharif, Z., Mansour, A., & Aggoune, E.-H. M. (2019). Internet-of-Things (IoT)-Based Smart Agriculture: Toward Making the Fields Talk. *IEEE Access : Practical Innovations, Open Solutions*, *7*, 129551–129583. doi:10.1109/ACCESS.2019.2932609

Bipasha Biswas, S., & Tariq Iqbal, M. (2018). Solar Water Pumping System Control Using a Low Cost ESP32 Microcontroller. *2018 IEEE Canadian Conference on Electrical & Computer Engineering (CCECE)*, 1–5. 10.1109/CCECE.2018.8447749

Cambra, C., Díaz, J. R., & Lloret, J. (2015). Deployment and Performance Study of an Ad Hoc Network Protocol for Intelligent Video Sensing in Precision Agriculture. In M. Garcia Pineda, J. Lloret, S. Papavassiliou, S. Ruehrup, & C. B. Westphall (Eds.), *Ad-hoc Networks and Wireless* (Vol. 8629, pp. 165–175). Springer Berlin Heidelberg. doi:10.1007/978-3-662-46338-3_14

Cambra, C., Sendra, S., Lloret, J., & Garcia, L. (2017). An IoT service-oriented system for agriculture monitoring. *2017 IEEE International Conference on Communications (ICC)*, 1–6. 10.1109/ICC.2017.7996640

Chand, A. A., Prasad, K. A., Mar, E., Dakai, S., Mamun, K. A., Islam, F. R., Mehta, U., & Kumar, N. M. (2021). Design and Analysis of Photovoltaic Powered Battery-Operated Computer Vision-Based Multi-Purpose Smart Farming Robot. *Agronomy (Basel)*, *11*(3), 530. doi:10.3390/agronomy11030530

Czymmek, V., Schramm, R., & Hussmann, S. (2020). Vision Based Crop Row Detection for Low Cost UAV Imagery in Organic Agriculture. *2020 IEEE International Instrumentation and Measurement Technology Conference (I2MTC)*, 1–6. 10.1109/I2MTC43012.2020.9128695

Faiçal, B. S., Freitas, H., Gomes, P. H., Mano, L. Y., Pessin, G., de Carvalho, A. C. P. L. F., Krishnamachari, B., & Ueyama, J. (2017). An adaptive approach for UAV-based pesticide spraying in dynamic environments. *Computers and Electronics in Agriculture, 138*, 210–223. doi:10.1016/j.compag.2017.04.011

Friha, O., Ferrag, M. A., Shu, L., Maglaras, L., & Wang, X. (2021). Internet of Things for the Future of Smart Agriculture: A Comprehensive Survey of Emerging Technologies. *IEEE/CAA Journal of Automatica Sinica, 8*(4), 718–752. doi:10.1109/JAS.2021.1003925

G, L., C, R., & P, G. (2020). An automated low cost IoT based Fertilizer Intimation System for smart agriculture. *Sustainable Computing: Informatics and Systems, 28*, 100300. doi:10.1016/j.suscom.2019.01.002

García, L., Parra, L., Jimenez, J. M., Lloret, J., & Lorenz, P. (2020). IoT-Based Smart Irrigation Systems: An Overview on the Recent Trends on Sensors and IoT Systems for Irrigation in Precision Agriculture. *Sensors (Basel), 20*(4), 1042. doi:10.339020041042 PMID:32075172

Hanif, A. S., Han, X., & Yu, S.-H. (2022). Independent Control Spraying System for UAV-Based Precise Variable Sprayer: A Review. *Drones (Basel), 6*(12), 383. doi:10.3390/drones6120383

Hasan, M., Uddin, K. N. W., Sayeed, A., & Tasneem, T. (2021). Smart Agriculture Robotic System Based on Internet of Things to Boost Crop Production. *2021 2nd International Conference on Robotics, Electrical and Signal Processing Techniques (ICREST)*, 157–162. 10.1109/ICREST51555.2021.9331091

Jones, K., Nowak, A., Berglund, E., Grinnell, W., Temu, E., Paul, B., Renwick, L. L. R., Steward, P., Rosenstock, T. S., & Kimaro, A. A. (2023). Evidence supports the potential for climate-smart agriculture in Tanzania. *Global Food Security, 36*, 100666. doi:10.1016/j.gfs.2022.100666

Kashyap, P. K., Kumar, S., Jaiswal, A., Prasad, M., & Gandomi, A. H. (2021). Towards Precision Agriculture: IoT-Enabled Intelligent Irrigation Systems Using Deep Learning Neural Network. *IEEE Sensors Journal, 21*(16), 17479–17491. doi:10.1109/JSEN.2021.3069266

Khan, N., Ray, R. L., Sargani, G. R., Ihtisham, M., Khayyam, M., & Ismail, S. (2021). Current Progress and Future Prospects of Agriculture Technology: Gateway to Sustainable Agriculture. *Sustainability (Basel), 13*(9), 4883. doi:10.3390u13094883

Khoa, T. A., Man, M. M., Nguyen, T.-Y., Nguyen, V., & Nam, N. H. (2019). Smart Agriculture Using IoT Multi-Sensors: A Novel Watering Management System. *Journal of Sensor and Actuator Networks, 8*(3), 45. doi:10.3390/jsan8030045

Kirina, T., Groot, A., Shilomboleni, H., Ludwig, F., & Demissie, T. (2022). Scaling Climate Smart Agriculture in East Africa: Experiences and Lessons. *Agronomy (Basel), 12*(4), 820. doi:10.3390/agronomy12040820

Kurgat, B. K., Lamanna, C., Kimaro, A., Namoi, N., Manda, L., & Rosenstock, T. S. (2020). Adoption of Climate-Smart Agriculture Technologies in Tanzania. *Frontiers in Sustainable Food Systems, 4*, 55. doi:10.3389/fsufs.2020.00055

Misra, N. N., Dixit, Y., Al-Mallahi, A., Bhullar, M. S., Upadhyay, R., & Martynenko, A. (2020). IoT, big data and artificial intelligence in agriculture and food industry. *IEEE Internet of Things Journal*, 1–1. doi:10.1109/JIOT.2020.2998584

Mizik, T. (2021). Climate-Smart Agriculture on Small-Scale Farms: A Systematic Literature Review. *Agronomy (Basel), 11*(6), 1096. doi:10.3390/agronomy11061096

Navarro, E., Costa, N., & Pereira, A. (2020). A Systematic Review of IoT Solutions for Smart Farming. *Sensors (Basel), 20*(15), 4231. doi:10.339020154231 PMID:32751366

Nciizah, A. D., & Wakindiki, I. I. C. (2015). Climate Smart Agriculture: Achievements and Prospects in Africa. *Journal of Geoscience and Environment Protection, 03*(06), 99–105. doi:10.4236/gep.2015.36016

Ojha, T., Misra, S., & Raghuwanshi, N. S. (2021). Internet of Things for Agricultural Applications: The State of the Art. *IEEE Internet of Things Journal, 8*(14), 10973–10997. doi:10.1109/JIOT.2021.3051418

Okolie, C. C., Danso-Abbeam, G., Groupson-Paul, O., & Ogundeji, A. A. (2022). Climate-Smart Agriculture Amidst Climate Change to Enhance Agricultural Production: A Bibliometric Analysis. *Land (Basel), 12*(1), 50. doi:10.3390/land12010050

Pérez-Ortiz, M., Peña, J. M., Gutiérrez, P. A., Torres-Sánchez, J., Hervás-Martínez, C., & López-Granados, F. (2016). Selecting patterns and features for between- and within- crop-row weed mapping using UAV-imagery. *Expert Systems with Applications, 47*, 85–94. doi:10.1016/j.eswa.2015.10.043

Qureshi, M. R. N. M., Almuflih, A. S., Sharma, J., Tyagi, M., Singh, S., & Almakayeel, N. (2022). Assessment of the Climate-Smart Agriculture Interventions towards the Avenues of Sustainable Production–Consumption. *Sustainability (Basel), 14*(14), 8410. doi:10.3390u14148410

Said, M. (2023, March 15). *Samia forms council to oversee food, agriculture—Daily News*. https://dailynews.co.tz/samia-forms-council-to-oversee-food-agriculture/, https://dailynews.co.tz/samia-forms-council-to-oversee-food-agriculture/

Selbonne, S., Guindé, L., Causeret, F., Chopin, P., Sierra, J., Tournebize, R., & Blazy, J.-M. (2023). How to Measure the Performance of Farms with Regard to Climate-Smart Agriculture Goals? A Set of Indicators and Its Application in Guadeloupe. *Agriculture, 13*(2), 297. doi:10.3390/agriculture13020297

Zhao, J., Liu, D., & Huang, R. (2023). A Review of Climate-Smart Agriculture: Recent Advancements, Challenges, and Future Directions. *Sustainability (Basel), 15*(4), 3404. doi:10.3390u15043404

KEY TERMS AND DEFINITIONS

Agroforestry: A practice where crops are integrated with trees and shrubs to provide various environmental and economic benefits.

Climate Change: A global change in the average weather conditions such as temperature and rainfall over a long period of time due to the increase in greenhouse gas emissions in the atmosphere.

Climate-Smart Agriculture: An approach that transforms agricultural systems towards climate resilient practices to sustainably increase productivity, reduce greenhouse gases, and attain food security.

Conservation Agriculture: Is a farming system that employs climate-smart agriculture practices such as minimum soil disturbance and diversification of plant species to achieve improved and sustainable agricultural production.

Internet of Things: A collective network of interconnected computing devices, sensors, unmanned aerial vehicles, and digital machines connected to the Internet. Devices have the ability to communicate by sending and receiving data from each other and implement remote sensing and actuation.

Smart Agricultural Systems: Are systems that employ advanced technologies such as Internet of Things, robotics, artificial intelligence, unmanned aerial vehicles, and sensors to perform agricultural processes and efficiently increase the quantity and quality of yield.

Unmanned Aerial Vehicle: Also known as a drone. It is a flying robot/aircraft that is guided autonomously by a remote control.

Chapter 5
Digital Payments Systems for Emerging Economies:
Case of Tanzania

Bossi A. Masamila
The Open University of Tanzania, Tanzania

George S. Oreku
The Open University of Tanzania, Tanzania

Edephonce N. Nfuka
The Open University of Tanzania, Tanzania

ABSTRACT

Innovative digital payment systems (DPS) are a crucial solution for greater financial inclusion assisting low-income households in overcoming poverty using lower-cost methods for managing their finances. The advancement in internet communication technologies and the arrival of e-commerce and e-business simulated digital payment systems providesvarious electronic payment options such as payment cards, mobile payments, mobile wallets, electronic cash, and contactless payment methods. This chapter discusses the current state of the art in digital payment systems in emerging markets. Also, it analyzes the advantages of DPS in emerging economies, challenges in emerging economies, the economic impact of DPS in emerging economies, cyber security issues in DPS, and the future of the DPS in emerging economies.

INTRODUCTION

Digital technologies enable financial services such as transaction accounts, credit, savings products, and insurance to people without limited financial services. They are increasing the speed of transactions, security, and transparency (Bachas et al., 2018). They enable the development of sustainable financial products tailored to the needs of people with meager, erratic incomes. These technologies are lowering costs by maximizing economies of scale by removing barriers to providing financial services, such as

DOI: 10.4018/978-1-6684-6873-9.ch005

lack of identification, formal income, and geographic distance, which are the stumbling block in developing economies (Sun et al., 2016).

In emerging economies, mobile money has leveraged high mobile phone penetration to deliver a 'first wave' of digital financial services. GSMA, a website that tracks mobile money service deployment worldwide, reported over 850 million registered mobile money accounts across 90 countries, most of which are emerging economies. Their day transaction is worth more than $1.3 billion. In their publication of 2020, the World Bank reported that Sub-Saharan Africa is the leader in mobile money (Serrate et al., 2020). It has over a fifth of the adult population with mobile money accounts (UNCTAD, 2020). The report shows that these accounts can provide a basis for more sophisticated financial services, such as digital lending and insurance. In the digital economy, going cashless eases one's life and helps authenticate and formalize transactions. This helps curb corruption and the flow of black money, which increases economic growth.

According to Wakarima (2022), Africa accounts for 70% of the World's $1 trillion mobile money value. That is almost two-thirds of the global value of $767 billion, according to the GSMA, underlining that the region's banking future is secured by monetary digitization (Wachira, 2023). Digitization of payments has increased transparency and reduced the cost of financial transactions, leading to greater efficiency and economic growth. Once a payment system works effectively and efficiently, it becomes a game changer to an economy (Wachira, 2023). Increasing the use of electronic payments boosts consumption and GDP. Moreover, the impact increases as penetration rises.

This chapter will discuss Digital Payment technologies, followed by the Advantages of digital payment Systems. The Challenges of Digital Payment Systems will follow, the Economic Impact of Digital Payment Systems, Cybersecurity in Digital Payment Systems, and the Future of Digital Payments Systems. It will end with concluding remarks.

Digital Payment Technologies in Emerging Economies

A digital payment System (DPS), sometimes called an electronic payment system, transfers value from one payment account to another using a digital device such as a mobile phone, POS (Point of Sales), or computer. This section will describe the technologies used in digital payment systems in developing markets. Figure 1 presents critical themes identified for digital payment technologies. They have broadly classified into four leading digital payment technologies modes: card payments, e-payments, mobile payments, and cryptocurrencies (Bachas et al., 2018). Each digital payment technology is grouped under one of these theme categories, and each theme is discussed below and supported by relevant studies.

- **Card Payments:** Card payments are digital payment technology services made available by banks and other financial institutions to their customers. It is a more convenient payment form than other categories, such as e-payments, mobile payments, and cryptocurrencies. Cardholders can access their bank accounts through bank cards and make payments online or via POS machines. All card payment technologies are regarded as easy and convenient payment methods (Aldaas, 2021). Banking cards offer consumers more security, convenience, and control than other payment methods. The wide variety of cards available includes credit, debit, and prepaid. Payment cards give people the power to purchase items in stores, on the Internet, through mail-order catalogs, and over the telephone—the usage of Bank cards is more pronounced in towns and cities where banks and their corresponding outlets exist.

Figure 1. Digital payment technologies
Source: Khando et al. (2022)

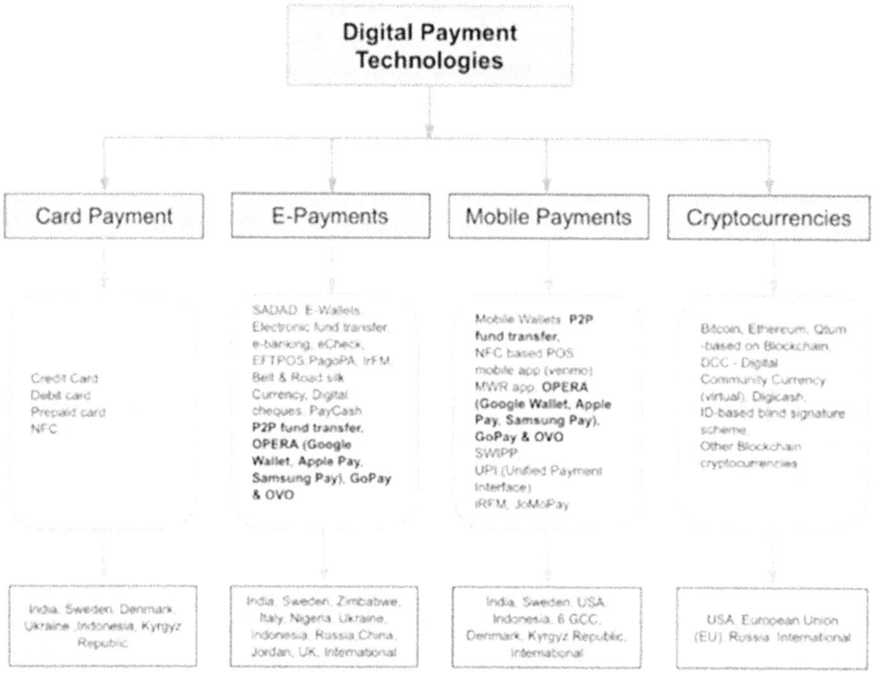

- **E-Payments:** E-payments or electronic payments are generally known as payment technologies that do not involve physical cash, bank drafts, or cheques. The transactions usually occur through internet services (Mader, 2016; Malusare, 2019). It can also refer to the banking products and services that are being delivered to customers automatically via the Internet. E-payment technologies refer to online payments that may or may not use mobile devices to complete transactions. E-payments can be accessed online through an e-payment website or online applications, e.g., a laptop, tablet, or desktop computer. Some digital payment technologies (e.g., Google Wallet, Apple Pay, Samsung Pay) can be classified as both E-payments (Torres, 2022).
- **Mobile Payment:** Mobile payments refer to payments for goods and services using mobile devices, including wireless handsets, PDAs, radio frequency devices, and NFC-based devices. Through the usage of mobile devices, mobile banking allows customers to perform various banking activities (UNCTAD, 2020). Mobile banking activities are conducted by using mobile internet technologies. Mobile payment technologies are increasingly popular for transactions, offering relatively high security online and in physical shops. In addition, mobile banking is a service provided by a bank or other financial institution that allows customers to conduct different financial transactions remotely using a mobile device such as a mobile phone or tablet. It uses software (an app) provided by banks and financial institutions, or its customers can use USSD and SMS to conduct financial transactions (Sahi et al., 2021).
- **Cryptocurrencies:** A cryptocurrency is a form of digital currency secured by cryptography that makes it nearly impossible to counterfeit or double-spend (Claeys et al., 2018). Most cryptocurrencies are decentralized networks based on blockchain technology and are secured

by encryption. For example, Bitcoin, as an emerging digital payment technology, is revolutionary in financial markets (Fama et al., 2019). It emerged as a peer-to-peer payment system combining modern cryptology and communications technology. It can meet the need for decentralization, controlling the money supply, estimating the amount of money in circulation, and reducing inflation (Karau, 2021).

Advantages of Digital Payment Systems in Emerging Economies

Digital payment systems introduce various new benefits for businesses, giving them the competitive advantage needed to stand out. The electronic payments ecosystem has two main end parties: buyers (consumers) and sellers (merchants) (Aldaas, 2021). The advent of electronic payments has greatly aided consumers' ability to optimize consumption decisions by giving them secure and immediate access to all of their funds on deposit or a line of credit. Merchants also benefit because there is less cash and check handling in the system, and they can access a large pool of customers with guaranteed payment (Srivastava, 2019).

Electronic payments play a critical role in the rapidly expanding e-commerce environment where payment by cash or check is not usually an option. The availability of electronic payment systems leads to a virtuous economic cycle whereby increased consumption leads to increased production, more jobs, higher income, and, ultimately, more substantial economic growth (Aldaas, 2021).

- **Electronic Payments Provide Access to Financial Resources:** They give consumers access to all available funds or lines of credit for a given transaction and give merchants peace of mind about payment guarantees, provided they follow appropriate payment procedures. In addition, access to credit helps calibrate periodic income with continuous consumption. They provide consumers with the means to participate in the digital economy. They reduce the costs associated with traditional methods such as cash and check (Radcliffe & Voorhies, 2012). For example, no fees are associated with credit or debit card transactions, and mobile payments typically have lower transaction fees than traditional methods (Patwardhan, 2018). With DFS, consumers have a wider variety of goods and vendors, and a broader international marketplace is available.
- **Security:** DPS has several levels of security. To begin with, unlike the currency, there is no chance of counterfeiting. Furthermore, typical DPS options like credit and debit cards require PIN verification for larger purchases. Cardless payment systems like Apple Pay are much safer, requiring biometric authentication such as fingerprint or facial ID. Not only that, but Apple Pay encrypts and fluidizes data, making it impossible to steal card information from a stolen phone. Further, trust in electronic transactions drives consumption (Torres, 2022). With electronic payments, consumers have recourse for fraudulent transactions. The peace of mind merchants have with guaranteed payment also extends to consumers, who feel more comfortable purchasing when they can pay with a card. This trust in the payment system eases friction, bolstering consumption and GDP growth (CIT Vericash, 2023).
- **Convenience:** DFS provides convenience and lower business costs. They can provide greater convenience for businesses and customers (Bachas et al., 2018). For example, customers can make payments using their mobile phones, and businesses can accept payments without handling cash. On the other hand, each small portion of friction that electronic payments eliminate from the system contributes to higher consumption and GDP.

- **Transparency:** Electronic transactions eliminate a substantial portion of the gray economy. It means better taxation. The self-employed and small businesses can use digital currencies for better taxation. With digital payment systems, all the transactions are recorded in an immutable ledger, thus providing better clarity for tracking the payments (Khando et al., 2022).

Challenges of Digital Payment Systems in Emerging Economies

Digital payment systems, despite their numerous benefits, come with their challenges. These challenges vary from country to country, depending on the socioeconomic factors and the technical, legal (regulations), and awareness levels of citizens. For instance, in some developing countries, digital payment systems successfully drive financial inclusion (Croxson et al., 2022). Businesses prefer digital payments because handling cash is expensive as it incurs expenses in obtaining cash from banks, reconciling the cash at the end of each day, storing cash, and transferring it back to their bank accounts (Croxson et al., 2022). Digital Payment System challenges in emerging economies could impact businesses and customers. Below is a summary of challenges in digital payment systems that are found in emerging economies:

Figure 2. Classification of digital payment technology challenges
Source: Khando et al. (2022)

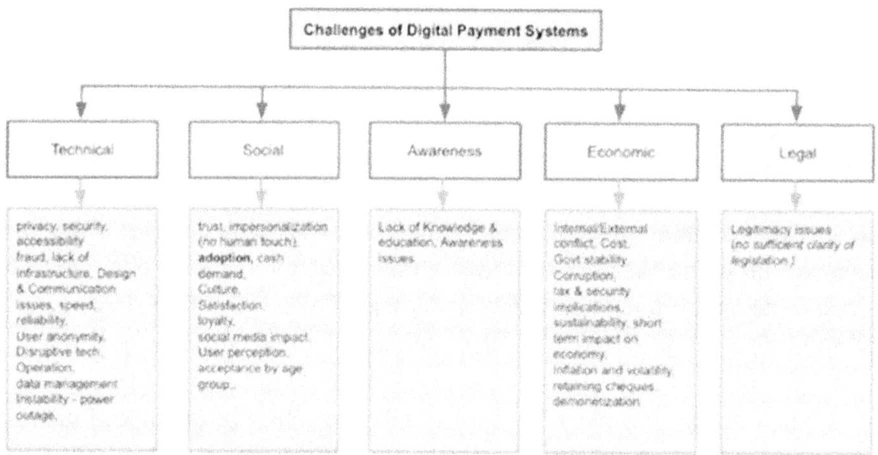

- **Technical Challenges:** DFS is subject to technical failures or downtime, like any other software dependent on technology. Furthermore, technical issues include privacy, security, access, fraud, lack of infrastructure, design and communication issues, speed, reliability, user anonymity, disruptive technology, operation, data management, and instability (Malusare, 2019). The technical challenges relate to 'safety and reliability issues and 'privacy issues.' Equally important, another digital payment challenge in emerging markets is technological illiteracy, especially among the older generation. Since they do not know how to use technology or Smartphone, they refrain from using online payment methods (Khando et al., 2022).

- **Social Challenges:** Social challenges of digital payment technologies are associated with social influence, which is connected to a person's feelings that their friends and acquaintances think they must use certain technologies. Their social circle influences the behavior of individuals, as this may preserve interrelationships and social harmony. Social challenges associated with digital payment technologies include trust, personalization (no human touch), risks, adoption, demands, culture, satisfaction, loyalty, social media impact, user perception, and acceptance by age group. For Instance, people see more risks in mobile devices, as they can be misplaced or stolen and may expose confidential information (Torres, 2022).
- **Awareness Challenges:** One of the biggest challenges confronting digital payments in Africa today is the lack of awareness and confidence among consumers and small businesses about the safety and security of these payment methods. Further, it could be emphasized that adopting multiple payment methods is related to consumer awareness as technology presents new solutions (Hyytinen & Takalo, 2009). The types of used payment methods depend on demographics, financial status, consumer academic achievement, and the continuous feedback process with commerce (Torres, 2022).
- **Economic Challenges:** Economic, in this review context, means the management of financial matters for a community, business, or family, and the digital payment technology challenges include internal and external conflict, cost, government stability, corruption, tax and security implications, sustainability, inflation, or volatility, retaining cheques and demonetization (Ozili, 2018). Other issues related to digital payment technologies include the technology's cost. The digital payment apps should be affordable for users to use the system. In July 2021, the Tanzanian Government introduced a new levy on mobile money transfer transactions, namely the "money transfer levy," to broaden the tax base and increase revenue collection. Equally important, DFS highly expensive because it includes set-up costs, machine costs, management costs, etc., and this mode of payment will take more time than the physical mode of payment.
- **Legal Challenges:** There are restrictive regulations in DPS. For instance, DPS systems require a large amount of information from end users, thus becoming difficult for users to apply it. In Africa, governments are slow to address the new technologies affecting financial services and adopt restrictive regulations impeding the spread of digital payment solutions. In Tanzania, Regulatory institutions include the Central Bank and Bank of Tanzania (BoT) for financial issues, and Tanzania Telecommunications Regulatory Authority (TCRA) regulates issues about communications infrastructure. For example, BoT signed an MOU with TCRA intending to share regulatory and supervisory information. Also, Tanzania is an Alliance for Financial Inclusion (AFI) member, which issued a Guideline note, "Mobile Financial Service: Supervision and Oversight of Mobile Financial Services," to its members (Masamila, 2014). Equally, there are challenges in legitimacy concerns, mostly cryptocurrencies, such as Bitcoin, that run on blockchain technology. In Tanzania, cryptocurrencies are not regulated under any law. Cryptocurrency is not legal tender, and users face the risk of unenforceability of cryptocurrency transactions as policymakers are cautious that cryptocurrency would be used for illegal activities, such as money laundering (BOT, 2019). Most publications suggest that investors consider Bitcoin's price trend, security risks, and legal policies (Claeys et al., 2018).
- **Multi-Currency and Payment Methods:** Global e-commerce means accepting various payment methods and currencies. eWallet payment processing, mobile payment processing, and acceptance of international credit/debit cards help online merchants compete in global markets by allowing

their customers to pay in their native currencies and method of choice. For merchants, multi-currency, cross-border transactions can require new bank accounts, new business entities, and new regulatory hurdles in each national market. For instance, Cellulant, a Nairobi-based company that operates in 35 African Countries, must connect to 257 payment methods, out of which almost 60 are mobile money wallets across Africa, and the rest would be about bank accounts, which we are directly connected to or could be connected to via a switch if there is a switch (A tool, run by a central financial body that facilitates communication between different payment service providers.) in a market

According to the report 2020 by UNCTAD (2020), several barriers face Tanzanians concerning using formal financial services provided by banks, MFIs, SACCOs, mobile money, and insurance providers (see Table 1).

Table 1. Reason for using formal financial services in Tanzania

Provider	Primary barrier	Secondary barrier
Banks	Insufficient income to consider opening an account	Cannot maintain minimum balance on the account, due to insufficient income
MFIs	Lack of awareness of how MFIs operate and where they are located	Insufficient income to become a MFI customer
SACCOs	Lack of awareness of how SACCOs operate, how to join them, and where they are located	Membership fee is perceived to be too high
Mobile Money	Non-users state that they do not engage in frequent transactions and hence do not need it	Non-users do not have the necessary device, i.e., phone, to be able to use services
Insurance	Lack of awareness of how insurance services work and how to obtain them	Perceived high cost of insurance and inability to afford insurance payments

Economic Impact of Digital Payment in Emerging Economies

Digitalization is reshaping society. It is how we work, produce, relate, exchange information, and entertain ourselves. Change is non-linear and proceeds with unexpected breakthroughs that create net economic value, social plot, and disruption. For digital transformation to enhance well-being, supporting a sustainable and inclusive digital society is crucial (Jain, 2022).

In 2020, Bill & Melinda Gates Foundation produced a report that shows the clear link between digital payment systems and the goals of G20 governments (Mureithi, 2022). The report urges governments to embrace digital payment systems as a path to growth, greater participation of users in the economy, and greater access to payments. Equally important, the G20 endorsed Principles for Innovative Financial Inclusion to guide policy and regulatory approaches (WB, 2014). The G20 Principles for Innovative Financial Inclusion spurred initial efforts and policy actions (UNCTAD, 2020).

Integrating digital payments into the economies of emerging and developing nations addresses crucial issues of broad economic growth and individual financial empowerment. Going cashless eases one's life and helps authenticate and formalize transactions. This helps curb corruption and the flow of black money, which increases economic growth (Jain, 2022). The expenditure incurred in printing and transportation of currency notes is reduced. If people invest money in the Bank, the Government will question them about that particular income source. Digitalization of payments improves transparency and culpability. The economy's liability progress can solely occur in a cashless economy.

In emerging economies, DPS can potentially promote women's economic empowerment by facilitating greater account ownership and asset accumulation, increasing women's economic participation. With DPS, payments via an account are deemed to provide the on-ramp to financial inclusion and, in many cases, the first account a woman has in her name and under her control (Zandi et al., 2016). With DPS, broader access to the financial system significantly reduces income inequality, boosts job creation, accelerates consumption, increases investments in human capital, and helps poor people manage risk and absorb economic shocks.

Integrating digital payments into the economies of emerging and developing nations addresses crucial issues of broad economic growth and individual financial empowerment. Going cashless eases one's life and helps authenticate and formalize transactions. This helps curb corruption and the flow of black money, which increases economic growth. The expenditure incurred in printing and transporting currency notes is reduced (Zandi et al., 2016). If people invest money in the Bank, the Government will question them about that particular income source. Digitalization of payments improves transparency and culpability. The economy's liability progress can solely occur in a cashless economy, and Figure 3 shows the Global Economic impact of DPS.

Figure 3. Global economic impact of digital payment systems
Source: Consultancy.uk (2020)

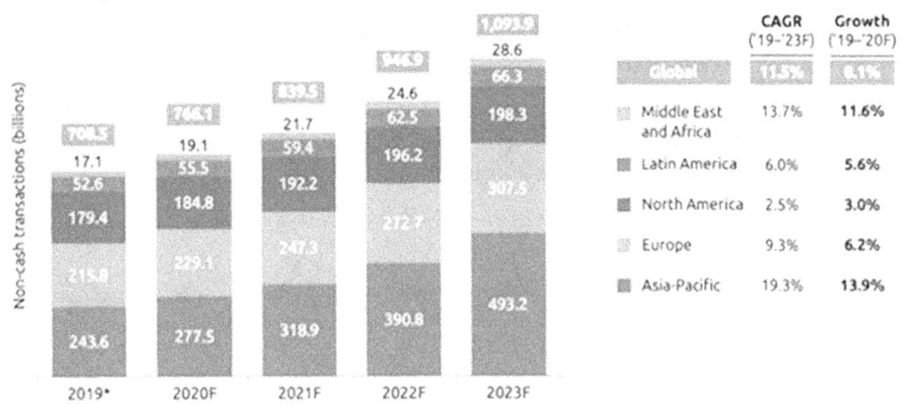

Digital payments can promote women's economic empowerment by facilitating greater account ownership and asset accumulation and increasing women's economic participation. Digital payments, particularly by governments and employers, enable the confidentiality and convenience women require in financial services. Payments via an account can provide the on-ramp to financial inclusion and, in many cases, the first account that a woman has in her name and under her control (Ozili, 2018). Opening an account can be an essential first step in an entrepreneur's introduction to the formal economy and can lead to the formalization of her small business. Broader access to and participation in the financial system can reduce income inequality, boost job creation, accelerate consumption, increase investments in human capital, and directly help poor people manage risk and absorb financial shocks (Mawejje & Lakuma, 2019). as shown in Figure 4 for Uganda.

Digital payment systems can conveniently and affordably connect entrepreneurs with banks, employees, suppliers, and new markets for their goods and services. These systems can accelerate business registration and payments for business licenses and permits by reducing travel time and expenses (Jain, 2022). Digital financial services can also improve access to savings accounts and loans. Electronic wage payments to workers can increase security and reduce the time and cost of paying employees. All these have the potential to affect the economy positively.

Figure 4. Economic effects of mobile money in Uganda
Source: Mawejje and Lakuma (2019)

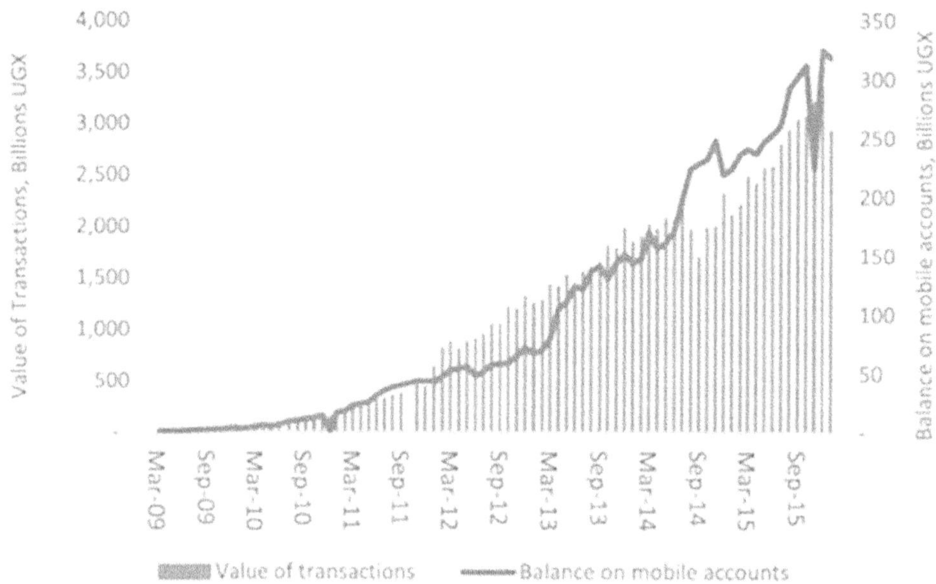

Source: Bank of Uganda

During the budget sessions in the Parliament in June 2022, the Minister for Information, Communication, and Information Technology, Mr. Nape Nnauye, attributed that the rapid digitalization is affecting all sectors of the economy in Tanzania, including the way Tanzanians access government services, how they pay for services, how they work, study, innovate, shop, socialize and receive services (Takwa, 2022). Figure 5 shows the number of Mobile Money Accounts in Tanzania.

According to Takwa (2022), the most crucial pillar of the digital economy is payment platforms, which include most Tanzanians. There are around 8 million bank accounts in populations of above 60 million people. As shown in the figure, Mobile Money Accounts have been increasing by an average of 10.7 percent annually since 2015. That is to say, in Tanzania, Mobile Money Accounts are contributing mainly to financial inclusion. This has been enhanced by the introduction of the Tanzania Instant Payment System (TIPS), an interoperable digital payment platform operated by the BoT; a government payment

Figure 5. Mobile money accounts in Tanzania
Source: Takwa (2022)

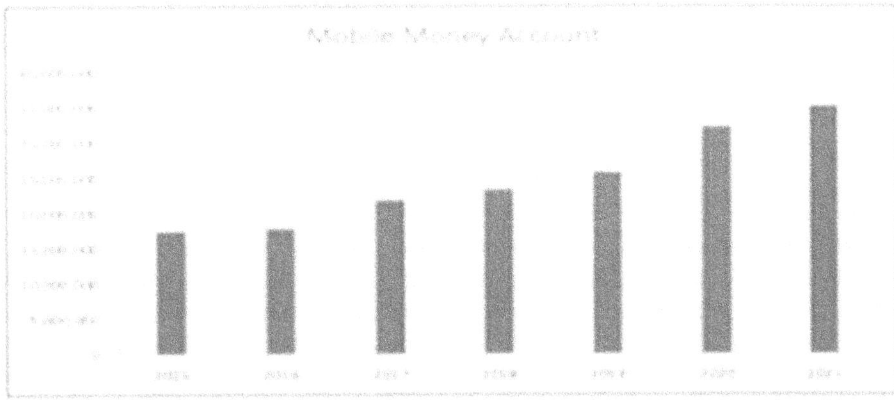

platform, interoperable mobile payment services operated by Mobile Network operators including M-Pesa, Tigo Pesa, Airtel Money, T-Pesa, EzyPesa, and Halo Pesa.

Cyber Security Issues in Digital Payments

New risks and vulnerabilities could undermine progress with this growing prosperity and digitization. Chief among these risks is the global rise of cybercrime. As emerging economies move online, citizens, computer systems, and information technology (IT) infrastructure become enticing targets for an increasingly professional cadre of cybercriminals. For instance, the report on the economic potential of cyber in Africa, with an estimated market value of 75 million USD in 2025, and the extent of cyber threats, especially regarding mobile malware and money transfers (CIT Vericash, 2023).

The risks to emerging economies arise from four areas: the complexity of supply chains, the need to maintain low costs to attract investment; the rapid spread of technology without adequate availability or awareness of training on technological risks; weak regulations; and the threat of mobile malware (Olifirov et al., 2021).

- **The Need to Remain Low Cost to Attract Investment:** Cost considerations are paramount on SME agendas. The need to be cost-effective means that investments to harden cyber security are often pushed back. This is compounded by many SMEs being unaware of the risks associated with a presence in cyberspace and often lacking knowledge of cyber-attack threats or the training to deal with them (Krishna et al., 2022).
- **The Complexity of Supply Chains:** The complexity of global supply chains adds to cyber risk. Further, most SMEs, which are the backbone of the businesses, may not know the intricacy of the global supply chains they are a part of and, thus, are unaware of potential losses due to breaches involving them (Olifirov et al., 2021).
- **The Rapid Spread of Technology Without Adequate Availability or Awareness of Training on Technological Risks:** The extent to which global value chains are integrated across borders today means that weakness in cyber security in emerging markets can quickly be passed on to ma-

ture ones via the supply chain. Compounding this problem is the widespread adoption of generic cloud, mobile and social technologies among smaller and medium-sized companies in emerging markets, even as these often serve larger companies in global supply chains (Verma et al., 2023).

- **Weak Regulations:** The risks associated with weak protection measures could affect developing countries more intensely due to their less strict safeguards and protection. The ability to protect customers and firms is a fundamental requirement for regular and online or Internet-based businesses. Without Internet security, developing countries could encounter significant difficulties promoting e-business and participating in online service industries (Akanfe et al., 2020).
- **The Threat of Mobile Malware:** Initial findings indicate that due to the borderless nature of cybercrime, many global trends also affect Africa, including the explosion of ransomware and social media scams and the proliferation of new malware and website vulnerabilities. However, because of how the IT infrastructure evolved in Africa, several cybercrime trends will become especially acute and pose a significant danger. Mobile malware, for instance, is a massive problem in Africa today and will continue to be a significant threat in the future (Singh & Rajput, 2019).

Future of Digital Payments in Emerging Economies

The future of DFS is envisioned as a digital paradise by many. The anticipated cashless society is a world where all financial transactions are carried out purely through non-analog means. Increasingly, we are seeing traditional banks and physical cash losing out to digital currencies and challenger FinTechs, with successive crises (Mützel, 2021). With more development in DPS, digital payments have gone from being rare to standard practice in emerging economies. In fact, for many, the question is no longer about whether we should use digital payments but how we make payments faster, better, and more secure. Such a transformation of the financial landscape has profound implications for business, society, and Government (Ghosh, 2021).

With the fintech industry gaining a solid footing in the developing market, more innovative and better payment modes will hit the market. The initiative will bring more safety and efficiency to digital transactions. Some markets have already adopted blockchain technology. Machine Learning, Artificial Intelligence, cloud-based payment facilities, and cryptocurrency are slowly being recognized. As part of aggressively achieving a digital economy, most developing economies have launched various initiatives to promote digital payments. The digital payments market is forecast to grow at a compound annual growth rate of 13.7 percent between 2021 and 2026 – a demand driven by greater convenience, favorable government policies, and evolving consumer behavior (CIT Vericash, 2023).

Moreover, this future will depend on the combination of digital native expectations and governments' desire to boost financial inclusion and reduce the use of cash. It will fuel rapid growth in electronic payment and bring a new breed of mobile and FinTech innovators into the payments market.

According to Statista (n.d.), the total transaction value in the Digital Payments segment in Tanzania is projected to reach US$3,268.00m in 2023. With a 14.20% annual growth projection, the total transaction will be worth US$5,559.00m by 2027. This is shown in Figure 6 below.

CONCLUSION

The World is experiencing an expanding use of digital technology, as does the payment system. The central banks are increasingly adopting the digital payment system to improve the efficiency of the financial

Figure 6. The future of DPS in Tanzania
Source: Statista (n.d.)

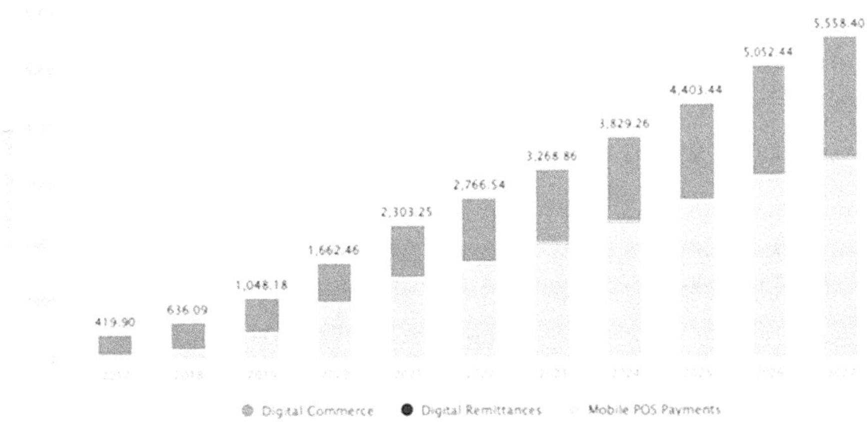

sector, which facilitates economic growth. While the challenges in digital payments are considerable, the paths to ongoing success are becoming more apparent. Adaptability is vital to success, as many options, technologies, partnerships, and customer considerations exist.

Digital payment systems are the connective tissue of every economic system. It facilitates purchasing goods and services (paying utility bills, insurance premiums, etc.) and sending money to friends, family, and business partners. It enables Governments to collect taxes and disburse social payments and suppliers to collect payments from buyers. In addition, broader adoption of digital payments—concerning both remittances and other expenses—can significantly advance the global financial inclusion agenda and support the priority areas of the Global Partnership for Financial Inclusion (GPFI).

Equally important, DPS payment usage also promotes consumer confidence and improves access to credit for the population. It also promotes financial inclusion for the most vulnerable by enabling those without access to the formal banking system a safe and efficient payment alternative to cash. Electronic payment usage also benefits governments, which can potentially collect more tax revenue thanks to a clear electronic trail and more transparent transactions that can be taxed more readily. This is more helpful in African countries with weak tax collection infrastructure. On the other hand, encouraging the growth of electronic payments gives consumers and merchants a choice and increases competition. Banks and consumers benefit when countries allow for competition and a level playing field (Zandi et al., 2016).

REFERENCES

Akanfe, O., Valecha, R., & Rao, H. R. (2020). Assessing country-level privacy risk for digital payment systems. *Computers & Security*, *99*, 102065. doi:10.1016/j.cose.2020.102065

Aldaas, A. (2021). A study on electronic payments and economic growth: Global evidences. *Accounting*, *7*(2), 409–414. doi:10.5267/j.ac.2020.11.010

Bachas, P., Gertler, P., Higgins, S., & Seira, E. (2018). Digital financial services go a long way: Transaction costs and financial inclusion. *AEA Papers and Proceedings. American Economic Association, 108*, 444–448. doi:10.1257/pandp.20181013

BOT. (2019). *Public notice on cryptocurrencies*. https://www.bot.go.tz/Adverts/PressRelease/sw/2020031307240424208.pdf

Claeys, G., Demertzis, M., & Efstathiou, K. (2018). *Cryptocurrencies and monetary policy*. Bruegel Policy Contribution.

Consultancy.uk. (2020). *Global market size of digital payments industry soares*. https://www.consultancy.uk/news/25975/global-market-size-of-digital-payments-industry-soares

Croxson, K., Frost, J., Gambacorta, L., & Valletti, T. (2022). *Platform-based business models and financial inclusion*. BIS Papers.

Fama, M., Fumagalli, A., & Lucarelli, S. (2019). Cryptocurrencies, monetary policy, and new forms of monetary sovereignty. *International Journal of Political Economy, 48*(2), 174–194. doi:10.1080/08911916.2019.1624318

Ghosh, G. (2021). Adoption of digital payment system by consumer: A review of literature. *International Journal of Creative Research Thoughts, 9*(2), 2320–2882.

Hyytinen, A., & Takalo, T. (2009). Consumer awareness and the use of payment media: Evidence from young Finnish consumers. *Review of Network Economics, 8*(2). Advance online publication. doi:10.2202/1446-9022.1175

Jain, S. (2022). *Harnessing digital financial inclusion under the G20 Digital Economy Agenda 2023*. ORF. https://www.orfonline.org/expert-speak/g20-digital-economy-agenda-2023/

Karau, S. (2021). Monetary policy and cryptocurrencies. *Proceedings of Paris December 2021 Finance Meeting EUROFIDAI-ESSEC*.

Khando, K., Islam, M. S., & Gao, S. (2022). The Emerging Technologies of Digital Payments and Associated Challenges: A Systematic Literature Review. *Future Internet, 15*(1), 21. doi:10.3390/fi15010021

Krishna, B., Krishnan, S., & Sebastian, M. P. (2022). Examining the relationship between national cybersecurity commitment, culture, and digital payment usage: An institutional trust theory perspective. *Information Systems Frontiers*, 1–29. doi:10.100710796-022-10280-7

Mader, P. (2016). Card crusaders, cash infidels and the holy grails of digital financial inclusion. *Behemoth-A Journal on Civilisation, 9*(2), 59–81.

Malusare, L. (2019). Digital payments methods in India: A study of problems and prospects. *International Journal of Scientific Research in Engineering and Management, 3*(8), 1–7.

Masamila, B. (2014). State of mobile banking in Tanzania and security issues. *International Journal of Network Security & its Applications, 6*(4), 53–64. doi:10.5121/ijnsa.2014.6405

Mawejje, J., & Lakuma, P. (2019). Macroeconomic effects of Mobile money: Evidence from Uganda. *Financial Innovation, 5*(1), 1–20. doi:10.118640854-019-0141-5

Mureithi, C. (2022, April 4). *Why Africa's digital payment landscape is still highly fragmented.* Quartz. https://qz.com/africa/2149097/why-africas-digital-payment-landscape-is-still-highly-fragmented

Mützel, S. (2021). Unlocking the payment experience: Future imaginaries in the case of digital payments. *New Media & Society*, *23*(2), 284–301. doi:10.1177/1461444820929317

Olifirov, A., Makoveichuk, K. A., & Petrenko, S. (2021). *Cybersecurity Measures of the Digital Payment Ecosystem.* Academic Press.

Ozili, P. K. (2018). Impact of digital finance on financial inclusion and stability. *Borsa Istanbul Review*, *18*(4), 329–340. doi:10.1016/j.bir.2017.12.003

Patwardhan, A. (2018). Financial inclusion in the digital age. In Handbook of Blockchain, Digital Finance, and Inclusion (vol. 1, pp. 57–89). Elsevier. doi:10.1016/B978-0-12-810441-5.00004-X

RadcliffeD.VoorhiesR. (2012). A digital pathway to financial inclusion. Available at SSRN 2186926.

Sahi, A. M., Khalid, H., & Abbas, A. F. (2021). Digital payment adoption: A review (2015-2020). *Journal of Management Information & Decision Sciences*, *24*(7).

Serrate, J. S., Lopez, C., Unver, H., Drobyshovsky, S., & Trunin, P. (2020). Digital money is here: G20 (Thinking) must go digital. A systemic agenda is necessary to steer the risky transition process and reap long-term benefits. *G20 Insights*. https://www.g20-insights.org/policy_briefs/digital-money-is-here-g20-thinking-must-go-digital-a-systemic-agenda-is-necessary-to-steer-the-risky-transition-process-and-reap-long-term-benefits/

Singh, P., & Rajput, R. S. (2019). Cybersecurity analysis in the context of digital wallets. *International Journal of Advanced Studies of Scientific Research*, *4*(3).

Srivastava, N. (2019). Digital Financial Services: Challenges and Prospects for Liberalized and Globalized Indian Economy. *Proceedings of 10th International Conference on Digital Strategies for Organizational Success*. 10.2139srn.3309294

Statista. (n.d.). *Mobile POS Payments—Tanzania | Statista Market Forecast.* Statista. Retrieved 1 April 2023, from https://www.statista.com/outlook/dmo/fintech/digital-payments/mobile-pos-payments/tanzania

Sun, T., Spiess, K., & Kulakoglu, A. (2016). *G20 High-Level Principles for digital Financial inclusion*. https://www.gpfi.org/sites/gpfi/files/G20%20High%20Level%20Principles%20for%20Digital%20Financial%20Inclusion.pdf

Takwa, E. (2022, December 30). *How digitalisation accelerates Tanzania's economic growth—Daily News*. https://dailynews.co.tz/how-digitalisation-accelerates-tanzanias-economic-growth/, https://dailynews.co.tz/how-digitalisation-accelerates-tanzanias-economic-growth/

Torres, N. M. S. (2022). *Awareness of new payment technologies in the digital banking transformation-Accelerated by the COVID 19 pandemia* [PhD Thesis].

UNCTAD. (2020). United Republic of Tanzania Rapid eTrade Readiness Assessment. United Nations.

Vericash, C. I. T. (2023, January 19). Digital Payments in Africa. *CIT Vericash*. https://citvericash.com/digital-payments-in-africa/

Verma, S., Sharma, J., Kaushik, K., & Vyas, V. (2023). Mounting Cases of Cyber-Attacks and Digital Payment. In Cybersecurity Issues, Challenges, and Solutions in the Business World (pp. 59–80). IGI Global.

Wachira, A. C. (2023, March 3). Global Finance Magazine - Africa: Digital Payments Progress. *Global Finance Magazine*. https://www.gfmag.com/magazine/march-2023/africa-digital-payments-progress

Wakarima. (2022, May 13). *Africa accounts for 70% of the World's $ 1 trillion Mobile Money Market—Kenyan Wallstreet*. https://kenyanwallstreet.com/africa-accounts-70-of-the-worlds-mobile-money/

WB. (2014, September 8). *The opportunities of digitizing payments: How digitization of payments, transfers, and remittances contributes to the G20 goals of broad-based economic growth, financial inclusion, and women's economic empowerment - GSDRC*. https://gsdrc.org/document-library/the-opportunities-of-digitizing-payments-how-digitization-of-payments-transfers-and-remittances-contributes-to-the-g20-goals-of-broad-based-economic-growth-financial-inclusion-and-womens/, https://gsdrc.org/document-library/the-opportunities-of-digitizing-payments-how-digitization-of-payments-transfers-and-remittances-contributes-to-the-g20-goals-of-broad-based-economic-growth-financial-inclusion-and-womens/

Zandi, M., Koropeckyj, S., Singh, V., & Matsiras, P. (2016). *The Impact of Electronic Payments on Economic Growth*. Academic Press.

Chapter 6
Digital Technologies and Resources for Learning Under Lockdown

Oluwabunmi Dorcas Bakare
https://orcid.org/0000-0002-4665-3969
Lead City University, Nigeria

Nosakhare Okuonghae
https://orcid.org/0000-0002-2281-6217
Glorious Vision University, Ogwa, Nigeria

ABSTRACT

Digital technologies like smartphones, social media, the internet, software applications, websites, and e-books are redefining the educational landscape, which was accentuated amid the COVID-19 pandemic. This chapter discussed the impact of digital technologies in enabling academic institutions to perform their noble responsibilities in delivering instructions virtually during the lockdown. The effects of using these technologies and the challenges encountered by developing countries in migrating to the digital environment amid the lockdown with particular reference to the educational ecosystem in Nigeria was the focal point in the chapter. Striking among these challenges is the issue of compatibility, the high cost of internet data, inadequate digital literacy skill, and environmental distraction. Thus, it was recommended that administrators of academic institutions and regulatory bodies such as the National Universities Commission (NUC) must provide lecturers and students at all levels with adequate training to ensure operational productivity in the use of digital technologies and resources.

INTRODUCTION

The phenomenon of the digital revolution is universally accepted as one of the most transformational innovations in recent human history. Digital innovation has enabled smarter service delivery across various sectors of our society, particularly the educational landscape. In support of this assertion, Bresciani,

DOI: 10.4018/978-1-6684-6873-9.ch006

Ferraris, Romano, and Santoro (2021) affirmed that all sectors and types of organizations are somehow affected in one way or the other by digital technologies such as social media, mobile devices, and cloud computing which offer unique opportunities in unprecedented ways. Interestingly, more of these technologies are being developed yearly by tech giants and introduced into the market to create more value and improve competitiveness among users (Majchrzak, Markus & Wareham, 2016). This paper focuses on the realistic effect of digital technology on learning settings, in which the physical learning environment is replaced by cyberlearning environments through the use of smart electronic devices which according to Mogas, Palau, Fuentes and Cebrian, (2022) are all hinged on the 4th Industrial Revolution (4th IR), thus creating paradigm shifts in the educational ecosystem.

The unique functionality of these devices is most appreciated in providing improved communication between people across various geographical locations and time zones, thus barring all geographical limitations. This submission was well enunciated by Bakare (2018) who asserted that the use of digital technologies (such as social media) is not inhibited by time, means, and location due to its ubiquitous nature. Jobirovich (2021) referred to these technologies as a set of combined methods, production processes, and software and hardware for editing, storage, distribution, and use aimed at redefining the phase of the educational landscape. As noted already, this technology is a tool for remote communication between teachers and students for knowledge sharing and information dissemination as it supports face-to-face communication through teleconferencing.

More appealing about this digital innovation is its ability to make information accessible in other formats (e-resources) and also the convenience it brings to bear in the learning processes. Students' can attend classes from the comfort of their homes, and the tutor can provide them with the relevant information resources from any location just with the click of a button. In addition, digital technology allows lecturers to configure their instructional material to suit the new digital learning environment, and assess as well as grade students online seamlessly. The need for effective integration and utilization of this system became reinforced by the global pandemic in 2019 (Obiakor & Adeniran, 2020) which redefined the educational scenery globally. This paradigm shift in the worldwide educational ecosystem was not herculean for academic institutions in developed countries. But on the other hand, was a struggling process for most African countries of which Nigeria was not an exception (Bakare & Ademakinwa, 2020) as the infusion of these technologies into the nitty-gritty of the instructional life-cycle was alien since the system had been weaved round face-to-face form of teaching methodology (Agbele & Oyelade, 2020).

The COVID-19 Pandemic

The discovery of Covid-19 in China threw the world into serious pandemonium. Medical experts and front-line regulatory agencies such as the World Health Organization (WHO) after several clinical analyses declared the virus a pandemic and warned the world of its severity. According to the World Health Organization (WHO, 2020), the virus spread through contact from the droplets (saliva or discharge) of an infected person to another, through the process of coughing or sneezing. Covid-19 as it is widely known is a shortened version of Corona Virus Disease-19. The virus can spread quickly from one host to another, invariably the virus is transmitted when an infected person touches or exchanges body fluids with an individual (WHO, 2020).

The proposed precautionary measure includes wearing a nose mask, regular hand washing, maintaining a social distance of at least 1 meter, and avoidance of large gatherings. Also, most institutions involving human interaction except essential service providers such as medical centres and media houses were shut down as Bakare and Ademakinwa (2020, p.60) opined this was a precautionary method to ensure that 'human contacts were reduced to the barest minimum to forestall the risk of people being infected by the highly contagious virus'. To further curtail the spread of the virus, it became imperative for national governments to initiate a lockdown, that is, nations globally were forced to shut their borders to visitors, especially from affected countries. However, some experts thought that the best way to curb the pandemic was to observe social distancing while scientists were working frantically to develop vaccines to combat the virus. Available records suggest that patients may begin to manifest symptoms within 14 days or in rare cases 5 days, infected persons were known to display signs of coughing, sneezing, fever, and shortness of breath (Guner, Hasanoglu & Aktas, 2020).

With the lockdown in place, a developing nation like Nigeria had a difficult time grappling with the effect of managing crucial sectors like education. This is because the learning process in this clime is predominantly conducted within the classroom setting which may customarily be referred to as the traditional teaching method. The traditional face-to-face approach requires students to attend lectures physically. In fact, in many institutions, students are not only required to attend lectures but as a matter of policy are expected to meet about 70% of class attendance before they could be permitted to partake in any examination. As a direct consequence, the process of teaching, learning, and assessment between the teachers and students, revolves around the classroom environment. Of course, the limitation of this traditional approach to learning is inherent in its nature of being confined to the physical structure of the school environment, and given the Covid-19 restriction policy, was a fundamental problem that needed urgent solutions. This is because students' and teachers' or lecturers' minds have been trained or conditioned to this physical domain, and migrating to the virtual space necessitated by the advent of the pandemic was taskful. This is in tandem with the findings of Agbele and Oyelade (2020) who averred that the Pre-Covid-19 educational domain in Nigeria made students and lecturers disadvantaged in the usage of digital technologies within the learning environment as both parties were accustomed to a traditional set-up of face-to-face lectures in the normal classroom settings.

The Global Perspective of the Learning Process

Learning for man is a lifelong affair and need not be restricted to a particular environment for the students to explore their intellectual capabilities seamlessly. This will in essence ensure that students are well-orientated through the vital tool of Education which has played a great role in the transformation of societies right from pre-recorded history. Okiy (2012) as cited in Ajoke (2022) remarked that education is an instrument of excellence for national development that focuses on developing an individual intellectual, psychological, social, vocational, religious, or moral capacity. Suffice it to say that each of these items constitutes the element or goal of education. The realisation of these objects of education is usually achieved through formal educational arrangements by an established school system. To promote systemic change in human existence, the United Nations through its policy framework known as Sustainable Development Goals (SDGs), recognised education as one of the critical pillars of the SDGs (Bakare & Okuonghae, 2022).

To achieve an inclusive, and equitable quality education for all, there must be a stable educational program to provide the needed lifelong learning irrespective of the country. Within the Nigerian domain, the global framework on educational pursuit is rigidly affirmed by its extant Constitution to the extent that it is the obligatory right for every citizen to have a quality education. The said provision has been widely criticised because it is couched under the infamous Chapter 2 of the Constitution of the Federal

Republic of Nigeria 1999 (as amended) which is widely regarded as non-justiciable. This has led to the establishment of educational institutions by the Federal and State government, religious bodies and individuals. At this point, it should emphasise that intellectual, psychological, moral, or vocal development is not restricted to the school environment.

However, it must be stressed also, that the school environment offers the teachers and the students the immense utility of coming together to interact socially and in the process, achieve the aim of mentorship and transfer of knowledge. This aligns with the conclusion of Bakare and Ademakinwa (2020, p. 60) which affirmed the 'significance of mentoring as a way of providing emotional and instrumental support needed by students to achieve their goals'. Notwithstanding, the social reality during and after the lockdown indicates that this sole mode of learning, is unsustainable. Unfortunately, for decades, this has been the approach within the Nigerian educational system which is a bane constraining innovation, upskilling, re-learning, and unlearning that is redefining the global educational landscape. Bakare and Ademakinwa (2020) revealed that Private Universities such as Lead City University, Bowen University, and Covenant University rose to the challenge of adopting digital technologies for graduate students' mentorship amid the pandemic while Public Universities were silent in this respect.

Historically, the use of digital tools and resources for learning in Nigeria is not new, however, it has evolved; though its actualization has mostly been on paper and not in reality. The idea may be remotely traced to 1983 when the long-distance education system was introduced in Nigeria under the National Open University Act (NOUA) 1983. The National Open University of Nigeria was established to advance learning throughout Nigeria mainly by correspondence and closely supplemented by lectures; broadcasts by radio and television as well as by occasional seminars; tutorial, and counseling services organised through a network of local study centres (Section 1(3) (a), NOUA).

This chapter will discuss the effect of digital technology as a response strategy by educational institutions in providing learning to their teeming pupils and students under the lockdown. The chapter will equally examine the challenges encountered by developing countries in migrating to the digital environment during the lockdown as well as its implications for the educational ecosystem in Nigeria. We acknowledge that vaccines have been developed to combat the virus, and life has returned to normalcy. However, it appears that the integration of digital technology in every form of learning has been accepted as the new normal, a paradigm shift brought to bear by the pandemic.

Nature of Digital Technology

Digital technologies like most disruptive technologies offer a huge potential to the world by enhancing rapid connectivity, access to information, and prompt service delivery. More reason, Frolova, Ryabova and Rogach (2019, p. 781) averred that the 'digital technologies in education contribute to the growth of academic performance, the increase of interest in learning due to the active inclusion in the process of new knowledge generation.' While commenting on the impact of digital technology in transforming societies, the United Nations (U.N.) stated that digital infrastructure is key to human modern survival. They pointed out that digital technology is relevant in the health sector through the use of artificial intelligence for examining the patient. In the educational scenery, the same can be said as the use of versatile software applications such as Zoom, Google Meet, and Microsoft Teams, are available to facilitate virtual or long-distance learning. For developing countries, this is a game changer, most especially for Nigeria as a lot is expected from her technologically and educationally being the giant of Africa.

The hallmark of this inclusion in academic activities is that it helps to facilitate pedagogic participation and strengthen the existing traditional system. As a result, digital technology is considered to be a major catalyst in achieving the educational element of the UN sustainable development goal 4 which emphasizes inclusive education for all. However, it must be emphasized that digitization itself is an enabler and not a replacer, thus, digital tools seek to support the traditional system by enhancing learning in the digital environment. This technology gained popularity amidst the Covid-19 pandemic to help academic institutions deliver contactless services without any restrain.

Essentially, digital technologies enable virtual learning which utilizes a web-based communication platform to facilitate different learning programs without limitations of space, location, and time. Olaniyi and Akinyoola (2021) expanded the role of the digitized system within the context of library services. According to them, digital technology optimizes the user mode of research through direct access to information, multimedia content, video/audio simulation, electronic-based inquiry, and assessment. Lund and Wang (2019) opined that the virtual environment allows for digital resource utilization which can enhance research, facilitate breakthroughs and contribute to new knowledge which Markus (2020) remarked as having a positive effect on students' creativity and academic performance. He traced this to the collaborative ability and the learner-centric ability of the digitized system. According to the study, students can work with peers online and drop questions for the tutor based on their research.

The adoption and exploitation of digital technology, however, requires basic digital literacy skills to effectively navigate the digital space. Essentially, access to electronic or digital information is dependent on the level of literacy skills possessed by an individual. Digital literacy skill is highly relevant in accessing information as the study of Fakunle, Bakare, and Adeyeye (2022, p. 1) revealed that "the majority of the undergraduates sampled in Private Universities in Oyo State, Nigeria frequently updated their digital skills to decrease their inability of accessing online materials which help in increasing their digital knowledge". The fact that developing countries have witnessed tremendous growth in the use of the Internet, shows the prime role of digital facilities. However, the cost factor may be a hindrance to the effective utilization of digital technologies and resources may take the following form;

Electronic Database

The database is a key feature of modern learning. Most institutions have databases where internal information resources are collected, curated, and made available for future use. However, many universities, colleges, and research institutes rely on external online databases for their information need. Ajani, Ismaila, and Ayodele (2021) assert that for learning to take place in a university, both the lecturers and the students need access to different databases. They went further to state that the use of online databases is instrumental for research and teaching activities, especially during the lockdown. The challenge with the use of these resources is the inability of users to search and retrieve information for personal use. Closely related to the former is the issue of awareness. In a study conducted at Kwara State University concerning the use of proprietary databases, findings revealed that only a few lecturers were aware of the subscribed online databases by their institution (Ajani, Ismaila, & Ayodele, 2021). These platforms which are often proprietary require a subscription from the parent institution. Staff and Students can gain access from the comfort of their homes provided they are registered with the school. With the personal login detail, the user can have access to the resources remotely from any location. E-database provides a wide range of information resources to both undergraduate and postgraduate students for their academic use. At Kuwait University, Hendal, (2020) showed electronic databases and e-journals were the most preferred electronic resources used by the faculty members for writing research papers during the Covid-19 Pandemic. The most common databases for academic research and learning are; Scopus, Agora Ebsco host, ProQuest, Jstor, Hinary Hein online, PubMed, Eric, OARE, DOAJ, ARDI, Law Pavillion Google Scholar, etc.

Social Media

According to Calderaro (2018), social media is a dynamic tool that enables interaction and collaboration among users with the view of sharing information and idea. In the academic space, social media is handsomely useful in facilitating scholarly interaction between scholars from different fields and locations. Similarly, Bakare & Bakare (2021) affirmed social media technologies as an emerging technological trend and a veritable tool for the provision of pervasive library services. Lund and Wang (2019) asserted that social media are effective in inducing widespread communication between individuals simultaneously. The essence of social media was captured by Iyanda (2019) when she described social media as web-based applications that facilitate communication, enhance the dissemination of files or sharing of multimedia content, enable group interaction, uploading and download multimedia content. While speaking on the dynamic nature of social media, Lund and Wang (2019) declared that Zoom is a type of social media software application that enables users to connect in real-time video calls. Importantly, he noted that the Zoom application enables distance education and teleconferencing. Sobaih, Palla, and Baquee (2022) studied the use of social media technologies for e-learning activities by higher education students in India amid the Covid-19 pandemic, and concluded that social media promote learning, increased student participation, and content sharing. In line with earlier studies by Greenhow and Askari (2017), Cain (2018), Greenhow and Chapman (2020), and Abi-Jaoude, Naylor, and Pignatiello (2020) all noted that educators may find it difficult to use because of privacy issues. Another area of concern is that excessive use of social media could harm the mental health of the student. However, their finding showed that the use of social media for learning purposes had a significant impact on a student's overall academic performance. World Bank (2021) commended the Edo State Government of Nigeria for advancing digital education during the pandemic through the use of WhatsApp along with other platforms to organize e-classes for government-owned primary and secondary schools in the State. Other examples of social media include; Twitter, Facebook, Google Duo, and Google meet.

Mobile Websites

Mobile Websites is a mobile interface website that allows the user to access the web with their mobile device. It is a user-friendly gateway that enables users to browse with a smaller smartphone screen. Olaniyi and Akinyoola (2021) assert that mobile websites were an essential information tool during the covid-19 pandemic due to their peculiarity in aiding users to view, upload, and publish content remotely. Teachers were able to provide links to academic sites, and students without mini computers or personal computers were not shut out of every academic activities. According to Olaniyi and Akinyoola (2021), mobile websites proved to be crucial amidst the pandemic because they allowed for easy remote access to the website without hindrances due to the specification of the individual's mobile device. Students could view information materials such as e-books, watch e-videos and upload assignments. In Edo State Nigeria, instructional materials including audio lessons were uploaded online through the Edo State

Universal Basic Education Board (SUBEB)'s websites for both pupils and teachers to access via mobile devices (World bank, 2021).

Institutional Repository

An Institutional Repository (IR) is an online or digital archive for preserving the intellectual capital of an institution. Since it was first developed by the University of Edinburgh and subsequently used by other types of institutions like colleges and research institutes, the goal is the same, to enhance free access to research out and to facilitate further research. (Saini, 2018). Crow (2002) described IR as the digital collection of the research output of one university or a community of different universities to provide a timely response to the issues facing academic institutions. The success of such innovation depends on the technical implementation of its policy. Harnad, Steve, McGovern, and Nancy (2009) opined that most institutions make it mandatory for lecturers to submit their course notes and other materials in the institutional repository. Crow (2002) is of the view that a modern academic institution must have an intellectual database from which it can draw knowledge. This is particularly important because the aim of an IR is focused on proving open access to the collective intellectual innovations of the institution. This tends to give the institution global visibility and enhance learning at the same time. Needless to say, an IR is an asset to any institution. It is an archive in digital format of the scholarly research output by staff and students in the institution including research thesis, technical reports, seminar papers, dissertations, conference proceedings, administrative documents, etc.

Saini (2018) in his literature search observed that there are two main categories of repositories. The first is a repository that contains all the subjects of the study of an institution which can be the general-based repository of an institution or a repository with special attention to a specific subject which is deemed the choice or specialised repository depending upon the interest, nature as well as the capacity or specialization of an institution. However, Darby, Jones, Gilbert, and Lambert (2009) identified three kinds of institutional repositories which are institutional, subject, and funder repositories; these three have a slight similarity to each other in their purpose, usage, and software interface. The same can be differentiated in their scope, sources of authorship, and funding criteria.

During the pandemic, most institutions around the world reinvented themselves by solely taking their mode of instructional learning online. These universities in Europe and America encourage their students to participate in virtual conferences, research, and symposium presentations. Some of the presentations were not only archived in the school repository but students were also given access to the university's repository to support their research. Symulevich and Hamilton (2022) reported that the outcome of the conferences and symposiums at the University of South Florida (USF), was 55 presentations which were uploaded to the University's repository. This resulted in a worldwide download of 2,068 files from 53 countries. At Longwood University located in South Central Virginia, 200 presentations were uploaded to the institutional repository. An average of 16, 190 files were downloaded from the university repository. The metrics show that the downloads were from 124 countries around the world. This remote accessibility of these intellectual contents by people all over the world outlines Daniel C. Gilman's view on the duty of a university in advancing knowledge. According to the renowned former president of John Hopkins University as cited by Montgomery, Hartley, Neylon, Gillies, Gray, Herrmann-Pillath, Huang, Leach, Potts, Ren, Skinner, Sugimoto, and Wilson (2019) asserts:

It is one of the noblest duties of a university to advance knowledge, and to diffuse it not merely among those who attend the daily lectures, but far and wide. (p. 1)

In this era of the global pandemic, Gilman's idea represents the present-day institutional repositories (IR). Institutional Repositories provide an opportunity for an organization to share its academic treasures with a vast community of users, allowing all interested students or researchers access to the findings and insights produced by its members. An IR ensures the long-term preservation of vital academic results. Increasingly, the potential of institutional repositories is being realised by librarians, researchers, and university administrators (Jones, Andrew & MacColl, 2006). In developing an IR, the library plays a key role because the essence of IR is linked with the library functions within the university setting, that is, in meeting the information needs of its patrons.

Consequently, an IR has proven to be an effective platform for researchers to showcase their wealth of research output within the university community as well as to the global academic space. Jones, Andrew, and MacColl, (2006) remarked that from the university administrators' point of view, IR helps to increase the global visibility of their institutions and to showcase the contribution to global intellectual wealth. The beauty of such an archive is that it embraces all kinds of material including teaching aid, course wears, institutionally authored materials, and textbooks. It is no brainer that copyright issue does not affect the use and reuse of such material except those authored by individuals outside the institution and of which the author has not granted open access privilege. The effective development, of IR, would have made it easy for many institutions in developing countries including Nigeria to move online rather than shut down amid the pandemic.

Three years before the pandemic, the State of Nigerian Universities repository was studied by Ukwoma and Okafor (2017) and the study revealed that the University of Nigeria, Nsukka (UNN) had the highest volumes of contents with 21, 461 files. However, both University of Nigeria, Nsukka, and the Federal University of Technology, Akure had the highest varieties of intellectual content. Finding also revealed that Covenant University and UNN archived more Journal articles. Like the University of South Florida and Longwood University in the United States of America, the five Nigerian universities acquired the majority of their contents from the research output of their post-graduate schools. The study of Bakare and Ademakinwa (2020) revealed that the University of Benin (UNIBEN), University of Portharcourt (UNIPORT), University of Ilorin (UNIILORIN), and the University of Calabar (UNICAL) research articles during the pandemic were mainly in preprints and were published on Research Gates which is an online repository. Despite the level of organization of these institutional repositories around the country, it has not translated to any meaningful usage. Especially during the lockdown and this failure may not be unconnected to a lack of awareness of the role of the institutional repository in advancing academic activities within the digital space.

Application of Digital Technology for Learning During the Lockdown

In the wake of the COVID-19 global Pandemic, all institutions involving human interactions including formal learning centres in both basic and tertiary institutions were shut down globally. Consequently, the students were asked to proceed on indefinite vacation pending the containment of the pandemic. This translated to either an institution accepting the sole technological tide of teaching and learning as well as students' assessment with utmost academic integrity or being left behind. The global north embraced this paradigm shift without any inhibition while it was mostly a difficult terrain for most of the global south countries of which Nigeria is not an exception.

Adedoyin and Soykan (2020) averred that educational institutions migrated online for various activities which could either be synchronous or asynchronous teaching methods. Irrespective of these teaching methodologies, Hrastinski (2008) averred that for digital online learning to be effective, the tutors and important stakeholders must appreciate the addition to comprehend its benefit as well as its limitations. The concept of digital learning and e-learning or online learning are terms having similar meanings because they all involve the use of technology in the form of the internet, social media platforms, email, text audio-visual conferencing tools to deliver instruction for academic purposes and to develop instructional materials (Dhull & Sakshi, 2017; Fry 2001, cited in Adedoyin & Soykan, 2020).

Prior to the Covid-19 pandemic the trend in Nigeria's educational system whether in primary, post-primary, or tertiary schools, was the same. The involvement or integration of digital technology and resources in the process of teaching, learning, and assessment was grossly limited, which was a fundamental bane of this system that the lockdown brought to bear but at the same time rectified. In Nigeria, available records show that private universities were at the forefront in accepting and assimilating Information Communications Technology (ICT) for instructional delivery. While many stakeholders were averse to this new approach, others were indifferent but waited patiently for the reopening of the physical classrooms, many private institutions responded to the pandemic by migrating online for their academic activities through the use of digital media, applications and software such as Microsoft Team, Zoom, Google Meet, Telegram, WhatsApp, etc. (Bakare & Ademakinwa, 2020). Unfortunately, some institutions like the Nigeria Law School, the statutory body responsible for training lawyers in Nigeria, remained adamant about the new approach. According to them, the training of lawyers cannot be adequately carried out through virtual or remote learning. This stance aligns with the rigid nature of the legal profession in Nigeria.

However, given the Covid-19 Pandemic, the Chief Justice of Nigeria, Hon, Justice I.T Muhammad made it clear that the legal profession cannot continue in its traditional mode of physical mode justice delivery. Therefore, in a circular with Ref. No NJC/CIR/HOC/II/660 the National Judicial Council (NJC) through the Chief Justice of Nigeria, issued guidelines on virtual hearing to ensure that hearing and determination of urgent and time-bound cases, interlocutory applications, fundamental right matters, adoption of addresses, ruling and judgment using approved digital platforms like Zoom, Google meet, Skype or any other video and audio-conferencing platforms approved by the Court. Although the adoption of this novel procedure for justice delivery in Nigeria was the subject of intense debate among legal practitioners regarding the Constitutionality or otherwise of conducting a virtual hearing. In all, NJC's attempt at integrating digital technologies into legal proceedings in terms of virtual hearings in courts dispels the myth that law cannot be taught with digital technologies. The Law profession like other related disciplines can be taught virtually which is just a matter of adaptation.

Advantages of Digital Technology for Learning During the Lockdown

Digital technologies redefined the landscape of learning across all levels of the educational cadre amid the pandemic without any inhibition and even afterward. This is therefore showcasing its significant role in ensuring that institutions maintained academic responsibility. Digitalized system of learning comes with substantial advantages without diminishing the standard or services being rendered. In a nutshell, digital technologies during the lockdown facilitated the learning process in line with the institution's curriculum by allowing teachers to impart knowledge and share educative information resources with students. The array of digital platforms, applications, and software for learning via the use of ICT was remarkable. Specifically, it provided the following benefits such as learning flexibility, information storage, social connectivity, improve communication ability, parental involvement in the learning process, and unlimited access to information.

Learning Flexibility

Digital learning allows for flexibility in timing and lesson delivery mode. The student who is slow in learning can collect, preserve and store lectures for future use. Besides, students and teachers can interact, learn and with ease depending on the learning capability of the students. Similarly, it affords lectures to be adjourned to a more convenient time and platform that is suitable for both parties which is an antithesis of physical classes.

Information Storage

It is a known fact that student cognitive abilities differ greatly and digital technology usage amid the lockdown for teaching and learning was able to bridge this gap. The inability of students to recollect example given in class, affect their optimal participation in systematical subjects like math which requires a step-by-step procedure. However, during the lockdown, students with the help of digital storage devices could rewind or replay lessons after a live class to catch up with the missed points. Most synchronous learning devices like WebEx, Microsoft Teams and Zoom have these features built into them. This point illustrates the unique ability of digital learning over the traditional method. Recording a lecture allow students in-depth understanding as the student may have to go over the lesson over and over again till the lesson is well understood.

Social Connectivity

Digital learning builds a relationship over the internet among students as well as between lecturers and students. This relationship often helps in advancing the academic performance of the student as there are students who are very timid to ask questions in physical classes. With digital platforms, some students can express themselves, make new friends, and at the same time be well engaging as they see these technologies as allowing them to be open and free to share their thoughts.

Improved Communication Ability

A great deal of the world of written and verbal communication is required for online learning. Although teleconferencing is part of online learning a lot of communication between students and tutors requires adequate self-expression in both worlds. Sometimes to convey your message you have to be skillful since you cannot rely on facial cues which are common with physical interaction. The catch here is that students' vocabulary had to be improved to be able to get the best during the virtual teaching process.

Parental Involvement in the Learning

Parents who cared less about how their children surfed the net, were fully integrated into the digital learning process of their wards. Typically, younger pupils needed assistance with this new method of learning and it was an opportunity for busy parents who were not present in their wards' educational activities previously due to one reason or the other to be part and parcel of this digital learning. Those who were too young to have their gadgets had to rely on their parents to receive lectures and submit their homework. This new development allowed parents to make contributions and comments. On the part of the tutor, the idea that parents were sitting beside their children at home, made them act professionally and work harder.

Rapid and Convenient Access to Information

Digital technology provides great utility in information sharing. During the lockdown, academic activities could not be hindered because apart from teaching through teleconferencing platforms like zoom or the use of voice notes on platforms like Telegram. Digital academic material for learning such as e-books, e-journals, PDFs, tutorial videos, courseware, and lecture notes were all made available to the student over the digital space. It saves the students the challenges of procuring the materials physically. However, it must be emphasized that this should not use as an excuse for a teacher to assist their student to infringe the intellectual property right of the authors. Literary and academic works in the digital environment are also covered by copyright laws.

It Is Entertaining and Engaging

Experienced teachers and module tutors often make use of emojis and short video skit interlude during their online lectures. This innovation helps reduce students' tension and keep their focus. Engaging students online for a long period is not an easy task because there are a lot of distracting elements that can divert their attention. For more reasons, tutors are meant to bring to bear the engaging power of digital technologies in their student-tutor interactions as such exercises enhance learning.

Positive and Negative Effects of Using Digital Technology

There is a widespread use of digital technologies such as social networking sites (SNS) (like Facebook, Twitter, WhatsApp, Telegram, YouTube, and LinkedIn) and mobile devices among youths. These technologies provide people especially young adults with the opportunity to connect with friends, classmates, family members, and mentors. Nowadays, it is very common for young people to share their thoughts and feelings on social media. Bryant, Sanders-Jackson, and Smallwood (2006) rightly noted that young people who find it difficult to express their feelings in a face-to-face conversation can do so through social media without being shy. Apart from sharing videos, pictures, and general information on social media, young adults also employ these tools for educational purposes. Gok (2015) while discussing the positive effect of social networking sites among students observed that SNS allow young adults to discuss class materials, share academic or school-related information, and plan for a project. Generally speaking, students at different levels use some of these media to achieve learning objectives. Many people have started exploring platforms like Telegram for academic discussions. Telegram has several benefits. Unlike WhatsApp, new members admitted into a group could access previous information or discussion. Also, it can accommodate a larger number of members.

The use of the internet and other technological devices may be useful in many ways. However, excessive and unhealthy use has resulted in many social and health problems among young people, resulting in great concern for modern society. Studies have shown that kids and young adults spend an average of 2-3 hours a day texting, gaming, and watching irrelevant videos (Vanderloo, Carseley, Aglipay, Cost, Maguire & Birken, 2020). This excessive use may lead to a series of side effects. Normal use of the internet according to Shapiro (1999) should be between 2, 5 to 8 hours a week. Well, the prescription Shapiro may not be realistic today because people depend so much on the internet for virtually everything. Scholars in recent studies tend to recommend 1 hour/per day for children aged 2 to 4 years to avoid the adverse risk (Vanderloo et al, 2020). Those addicted to the internet are known to have less interest in social activities, and increased feelings of loneliness, self-esteem, lack of self-control, and shyness. It can also lead to poor academic performance which may bring about a sense of guilt and personal crisis (Eldeleklioglu, & Vural, 2013; Bozoglan, Demirer & Sahin, 2013; Yao & Zhong, 2014). According to Schill (2011) cited in Gok (2015), other side effects may include; stress, anxiety, mental health problems, and severe loss of personal productivity.

The Challenges Encountered in Using Digital Technology

Digital inclusion came with several challenges for the educational system. As noted above, many institutions responded to the pandemic by migrating to the online space for carrying on the academic activities of teaching, learning, supervision, and assessment. However, this system is fraught with a myriad of challenges. On their part, Adedoyin and Soykan (2020), Ribeiro (2020), and Aiyedun, Ogunode, and Aiyedun (2021) highlighted the following challenges that were encountered by an academic institution in migrating to the digital environment; compatibility, heavy workload, epileptic power supply, high cost of internet facility, inadequate digital literacy skill, economic factor, the challenge of supervision and assessment as well as environmental distraction. This is in tandem with the findings of Bakare and Ademakinwa (2020) who affirmed these myriads of challenges as militating factors against the inactivity of most public universities in Nigeria amid the pandemic.

Summary

The emergence of digital technologies and resources have proven to be an essential tool in facilitating smarter service delivery across various sectors of human networking systems. Concerning the educational scenery, the utility of digital technologies is amazing, especially in enhancing the learning and research process. The study highlighted the significance of digital technologies on the teachers as well as the students. It noted that digitalized learning system, although not new in Nigeria, is efficient for the learning process. However, the level of usage increased tremendously during the Covid-19 P era across all educational cohorts in varying degrees. Markus (2020) summed up the benefit of this innovation as learner-centric, learning-centric, collaborative development and enables students to carry out research and then drop their queries online for the teacher to respond synchronously or asynchronously across platforms.

CONCLUSION

The process of learning has evolved in style and scope. Recent transformation in the learning process during the lockdown was occasioned by the massive intrusion of digital technologies into educational activities. Prior to the Covid-19 pandemic, the educational instructional method was through the physical interaction between the teachers and their students within the four walls of the classroom. With the restrictive measure of the Covid-19 pandemic, this traditional approach to learning became unsustainable. This development necessitated the adoption of digital technologies and digital information resources. Digital technologies offer teachers and students the requisite avenue to interact, impart knowledge and share information from the comfort of their homes. This approach tends to make learning more flexible and interesting as it enhanced open access to information as well as eases tension common in the classroom environment. Similarly, it creates room for social interaction between the students. In addition, it eliminates hazards faced by parents and students every day while running to school, it also eliminates the problem of gun violence and physical bullying in schools through which several students have lost their lives.

RECOMMENDATIONS

Given the enormous benefit and opportunities provided by digital technologies to relevant stakeholders in the academic ecosystem, particularly in maintaining the standard of learning, despite the lockdown, it is useful to make the following recommendations:

1. Regulatory bodies like the National Universities Commission (NUC) should develop a policy framework for the adoption and integration of digital technologies in all academic activities to support the overall educational goal of the nation. This policy will ensure the effective optimization of digital technologies, at the same time, guide against abuse and wrongful use.
2. Administrators of academic institutions must provide teachers at all levels with adequate training to ensure operational productivity in the use of digital technologies and resources. This will help eradicate the fear and disinterestedness shown by many stakeholders who are averse to this new paradigm.
3. Educational administrators should engage experts to guide and train students on the use of the digital space. Specifically, in observing the famous principles of "netiquette" and navigating cyberspace to avoid cyberbullying.
4. The Federal Government, State Governments, as well as school proprietors, should seek ways of addressing some of the peculiar challenges facing the adoption of digital technologies and resources in the educational sector.
5. In addition, it is recommended that migrating online to learn with its seeming benefits, should not lead to the complete displacement of the traditional method of face-to-face instructional delivery, rather, in line with international best practices, there should be a fusion of both systems(hybrid)

Impact of the Study

The study is impactful to:

1. **Academic Instructors:** The new paradigm occasioned by the novel pandemic has revealed the need to evaluate the efficacy of the traditional face-to-face learning style as the only means of education, and has shown that digital inclusion is necessary to forestall the closure of academic institutions in the face of future pandemics.
2. **Society:** Society will work smarter and this will further go a long way in addressing the gap in technological usage between developed and developing countries. Again, it will be Nigeria's part of the global community.
3. **Policy:** Relevant stakeholders in the educational sector like the National Universities Commission and the Council of Legal Education should formulate policies for the adoption and integration of digital technologies in all academic activities.
4. The study has helped to further dispel the myth that the teaching and learning process cannot be achieved remotely.

REFERENCES

Abi-Jaoude, E., Naylor, K. T., & Pignatiello, A. (2020). Smartphones, social media use, and youth mental health. *Canadian Medical Association Journal*, *192*(6), E136–E141. doi:10.1503/cmaj.190434 PMID:32041697

Adedoyin, O. B., & Soykan, E. (2020). Covid-19 Pandemic and online learning: The challenges and opportunities. *Interactive Learning Environments*. Advance online publication. doi:0.1080/10494820.2020.1813180

Afolasade, A. A., & Oluyomi, S. P. (2021). *Nigeria Law Students' Perception of Online Teaching: Appraisal of COVID-19-Imposed Online Classes*. Asian Journal of Legal Education. doi:10.1177/23220058211061915

Agbele, A. T., & Oyelade, E. A. (2020). Impact of COVID-19 on the Nigerian educational system: Strengths and challenges of online/virtual education. *Asian Journal of Education and Social Studies*, *13*(1), 26–35. doi:10.9734/ajess/2020/v13i130322

Aiyedun, O. T. G., Ogunode, N. J., & Aiyedun, C. T. (2021). Assessment of Virtual Learning During COVID-19 Lockdown in Nigerian Public Universities, Academicia Globe. *Inderscience Research.*, *2*(5), 159–175.

Ajadi, T. O., Salawu, I. O., & Adeoye, F. A. (2008). E-Learning and Distance Education in Nigeria. *The Turkish Online Journal of Educational Technology*, *7*(4), 7.

Ajani, F. O., Ismaila, Y. A., & Ayodele, R. O. (2021). Assessment of Library Database Utilization for Academic Activities Among Kwara State University Lecturers During Covid-19 Pandemic Period. *Journal of Applied Information Science and Technology*, *14*(2), 89–97.

Ajoke, B. S. (2022). The Place of Libraries and Information Communication Technology in Education and National Development in Nigeria. Nigeria Library Association.

Bakare, O. D. (2018). *The use of social media technologies (SMTs) in the provision of library and information services in academic libraries of South-West, Nigeria* [Doctoral dissertation].

Bakare, O. D., & Ademakinwa, A. O. (2020). The Impact of Covid-19 on Mentorship of Graduate Students in Nigerian Universities. *Journal of Nigerian Association of Pastoral Counsellors, 1*(1), 50–65.

Bakare, O. D., & Okuonghae, N. (2022). Information Managers as Change Agents in Achieving Sustainable Development in the 21st Century. *Journal of Environmental Science and Economic, 1*(2), 68–78.

Bakare Dr, O. D., & Bakare Dr, B. M. (2021). *Global Technological Trend in Academic Libraries. Information & Media Studies*. FIMS.

Bozoglan, B., Demirer, V., & Sahin, I. (2013). Loneliness, self-esteem, and life satisfaction as predictors of Internet addiction: A cross-sectional study among Turkish university students. *Scandinavian Journal of Psychology, 54*(4), 313–319. doi:10.1111jop.12049 PMID:23577670

Bresciani, S., Ferraris, A., Romano, M., & Santoro, G. (2021). *Building a Digital Transformation Strategy. In Digital Transformation Management for Agile Organizations: A Compass to sail the Digital World.* Emerald Publishing Limited. doi:10.1108/978-1-80043-171-320211002

Bryant, J. A., Sanders-Jackson, A., & Smallwood, A. (2006). IMing, text messaging, and adolescent social networks. *Journal of Computer-Mediated Communication, 11*(2), 577–592. doi:10.1111/j.1083-6101.2006.00028.x

Cain, J. (2018). It's Time to Confront Student Mental Health Issues Associated with Smartphones and social media. *Am. J. Pharm. Educ., 82*, 6862.

Calderaro, A. (2017). Social Media and recruitable. *International Journal of Digital Technologies, Research, Knowledge and Education, 4*(6), 169–180.

Chambers Harrap. (2009). *Chambers Concise Dictionary* (2nd ed.). Author.

Crow, R. (2002a). *Case for Institutional Repositories: A SPARC Position Paper*. Washington, DC: The Scholarly Publishing and Academic Resources Coalition. Retrieved from http://www.arl.org/sparc/bm~doc/ir_final_release_102.pdf

Darby, R. M., Jones, C. M., Gilbert, L. D., & Lambert, S. C. (2009). Increasing the productivity of interactions between subject and institutional repositories. *New Review of InformationNetworking, 14*(2), 117–135. doi:10.1080/13614570903359381

Dhull, I., & Sakshi, M. S. (2017). Online Learning. *International Education and Research Journal, 3*(8), 32–34.

Eldeleklioglu, J. & Vural, M. (2013). Predictive effects of academic achievement, internet use duration, loneliness and shyness on internet addiction. *Hacettepe Universitesi Egitim Fakultesi Dergisi, 28*(1), 141-151.

Fakunle, S. M., Bakare, O. D., & Adeyeye, S. V. (2022). Digital Literacy Skills as Determinants of Library Use by Undergraduate Students of Private Universities in Oyo State, Nigeria. *Library Philosophy and Practice, 7054*. https://digitalcommons.unl.edu/libphilprac/7054

Frolova, E. V., Ryabova, T. M., & Rogach, O. V. (2019). Digital Technologies in Education: Problems and Prospects for" Moscow Electronic School" Project Implementation. *European Journal of Contemporary Education*, *8*(4), 779–789.

Greenhow, C., & Askari, E. (2017). E. Learning and teaching with social network sites: A decade of research in K-12 related education. *Education and Information Technologies*, *22*(2), 623–645. doi:10.100710639-015-9446-9

Greenhow, C., & Chapman, A. (2020). Social distancing meets social media: Digital tools for connecting students, teachers, and citizens in an emergency. *Inf. Learn. Sci.*, *121*(5/6), 341–352. doi:10.1108/ILS-04-2020-0134

Guner, H. R., Hasanoglu, I., & Aktas, F. (2020). COVID-19: Prevention and control measures in the community. *Turkish Journal of Medical Sciences*, *50*(9), 571–577. doi:10.3906ag-2004-146 PMID:32293835

Hendal, B. A. (2020). Kuwait University Faculty's Use of Electronic Resources During the Covid-19 Pandemic. *Digital Library Perspectives*, *36*(4), 429–439. doi:10.1108/DLP-04-2020-0023

Jobirovich, Y. M. (2021). The Role Of Digital Technologies In Reform Of The Education System. *The American Journal of Social Science and Education Innovations*, *3*(04), 461–465. doi:10.37547/tajssei/Volume03Issue04-73

Jones, R., Andrew, T., & MacColl, J. J. (2006). The Institutional Repository. Chandos Publishing (Oxford) Limited.

Lund, B. D., & Wang, T. (2019). Effect of virtual reality on learning motivation and academic performance. *Kansas Library Association College Proceedings*, *9*(1), 1–7.

Majchrzak, A., Markus, M. L., & Wareham, J. (2016). Designing for digital transformation: Lessons for information systems research from the study of ICT and societal challenges. *Management Information Systems Quarterly*, *40*(2), 267–278. doi:10.25300/MISQ/2016/40:2.03

Markus, D. G. (2020). Is the online learning, good in the Midst of Covid -19 Pandemic? The case of ETL Learners. *Journal of Sinestesia*, *10*(1), 1–10.

Mogas, J., Palau, R., Fuentes, M., & Cebrián, G. (2022). Smart schools on the way: How school principals from Catalonia approach the future of education within the fourth industrial revolution. *Learning Environments Research*, *25*(3), 875–893. doi:10.100710984-021-09398-3

Montgomery, L., Hartley, J., Neylon, C., Gillies, M., Gray, E., Herrmann-Pillath, C., Huang, C., Leach, J., Potts, J., Ren, X., Skinner, K., Sugimoto, C., & Wilson, K. (2019). Universities. *Works*.

Obiakor, T., & Adeniran, A. (2020). *Covid-19. Impending Situation threatens to Deepens Nigeria's Education crisis*. Centre for the Study of the Economic Africa. Available at https://media.africaportal.org/documents/covid-19-impendingsituation-threatens-to-Deepens-Nigerias-Education-pdf

Olaniyi, E. T., & Akinyoola, O. G. (2021). Implication of digital Innovations for Academic Libraries amidst the covid-19 Pandemic. *Lagos Journal of Library & Information Science., 10*(1/2), 62–79.

Red Cross. (2020, April 21). *What social distancing means.* https://www.redcross.org/about- us/news-and-events/news/2020/coronavirus-what-social-distancing-means.html

Ribeiro, R. (2020, April 14). How university faculty embraced the remote learning shift. *EdTechMagazine.* https://edtechmagazine.com/higher/article/2020/04/how-university-faculty-embraced-remote-learning-shif

Saini. (2018). Understanding the role of institutional repository in digital preservation in Academic libraries: A Review of Literature. *Library Philosophy & Practice, 1904.*

Schill, R. (2011). *Social networking teens are more likely to drink, and use drugs, study finds.* Retrieved on March 01, 202e from the website: https://jjie.org/teens-on-facebook-more-likely-drink-or-use-drugs-study-finds/

Shapiro, J. S. (1999). Loneliness: Paradox or artifacts? *The American Psychologist, 54*(9), 782–783. doi:10.1037/0003-066X.54.9.782

Sobaih, A. E. E., Palla, I. A., & Baquee, A. (2022). A Social Media Use in E-Learning amid Covid-19 Pandemic: Indian Students Perspective. *International Journal of Environmental Research and Public Health, 19*(9), 5380. doi:10.3390/ijerph19095380 PMID:35564771

Symulevich, A., & Hamilton, M. (2022). Using Open Access Institutional Repositories to Save the Student Symposium during the COVID-19 Pandemic. *Information Technology and Libraries, 41*(1). Advance online publication. doi:10.6017/ital.v41i1.14175

Ukwoma, S. C., & Okafor, V. N. (2017). Institutional Repository in Nigerian Universities: Trends and Development. *Library Collections, Acquisitions & Technical Services, 40*(1-2), 46–57. doi:10.1080/14649055.2017.1331653

W.H.O. (2020). *Coronavirus disease (COVID-19) pandemic.* World Health Organization. https://www.who.int/emergencies/diseases/novel-coronavirus-2019

World Bank. (2021). *Remote Learning During Covid-19 Lockdown is Preventing Learning Loss in Nigeria.* https://www.worldbank.org/en/news/feature/2021/12/08/remote-learning-during-covid-19-lockdown-is-preventing-learning-loss-in-nigeria

Yao, M. Z., & Zhong, Z. (2014). Loneliness, social contacts, and Internet addiction: A cross-lagged panel study. *Computers in Human Behavior, 30*, 164–170. doi:10.1016/j.chb.2013.08.007

Chapter 7
Digitising Standardised Educational Assessment in Africa Using Computerised Adaptive Testing:
Transdisciplinary Framework for Action

Jumoke I. Oladele
University of Johannesburg, South Africa

Mdutshekelwa Ndlovu
University of Johannesburg, South Africa

ABSTRACT

The experience of the COVID-19 pandemic has revealed a need for the educational sector in Africa to adopt innovative ways for assessment by leveraging technology with the increasing number of student enrollments at all levels of education. A systematic approach is also required to circumvent the challenges faced by developing countries transdisciplinary. Transdisciplinarity is still evolving and has been proved to be a viable tool for engagement, societal impact, new partnerships, fresh ideas, reality checks, new capacities, and systemic thinking leading to new career possibilities. This study conducted a documentary analysis of standardised examination administration in Africa and proposed a framework for action adopting a transdisciplinary approach to research for problem-solving. The study used a qualitative approach for collecting and analysing data from reports and documents supported by empirical findings from existing literature. The study created a framework for action through which the gains of the transdisciplinary approach can be translated to practice.

DOI: 10.4018/978-1-6684-6873-9.ch007

INTRODUCTION

Education has been regarded as a key indicator of development. Nations worldwide are now gearing efforts at increasing access to quality education for citizens. Quality is reflected in the teaching and learning process, human capital development, instructional resources and support facilities. Didham and Ofei-Manu (2015) stressed that education has a long history as an international priority, and the right to education was first enshrined in the Universal Declaration of Human Rights in 1948. Therefore, improving education and ensuring all people are afforded a high standard of education has been reaffirmed as a key global goal of development under the post-2015 development agenda.

In 2015, the international community, through the efforts of the United Nations and Heads of states of the 193 Member Nations, launched the Sustainable Development Goals (SDGs) as a new developmental strategy for 2030. This strategy, which is otherwise known as Agenda 2030, is framed into 17 Goals, with Goal 4 being targeted at ensuring inclusive and quality education for all while promoting lifelong learning as well as building and upgrading educational facilities that are child, disability and gender-sensitive and to provide, safe, non-violent, inclusive and effective learning environments for all (Ugwuegbe et al., 2018). SDG Goal 4 is pivotal to the other 17 Sustainable Development Goals (Oladele et al., 2021).

The synthesis report of the United Nations Secretary-General (UNSG) on the post- 2015 development agenda stated that "high-quality education and life-long learning" and the capacity of teachers are key factors in empowering youth as a "globally connected engine for change". World Economic Forum (2015) have also adduced a high level of importance to education as a strong system that broadens access to opportunities, improves health, and bolsters the resilience of communities; while fueling economic growth in a way that can reinforce and accelerate these processes. As such, there is a consensus on the relevance of education in the SDG agenda.

According to Ghavifekr and Rosdy (2015), integrating information and communication technologies (ICT) in education generally means technology-based teaching and learning process that closely relates to utilising learning technologies in schools. ICT is a backbone for teaching, learning and assessment, considered a key component in the pedagogical process (Githiru, 2018; Majid, 2019). The use of ICT in assessment is now common where it utilises digital devices which help construct assessment tasks. It could be delivered as computer-assisted assessment, computer adaptive testing, e-portfolio, and digital rubrics. These delivery forms provide immediate grading and feedback to students (Bethany Christian Institute, 2018). As such, technology is transforming learning and assessment through enhanced question types, real-time feedback, increased accessibility, adapts to learner ability and knowledge, embedded with the learning process and assessment for ongoing learning (Thomas, 2016).

Pedagogical processes in developing nations suffered considerable setbacks with the Covid-19 Pandemic due to non-access to technology support for teaching-learning with assessment as an integral aspect of this process. Educational assessment has a range of predicted effects on learners' attainment to indicate the extent to which educational objectives are achieved (Mons, 2009). It also serves as a link between schools and national-level administrators. Educational assessment can either be teacher-made or standardised. The teacher normally prepares teacher-made tests to measure the classroom teaching outcomes in line with a specified curriculum. With standardised assessment, candidates are presented with the same questions scored consistently, comparing the relative performance of students usually practised with large-scale tests administered to large populations of students (Hodder Education, n.d.).

Some formats for administering standardised tests include multiple-choice, true-false questions, short-answer questions, essay questions, or a mix of question types. While standardised tests were traditionally presented on paper and completed using pencils, many still are; they are increasingly being administered on computers connected to online programs and widely used for large-scale testing situations because computers can score them quickly, consistently, and inexpensively (Great Schools Partnership, 2015). Worthy of note is that open-ended essay questions usually scored by humans are now done using computers and deployed through platforms like FastTest, following the same pattern of setting a common set of guidelines or rubrics to promote consistent evaluations from essay to essay (Oladele, 2022).

While ICT unarguably brings value to the table for educational assessment, it also comes with challenges such as lack of hardware, shortage of technology experts, slow network connection, high cost of Internet, erratic power supply and economic and location disparities with access to digital technology in sub-Saharan Africa among others (Pelgrum, 2001; Mourdoukoutas 2019; Oladele et al., 2021). Also, the digital dividends, described as "broader development benefits from using digital technologies", have not been evenly distributed. "For digital technologies to benefit everyone everywhere requires closing the remaining digital divide, especially in internet access (World Bank's World Development Report, 2016; Matthew, 2018).

These challenges call for research to provide solutions. Burnett (2011) evaluated the benefits of technological novelties and the need to integrate them into teacher education. Lei (2009) examined the technology requirement for preservice teacher training. The lack of technological know-how necessitates a systematic technology preparation to aid learning using classroom and assistive technologies. More importantly, it helps them connect technology and teaching for meaningful learning. Coccoli et al. (2014) conducted a study which analysed performance enhanced through ICT to enhance the quality of pedagogical practices. Gruszczynska and Pountney (2013) also examined the role of ICT in teacher education curriculum development.

Oladele et al. (2021) examined Google Classroom for online instructional delivery. Their findings revealed that it is a useful innovation and cost-effective instructional approach for teaching and learning in higher education. Also, a review of Standardised Assessment Development Procedure and Algorithms for Computer Adaptive Testing by Oladele and Ndlovu (2021) showed a positive direction for standardised testing. Most of these studies are on digitisation for teaching and learning, while the aspect of digitisation for standardised educational assessment is sparse in the African literature. In addition, much is required in towing the path to digitised assessment practices for successful implementation, which is the gap this study is poised to fill.

The Problem

Teaching and learning in the 21st Century require technological integration owing to current realities in developing countries. The world is just recovering from the Covid-19 Pandemic, which resulted in lockdowns which affected the educational sector like others. The COVID-19 Pandemic undoubtedly shocked the educational sector in Africa to its roots occasioned by the lockdowns, which became necessary to curb the spread of the COVID-19 virus, having established that it was transmitted through physical contact. While developed countries could transfer their curriculum to the online mode, teaching and learning in higher education in developing countries were left struggling with the online teaching and learning mode. In contrast, others had to stop all teaching and learning activities altogether. The Pandemic also affected standardised examination bodies who were saddled with the responsibility of maintaining internationally accepted procedures, providing qualitative and reliable educational assessment and promoting sustainable human resources development, mutual understanding and international cooperation (Enang, 2021).

Particularly in 2020, examination bodies in Africa had to compulsorily postpone their examinations, considering that they administered examinations through paper-pencil testing. One of the major reasons for this occurrence was the lack of access to educational assessment platforms through which the extent to which learning has been achieved can be ascertained. This occurrence altered the higher education academic calendar, with students losing that year of entry into higher learning institutions. However, as the world is gradually recovering from the COVID-19 Pandemic experience, examination bodies are returning to "business as usual" by administering external examinations. The question of how many standardised examination bodies move from the age-long paper-pencil administration to more technology-enhanced modes of test administration requires thought-leading answers.

Digitalised educational assessments have moved through 4 generations of linear computerised testing (which is at par with paper-pencil assessments), computerised adaptive testing-CAT (tailored to the ability levels of examinees, continuous measurement (using calibrated measures to continuously and unobtrusively estimate dynamic changes in the student's achievement trajectory and intelligent measurement (producing intelligent scoring, interpretation of individual profiles, and advice to learners and teachers using knowledge bases and inference procedures (Oladele et al., 2020). Quite commendable is that the African continent has explored the first generation of deploying paper-pencil tests using computer terminals. However, developed countries have extensively explored the second generation for over three decades and are currently in the fourth. Hence, CAT is an emerging African research area requiring a tractable framework.

Krumsvik (2006) examined ICT-related challenges faced by teacher education in Norway while stressing the need for a progressive learning curve leading to home-grown solutions in implementing ICT for teaching and learning. Jukes and Dosaj (2006) examined digital literacy indicators among immigrant teachers, and their study revealed that digital literate teachers are more productive than their non-literate counterparts. Prensky (2001) explained that the younger generation is more responsive to ICT than the older one as they are more open-minded and empirically proved to aid learners. These findings showed that students' technology interest could be leveraged for teaching learning and assessment. Education is unarguably important in achieving the SDG 2030 development agenda. However, a carefully developed implementation framework premised on a functional and scalable approach is required to ensure sustainability. This study examined current standardised assessment practices in Africa through document analysis and proffering a framework for action through a transdisciplinary approach to research for problcm-solving.

METHODOLOGY

This study employed a qualitative research design of case study type, which entails collecting and analysing data derived from reports and documents as an interpretive transdisciplinary research methodology. This design is deemed appropriate for exploring and understanding the impact of COVID-19 on examination administration while developing a transdisciplinary framework for action on digitalisation for educational assessment in Africa. The population of this research was all examination bodies in Africa. Inclusion criteria for analysed documents were based on educational assessment bodies in Africa concerning test administration. As such, the study involved the use of secondary sources of data collection. Documentary analysis was approached expositorily in analysing the collected study data and supported with relevant literature for explanation building. This approach was geared towards formulating a framework for action for digitalising standardised educational assessments in Africa.

Ethical Considerations: This study was exempted from the requirement to obtain informed consent by the University of Ilorin Ethics Committee as no human participant was involved.

Findings

The documentary analysis was carried out to examine the current mode of test administration deployed by African examination bodies. Findings reveal that in West Africa, standardised examinations are conducted on a regional and national basis. The West African Examinations Council (WAEC) is an examination board established by law in 1952 to determine learners' competencies after three years of secondary education in the English-speaking West African countries, with headquarters in Accra, Ghana. WAEC is responsible for conducting the Senior Certification examinations and awarding certificates comparable to those of equivalent examining authorities internationally in Anglophonic countries of West Africa (Ghana, Nigeria, Sierra Leone, Liberia, and The Gambia) (Okoye & Nwafor, 2009). Some national examination bodies which perform similar roles to that of WAEC are National Examination Council- NECO, Joint Admissions and Matriculation Board- JAMB (Nigeria), National Board for Professional and Technical Examinations-NABPTEX (Ghana), and Gambia Basic Education Certificate Examination- GABECE (Gambia).

Similar to operations in West Africa, standardised examinations are conducted regionally and nationally in East Africa. At the regional level, the East African Examinations Council (EEAC) is responsible for secondary-level testing, being an agency of the East African Community established by The East African Examinations Council Act in 1967 (Kiwanuka, n.d.). Some national examination bodies with similar responsibilities to EEAC are The National Examinations Council of Tanzania- NECTA (Kitta & Afeli, 2017); Uganda National Examinations Board (UNEB) which awards the Uganda Advanced Certificate of Education (UACE); the gateway to university and tertiary institutions (UNESCO-Institue of Statistics, 2015; Allen et al., 2016), Malawi National Examinations Board (MANEB) (Devex, 2022) and The Kenya National Examinations Council- KNEC (KNEC, 2021) among others.

Standardised examinations for the senior phase of education in Southern Africa are decentralised as each country has designated agencies and departments that manage their examination. In South Africa, secondary school-leavers take two assessments which are the national school-leaving examination, the National Senior Certificate (NSC), which is a statutory requirement for entry into Higher Education and the National Benchmark Tests (NBTs) (Prince, 2017). The Department of Basic Education is responsible for conducting the National Senior Certificate (NSC) examinations, commonly called "matric". The national school-leaving examination is a standardised examination conducted to assess the culmination of twelve years of formal schooling. It serves as a barometer of the health of the education system (Department of Basic Education, 2021). The NBTs is a project deployed by the Centre for Educational Testing for Access and Placement (CETAP) to assess new entrants into the university students' academic readiness as a complement to secondary school results. The NBTs assess aspects of prior learning in competency areas of Academic Literacy (AL), Quantitative Literacy (QL) and Mathematics (MAT) that directly impact the university students' success in the first year. AL and QL are combined in the AQL test and written in a three-hour morning session; the MAT is written in a three-hour afternoon session. Both are administered as computer-based onsite standardised examinations across South Africa following pre-scheduled dates (University of Cape Town, 2022). Lesotho, also in Southern Africa, has her national Examinations Council responsible for conducting public examinations on behalf of the Ministry of Education and Training. The body awards the Lesotho General Certificate of Secondary Education GCSE (Examinations Council of Lesotho, 2022).

All these examinations are administered using the paper-pencil administration mode except for the Universities Matriculation Examination (UME) conducted by JAMB in Nigeria and the National Benchmark Tests conducted by CAE in South Africa; both deployed as the linear CBT modes. These reveal that high stake assessment practices in Africa rely heavily on pencil-and-paper tests (PPT) and, at best, the linear computer-based administration modes in the first generation of computerised testing (Oladele et al., 2020).

CBT mode of administration is a remarkable improvement over the PPT, such as increased test security and professionalism, consistent testing environment, more frequent testing opportunities window or on-demand suitable for countries with a large population, scheduling in real-time, potential for on-demand, more accurate and instant feedbacks, precise with ability estimation, flexibility, and quality control (Noyes & Garland, 2008; Surpass, 2019). Because of these advantages with test administration, CBT has become the de facto standard for large-scale, high-stakes assessments. However, the decision for this assessment mode should be made cautiously, considering the African context (Blazer, 2010). Despite the attractive advantages of linear CBT, continuous improvements are required for educational assessments driven by technological advancements, which are fast becoming a way of life and shaping life operations with the potential of bringing about life-long changes (Manyika et al., 2018). A report on the use of ICT formative and summative assessments revealed that new technologies create both the need for education to provide students with higher-level thinking skills, particularly the aspects of creative and critical thinking, and the opportunity to teach and assess those skills accurately (Harlen & Deakin, 2003).

Technology-driven assessments such as Computer Adaptive Testing (CAT) have greater potential to enhance standardised assessment processes and cognitive outcomes (Gathitu, 2010). CAT is an assessment system that uses AI algorithms based on Item Response Theory to tailor items according to the examinee's ability level, thereby increasing the examination process's efficiency (Oppl et al., 2017; Thompson, 2019; Oladele et al., 2020). CAT has been widely adopted for standardised testing in developed countries. The Armed Services Vocational Aptitude Battery (ASVAB) in the United States has been administered using CAT for over a decade, formerly a conventional paper and pencil test (ASVAB, 2022). The Graduate Management Admission Test (GMAT) is administered worldwide to more than 200,000 candidates annually in more than 400 testing centres using CAT (GMAT, 2022). CAT has also been instrumental in administering a variety of licensing and certification examinations for health professionals in the United States, Isreal, Australia, and Canada (Mutisya, 2020; Ogunjimi et al., 2021). Mutisya's (2020) findings revealed a positive perception of Adopting CAT for educational assessment while stressing that the Government of Kenya has an ICT policy that aims at improving the lives of her citizens by ensuring ICT services across the country are accessible efficient, reliable and affordable. Oladele et al. (In Press) examined the perception and prospects of educational assessment administrators using Computer Adaptive Testing. Findings from the study also revealed a positive perception of CAT. Furthermore, the prospect of adopting the technology by examination bodies in Nigeria is relatively high once circumventing the mitigating challenges. These findings are a pointer in the right direction, as positive perceptions are part of the underlying mechanism for progressive action for just transition (Alfauzan & Hussain, 2017; Slycan Trust, 2021).

Framework for Action

This study proposes a framework for action through transdisciplinarity based on the Nicolescuian philosophical axioms of ontology, epistemology, logic and axiology. Transdisciplinarity is a fast-developing field with about four decades of practice. However, the field is gaining relevance due to the need for a critique of the standard configuration of knowledge (Oladele, 2022). This need calls for a paradigm shift from individual to systemic thinking for problem solutions sustainably and relevant to all disciplines (Reynolds, 2018; Maracha, 2018; Harwood, 2019). Transdisciplinarity involves realistic goal setting, cross-disciplinary collaboration, stakeholders' participation, and academic and conventional knowledge with a thematic umbrella (Utrecht University, 2022). As such, it integrates knowledge across academic disciplines and with non-academic stakeholders to address societal challenges guided by the principle of scientific rigour for societal relevance (Morton et al., 2015). Transdisciplinarity ensures a holistic view of reality as filtered by that developer's sensory input and perception of that reality while opening limitless possibilities for the mind concerning problem-solving.

The transdisciplinary framework for action in this study is proposed for charting a pathway for digitising educational assessment in Africa while leveraging technological advancement for quality education succinctly espoused by the Sustainable Development Goals 4. These comprised four Nicolescuian philosophical axioms (ontology, epistemology, logic and axiology), shaping the transdisciplinary research methodologies as shown in Figure 1.

Figure 1. Framework for action for digitising standardised educational assessment in Africa

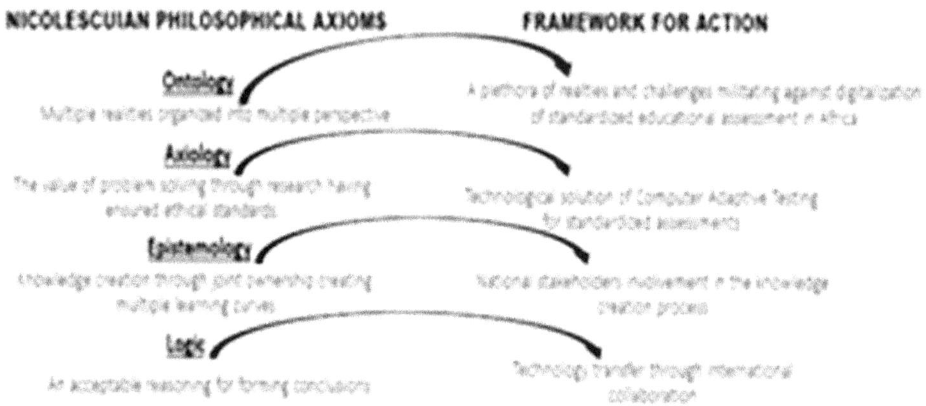

As shown in Figure 1, ontology connotes multiple levels of reality which applies to the current state of digitisation of standardised assessment in Africa. The finding of this study revealed that high stake assessment practices in Africa rely heavily on pencil-and-paper tests. This finding is the current reality coupled with many challenges such as power shortage, poor internet access, advancing technological know-how, low computer literacy, and large classroom situations (Oladele et al., 2021). Tackling these challenges, especially in power supply and internet access, is required for technology to benefit everyone everywhere (World Bank's World Development Report, 2016).

Axiology which speaks to the value of problem-solving through research while adhering to ethical standards in this framework, recommends Computer Adaptive Testing (CAT) as a technological solution for standardised assessments in Nigeria while serving as a model for Africa. This study's findings, which revealed that the JAMB has successfully deployed educational assessment using the linear computerised assessment mode, show that the organisation is in the proper position to explore CAT. This position is apt, having deployed JAMB using the CBT format (Editor, 2016; Punch, 2021). The experiences gathered over the years would surely be of value while moving through the CAT learning curve. This recommendation would also aid the accurate placement of students in various courses in higher learning institutions. It may render post-UTME examinations unnecessary currently employed for validating students' UTME scores with time.

The third philosophy premised on epistemology presents knowledge as complex, emergent, cross-fertilised and embodied through joint ownership. This aspect can be achieved through national stakeholders' involvement in the knowledge creation process, which brings together various expertise for evolving through the learning curve with digitising educational assessments deployed through CAT. Some of the related expertise construed as relevant stakeholders in this framework are educational technologists, computer programmers, educational test administrators, psychometricians, electrical engineers, innovation specialists, universities/ research institutes and the government, among others. Putting together the various expertise would engender a broad-based solution in the context of Nigeria. Slycan Trust (2021) puts just transition (JT) as the transformation of economies and societies toward sustainability. JI is premised on a holistic approach to problem-solving. It functions by leveraging opportunities and choosing pathways of transformation that translate into resilience for all through institutional arrangements and policy coherence for economic development. It also comprises changes in livelihoods and ways of life, business practices and methods, the rise of new sectors and the replacement of others through a social dialogue that includes all relevant stakeholders and addresses existing inequalities. Recognising the different contexts, impacts, vulnerabilities, and needs across communities, sectors, countries, and regions is germane to achieving sustainability (Slycan Trust, 2021). JT remains relevant as studies have shown that home-grown solutions through collective efforts employ cutting-edge innovation, which is key to economic recovery (Ndagijimana & Gomera, 2022).

Logic speaks to inclusive and acceptable reasoning for forming conclusions to facilitate contradiction(s) and reconciliation(s). In this framework, logic relates to technology transfer mechanisms through international collaboration. Undoubtedly, technology has been well explored for educational assessment in developed countries. A smart learning route is to open up channels for international collaboration through which the door for technology transfer is opened. According to Eaton (2018), the relationship between technology, teaching-learning and testing is a complex one with related factors such as but not limited to instructors' confidence and competence in using technology for teaching; the kinds of technology that are available in a particular learning context; institutional policies on how money is spent on technology and what kind of technology is licensed or purchased as well as whether students bring their own devices or use a technology provided by their various learning institutions. If Sustainable Development Goals are to be achieved by 2030, Information and Communication Technology (ICT) in education cannot be overemphasised. A classical example of a technology transfer mechanism is seen in the recent Accenture/UJ 4th Industrial Revolution (4IR) internship programme for designing, developing and delivering new software, applications and technology solutions driven through a systemic technology transfer mechanism. Systems thinking is key to process improvements considering that "everything connects to everything else" (Dash, 2020). This type of initiative would aid upskilling for the 4IR and provide valuable experience for success with digitisation applicable to educational assessments.

A review of standardised assessment development procedures and algorithms for computer adaptive testing by Oladele and Ndlovu (2021) showed an exciting direction for ensuring accuracy in ability estimation with standardised educational assessments characterised by high-ended adaptive technologies such as CAT in the realm of AI made possible by the fourth industrial revolution. Using this framework for action, Africa can move from paper-pencil/linear CBT to assessment digitisation deployed with CAT through national stakeholders' involvement in the knowledge creation process which brings together relevant expertise in the fields of educational technologists, computer programmers, educational test administrators, psychometricians, electrical engineers, innovation specialist, universities/research institutes and the government. Also, the door for international collaboration should be open for technology transfer mechanisms.

A framework for CAT by Thompson and Weiss (2011) revealed that feasibility studies are the first and a major step in the CAT adoption decision process. Some progress has been made with feasibility CAT studies in the African context on CAT test length (Ogunjimi et al., 2021), CAT performance for Postgraduate training assessments (Oladele, 2021) and ability estimation for CAT (Oladele et al., 2022), among others. While a handful of lessons can be learnt from existing research, feasibility studies are necessary for each testing programme projected for CAT adoption to adequately answer questions encountered during the development of a CAT and for a legally defensible documentation process.

Limitation of the Study

The difference between disciplines is one potential challenge to collaboration. Many disciplines have developed their internal guidelines, norms, and rules. Thus, working transdisciplinarily can generate many challenges due to research practice and implementation differences. Failure to identify and reconcile such differences can affect the integrity of the research process and its findings and even end a collaboration.

REFERENCES

Accenture/UJ 4IR internship programme. (2022). *4IR Internship Opportunity*. https://bit.ly/3y296nb

Alfauzan, A. H., & Hussain, A. G. (2017). Attitude towards and Perception of Literature in EFL Setting: A Case Study on QU Male Undergraduate Students. *English Language Teaching*, *10*(1), 1–17. doi:10.5539/elt.v10n1p1

Allen, R., Elks, P., Outhred, R., & Varly, P. (2016). *Uganda's assessment system: A road-map for enhancing assessment in education*. Health & Education Advance & Resource Team. https://www.heart-resources.org/wp-content/uploads/2016/10/Final-report-Enhancing- Uganda's-Assessment-System-September-2016.pdf

Armed Services Vocational Aptitude Battery. (2022). *The Armed Services Vocational Aptitude Battery*. https://www.officialasvab.com/

Bethany Christian Institute. (2018). *ICT in assessment*. BCI. https://sites.google.com/site/bethanycollegeofteacheredn/ict-in-assessment

Blazer, C. (2010). *Computer-Based Assessments*. Information Capsule. 0918. Research Services, Miami-Dade County Public Schools. https://files.eric.ed.gov/fulltext/ED544707.pdf

Burnett, C. (2011). Shifting and Multiple Spaces in Classrooms: An Argument for Investigating Learners' Boundary-Making around Digital Networked Texts. *The Journal of Literacy and Technology*, *12*(3).

Coccoli, M., Guercio, A., Maresca, P., & Stanganelli, L. (2014). Smarter universities: A vision for the fast-changing digital era. *Journal of Visual Languages and Computing*, *25*(6), 1003–1011. doi:10.1016/j.jvlc.2014.09.007

Dash, S. R. (2020). *Systems thinking: The key to process improvements*. UX Collections. https://uxdesign.cc/systems-thinking-the-key-to-process-improvements-ec8a0f71f628

Department of Basic Education. (2021). *NSC Examinations*. https://www.education.gov.za/Curriculum/NationalSeniorCertificate(NSC)Examinations.aspx

Devex. (2022). *Malawi National Examinations Board (MANEB)*. https://www.devex.com/organizations/malawi-national-examinations-board-maneb-133621

Didham, R. J., & Ofei-Manu, P. (2015). *The role of education in the sustainable development agenda: Empowering a learning society for sustainability through quality education*. ResearchGate. Available online at: https://www.researchgate.net/publication/280458119

Eaton, S. E. (2018). The Impact of Technology on how instructors Teach and how students Learn. In R. J. Harnish, K. R. Bridges, D. N. Sattler, M. L. Signorella, & M. Munson (Eds.), *The Use of Technology in Teaching and Learning*. Retrieved from the Society for the Teaching of Psychology website: http://teachpsych.org/ebooks/

Enang, W. (2021). *5 Functions of West African Examinations Council*. Pro guide. https://proguide.ng/functions-west-african-examinations-council/

Examinations Council of Lesotho. (2022). *Background*. https://www.examscouncil.org.ls/web/aboutUs

Gathitu, L. N. (2010). *Examination representation using adaptive testing: application in interview process* [Doctoral dissertation]. University of Nairobi. http://erepository.uonbi.ac.ke/bitstream/handle/11295/13095/Gathitu_Examination?sequence=3

Ghavifekr, S., & Rosdy, W. A. W. (2015). Teaching and learning with technology: Effectiveness of ICT integration in schools. *International Journal of Research in Education and Science*, *1*(2), 175–191. doi:10.21890/ijres.23596

Githiru, T. (2018). *How Technology Can Improve Africa*. Techweez. Available online at: https://techweez.com/2018/05/15/technology-can-improve-africa/

Graduate Management Admission Council. (2022). *GMAT Exam Structure: An Assessment of the Skills That Matter Most in Business*. https://www.mba.com/exams/gmat/about-the-gmat- exam/GMAT-exam-structure

Great Schools Partnership. (2015). *Glossary Of Education Reform: Standardized Test Definition*. Great Schools Partnership. https://www.edglossary.org/standardized-test/

Gruszczynska, A., Merchant, G., & Pountney, R. (2013). Digital Futures in Teacher Education": Exploring Open Approaches towards Digital Literacy. *Electronic Journal of e-Learning*, *11*(3), 193–206.

Harlen, W., & Deakin, C. R. (2003). A systematic review of the impact on students and teachers of the use of ICT for assessment of creative and critical thinking skills. In *Research Evidence in Education Library*. EPPI-Centre, Social Science Research Unit, Institute of Education, University of London. https://eppi.ioe.ac.uk/cms/Default.aspx?tabid=109

Harwood, S. A. (2019). Systems thinking and sustainable development. Encyclopedia of Sustainability in Higher Education, 1892-1897. doi:10.1007/978-3-030-11352-0_399

Hodder Education. (n.d.). *RS Assessment*. www.hoddereducation.co.uk/rsassessment

Jukes, I., & Dosaj, A. (2005). *Understanding Digital Kids (DKs): Teaching & learning in the new digital landscape*. The Info Savvy Group.

Kitta, S., & Afeli, S. (2017). *Examinations and Competitive Exams in Tanzania*. Regional Workshop on National Learning Assessment Systems in sub-Saharan Africa: Knowledge sharing and needs assessment, Dakar, Senegal. http://education2030-africa.org/images/talent/atelier061217/PPT_Tanzania.pdf

Kiwanuka, B. P. (n.d.). *The East African Examinations Council*. https://www.thecommonwealth-ilibrary.org/index.php/comsec/catalog/view/262/259/1971

Krumsvik, R. (2006). *ICT-initiated school development in lower secondary school* [Doctoral dissertation]. The University of Bergen.

Lei, J. (2009). Digital natives as preservice teachers: What technology preparation is needed? *Journal of Computing in Teacher Education*, *25*(3), 87–97.

Majid, I. (2019). ICT in Assessment: A Backbone for Teaching and Learning Process. *United International Journal for Research & Technology*, *1*(3), 38-40. https://uijrt.com/articles/v1/i3/UIJRTV1I30006.pdf

Manyika, J., Chui, M., Bughin, J., Dobbs, R., Bisson, P., & Marrs, A. (2018). *Disruptive Technologies: Advances that will Transform Life, Business, and the Global Economy*. McKinsey Global Institute.

Maracha, V. (2018). Systems thinking and collective problem-solving practices. System analysis in economics. In *Proceedings of the V International research and practice conference–biennale*. Prometheus Publishing House. 10.33278/SAE-2018.eng.269-272

Matthew, K. (2018). The digital divide – Where are we now? *IIT News Africa*. https://www.itnewsafrica.com/2018/08/the-digital-divide-where-are-we-now/

Mons, N. (2009). Theoretical and real effects of standardised assessment. *Eurydice Network*. https://citeseerx.ist.psu.edu/viewdoc/download?doi=10.1.1.174.4813&rep=rep1&type=pdf

Mourdoukoutas, E. (2019). *Digital revolution holds bright promises for Africa*. United Nations Africa Renewal. https://www.un.org/africarenewal/magazine/december-2017-march- 2018/digital-revolution-holds-bright-promises-Africa

Mutisya, T. M. (2020). *Adoption Of Computer Adaptive Testing In Educational Assessment In Kenya* [Doctoral dissertation]. University of Nairobi. http://erepository.uonbi.ac.ke/bitstream/handle/11295/153171/TITUS%20MUTIE%20MUTISYA%20FINAL%20PROJECT%20.pdf?sequence=1&isAllowed=y

Ndagijimana, U., & Gomera, M. (2022). *Rwanda's Home-grown Solutions are key to Economic Recovery*. United Nations Development Programme. https://www.undp.org/rwanda/rwanda%E2%80%99s-home-grown-solutions-are-key-economic-recovery-dr-Uzziel-ndagijimana-and-maxwell-gomera

Noyes, J. M., & Garland, K. J. (2008). Computer-vs. paper-based tasks: Are they equivalent? *Ergonomics, 51*(9), 1352–1375. doi:10.1080/00140130802170387 PMID:18802819

Ogunjimi, M. O., Ayanwale, M. A., Oladele, J. I., Daramola, D. S., Jimoh, I. M., & Owolabi, H. O. (2021). Simulated Evidence of Computer Adaptive Test Length: Implications for High Stakes Assessment in Nigeria. *Journal of Higher Education Theory and Practice, 21*(2), 202–212. businesspress.com/JHETP/JHETP21-2/16_OladeleFinal.pdf

Okoye, R. O., & Nwafor, V. C. (2009). A Comparison of SSCE Questions Set by the West African Examinations Council and the National Examinations Council, Nigeria. *African Research Review, 3*(5). Advance online publication. doi:10.4314/afrrev.v3i5.51159

Oladele, J. I. (2022). Estimating Measurement Error in University Students' Work Experience Programme (SWEP) Assessment using Generalizability Theory: Implications for Transdisciplinarity in Engineering Training. *Transdisciplinary Journal of Engineering & Science, 13*. Advance online publication. doi:10.22545/2022/00185

Oladele, J. I. (2022). Review of FastTest for Electronic Item Banking for Standardised Assessments: Implications for the Fourth Industrial Revolution and Covid-19 interjections. *Journal of Research and Reviews in Social sciences Pakistan, 5*(1). https://journal.kinnaird.edu.pk/online-first/

Oladele, J. I., Ayanwale, M. A., & Owolabi, H. O. (2020). Paradigm Shifts in Computer Adaptive Testing in Nigeria in Terms of Simulated Evidence. *Journal of Social Sciences, 63*(1-3), 9–20. doi:10.31901/24566756.2020/63.1-3.2264

Oladele, J. I., Bamidele, S.T., Ndlovu, M., & Owolabi, H.O. (2022). Adoption of Computer Adaptive Testing for Standardized Educational Assessment: Case Studies from West and South Africa. *Qualitative Report.*

Oladele, J. I., Koledafe, O. S., & Daramola, D. S. (2021). Prospects for Online Instructional Delivery Using Google Classrooms: Implications for Higher Education in Sub-Sahara Africa. *Journal of Digital Learning and Education, 1*(3), 92–108. doi:10.52562/jdle.v1i3.227

Oladele, J. I., & Ndlovu, M. (2021). A Review of Standardised Assessment Development Procedure and Algorithms for Computer Adaptive Testing: Applications and Relevance for Fourth Industrial Revolution. *International Journal of Learning, Teaching and Educational Research, 20*(5), 1–17. Advance online publication. doi:10.26803/ijlter.20.5.1

Oladele, J. I., Ndlovu, M., & Spangenberg, E. D. (2022). Simulated computer adaptive testing Method Choices for ability estimation with empirical evidence. *The International Journal of Evaluation and Research in Education, 11*(3). https://ijere.iaescore.com/index.php/IJERE/issue/view/565

Oloyode assumes office at JAMB, commends Ojerinde for adopting CBT. (2016). *The Government Business Journal*. https://govbusinessjournal.ng/2016/08/08/oloyode-assumes-office-at-jamb-commends- ojerinde-for-adopting-cbt/

Oppl, S., Reisinger, F., Eckmaier, A., & Helm, C. (2017). A flexible online platform for computerised adaptive testing. *International Journal of Educational Technology in Higher Education, 14*(1), 1–21. doi:10.118641239-017-0039-0

Pelgrum, W. J. (2001). Obstacles to the integration of ICT in education: Results from a worldwide educational assessment. *Computers & Education, 37*(2), 163–178. doi:10.1016/S0360-1315(01)00045-8

Prensky, M. (2001). Digital natives, digital immigrants part 1. *On the Horizon, 9*(5), 1–6. doi:10.1108/10748120110424816

Prince, R. (2017). The relationship between school-leaving examinations and university entrance assessments: The case of the South African system. *Journal of Education (University of KwaZulu-Natal),* (70), 133-160. http://www.scielo.org.za/scielo.php?script=sci_arttext&pid=S2520-98682017000300007

Punch. (2021). *Hitches in the conduct of UTME, inexcusable*. Punch. https://punchng.com/hitches- in-the-conduct-of-utme-inexcusable/

Reynolds, M., Blackmore, C., Ison, R., Shah, R., & Wedlock, E. (2018). The role of systems thinking in the practice of implementing sustainable development goals. In *Handbook of sustainability science and research* (pp. 677–698). Springer. doi:10.1007/978-3-319-63007-6_42

Slycan Trust. (2021). *Issue Paper: Challenges and Opportunities for a Just Transition*. ReliefWeb. https://www.slycantrust.org/knowledge-resources/issues-paper-challenges-and-opportunities-for-a-just-transition

Surpass. (2019). *Computer Adaptive Testing: Background, benefits and case study of a large-scale national testing programme*. Surpass. https://surpass.com/news/2019/computer- adaptive-testing-background-benefits-and-case- study-of-a-large-scale-national-testing-programme/

Thomas, S. (2016). *Future Ready Learning: Reimagining the Role of Technology in Education*. 2016 National Education Technology Plan. Office of Educational Technology, US Department of Education. https://eric.ed.gov/?id=ED571884

Thompson, N. A. (2019). *What Is Computerized Adaptive Testing?* Assessment System Corporation. https://assess.com/what-is-computerized-adaptive-testing/

Thompson, N. A., & Weiss, D. A. (2011). A Framework for the Development of Computerised Adaptive Tests. *Practical Assessment, Research & Evaluation, 16*(1). Advance online publication. doi:10.7275/wqzt-9427

Ugwuegbe, U., Iloh, E. & Urama, N.E. (2018). *Meeting the 2030 SDG in Nigeria: The Role Of Entrepreneurship Development.* AfriHeritage Policy Brief No. 16.

UNESCO-Institute of Statistics. (2015). *Uganda National Examinations Board – Government*. http://nada.uis.unesco.org/nada/en/index.php/catalogue/105

University of Cape Town. (2022). *Centre for Educational Assessment (CEA).* http://www.ched.uct.ac.za/ched/cetap

Utrecht University. (2022). *Why transdisciplinary research?* https://www.uu.nl/en/research/transdisciplinary-field-guide/get-started/why-transdisciplinary-research

World Bank's World Development Report. (2016). *Digital Dividends.* Washington DC: International Bank for Reconstruction and Development/The World Bank.

World Economic Forum. (2015). *Future of Economic Progress: Why education is the key to sustainable development.* https://www.weforum.org/agenda/2015/05/why-education-is- the-key-to-sustainable-development/

Chapter 8
ICT Skills Training for the Deaf to Enhance Employment Prospects

Cosmas Boniface Mnyanyi
The Open University of Tanzania, Tanzania

ABSTRACT

The chapter is on ICT skills training for the deaf to enhance employability prospects to improve social-economic development. Deaf employment is a global issue. ICT skills training might reduce the challenge. Little is known about ICT skills training for the deaf. The author interviewed 5 parents and 15 ICT skills training for the deaf graduates at the Open University of Tanzania. Data were collected using an interview guide with support from an experienced sign language interpreter. Findings indicated that ICT skills training increased participation in learning, employment, networking, and social inclusion. However, they faced challenges related to community perception, resources availability, affordability, connectivity, funding, and availability of ICT skills training opportunities that met their special learning needs. Based on the results, people with disabilities have to learn ICT skills that meet their unique special needs to reduce the negative effects of the impact of disruptive technologies and employability in the 4th Industrial Revolution.

INTRODUCTION

Deaf employment is a global issue due to shortages of training opportunities that respond to their needs, including ICT skills training. Delayed, creation of ICT skills training for the deaf increases negative impact of the disruptive technologies on the socio-economic development (Melnyk, et al., 2019; Sineviciene, et al., 2021). With the implementation of inclusive education, it is not yet known how educators including the teachers can facilitate ICT skills training for the deaf to enhance their employability status in the 4th industrial revolution characterised by use of technology. In many cases people who are deaf use sign language interpreters and thus likely to increase burden to employers and reduce chances for employment. With ICT skills, a person who is deaf can communicate directly using ICT tools. The

DOI: 10.4018/978-1-6684-6873-9.ch008

paper contributes to Sustainable Development Goals (SDGs) 4 (quality education),8 (on decent work and economic growth), 9 (on industry, innovation and infrastructure), 10 (on reducing inequalities), and 17 (on partnerships for the goals). The paper also contributes to innovation toward ICT skills training Policy or practice implications including setting up ICT skill training centres for the deaf to improve their chances of accessing lifelong learning opportunities for increasing employability chances.

The Open University of Tanzania started ICT skills training for the deaf in 2015 with a view to create opportunities for ICT skills training and improve access to on line job-seeking skills. Persons who are deaf face challenges related to communication as they use sign language and less opportunities are availed to learning sign language. With inclusion, we find a need to create inclusive social and working environment for all.

The chapter addresses importance of enhancing ICT skills training opportunities for enhancing employment prospects for the deaf to prepare them for the fourth industrial revolution responding to questions: what is the status on the availability of ICT skills training for the deaf? What are the strategies used to facilitate ICT skills training for deaf for enhancing their employability status? What are the status of availability of *ICT infrastructure* to facilitate ICT skills training for the deaf?

BACKGROUND

Information, communication, and technology (ICT) skills training for the deaf people with disabilities is important for realizing employment, job creation and contributing to personal and national development (Ajrun, 2021; Enkhtsogt & Kim, 2018; Ngonyani & Mnyanyi, 2021; Thompson, 2018; Ullmann, et al., 2018). Delayed, creation of ICT skills training to persons who are deaf increases negative impact of the disruptive technologies on the socio-economic development related to personal freedom, reduced employment chances, loss of jobs, reduced participation in digital economy, increased illiteracy and reduced creativity in social network (Melnyk, et al., 2019; Muza & Debnath, 2021; Sineviciene, et al., 2021). According to WHO projections, approximately 2.5 billion individuals will have hearing loss by the year 2050, at least 700million of them would need rehabilitation services (WHO, 2021). Furthermore, the World Federation of the Deaf (WFD), an international non-governmental organization in 2013 estimated around 72 million deaf persons and that More than 80 percent of these 72 million people, resided in developing nations, where the government frequently has little knowledge of their needs. It is estimated that the number of people with disabilities is on the increase, accounting for about 15% of the population, indicating a need to have in place systems that support disability inclusion (World Health Organisation [WHO], 2011; WHO, 2018; Thomson, 2018).

Globally there are efforts to ensure accessibility to ICT technology for persons with disabilities like the emergency of artificial intelligence and development of applications that enable persons with disabilities to use technology (Borg & Larsson, 2011; Raja, 2016; Bjelčić & Švelec, 2019). Little is known about how deaf people access ICT skills training in Tanzania. It is unknown how teachers can facilitate ICT skill training and modify available ICT curricular to meet the needs of people with disabilities in the implementation of inclusive education in schools (Ngonyani & Mnyanyi, 2021). Nurturing ICT skills training for the deaf require adaptations in the curricular so it is made accessible. With the widespread use of ICT worldwide, there is a need to ensure everybody has an opportunity to learn and use it to improve their capability to participate in the global economy. Drawing on resource-based and dynamic capability theory, the deaf community has to be engaged in developing the capacity to use ICT skills to improve their employability and to gain competitive job performance (Khin & Ho, 2018).

The ICT assistive technology (ICT-AT) supports people with disabilities to create skills leading to independence, social integration, educational success, employment opportunities, and communication (Mavrou, et al., 2017; Kasesera, 2012; UNDESA 2012). According to Raja (2016), whereas ICT to non-disabled individuals makes things easier, for persons with disabilities makes things possible. People with disabilities face difficulties in accessing education and employment do face challenges related to communication; social skills; academic skills; vocational skills; and independent living skills (Parmenter, 2011; Kett, 2012). Lack of skills needed in the labour market makes people who are deaf vulnerable to poverty, which is the major obstacle to achieving most of the sustainable development goals. To break the digital divide, ICT skills training has to be integrated into school curricular implemented in inclusive education (Raja, 2016; AlSadrani, et al., 2020; Rodríguez-Abitia, et al., 2020; Pittman, Severino, et al., 2021). According to Mavrou, et al. (2017), there is a need to break barriers related to incompatibility of ICT technologies and insufficient ICT skills training opportunities for people with disabilities. In developing countries, including Tanzania, people with disabilities face challenges related to the availability of ICT skills training and unfriendly infrastructure for specific disabilities, for example, ICT sign language for the deaf (Al-Sarayrah et al., 2021; Ngonyani & Mnyanyi, 2021).

The Open University of Tanzania (OUT) delivers its teaching, learning, and research through the use of open and distance learning approaches and technologies. OUT is a government-owned university established under the Open University of Tanzania Act in 1992, which was repealed by the University Act in 2005. The Open University of Tanzania started enrolling people with visual impairment in 1997 and started an ICT skills training for people with visual impairment in 2011 with support from Sightsavers International and the Tanzania Education Authority (TEA). The university also started an ICT class for the deaf (2015) with support from Deaf Aid. The paper focus setting up ICT skill training centres for the deaf to improve their chances for jo skills training, learning online, or making an online job; providing a chance for the deaf to create job-related sign language to use when they learn so they thrive both in schools and in the community; using ICT skills training for job related skills and link deaf job seekers with employers. For enhancing deaf employability skills, the University hired a deaf and a sign language interpreter, for the two the deaf is the facilitators for the fellow deaf in the skills training sessions and the sign language interpreter supports the deaf facilitator and the non-deaf community when communicating with the deaf community. The intervention broke the communication barriers between the deaf and the blind communities after all had ICT skills training and can communicate using emails and social media.

People With Disabilities' Employment Status

The capacity of individuals with disabilities to uphold a satisfactory quality of life for themselves and their families is significantly reliant on their employment status. Furthermore, their ability to engage fully in society is influenced by this crucial factor. The concept of work is a fundamental aspect of human existence, and in numerous cultures, the capacity to engage in work is regarded as a crucial means through which individuals can offer their unique contributions to their respective societies.

According to the World Health Organization (WHO) and Word Bank report on disability (2011), people with disabilities have the right to work on an equal basis with others; this includes the opportunity to earn a living by working freely chosen or accepted in an open, inclusive, and accessible labour market and work environment. The question then is how we make a work environment accessible to People with disabilities, especially in developing countries where there are shortages of resources and inadequate ICT skills training opportunities. According to Kasesera (2012), disability is associated with the exclusion of people with disabilities from the rest of society due to various cultural attitudes, perceptions, and environmental factors. It is a common phenomenon, especially in developing countries, that People with disabilities are on the increase (NBS, 2008; Mnyanyi, 2014) due to inadequate health care systems and opportunities to access education, economic, and social services. The increase of people with disabilities in developing countries calls for creating more skill training opportunities for People with disabilities so they can become independent and included in social and economic activities. Stainton et al. (2006) pointed insufficient training and relatively low educational levels, a lack of accessible transportation, employer discrimination, and disincentives to employment resulting from income and disability support programs, among other things, prevent the recruitment of people with disabilities including the deaf into social economic programs and employment sectors.

According to the Human Rights Report (2012) people living with disabilities in Tanzania face challenges related to shortages of universal access in structural buildings, People with disabilities living in extreme poverty, the high unemployment rate among People with disabilities, and poor provisions of education and health services. In Tanzania, people with disabilities experience challenges related to access to education (Mkumbo, 2008), access to health services (Kweka, 2010), and access to employment (Edwards, Rentschler, Fujimoto & Le, 2010; Morwane,2021) and are mostly poor. One way to improve the situation of People with disabilities is to promote their rights to employment opportunities (Heyer, 2008) through skills development strategies, vocational rehabilitation, and quota registration or anti-discrimination legislation. Strategies for promoting the rights of people with disabilities are critical, not only in terms of their economic rights, but also of their broader social and political rights, which are inextricably linked to economic empowerment (ILO, 2004).

In Tanzania, the Disability Survey 2008 indicated that nine percent of children with disabilities under the age of 18 years had no father, 1.8 percent had no mother, and 1.3 percent had no both parents; about half of PWDs aged 15 years and above reported having problems with the availability of information in accessible format; fifty percent of children with disabilities were either born with disabilities or acquired before the age of one year; and two percent of children with disabilities were using assistive devices. The facts presented in the Disability Survey 2008 indicate that people with disabilities face challenges in accessing social services, including education that would lead to skills training to improve their quality of life. According to WHO (2011), "disability is the umbrella term for impairments, activity limitations, and participation restrictions, referring to the negative aspects of the interaction between an individual (with a health condition) and their contextual factors (environmental and personal factors). Disability affects 7.8 percent of Tanzania's population (Mnyanyi, 2014; National Bureau of Statistics, 2008).

Disability worldwide, including in Tanzania, is on the increase, necessitating the development of strategies to best support people with disabilities. According to a national survey on disability in Tanzania in 2008, only 3.1 percent of households headed by people with disabilities indicated that people with disabilities had no problems on finding jobs. People with disabilities face widespread barriers to accessing services in health care (including rehabilitation), education, transport, and employment (WHO 2012). There are many barriers in society that make people with disabilities seem low-class because they can't live the way they want to; they do not have a high enough level of education; they do not have a job; they don't have a lot of money; and they have restrictions on what they can do in their lives, making them more dependent.

People With Disabilities' Transition to Work

There is still a mismatch between vocational training and the labour market, with far more effects for people with disabilities, as these People are often taught skills thought to be appropriate to them, such as craft work, with limited scope for business expansion, rather than those skills linked to specific labour market requirements (Alpha, et al., 2021; Kett, 2012). The challenges to increasing access to employment for People with disabilities are a result of the paucity of opportunities (including education, training, and employment) as well as a lack of expectations (by themselves and others) and a lack of support mechanisms for people with disabilities (Kett, 2012). One of the strategies to empower people with disabilities is to create equal opportunities in employment that require training them in employable skills. According to Turmusani (2012), employability (ability to obtain, maintain, and retain employment) does inform labor market policy, determining its size, operation, and future direction linked to employment and labour market policies, supply and demand.

According to Tororei (2009) and the European Agency for Development in Special Needs Education (EADSNE) report (2002), factors influencing transition from skills training to work include issues related to policy implementation; the involvement of students (and their families); guidance; the use of Individual Plans (IEP); and cooperation and collaboration between stakeholders. This is also the case in developing countries, including Tanzania. There are policies that are not implemented, resulting in poor stakeholders' involvement. For example, in Tanzania we have the Education and Training Policy 1995; Education and Training Policy 2014; the Disability Policy 2004; Disability Act (2010); and the Employment Act (2008. Yet, very few people with disabilities have access to skills training that enhance access to employment, self-employment and participate in creating employment opportunities.

In the Tanzania employment Act, one of the specific objectives is to "Promote equal access to employment opportunities and resources endowments for marginalized and vulnerable groups, including women, youth and People with Disabilities (PWDs)" (URT, 2008). Within the document a policy statement of the objective 3 states "The government in collaboration with other stakeholders will educate and establish capacity building programmes for vulnerable and marginalized groups including with disabilities, women and youth to enable them participate fully in productive activities". Regardless of having legislation that protects against discrimination in employment in Tanzania yet few people with disabilities are employed (Tororei, 2009). This calls for stakeholders to create skills development opportunities including ICT skills training so that the deaf can get opportunity to learn skills that will enhance their chances of accessing employment in equal basis.

In accessing employment for all, there are a variety of models used to facilitate transition from schools to employment (including work placements, work experience, training schemes, and accreditation); the support available; networks; as well as policy measures. These models cannot be used without the skills of people with disabilities having those skills related to needed job skills. According to Freedman (2008) and Tripney, et al. (2019), employment challenges for people with disabilities are more common in low- and middle-income countries due to a lack of access to basic education, vocational skills training, and/or higher education opportunities.

ICT for the Deaf

Literature indicates people who are deaf face challenges related to how to meet their learning demands, time, technological issues, lack of connectivity, and digital devices (Makeshine et al., 2021). Researchers proposed some solutions to increase efficiency, effectiveness, helpfulness, and learnability among deaf individuals like translation of text into sign-language (Al-Sarayrah et al., 2021). According to Yeratziotis and Van Greunen (2013) deaf community face challenges in accessing ICT as a result of challenges related to user interface design for the Deaf, e-learning multimedia, sign language and literacy levels. In developing countries, including Tanzania, deaf community is facing challenges of having low access to ICT skills training. As a means to increase access to ICT skills, one option was to use same ICT tools without additional costs so as to create inclusion at the Open University of Tanzania (OUT).

ICT for the deaf at OUT started in April 2015 with support from Deaf Aid. In the first ICT training, OUT facilitates ICT training for people who are visually impaired and those who are deaf. For the deaf, they follow the CISCO curriculum. As such, they are trained in both the use of ICT tools and maintenance. Upon completion of the course, deaf people are expected to be able to troubleshoot and repair personal computers, at the same time being able to use ICT. Selection of students to join the course is based on only one criterion: that they are deaf. The choice of the selection based on disability only takes account of access to education for people with disabilities being so low and that those who manage to enter the education cycle do not have the necessary support and thus end up failing to master the curriculum content.

METHOD

The study used a hermeneutic phenomenological approach to capture the participants' narrative accounts, which reflects how they interpret and express their experiences, nature, and meaning through interviews (Kafle, 2011; Finlay, 2009). All participants had no employment and or attachment to a working place. None of the deaf youth had attended ICT skills training program. Data were collected at the Open University of Tanzania (OUT) in the Assistive Special Technology Unit (ASTU). Approval was sought to the OUT research and publications unit. Participants were studying at the OUT -ASTU, the ASTU at OUT runs an ICT skills laboratory for the deaf. The ICT laboratory for the deaf started in 2015. Participants were purposefully selected. The condition was that one must have participated in ICT skills training at the Open University of Tanzania. A total of 20 people with hearing impairment were interviewed. Of whom, 15 were people who are deaf and 5 were parents of youth who are deaf. Of the 15 people who are deaf, 6 had completed initial training and were attached to employers for their industrial training. Data collection was conducted through face-to-face interviews with support of a sign language interpreter and analysed using content analysis.

FINDINGS AND DISCUSSION

Participants had mixed views with regard to ICT skills training opportunities for enhancing people who are deaf employability status. Participants talked about the availability of ICT skills training opportunities, which can be described as the *availability of ICT skills training opportunities*. There were participants who talked about how they can be facilitated, reflecting their diversity, which can be termed *capacity building* for ICT skills training for people who are deaf facilitators. On the other hand, participants talked about the availability of *ICT infrastructure* and *ICT content* reflecting the diverse needs of participants and how content can be delivered to people who are deaf. This can be termed *communicatio*n. Similarly, participants talked about challenges and strategies to enhance ICT skills training opportunities.

Availability of ICT Skill Training Opportunities

Participants talked about the availability of ICT skills training, reflecting on efforts made during the early 21st century where ICT skills training opportunities on how to use computers were made accessible to the community (Mnyanyi, Mbwette & Bakari, 2010). People with disabilities had qualitatively different views on the availability of skills training opportunities because fewer efforts were made to ensure people with disabilities access ICT classes; there was a lack of awareness in the community; and there was a shortage of information about the availability of skills training opportunities. With regard to community awareness, participants talked about the belief systems that people with disabilities, especially the deaf, cannot learn ICT.

I had no idea that Tanzania offered ICT training for deaf people. I wasn't certain that I could learn, either. I informed my parents what I learned from my pal. Despite my parents' advice to stay away from the training, I chose to enrol in the ICT course. I can now use a computer and a phone thanks to my ICT training. I have the skills necessary to get a job. (Resp1: Deaf)

I got a chance to be trained in ICT in Kenya at Deaf Aid. In Tanzania, there was no opportunity for the deaf to learn ICT. I am happy that now at OUT, one can learn ICT skills for the deaf. I was happier to find that I became a teacher for my fellow deaf students. I am so proud to find a class where a deaf teacher facilitates ICT skills training for fellow deaf people. (Resp2: Deaf)

People who are deaf had an opinion on what they experienced during the teaching and learning process at the Open University of Tanzania. All respondents originally believed learning would be difficult and that they could not perform. With time, after had a session of creating ICT sign language (https://www.out.ac.tz//vis/#) to use during their training, they found themselves capable of learning ICT skills and computer application software. The deaf, they had a deaf ICT skills training facilitator supported by a sign language interpreter during development of ICT sign language. Later the sessions were facilitated by the deaf ICT skills training facilitator.

When I heard about ICT skills, I found it something very difficult and special for some people. When I saw a laptop or a computer, initially, I was afraid to touch it, thinking that I could destroy it. But when I started learning, I discovered ICT is normal and I can use, repair, and troubleshoot problems on computers. I feel ICT is a tool for making all people feel happy and communicate. I can now send email, use Facebook and even do online exams. I am now doing an internship at a big company, TTCL. I am so comfortable. (Resp 6: Deaf)

ICT skills training requires encouragement and a role model. People with disabilities have few role models that can be used to enhance their likelihood of enrolling in ICT skills training classes.

Skills Development for the Deaf

Respondents indicated most people who are deaf and unable to use ICT had less opportunity to find jobs. The reason brought was that jobs are advertised online and that they do not have the ICT skills to access the online jobs. According to Hall (2019) deaf students face challenges when placed in an environment with less use of sign-language. Most of the work environment do not use sign language as deaf find it challenging to decode a language in the absence of linguistic guidance (Braithwaite, 2015). Parents of children who are deaf were unsure of the job market acceptance for their children. Parents in this study also stated that they were unaware of the places where their children could enrol to learn job market skills; ICT skills training; they faced difficulties with fee payment; accommodation payments; and the availability of support staff during the teaching and learning process.

There is a challenge about where to enroll our people with disabilities for skills training. In my case, I thank TBC1, which had a special programme for people with disabilities called "Pambazuko". I think there is a need to disseminate information about the availability of ICT skills training. Above all, it is only at OUT in Dar es Salaam. What about those living in different regions? There is a need, therefore, to create accommodation for people with disabilities so that many can benefit. As OUT is in all regions in Tanzania, there is a need to provide such services in regional centres. (Resp 1, Parent of Deaf Youth)

I would like my child to learn ICT skill at OUT but do not have money to pay for accommodation, transport, and fees. As I stay far from Dar Es Salaam. (Resp 5: Parent of Deaf youth)

Being a new experience to the deaf community in Tanzania, learning of ICT skills, where facilitators are also deaf, had some challenges about how one can obtain job placement. Most employers had a view that deaf community cannot work independently without the need of a sign language interpreter. It is until some employers accepted and started working with the deaf. To increase chances for employment, the University through the office of Assistive Special Technologies Unit (ASTU) arranged for placement by seeking places for industrial training and each student had a letter asking employers to employ the deaf youth after industrial training period. According to Prior and Conway (2008), deaf people face challenges to find and maintain jobs, even more difficulty if they have other types of disabilities apart from only being deaf.

I have decided my child will enrol at OUT to learn IT skills. But I am unsure of employment after graduation. I am not sure whether skills obtained at OUT will help my child get at least a job to improve his quality of life. It is a new experience for me as I have never heard of a deaf person learning ICT. Because it is a new experience, I think employers might also want to practice and see the results. I am not sure about how my child will be supported in the job environment. (Respondent 2: Parent of a Deaf youth)

I have learned skills in computer maintenance, but when seeking a job, employers are unsure that I can do the job. Since I got trained at OUT, I have not found a place to work. If any jobs for PC maintenance are announced publicly, I can apply. I have a communication challenge to starting my own business. I am deaf. (Resp 7: Deaf)

In this case, one can say that people with disabilities face challenges related to participation. In most cases, challenges to employment are not related to their impairment but because of a lack of information about job availability, inadequate training and comparatively low education levels, lack of accessible transportation, and employer awareness about disability challenges (Parmenter, 2011). Respondents talked about how ICT can prepare them for the labour market as most people had a belief that *skills* trained for people with disabilities are not related to the job market. Some had the view that vocational training centres for people with disabilities should be established and that the vocational training curriculum should focus on research findings on current job market skills.

I am happy that my child has been accepted to study an ICT course at OUT. It is my expectation that the skills he obtains will help him advance further. You know, ICT is everything. But I am not sure that skills needed for employment purposes are known. (Resp 3: parent of a deaf youth)

Learning ICT was an avenue to deaf inclusion at workplace. The ICT skills with PC maintenance skills, made deaf people to employed as the company or any employer would use emails and other forms of online communication to give instructions to employees.

I got a job at Company A, when I submitted an introduction letter from OUT. They read and later decided to give me a PC that was not working. I repaired the PC, and the boss decided that I can start working with him. When I started working at Company A, I was not sure that I could perform. I received support from my supervisors and later continued working very well. Good supervisors will encourage people with disabilities to work better. At Company A, I have my own PC. My supervisor sends me job schedule through email what I should perform and at the end of the day I report back. (Resp 12: Deaf)

For research institutions, there is a need to support people with disabilities in employment through designing vocational skills needed in the job market and having programmes to support employers in designing accessible environments. At the same time, vocational skills for people with disabilities should also include training related to independent living and social skills (Riches, et al., 2018; Blackman & Maynard, 2009). These findings suggest that when improving ICT skills training for people with disabilities, the computing, communication, content, and capacity building (4Cs in ICT) (Mavrou et al., 2017) must be improved. Within the 4Cs, the three pose challenges as little is known with regard to communication, content, and capacity building. In the case of communication, the challenge is how to facilitate learning, as Bisanda (2016) asserts that communication barriers pose challenges to ICT skills training for the deaf. When people with disabilities are hired for work, they have proven to have high retention rates; comply with organizational goals; are highly motivated; have low sickness absence; and increase work morally (Agale, 2017; Dewson et al., 2005).

Strategies to Increase ICT Skills Training and Learning Opportunities for the Deaf

Respondents had different views on supporting individuals with disabilities in their skills development. There are some who commented to establish courses related to skills development for people with disabilities; create sheltered employment; peer work relations; and train employers, as seen in Table 1.

For increasing employability chances for the deaf, issues related to government intervention, awareness creation to the public, employer perceptions and acceptability, training institutions' awareness of disability, and linking employers and people with disability have to be addressed. According to Omar et al. (2022), human capacity is the most overlooked, hence producing a challenge on how training can be created and implemented to empower people who are deaf and those with other disabilities. These concerns are linked to the four Cs of ICT: computing, communications, content, and human capacity (Mavrou et al., 2017). The results show that it is hard to help deaf people if you believe in resource-

Table 1. Proposed strategies to enhance skills training for people with disabilities (N=15)

Proposed Strategy	N	%
Establish ICT skills training centres for people who are deaf	10	67%
Have sheltered employment (learn skills while working)	8	53%
Use people with disabilities in skills training as facilitators	9	60%
Train employers on how to support people with disabilities	12	80%
Provide internship for the deaf in workplaces	10	67%
Create awareness to skills training providers to include the deaf	12	80%
Create awareness to the community on availability of skills training opportunities for people with disabilities	15	100%
Linking the deaf jobseekers with employers	10	67%
Provide the deaf with the on-job support	5	33%
Improved communication between the service providers and families	10	67%
Government intervention and support in establishing skills development courses for people with disabilities	15	100%

Source: Field work (2022)

based theory, which says that a company's success is due to unique, rare, and hard to copy resources (Jurado-Caraballo, et al., 2022; Miethlich & Oldenburg, 2019). People who are deaf needs sign-language interpretation experts. On the other hand, with use of ICT deaf people can work well without a need of sing language interpreter. There is a need to create ICT skill training for the deaf so we increase their chance of being employed, establish their own business and or participate in online learning.

FUTURE RESEARCH DIRECTIONS

With glowing use of ICT in all aspects of life, deaf community, if not given opportunity for ICT skills training are likely to be face challenges in socio-economic development. Rarely one finds an opportunity for ICT skills training for the deaf. The ICT skills training for the deaf is one of the impacts of disruptive technologies on the socio-economic development as increases participation chances to the deaf community that faces challenges in improving quality of life through skills training and employment. The chapter calls for stakeholders to increase funding that will enhance ICT skills training opportunities for the deaf as an avenue for lifelong learning and updating job skills for improving their work performance. Similarly, the chapter calls the government, institutions and stakeholders to facilitate awareness campaign toward development of skills-based sign-language in vocational education institutions for enhancing access to skills training for the deaf including ICT sign language for training the deaf.

CONCLUSION

People Who are deaf like other people with disabilities represent a large proportion of unemployed people especially in developing countries. Results support resource-based theory and dynamic capability theory that link digital orientation and digital capability to digital innovation. In the case of resource use, commitment and limited capabilities impede digital transformation, more so to the deaf community who rarely in developing countries find an opportunity to learn ICT skills. With increasing use of online platforms for training and employment opportunities, there is a need to create ICT skills training for the deaf so they can participate in social and economic development. Challenges facing ICT skills training for the deaf are related to human, fiscal, communication, capacity building for facilitators, content and physical resources. The study calls for government intervention by refining policies and practice guidelines in order to increase access to lifelong learning education, ICT skills training and online learning to enhance participation in decent jobs. Similarly, research suggests increased research on ICT skills training for people with disabilities if we are to create a community that embrace equity and equality among all members of the community.

ACKNOWLEDGMENT

This research was supported by the Open University of Tanzania.

REFERENCES

Agale, M. P. A. (2017). *Employers' perception about capabilities of persons with disabilities in the Kassena-Nankana municipality in the upper east region of Ghana* [Doctoral dissertation]. University of Education, Winneba.

Ajrun, N. (2021). Bridging the Digital Divide Affecting People with Disabilities in Malaysia. *International Journal of Disability Development and Education*, 1–13.

Al-Sarayrah, W., Al-Aiad, A., Habes, M., Elareshi, M., & Salloum, S. A. (2021). Improving the deaf and hard of hearing internet accessibility: JSL, text-into-sign language translator for Arabic. In *International Conference on Advanced Machine Learning Technologies and Applications* (pp. 456-468). Springer. 10.1007/978-3-030-69717-4_43

Alpha, K., Onsoti, N., & Kituyi, A. (2021). The Project Planning and Implementation in Rwanda National Union of Deaf Project Kicukiro District. *Journal of Advance Research in Business Management and Accounting*, *7*(4), 1–15. doi:10.53555/nnbma.v7i4.976

AlSadrani, B., Alzyoudi, M., Alsheikh, N., & Elshazly, E. E. (2020). The digital divide in inclusive classrooms. *International Journal of Learning, Teaching and Educational Research*, *19*(3), 69–85. doi:10.26803/ijlter.19.3.5

Bisanda, E. T. (2016). Empowering learners for effective open and distance learning. In *Third Open and Distance Learning Conference in Namibia* (p. 8). Academic Press.

Bjelčić, N., & Švelec, D. (2019). New perspectives for people with special needs according the development of new generation ICT technologies. In *2019 42nd International Convention on Information and Communication Technology, Electronics and Microelectronics (MIPRO)* (pp. 392-397). IEEE.

Blackman, S., & Maynard, D. M. (2009). In Their Own Words: Exploring the Phenomenological Field of a Sample of Employed Persons Who Are Deaf in Barbados. *International Journal of Disability Management Research*, *4*(1), 12–18. doi:10.1375/jdmr.4.1.12

Borg, J., Larsson, S., & Östergren, P.-O. (2011). The right to assistive technology: For whom, for what, and by whom? *Disability & Society*, *26*(2), 151–167. doi:10.1080/09687599.2011.543862

Braithwaite, B. (2015). Deaf perspectives on deaf education: An ethnographic study from Trinidad and Tobago. *Caribbean Educ. Res. J.*, *3*(1), 18–26.

Dewson, S., Ritchie, H., & Meager, N. (2005). *New Deal for Disabled People: Survey of employers.* Department for Work and Pensions Research Report No.301. DWP.

Edwards, D., Rentschler, R., Fujimoto, Y., & Le, H. (2010). Why has the rising economic tide failed to float the disability employment boat? A call to action: Business, community, government and people power. *The International Journal of Diversity in Organisations, Communities and Nations*, *10*(1), 117–127. doi:10.18848/1447-9532/CGP/v10i01/39810

Enkhtsogt, T. A., & Kim, Y. (2018). Major Principles of ICT Policy for Improving ICT Integration in Education for Students with Disabilities in Mongolia. *Asia-Pacific Collaborative Education Journal*, *14*(2), 21–32.

European Agency for Development in Special Needs Education. (2002). Transition from School to Employment: Main problems, issues and options faced by students with special educational needs in 16 European countries. Summary Report October 2002. Brussels: EADSNE.

Finlay, L. (2009). Debating phenomenological research. *Phenomenology & Practice*, *3*(1), 6–25. doi:10.29173/pandpr19818

Freedman, D. H. (2008). *Improving skills and productivity of disadvantaged youth.* ILO Working Paper.

Hall, M. L., Hall, W. C., & Caselli, N. K. (2019). Deaf children need language, not (just) speech. *First Language*, *39*(4), 367–395. doi:10.1177/0142723719834102

Heyer, K. (2008). Rights or quotas? The ADA as a model for disability rights. In L. B. Neilsen & R. L. Nelson (Eds.), *Handbook of employment discrimination research III* (pp. 237–257). Springer.

ILO. (2004). *URT: Employment of People with Disabilities-The Impact of Legislation in East Africa*. ILO.

Jurado-Caraballo, M. Á., Quintana-García, C., & Rodríguez-Fernández, M. (2022). Trends and opportunities in research on disability and work: An interdisciplinary perspective. *Business Research Quarterly*, *25*(4), 366–388. doi:10.1177/2340944420972715

Kafle, N. P. (2011). Hermeneutic phenomenological research method simplified. *Bodhi: An Interdisciplinary Journal*, *5*(1), 181–200.

Kasesera, J. (2012). Assessing the impact of mainstream vocational training in developing capabilities of people with and without disabilities. A case of Danhiko Training Institution in Harare, Zimbabwe. Institute of Social Studies.

Kett, M. (2012). *Skills development for youth living with disabilities in four developing countries. Paper commissioned for the EFA Global Monitoring Report 2012, Youth and skills: Putting education to work.* UNESCO.

Khin, S., & Ho, T. C. (2018). Digital technology, digital capability and organizational performance: A mediating role of digital innovation. *International Journal of Innovation Science*. Advance online publication. doi:10.1108/IJIS-08-2018-0083

Kweka, J. (2010). *Employment of people with disabilities in Dar es Salaam Tanzania: An assessment of the proportion of people with disabilities in the workplace*. Retrieved on August 1, 2022 from: http://www.radardevelopment.com/fileadmin/downloads/CCBRT_Disability_Employment_Survey.pdf

Loyilane, P. (2008). *We should be given a chance: Identifying barriers and enablers from disabled people's employment in the office of the Premier of the Eastern Cape Provincial Government, South Africa* [Unpublished Masters Thesis]. University of Cape Town.

Maebara, K., Yamaguchi, A., Suzuki, T., & Imai, A. (2022). A Qualitative Study on The Function of Information and Communication Technology Utilization in Teaching Students with Intellectual Disabilities: Implications for Techniques of Teaching/Job Coaching. *Journal of Intellectual Disability-Diagnosis and Treatment*, *10*(1), 13–20. doi:10.6000/2292-2598.2022.10.01.2

Makeshine, S., Viriyavejak, C., & Sovajassatakul, T. (2021). The impact of Distance Learning for Deaf and Hard of Hearing students during the COVID-19 pandemic in Thailand. In T. Bastiaens (Ed.), Proceedings of EdMedia + Innovate Learning (pp. 7-14). Association for the Advancement of Computing in Education (AACE).

Mavrou, K., Meletiou-Mavrotheris, M., Kärki, A., Sallinen, M., & Hoogerwerf, E. J. (2017). Opportunities and challenges related to ICT and ICT-AT use by people with disabilities: An explorative study into factors that impact on the digital divide. *Technology and Disability*, *29*(1-2), 63–75. doi:10.3233/TAD-170174

Melnyk, L., Dehtyarova, I., Kubatko, O., Karintseva, O., & Derykolenko, A. (2019). Disruptive technologies for the transition of digital economies towards sustainability. *Економічний часопис-XXI*, (9-10), 22-30.

Miethlich, B., & Oldenburg, A. G. (2019). The employment of persons with disabilities as a strategic asset: A resource-based-view using the value-rarity-imitability-organization (VRIO) framework. *Journal of Eastern Europe Research in Business and Economics*, *1*, 1–13. doi:10.5171/2019.667087

Mkumbo, K. (2008). *Do children with disabilities have equal access to education? A research report on accessibility to education for children with disabilities in Tanzanian schools*. Retrieved on November 1, 2013 from: http://www.hakielimu.org/hakielimu/documents/document131Children_disabilities.pdf

Mnyanyi, C. B. (2014). Changing Teachers' Practices in Regular Schools Enrolling Children with Visual Impairment: An Action Research Project in Tanzania. Abo Akademi University Press.

Mnyanyi, C. B. F., Bakari, J., & Mbwette, T. S. A. (2010). *Implementing E-learning in Higher Open and Distance Learning Institutions in Developing Countries: The Experience of the Open University of Tanzania*. Paper presented at the 5th MIT LINC 2010 Conference, Boston, MA.

Morwane, R. E., Dada, S., & Bornman, J. (2021). Barriers to and facilitators of employment of persons with disabilities in low-and middle-income countries: A scoping review. *African Journal of Disability*, *10*, 10. doi:10.4102/ajod.v10i0.833 PMID:34230882

Muza, O., & Debnath, R. (2021). Disruptive innovation for inclusive renewable policy in sub-Saharan Africa: A social shaping of technology analysis of appliance uptake in Rwanda. *Renewable Energy*, *168*, 896–912. doi:10.1016/j.renene.2020.12.091 PMID:33942003

National Bureau of Statistics. (2008). *Tanzania disability survey*. Dar es Salaam: NBS.

Ngonyani, J., & Mnyanyi, C. (2021). Assessing the relevance of assistive technologies for people with disabilities in higher learning institutions: A case of university of Dar es salaam in Tanzania. *European Journal of Special Education Research*, *7*(2). Advance online publication. doi:10.46827/ejse.v7i2.3712

Omar, M. K., Puad, M. H. M., Yaakub, M., & Muslim, M. (2022). Employability Skills Requirement for People with Disability (PWD) Job Success. *Specialusis Ugdymas*, *2*(43), 367–385.

Parmenter, T. R. (2011). *Promoting training and employment opportunities for people with intellectual disabilities: international experience*. ILO.

Pittman, J., Severino, L., DeCarlo-Tecce, M. J., & Kiosoglous, C. (2021). An action research case study: Digital equity and educational inclusion during an emergent COVID-19 divide. *Journal for Multicultural Education*, *15*(1), 68–84. doi:10.1108/JME-09-2020-0099

Prior, S., & Conway, M. (2008). 'All the Doors are Closing': National Deaf Services Users' Thoughts and Views on Deafness, Mental Health and Employment. *British Journal of Occupational Therapy*, *71*(3), 95–102. doi:10.1177/030802260807100304

Raja, D. S. (2016). *Bridging the disability divide through digital technologies. Background paper for the World Development report*. The World Bank.

Riches, V., Gadow, F., & MacDonald, J. (2018). Transition from university to employment. In *People with intellectual disability experiencing university life* (pp. 255–266). Brill.

Rodríguez-Abitia, G., Martínez-Pérez, S., Ramirez-Montoya, M. S., & Lopez-Caudana, E. (2020). Digital gap in universities and challenges for quality education: A diagnostic study in Mexico and Spain. *Sustainability (Basel)*, *12*(21), 9069. doi:10.3390u12219069

Sineviciene, L., Hens, L., Kubatko, O., Melnyk, L., Dehtyarova, I., & Fedyna, S. (2021). Socio-economic and cultural effects of disruptive industrial technologies for sustainable development. *International Journal of Global Energy Issues*, *43*(2-3), 284–305. doi:10.1504/IJGEI.2021.115150

Thompson, S. (2018). Mobile Technology and Inclusion of Persons with Disabilities. K4D Emerging Issues Report. Brighton, UK: Institute of Development Studies.

Tororei, K. (2009). The right to work: A strategy for addressing the invisibility of people with disability. *Disability Studies Quarterly*, *29*(4). Advance online publication. doi:10.18061/dsq.v29i4.973

Tripney, J., Hogrebe, N., Schmidt, E., Vigurs, C., & Stewart, R. (2019). Employment supports for adults with disabilities in low-and middle-income countries: A Campbell systematic review. *Research on Social Work Practice*, *29*(3), 243–255. doi:10.1177/1049731517715316

Turmusani, M. (2012). The employability of people with disabilities and groups at risk in enterprises of skills development: International Perspective of Convention on the Rights of People with Disabilities (CRDP). *Revue Développement humain, handicap et changement social, 20*(3), 7-24.

Ullmann, H., Jones, F., Williams, R. C., & Williams, D. (2018). *Information and communications technologies for the inclusion and empowerment of people with disabilities in Latin America and the Caribbean*. Academic Press.

UNDESA. (2012). *Building a better tomorrow: the voices of young people with disabilities*. Department of Economic and Social Affairs.

World Health Organization. (2018). *Deafness and hearing loss*. WHO.

World Health Organization. (2021). *World Report on hearing*. WHO.

World Health Organization & World Bank. (2011). *World report on disability 2011*. World Health Organization.

Yeratziotis, G., & Van Greunen, D. (2013). *Making ICT accessible for the deaf. In 2013 IST-Africa Conference & Exhibition*. IEEE.

Chapter 9
Impact of Disruptive Technologies on the Socioeconomic Development of Emerging Countries:
Digital Tech and Resources for Learning Under Lockdown

Solomon Odei-Appiah
Ghana Institute of Management and Public Administration, Ghana

ABSTRACT

In the COVID-19 pandemic crisis, educational institutions had to be temporarily shut down by their respective governments around the world in order to contain the spread of the virus. The pandemic globally engendered new ways of teaching and learning amidst the restrictions. Schools in emerging countries are mostly dependent on the traditional face-to-face method of teaching and learning and barely had any substantial experience in virtual education prior to the outbreak. Moreover, many countries lack adequate infrastructure for ICTs and internet usage. Nonetheless, these countries also adopted various digital technologies for virtual teaching and learning. This chapter discusses digital technologies and resources for learning in emerging countries under lockdown and proposes a research model for evaluating their impact amidst the effects of the digital divide.

INTRODUCTION

During the outbreak of the COVID-19 pandemic, many preventive measures which were non-medicinal were recommended. These included self-isolation, social distancing and a high level of personal hygiene paramount of which is frequent hand washing. In addition to these measures, educational institutions had to be temporarily shut down by their respective governments all around the world in order to con-

DOI: 10.4018/978-1-6684-6873-9.ch009

tain the spread of the virus (Bayham & Fenichel, 2020; Remuzzi & Remuzzi, 2020; Viner et al., 2020). This happens to be not the first time that schools had to be closed amidst a pandemic. The 1918 to 1919 Spanish flu, the 1958 Asian flu, the Hong Kong originated pandemic flu in 1968, the outbreak of Swine flu in USA and Mexico in 2009, and the 2014 Ebola disease, all resulted in school closures in affected parts of the world. During the spread of infectious diseases, restriction of movements and for that matter closure of schools have been found to be an effective way to slow down the spread of the disease (Oloyede et al., 2022).

It is very likely for developing countries to suffer the impact of the pandemic the more with regards to disruption of educational processes (Mathrani et al., 2021). This is from the fact that from elementary to tertiary levels, most schools in Africa for instance are dependent on the traditional face-to-face method of teaching and barely have any substantial experience in virtual teaching prior to the outbreak of the pandemic.

Nevertheless, to protect students' health against the disease without compromising the educational process, reinforcement of infection control measures needs to be complemented with distance learning in the form of online learning to avoid crowding which fuels the spread of the virus. As a result, many schools in developing countries have also adopted various digital technologies used for virtual teaching and learning. In emerging countries, the efficacy of virtual teaching and learning can be influenced by a myriad of factors prominent of which is the digital divide (Mathrani et al., 2021) in addition to the socio-economic condition of the country and its people (Noor et al., 2022), skillsets and motivation of both teachers and learners, (Mehta et al., 2016; Towers et al., 2019) and many others.

Most developing countries were ranked the least in the 2017 edition of the ITU-IDI Telecommunication Infrastructure & Access Index (ITU, 2017). This is an indication of how disadvantaged such countries are regarding the digital divide. Though the digital divide negatively impacts emerging economies the most, majority of studies on the phenomenon are conducted in the developed world. The few digital divide studies with developing country contexts also suffer the limitation where the only key variable used to measure the phenomenon is access to ICT infrastructure (Bertot et al., 2011). Rahman (2015) therefore posits that using technological determinism to explain the digital divide is inadequate. It is therefore suggested that different dimensions be used to examine the digital divide rather than just the categorization into the "haves" and the "have-nots". Moreover, extant literature on teaching and learning technologies in the Covid-19 pandemic lack a focus on how multidimensional digital divide affects the use and impact of such technologies. This chapter fills these gaps by proposing a conceptual model for evaluating the use of digital technologies and resources for learning under lockdown in emerging countries. The next section provides an overview of the most common of such technologies and resources.

Overview of Digital Technologies for Online Teaching and Learning

Improvement in telecommunication networks over the years has given way to the successful development of web conferencing applications and solutions for business communications. Web conferencing is a multimedia communications system in which computer screens, individual applications or web contents can be shared among connected computers in real-time. Web conferencing can be used to support teamwork, organize and conduct seminars or business meetings, deliver lead presentations and provide customer-relation support. These functionalities enable for its use recently for conducting online teaching and learning (education). Some applications for web conferencing offer many other sophisticated features well-suited for real-time interactions between teachers and learners. These include whiteboarding, chat discussions, polling, annotating and others (Islam, 2019). With the use of the Internet and other electronic technologies, web conferencing provides a media space for thousands of participants across the world separated by distance and time to exchange ideas, knowledge or information. Though a web conference platform can be accessed through a web browser, downloading and installing the application client provides a better experience. Web conferencing is driven by the TCP/IP connections of the Internet. Early stages of web conferencing solutions only involved the exchange of text messages over the Internet until over time the integration of audio and eventually video was achieved (Alqurashi, 2019). Generally, web conferencing refers to different kinds of collaborative services including webcasts, webinars (web seminars) and peer-level web meetings provided on the Internet (Oloyede et al., 2022).

Webcasts

A webcast (contracted from 'web' and 'broadcast') refers to a broadcast over the Internet and it can be delivered either live or on-demand (Sun & Liu, 2019). As a form of web conferencing, a webcast integrates audio and video conferencing to transmit prerecorded or live events over the Internet using the streaming technology. The communication mode of a webcast is one-to-many and similar to the traditional TV and radio broadcast, its deployment is usually in a non-interactive context (Zamfir et al., 2022). A noteworthy difference between a webcast and the conventional TV and radio broadcast is its transmission over the Internet using media streaming technology. In webcasting there is usually a host or hosts and a large audience with the required multimedia application and devices to access the broadcast on the Internet though no interaction can happen between the two parties (Zoumenou et al., 2015). Webcasting can extensively be used by educational institutions especially universities which offer some form of distance learning (Das, 2021).

Webinars

A webinar (a blend of 'web' and 'seminar') is an interactive web-based seminar, lecture, teaching, workshop or meeting held virtually (Lieser, 2018) with its attendance exclusive to an online audience. This distinguishes a webinar from a webcast which involves the presence of a physical audience. As another category of web conferencing, there are many sophisticated features in a webinar and these include document/file sharing, white-barding, chat, polling, shared desktop, and others, making it particularly useful for teaching and learning. The basic design of a webinar enables unicast (one-to-one), broadcast or multicast (one-to-many), multi-peer (many-to-many) and anycast (many-to-one) forms of communications. It is considered as more collaborative given its use of interactive features for communication between the host(s) and audience (Lieser, 2018). In a webinar, the speaker or host can share PowerPoint presentations, web pages, videos and other multimedia content with the audience. Comprised of both visual and audio components, the visuals of a webinar can be shared using a web conferencing tool or browser. The broadcast of a webinar's audio portion is usually done through the speakers and media players of the audience's computer or through a telephone.

Selected Web Conferencing Solutions for Online Teaching and Learning

There are many different web conferencing solutions with some being more popular than others. Despite having varying costs and features, they can all be used for the various forms of communications be it

Unicast, Multicast and Anycast. Some come with more options and affordable features while others are considered more effective for teaching and learning than others. The selection and discussion of the web conferencing solutions here were based on their technical features, educational support, technical specifications, data rate requirements and use cases. These five criteria are considered necessary to ensure the effective use of these tools for teaching and learning (Pozo et al., 2021). During lockdown in the pandemic, most of these tools were offered for free and as such their cost was not necessarily included in the criteria.

Zoom

Zoom is provided by the Zoom Video Communications Inc. it is a tool that enables users to join webinars or meetings on the Internet with the aid of the zoom application on desktop, as well as the mobile app on Android, iOS and others. Aside video conferencing, zoom provides instant messaging, recording, voice calling and screen sharing (Robertson, 2020). Video sharing on the screen can happen between up to 49 participants at the same time while up to 1000 participants depending the chosen plan, can also join the meeting with any device. Both free and paid versions are available for use with the free version allowing only up to 40 minutes meeting time for multiple participants but allows for an unlimited number of meetings. The free version is the best option for those working solo with additional two or three people collocated. The Zoom Pro is good for those working with a small team with at least a member who works full-time or part-time remotely so there can be effective collaboration regardless of where the meeting is hosted. With this tier, hosts can create personal meeting IDs necessary for recurring meetings. It also allows the recording of meetings in the cloud or on users' devices and group meeting durations are pegged at 24 hours. For small to medium-sized businesses which hold regular meetings among multiple teams, the Zoom Business is the best option. Zoom Enterprise is best-suited for businesses with thousand or more employees and it offers unlimited storage in the cloud for meeting recordings.

Zoom has a special educational package which enables users to chat during meetings. The data rate requirements for zoom are 800 kbps for upload and 1.0 Mbps for download of high-quality video. Operating systems that support zoom include the following and their later versions: Windows XP, Mac OS 10.7, Ubuntu 12.04, Oracle Linux 6.4 and others. Browsers like Chrome, Firefox, Edge and Safari work with zoom. The hardware requirements of systems that can run zoom are a minimum of 1 GHz processor speed and 4 GB RAM. Security features for zoom include encryption provided by its architecture for communication and content sharing (Oloyede et al., 2022). Moreover, users can be removed, kept in waiting rooms by the host, and meeting rooms can be locked and password protected.

Skype

As a communication tool, skype allows both audio and video conferencing, screen sharing, instant messaging and recording of meetings. Users can use skype on desktop computers, tablets, smart phones, smart watches and Xbox 1 game console via the Internet. Acquired in 2011 by Microsoft, skype can be used free of charge. Users need to register for a skype ID which will be required to contact other skype users. Up to 50 participants from anywhere can attend a meeting on skype with different devices. Skype offers services to enable users use tier accounts to make calls to mobile phones and landlines and also send SMS. However, the charging rate for this varies among countries. When users are offline, messages can be sent to them so they can be retrieved as soon as the user comes online. The desktop application can be installed on Windows, Linux and Mac OS while it can also be used on android, iOS, Nokia X and others. For educational purposes, skype is widely used by many teachers as well as students as it also provides services like Skype in the classroom. The bandwidth required for using skype is determined based on the number of participants and type of call. 30 kbps is required for both upload and download when just calling while 128 kbps (upload) and 4 Mbps (download) is needed for video calling among seven or more users. Without downloading the app, Skype cannot be used on web browsers and the system's lack of an end-to-end encrypted VoIP does not make it very secure (Das, 2021).

Google Classroom

This is a Google provided free web service for schools and universities. For the purpose of meeting classroom requirements, Google classroom provides the avenue for assignments and file sharing among teachers and students. Other Google services like Google Calendar, Google Drive, Gmail and Google documents are integrated. Students can be invited to the classroom through the institution's database or by using private codes. Up to 20 teachers can be allowed for one class while a class can be made of 1000 members comprising both teachers and students (Iftakhar, 2016). If members of a class or viewers belong to the same domain, they can perform live streaming and recordings can also be made to be saved on the Google drive. Google Classroom provides a feature where teachers can post announcements and students can then comment on them. It can be accessed not only through the web but also via devices running android and iOS. Google Classroom also allows the incorporation of YouTube videos.

CISCO Webex

Webex is a communication tool that offers audio conferencing, video conferencing, meeting, screen sharing, instant messaging and recording. It is considered as cost effective and up to 100 participants can be hosted on it for a video conference with its monthly price depending on requirements of the user. Webex also has a package purposely for education and classes (Webex, 2014). Participants can access the Webex platform using all kinds of devices and it is compatible with Windows XP, Mac 10.6 Snow Leopard and the later versions of these systems. Internet Explorer 8 and 9, Safari, Google Chrome and Mozilla 10 are some of the browsers Webex works on. It incorporates an end-to-end encryption service for security whiles it offers meeting passwords as well as data center security. Different features are offered to users based on their roles which include host, presenter, alternate host, attendee, site administrator and panelist (Webex, 2014).

GoToMeeting

Considered as user friendly (Oloyede et al., 2022), GoToMeeting is a web conferencing package which offers real-time collaboration, effective screen sharing, recordings between users, and the ability to broadcast the host's screen to others. Similar to most solutions, there are different packages and each has their offering. With the enterprise package, up to 3000 participants can be hosted for video conferencing. For some other packages, there are personal meeting rooms, high-definition video, and no limit on meeting time (Lipschutz, 2011). A user can choose to use either the device audio or a phone call and while in a meeting users can chat with each other. It works on devices running Android 2. And above, Windows XP and above, Mac OS Catalina (10.15) and Mac OS X 10.9. It requires a processor speed of 2 GHz and 2GB or more of RAM. For audio and video conferencing and screen sharing it requires a bandwidth of 700 kbps (Noll & Belur, 2018). Aside a security feature for locking meeting rooms, GoToMeeting provides an authentication based on Secure Socket Layer and an end-to-end encryption using the 128-bit Advanced Encryption Standard (AES). Participants have different access levels depending on whether they are an attendee, organizer, or a presenter (Pozo et al., 2021).

TeamViewer

Founded in Germany and taken over by Pemira in 2014, TeamViewer is noted for connecting and controlling remote devices and providing remote support. Every user has an ID and a password and these can be shared with other TeamViewers to allow them take control of the other's device (Drugarin et al., 2016). Different packages exist from the version to the paid one and these allow sessions lasting from three up to eight hours. Multiple conferencing solutions are provided by TeamViewer. Based on various hardware requirements and using VoIP, business calls can be made as well video conferencing. With the online meetings, communications can be established between for example teachers and learners, colleagues and customers. A secure and flexible file sharing feature is available as well as remote printing. A number of platforms support TeamViewer including Windows, Mac OS, Linux, Android and iOS. On Mac OS, many remote sessions can be run concurrently within browser tabs. For upload and download connections with TeamViewer, 1Mbit/s and 6Mbit/s is required respectively. Among other security features, it incorporates an end-to-end encryption using 256-bit AES and a two-factor authentication (Drugarin et al., 2016).

Google Hangouts

This is a communication tool from Google designed for keeping in touch with an individual or a group of people. Available functions include audio conferencing, video conferencing, recording, instant messaging and screen sharing. It can be used both on desktop or mobile devices and it is integrated into Gmail and Google+. It is compatible with multiple computing devices which when used, a chat history saved online allows for synchronization. An educational package is offered and 25 concurrent users can be allowed. It works on Windows, Mac OS, Ubuntu and Chrome. While it can be ran on both Android and iOS, it can easily be integrated into Google Chrome so that users need not to install a plugin which is required when using other browsers. Google products including Google voice, Google chat and Google Meet are integrated into Google Hangouts. For upload and download, it needs 256 and 512 kbps minimum respectively but for the best experience 900 kbps and 2 Mbps are recommended for more than two people on a call (Pozo et al., 2021). A number of security issues are raised in Google Hangouts because it doesn't provide end-to-end encryption although hangout messages are encrypted in addition to messages in transit.

Google Meet

As part of the G-suite, Google offers Google Meet as its premium video conferencing solution. Google Meet was originally paid but was made available for free only recently due to the Covid-19 pandemic. Google Meet allows anyone to create and join high-quality video conferences with up to 250 people without limitations on meeting time. It allows chat, screen sharing and high-definition calls but unlike hangout, additional effects such as emojis or status messages are not permitted. The screen layout can be changed to see the current speaker or other users. Users can easily join meetings on Google Meet using either desktop computers or mobile devices. It shares the same security features, system requirements and others with Google Hangout.

Apache OpenMeetings

As an open source software from the Apache software foundation, OpenMeetings is another conferencing solution that offer audio and video conferencing, collaborative document editing, white board, meeting recording, screen sharing instant messaging, and other groupware tools. It is supported by the Red5 media server, flash and HTML5. Its open-source nature allows developers from across the world to collaborate on its development though in 2011 the main project moved to Russia. OpenMeetings is considered easy to use and the app needs to be installed for use (Oloyede et al., 2022). OpenMeetings allows between 50 and 100 users for engagement concurrently. Each user can have by default 2 up to about 20 personal rooms always exclusively accessible by that user. The dashboard provides buttons for entering those rooms. It can run on most of the widely used operating systems such as Windows, Linux and Mac OS. There is no end-to-end encryption and its open nature makes it suffer some security vulnerabilities.

Adobe Connect

This is a web conferencing tool from Adobe Inc. that offers audio and video conferencing, meeting recording, remote training, polling, screen sharing, breakout rooms, individual muting and instant messaging. The meeting rooms in Adobe connect are organized into 'pods' and every pod is designated to perform a specific role such as whiteboard, chat, note and others. It offers different packages for both free and paid plans with associated different levels of features. Up to 1500 participants can be hosted depending on the choice of plan. It is touted to be the most flexible and secure web conferencing tool with extensible features (Das, 2021). It allows customization so that users can have personalized layouts, pods and images making them design their own experience. Adobe connect also provides a mechanism for measuring the level of engagement of the audience using the simultaneous breakout and multiple chat rooms. A presenter and the host can have behind the scene collaborations during a live session. Educational packages are also available which enable holding of virtual classes consisting of up to 200 participants. However, the package for webinars can have only up to 100 users. The recommended bandwidth requirement for meeting attendees or participants is 256 kbps minimum. Platforms like Windows, Linux, Mac OS as well as mobile devices are compatible with Adobe connect and can run on major browsers like Chrome (Connect 2014). It does not offer end-to-end encryption though transit encryption is provided using the Transport Layer Security. Passwords stored on its database are also encrypted.

Digital Divide and Digital Learning in Developing Countries Under Lockdown

The digital divide refers to "the gap among individuals, households, and businesses at different socio-economic levels with regard to both their opportunities to access ICTs and their use of the Internet for a wide variety of activities" (ITU, 2017). It is characterized with imbalances which include physical access to ICT, resources and skills required for the effective use of such technologies (ITU, 2017). The imbalances in material access for example, can pertain to schools and homes regarding total number of devices, replacement of devices, licensing and related service subscription fees (van Deursen & van Dijk, 2018). Access to ICTs is linked to economic, social, technological and cultural contexts (Mishra et al., 2020). The level of purchasing power among individuals determine the range of technological devices they participate in, thus from devices with simple features to those with advanced ones (Mathrani et al., 2021). Given the uneven distribution of household income in developing countries, there is a significant gap between the 'haves' and 'have-nots' and unfortunately this undermines the educational choices of an individual (Mishra et al., 2020).

During the pandemic crisis in 2020, it was realized that digital education could serve as a potent enabler for teaching and learning during lockdown. However, indications from studies (Aristovnik et al., 2020; George, 2020) suggest that not only should digital education be considered as backup response to teaching and learning during school closures but also as complementary to traditional in-person approaches to education. Nevertheless, the digital divide and many other challenges threaten the impact of these initiatives.

A recent study by Iivari et al., (2020) highlights how various levels of digital divide were induced by COVID-19 regarding digital teaching/learning in developing country contexts. There were situations where a lot of families faced lack of access to digital devices, internet and applications for learning. In another breadth, teachers, students and parents had serious limitations in terms of skills and competencies for proper use of digital technologies and media. It is also reported by Mishra et al., (2020) that in spite of the many digital tools such as those described above (for example Zoom, Google Meet, Google Classroom), one tool that was mainly used by teachers was WhatsApp. According to the teachers, the preference for this application was due to limited digital infrastructure like slow or poor network connectivity, expensive internet data packages and electricity outages, and in addition, they were more familiar with the use of WhatsApp in their daily activities as compared to other applications.

Theoretical Foundation and Research Model

The use and impact of the digital technologies described above will be evaluated through the lens of the DeLone & McLean (D&M) IS success model. The model provides an in-depth understanding of information system effectiveness by defining and explaining quality dimensions and their inter-relationships and how they in turn influence perceived benefits (Delone & Mclean, 2003; Ondego & Moturi, 2016). The D&M model comprises of information quality, system quality, user satisfaction, usage and net benefits as the dimensions for measuring information system success. Nevertheless, this study's focus will be on usage and how it impacts net benefits. To assess the impact of the digital divide on the use of these digital teaching/learning technologies, this study adapts the Integrated Model of Digital Inequality which is a consolidation of the fragmented concepts and constructs of the digital divide (Yu et al. 2018). The model posits that there are three determinants of the digital divide and they are access, resources and forces (Yu et al. 2018). In the proposed research model of this study as illustrated in Figure 1, the three determinants of the digital divide are used as moderators of the use of educational digital technologies (EDT) given that those determinants are constituted by the resultant contributions of their sub-constituents based on their presence/absence and strength/weakness (MacKinnon, 2011).

Information system use or usage can be described as the rate, frequency and degree of actual use of a system by individuals or groups/organisations as opposed to relying on manual ways of performing their activities (Delone & Mclean, 2003). The use of an EDT refers to the degree and manner of the utilization of the technology's capabilities. The use of information systems have been investigated in different

Figure 1. Proposed research model

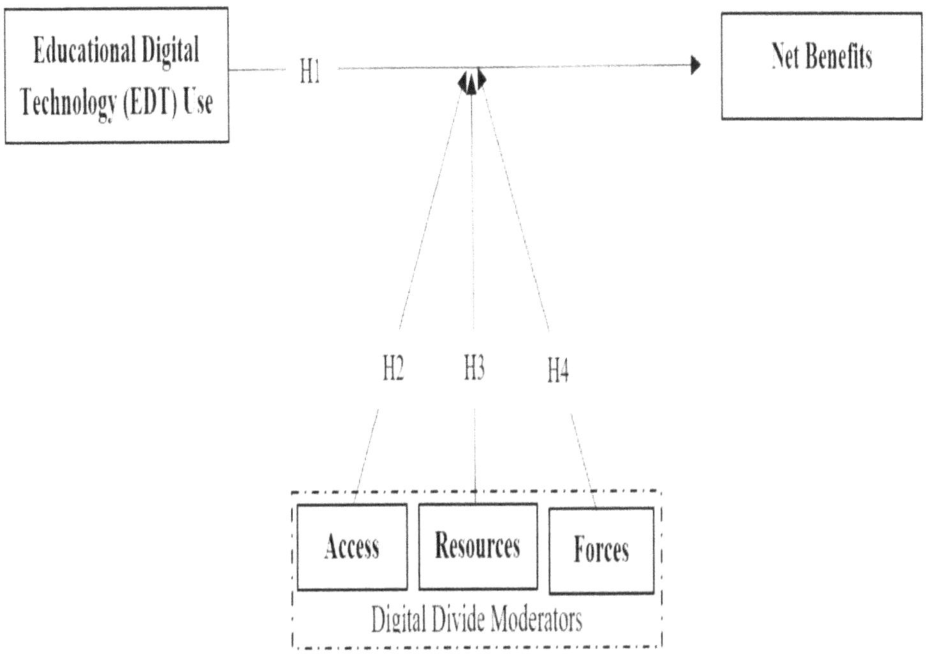

contexts and technologies to establish its relationship with net benefits (Aldholay et al., 2018; Owusu, 2020). In the context of technologies for teaching and learning under lockdown, it has been revealed that usage of such technologies have both positive and negative impacts on net benefits (Aristovnik et al., 2020; George, 2020). It is therefore hypothesized that:

H1: The use of EDT will have a positive impact on net benefits.

The digital divide denotes "the gap among individuals, households, and businesses at different socio-economic levels with regard to both their opportunities to access ICTs and their use of the Internet for a wide variety of activities" (ITU, 2017). Yu et al. (2018) conceptualizes the digital divide with three determinants which are access, resources and forces. Access is described as the entire ability of an individual to readily use certain ICTs in particular situations (van Dijk 2005). Access can be classified into material, motivational, cognitive and social access (Yu et al., 2018). Individuals with ready access to technology are those who are more likely to use the technology. It has been established by Oyelaran-Oyeyinka and Lal (2005) and Quibria et al. (2002) that ICT usage is impacted by access and Bélanger and Carter (2008) also found e-government use to be predicted by access. Moreover, the use of FinTech is found to be moderated by access (Odei-Appiah, Wiredu, and Adjei 2022). Thus, it is hypothesized that:

H2: Access moderates EDT usage in a way such that the relationship will be stronger with individuals with more access.

Resources as a digital divide determinant describes a stock of money, materials, social networks, infrastructure and other instruments on which users can rely for the realization of their general technology use (Yu et al., 2018). Six types of resources identified from literature are financial, material, cognitive, interpersonal, educational and psychological resources (van Dijk 2005). Examples of such resources include income and education and they have been found to have great impact on ICT usage

(Fuchs, 2009). E-government usage is also significantly predicted by education and income (Bélanger and Carter 2009). Odei-Appiah et al. (2022) in addition found resources to moderate the use of FinTech for financial inclusion. Therefore, it is hypothesised that:

H3: Resources moderate EDT usage in a way such that the relationship will be stronger with individuals with more resources.

Forces denote institutions, systems or stakeholder groups noted for alleviating or perpetuating digital inequality (Hsieh et al., 2008). These forces represent the attributes for controlling the structural distribution, quantity and quality of resources that individuals require to access ICT. Five classification of forces are namely personal, ideological, administrative and industrial forces (Yu et al., 2018). Peer pressure, racial influences and forces from ethnic groupings have been found to impact ICT usage (Agarwal et al., 2009) and Odei-Appiah et al. (2022) found resources to moderate FinTech use. It is thus hypothesised that:

H4: Forces moderate EDT usage in a way such that the relationship will be stronger with individuals with more forces.

CONCLUSION

The Covid-19 pandemic led to the closure of schools as one of the measures to contain the spread of the disease. During these times many digital technologies were deployed by nations to ensure teaching and learning continued in their schools. Many developing countries adopted a variety of these technologies which were not as usual to their teachers, students and parents as could be witnessed in developed parts of the world. This chapter discussed various technologies for online teaching and learning and a proposed research model illustrates how they impact on education in emerging countries amidst the digital divide. Many widely used web conferencing solutions including Zoom, Skype, Google Classroom and others prove to be strong enablers for teaching and learning in the absence of face-to-face interactions in schools. These technologies are not seen only as replacements for traditional approaches to education but going forward should be regarded as necessary complementary means of helping students acquire necessary competencies for the new digital economy. Nevertheless, challenges such as the digital divide, poverty, and lack of access to electricity should be addressed to realize the full potential of digital education in developing countries.

REFERENCES

Agarwal, R., Animesh, A., Prasad, K., & Smith, R. H. (2009). *Research note—Social interactions and the "digital divide": Explaining variations in internet use.* https://pubsonline.informs.org/doi/abs/10.1287/isre.1080.0194

Aldholay, A., Isaac, O., Abdullah, Z., Abdulsalam, R., & Al-Shibami, A. H. (2018). *An extension of Delone and McLean IS success model with self-efficacy.* Academic Press.

Alqurashi, E. (2019). *Technology tools for teaching and learning in real time.* https://www.igi-global.com/chapter/technology-tools-for-teaching-and-learning-in-real-time/225755

Aristovnik, A., Keržič, D., Ravšelj, D., Tomaževič, N., & Umek, L. (2020). Impacts of the COVID-19 Pandemic on Life of Higher Education Students: A Global Perspective. *Sustainability, 12*(20), 8438. doi:10.3390/su12208438

Bayham, J., & Fenichel, E. P. (2020). Impact of school closures for COVID-19 on the US health-care workforce and net mortality: A modelling study. *The Lancet. Public Health, 5*(5), e271–e278. doi:10.1016/S2468-2667(20)30082-7 PMID:32251626

Bélanger, F., & Carter, L. (2008). Trust and risk in e-government adoption. *The Journal of Strategic Information Systems, 17*(2), 165–176. doi:10.1016/j.jsis.2007.12.002

Bélanger, F., & Carter, L. (2009). The impact of the digital divide on e-government use. *Communications of the ACM, 52*(4), 132–135. doi:10.1145/1498765.1498801

Bertot, J. C., McClure, C. R., & Jaeger, P. T. (2011). *Public Libraries and the Internet: Roles, Perspectives, and Implications*. Google Books. https://books.google.com.gh/books?hl=en&lr=&id=NZ0zH-jF8tcC&oi=fnd&pg=PP2&dq=Bertot,+J.C.,+Jaeger,+P.T.+and+McClure,+C.R.+(2011),+Public+Libraries+and+the+Internet:+Roles,+Perspectives,+and+Implications,+ABC-CLIO,+Santa+Barbara,+CA.&ots=0ECU4QQpH0&sig=H1N

Das, K. (2021). Digital Technologies on Mathematics Education at the Covid-19 Lockdown Situation in India. *Indonesian Journal of Innovation and Applied Sciences, 1*(2), 95–104. doi:10.47540/ijias.v1i2.197

Delone, W. H., & Mclean, E. R. (2003). The DeLone and McLean Model of Information Systems Success: A Ten-Year Update. *Journal of Management Information Systems, 19*(4), 9–30. Advance online publication. doi:10.1080/07421222.2003.11045748

Drugarin, C., Draghici, S., & Raduca, E. (2016). *Team Viewer Technology for Remote Control of a Computer*. https://www.researchgate.net/profile/Cornelia-Victoria-Anghel-Drugarin/publication/311057172_Team_Viewer_Technology_for_Remote_Control_of_a_Computer/links/583c5d4408ae3cb636556e7a/Team-Viewer-Technology-for-Remote-Control-of-a-Computer.pdf

Fuchs, C. (2009). The role of income inequality in a multivariate cross-national analysis of the digital divide. *Social Science Computer Review, 27*(1), 41–58. doi:10.1177/0894439308321628

George, M. L. (2020). Effective Teaching and Examination Strategies for Undergraduate Learning During COVID-19 School Restrictions. *Journal of Educational Technology Systems, 49*(1), 23–48. doi:10.1177/0047239520934017

Hindman, D. B. (2000). *The Rural-Urban Digital Divide*. Academic Press.

Hsieh, J. J. P. A., Rai, A., & Keil, M. (2008). Understanding digital inequality: Comparing continued use behavioral models of the socio-economically advantaged and disadvantaged. *Management Information Systems Quarterly, 32*(1), 97–126. doi:10.2307/25148830

Iftakhar, S. (2016). *Google classroom: What works and how*. https://jesoc.com/wp-content/uploads/2016/03/KC3_35.pdf

Iivari, N., Sharma, S., & Ventä-Olkkonen, L. (2020). Digital transformation of everyday life – How COVID-19 pandemic transformed the basic education of the young generation and why information management research should care? *International Journal of Information Management, 55*, 102183. Advance online publication. doi:10.1016/j.ijinfomgt.2020.102183 PMID:32836640

ITU. (2017). Measuring the Information Society Report 2017 (Vol. 1). doi:10.1787/9789264244047-37-en

Lieser, P., Taff, S. D., & Murphy-Hagan, A. (2018). The Webinar Integration Tool: A Framework for Promoting Active Learning in Blended Environments. *Journal of Interactive Media in Education, 2018*(1), 1–8. doi:10.5334/jime.453

MacKinnon, D. P. (2011). Integrating Mediators and Moderators in Research Design. *Research on Social Work Practice, 21*(6), 675–681. doi:10.1177/1049731511414148 PMID:22675239

Mathrani, A., Sarvesh, T., & Umer, R. (2021). Digital divide framework: Online learning in developing countries during the COVID-19 lockdown. *Globalisation, Societies and Education, 0*(0), 1–16. doi:10.1080/14767724.2021.1981253

Mehta, S., Clarke, F., & Fleming, P. S. (2016). An assessment of student experiences and learning based on a novel undergraduate e-learning resource. *British Dental Journal, 221*(3), 131–136. doi:10.1038/sj.bdj.2016.563

Mishra, L., Gupta, T., & Shree, A. (2020). Online teaching-learning in higher education during lockdown period of COVID-19 pandemic. *International Journal of Educational Research Open, 1*, 100012. doi:10.1016/j.ijedro.2020.100012 PMID:35059663

Noor, R., Singh, D., Agarwal, A., Mansoori, S., & Ansari, M. I. (2022). Perception of dental students towards the online method of dental education during the COVID-19 pandemic. *Journal of Oral Biology and Craniofacial Research, 12*(2), 223–227. doi:10.1016/j.jobcr.2022.02.002 PMID:35186671

Odei-Appiah, S., Wiredu, G., & Adjei, J. K. (2022). Fintech use, digital divide and financial inclusion. *Digital Policy. Regulation & Governance, 24*(5), 435–448. doi:10.1108/DPRG-09-2021-0111

Oloyede, A. A., Faruk, N., & Raji, W. O. (2022). COVID-19 lockdown and remote attendance teaching in developing countries: A review of some online pedagogical resources. *African Journal of Science, Technology, Innovation and Development, 14*(3), 678–696. doi:10.1080/20421338.2021.1889768

Ondego, B., & Moturi, C. (2016). Evaluation of the Implementation of the e-Citizen in Kenya. *International Journal of Applied Information Systems, 10*(4), 13–21. doi:10.5120/ijais2016451486

Owusu, A. (2020). The impact of audio–visual technologies on university teaching and learning in a developing economy. *South African Journal of Information Management, 22*(1), 1–9. doi:10.4102ajim.v22i1.1235

Oyelaran-Oyeyinka, B., & Lal, K. (2005). Internet diffusion in sub-Saharan Africa: A cross-country analysis. *Telecommunications Policy*. https://www.sciencedirect.com/science/article/pii/S0308596105000479

Pozo, J. I., Pérez Echeverría, M. P., Cabellos, B., & Sánchez, D. L. (2021). Teaching and Learning in Times of COVID-19: Uses of Digital Technologies During School Lockdowns. *Frontiers in Psychology, 12*, 1511. doi:10.3389/fpsyg.2021.656776 PMID:33995217

Quibria, M. G., Ahmed, S. N., Tschang, T., & Reyes-Macasaquit, M. L. (2002). Digital divide: Determinants and policies with special reference to Asia. *ERD Working Paper Series, 27*, 1–16.

Rahman, A. (2015). Toward a Comprehensive Conceptualization of Digital Divide and its Impact on E- Government System Success. In *Advances in Business Marketing and Purchasing* (Vol. 23). https://www.scopus.com/inward/record.url?eid=2-s2.0-84943382451&partnerID=tZOtx3y1

Remuzzi, A., & Remuzzi, G. (2020). COVID-19 and Italy: What next? *Lancet, 395*(10231), 1225–1228. doi:10.1016/S0140 6736(20)30627-9 PMID:32178769

Robertson, J. (2020). *Zoom Guide*. Google Search. https://www.google.com/search?q=Robertson%2C+Julia.+2020.+Zoom+Guide.pdf&rlz=1C1CHWL_enGH964GH965&oq=Robertson%2C+Julia.+2020.+Zoom+Guide.pdf&aqs=chrome.69i57j69i60.1010j0j4&sourceid=chrome&ie=UTF-8

Sipior, J., & Ward, B. (2011). *The digital divide and t-government in the United States: using the technology acceptance model to understand usage.* Taylor & Francis. doi:10.1057/ejis.2010.64

Sun, J., & Liu, Z. (2019). Analysis of public satisfaction on the webcast in Taiyuan city, Shanxi Province. *2019 International Conference on Management, Finance and Social Sciences Research (MFSSR 2019) Analysis*. https://doi.org/10.25236/mfssr.2019.157

Thompson, K. M., & Afzal, W. (2011). A look at information access through physical, intellectual, and socio-cultural lenses. *OMNES: The Journal of Multicultural Society*, 2(2), 22–42. doi:10.15685/omnes.2011.12.2.2.22

Towers, A., Field, J., Stokes, C., Maddock, S., & Martin, N. (2019). A scoping review of the use and application of virtual reality in pre-clinical dental education. *British Dental Journal, 226*(5), 358–366. doi:10.1038/s41415-019-0041-0

van Deursen, A. J. A. M., & van Dijk, J. A. G. M. (2018). *The first-level digital divide shifts from inequalities in physical access to inequalities in material access.* doi:10.1177/1461444818797082

van Dijk, J. A. G. M. (2005). The Deepening Divide: Inequality in the Information Society. Thousand Oaks, CA: Sage, 2005, 240 pp., ISBN 141290403X (paperback). *Mass Communication & Society, 11*(2), 221–224. doi:10.1080/15205430701528655

Viner, R., Russell, S., & Croker, H. (n.d.). *School closure and management practices during coronavirus outbreaks including COVID-19: A rapid systematic review.* Elsevier. Retrieved June 30, 2022, from https://www.sciencedirect.com/science/article/pii/S235246422030095X

Webex, C. (2014). *How would you like to work together? Cisco Webex Events Cisco Webex Training Offer courses and training.* Luettavissa. Http://Www.Webex.Com/Products/Webconferencing.Html

Yu, B., Ndumu, A., Mon, L. M., & Fan, Z. (2018). E-inclusion or digital divide: An integrated model of digital inequality. *The Journal of Documentation, 74*(3), 552–574. doi:10.1108/JD-10-2017-0148

Zamfir, A.-M., Raccanello, D., Balbontín-Alvarado, R., Bezerra, D. da S., Burro, R., Cheraghi, M., Dobrowolska, B., Fagbamigbe, A. F., Faris, M. E., França, T., González-Fernández, B., Hall, R., Inasius, F., Kar, S. K., Keržič, D., Lazányi, K., Lazăr, F., Machin-Mastromatteo, J. D., Marôco, J., ... Aristovnik, A. (2022). Higher education students' achievement emotions and their antecedents in e-learning amid COVID-19 pandemic: A multi-country survey. *Learning and Instruction*, *80*(May), 101629. doi:10.1016/j.learninstruc.2022.101629 PMID:35578734

Zoumenou, V., Sigman-Grant, M., Coleman, G., Malekian, F., Zee, J. M. K., Fountain, B. J., & Marsh, A. (2015). Identifying Best Practices for an Interactive Webinar. *Journal of Family and Consumer Sciences*, *107*(2), 62–69.

KEY TERMS AND DEFINITIONS

Access: The total ability of an individual to readily use certain ICTs in particular situations.

Digital Divide: Unequal opportunities among individuals, households and businesses to access and use ICTs and the internet due to their varying socio-economic levels.

Forces: Institutions, systems, or stakeholder groups noted for alleviating or perpetuating digital inequality.

Resources: A stock of money, materials, social networks, infrastructure, and other instruments on which users can rely for the realization of their general technology use

Web-Conferencing: A multimedia communications system in which computer screens, individual applications, or web contents can be shared among connected computers in real-time.

Webcast: A broadcast over the Internet which can be delivered either live or on-demand.

Webinar: An interactive web-based seminar, lecture, teaching, workshop, or meeting held virtually with its attendance exclusive to an online audience.

Chapter 10
Impacts of Digital Payments on Socio-Economic Factors in Emerging Markets and Developing Economies

Ranjan Kumar
Asian Institute of Technology, Thailand

Maheshwor Shrestha
Asian Institute of Technology, Thailand

ABSTRACT

Digital payments are increasingly becoming popular worldwide, especially in underdeveloped and developing countries, despite the challenges these countries face regarding required infrastructure and digital literacy. Digital payments have emerged as an important tool for governments to distribute the funds for social welfare schemes to their citizens directly in their accounts with zero corruption and delays. Socio-financial inclusion of society's deprived and marginalized section is another advantage of digital payments. Having access to transaction accounts, credit, savings products, and insurance helps the poor raise their incomes and become more resilient. Paperless and cashless transactions are a huge advantage of digital payments. This chapter aims to discuss the impacts of digital payments on the socio-economic factors in emerging markets and developing economies. In addition, it highlights the solution and recommendations for policymakers.

INTRODUCTION

Digital payment is a payment method that is based on the Internet, where several transactions can be processed concurrently in an orderly, precise, and productive manner, which increases productivity (B. J. Ali & Anwar, 2021; Chaveesuk et al., 2021). The usage of internet-based modern banking services improves the accuracy and efficiency of money transfer activities. The Digital Payment System (DPS) is

DOI: 10.4018/978-1-6684-6873-9.ch010

becoming increasingly important for enforcing effective monetary policies through financial transactions (Lo Prete, 2022), and its effects on global economic and financial activity are visible (Aurazo & Vega, 2021). Those who opt to use the DPS reap the benefits of a swift and prompt settlement of payments instantaneously, which results in a reduction in both expenses and the amount of time spent (Balakrishnan & Shuib, 2021). Even though it has a lot of advantages, end-users had many problems with it when it was first introduced. These problems included regulatory norms, network issues, secrecy, safety, security, trust, confidentiality (Verkijika, 2018; Yang et al., 2012), and fraud (Chang et al., 2022). These problems led to the DPS not being very popular when it was first introduced. With the government's ongoing efforts to fix these problems and the regulatory authorities working to make the DPS work better, as well as the benefits that end-users enjoy, the system is becoming more popular in developing countries.

Through DPS, governments can ensure that social welfare schemes are delivered 100% to the beneficiaries cost-effectively without involving any middle layer. Indian government's scheme, "Direct Benefit Transfer (DBT)," is the best example where beneficiaries get their social welfare funds directly in their accounts without going to the banks or post offices (Varshney et al., 2021). This scheme helped the central government of India tackle corruption, which was a lot in this area where beneficiaries never received their 100% allotted funds. Therefore, digital payments can lead to financial inclusion for the marginalized section of society (Allen et al., 2016; Aurazo & Vega, 2021). Transparency is another big advantage of digital payments (Setor et al., 2021a). Digital technologies allow these services to reach people (Sardana & Singhania, 2018) who previously did not have access to them, including nearly two-thirds of adults in developing countries (Pazarbasioglu & Mora, 2020). It is because costs are going down as the technology is making the most of economies of scale. It is also making it possible to create long-lasting financial products that meet the needs of people with very low and unpredictable incomes (Sardana & Singhania, 2018). Technology is making it easier for people to get financial services, even if they don't have identification or a regular source of income.

By their digital nature, digital payments also provide opportunities for data mining (Mittal & Agrawal, 2022), which may pose a significant threat to users' privacy rights and raise the likelihood of cyber assaults, which may result in data leakage and exploitation (Tronnier et al., 2022). Regulations that are new or not complete can also leave room for non-compliance and abuse by service providers, who are not always upfront about how they monetize the data passing through their platforms. In addition, concerns are also growing about the power of tech giants, which is shown by Facebook's plan to start its digital currency platform (Brühl, 2020). In the same way, if a digital currency is not issued or controlled by a central bank, the supply may not be regulated. This could cause the currency's value to drop and inflation to get out of hand. Recent Bitcoin price variations due to Elon Musk's involvement are an outstanding example of this volatility (Shahzad et al., 2022). In terms of macroeconomics, digital currencies administered by a central bank may be able to prevent currency volatility and exchange rate risk if they are based on multiple currencies. On the other hand, even though there are many great things about the different digital payment options, businesses need to find a way to make them work together. Consequently, the authors aspire to provide an answer to the following question within the scope of this chapter: what are the impacts of digital payments in Emerging Market and Developing Economies (EMDEs)?

In summary, this chapter will analyze and synthesize the socio-economic impacts of digital payment in EMDEs and reflect its findings in the form of solutions and recommendations. This proposed chapter will discuss the impacts and demonstrate how digital payments are both a driver and a precursor of long-term sustainability for businesses, individuals, and governments. These impacts can be broadly classified as positive and negative. The positive impacts can be seen as operational efficiency, innovative solutions to challenging problems and fresh new opportunities. Negative impacts largely come in the form of new threats. This chapter will discuss these impacts in-depth with examples, cases, causes and probable solutions.

BACKGROUND

Many people imagine the future of money as a digital utopia (Fabris, 2019). A truly cashless society - a world where all financial transactions are conducted entirely through digital means. Increasingly, traditional banks and physical currency are losing to digital currencies (R. Ali et al., 2014) and challenger FinTechs. Successive crises, especially the coronavirus (COVID-19) pandemic, are speeding fundamental changes in how individuals and governments manage and govern money. Anne Boden, founder and chief executive officer of Starling Bank, said, "since the advent of the internet, digital payments have been virtually unavoidable" (Mills, 2022). Since the Bankers' Automated Clearing System (BACS) (Howcroft & Lavis, 1987) was first implemented in the 1960s, digital payment methods have been gaining ground while the use of cash has been on the wane. This trend has continued right up until the present day. The skyrocketed usage of digital payments has brought all-around effects on how society functions. Money is one crucial medium to exchange things in social transactions. Since money is ceasing its physical being to a digital being, more as a concept or a number that appears on the mobile phone screen, it has solved some of the challenges, brought in some opportunities and invited some new threats as well.

In just a few decades, digital payments went from being uncommon to becoming a standard practice. In reality, for many, the debate is not about whether one should use digital payments but how to make them faster, safer, and more convenient. With the number of bank branches and automated teller machines (ATMs) declining (R. Kumar et al., 2021), access to cash is dwindling. Digital payments are becoming more widespread, and the many wallets that existed a few years ago have now consolidated, with Apple, Google, and PayPal dominating. Table 1 provides a detailed overview of the digital payment definitions and their concept, allowing for a comprehensive understanding of the topic at hand. Digital payment systems like peer-to-peer payments, mobile wallets, mobile point-of-sale devices, and digital coins are becoming increasingly common (Aurazo & Vega, 2021). This gives businesses and customers a wide range of options, each of which promises transparency, efficiency, and convenience. Such a shift in the financial landscape will significantly affect industry, society, and government.

Furthermore, cashless payment systems can help the economy grow because they make payments easier and more convenient, which makes it easier for people to buy things (Aurazo & Vega, 2021; Ferrari, 2022; Frączek & Urbanek, 2021; R. Kumar et al., 2021; Lo Prete, 2022; Setor et al., 2021a). The main benefit of making payments digital is that, in theory, anyone with a smartphone can make payments and purchases across borders cheaply and quickly. Businesses can save time and money by not having to manually do things like reconcile, count, and handle cash. The government can also save money by not having to print as much cash. Studies show that countries with more robust and sophisticated financial systems experience stronger economic growth, faster poverty reduction, and greater income equality (Chiu & Wong, 2021; Fabris, 2019). The necessity of digital financial services in offering safe, low-cost, and contactless financial tools to consumers and governments has grown further even more clear as the world grapples with the COVID-19 crisis (Aurazo & Vega, 2021; Ferrari, 2022; Suyunchaliyeva et al., 2021).

Table 1. Digital payments definition and their concept

Definition	Concept	Source
"Digital Payment is a method of payment which can be made by the use of Banking cards, USSD, AEPS, E-wallets, UPI, etc. Both payer and payee use digital mode in to send and receive money. No hard cash is used in this process but completed with the help of Internet or online. It is a very convenient way to make the payments."	Digital payment	(Gupta et al., 2022)
"Digital payment is referred to any types of payments using digital instruments, including mobile payment, digital wallets, cryptocurrency, and electronic payment."	Digital payment	(Alkhowaiter, 2020)
"Any prevailing or new payment system that enables financial transactions to be conducted safely from one organization or individual to another via the internet."	E-payment	(Hidayanto et al., 2015)
"Online payment refers to the exchange of monetary value between payers and payees via the Internet."	Online payment	(Effah, 2016)
"Digital payments are defined as non-cash transactions processed through digital channels which the main form is mobile payment."	Digital payment	(Chen et al., 2019)
"The term digital payments refer to payments made by using digital instruments. The payee and the payer both use electronic modes to send and receive money."	Digital payment	(P. Kumar & Chaubey, 2017)
"E-payment is a technology which doesn't involve physical cash here the payment is made through the electronic medium."	E-payment	(Vinitha & Vasantha, 2017)
"E-payment is defined as the transfer of an electronic value of payment from a payee to a payer through an e-payment medium."	E-payment	(Sahu & Singh, 2018)
"Digital payment is a method of payment that is produced through digital methods. Both payer and payee use digital methods for sending and receiving cash in digital payments. It is called electronic payment as well."	Digital Payment	(Bisma et al., 2020)
"The term digital payment means the type of payment which is done through the digital mode."	Digital payment	(Sivathanu, 2019)

Moreover, the Covid-19 pandemic has also pushed governments to use digital payment platforms in their response efforts (as much as possible), both for distributing money to those in need and for paying key workers. In fact, due to these changes, governments have also eased their regulations on digital payment systems. For example, the Rwandan government abolished digital transfer fees and raised the maximum limit on online transactions (Ngamije, 2021).

Impacts of COVID-19

The recent global outbreak of the coronavirus has hastened the transition to digital payment methods and increased their use (more specifically cashless payments). Many people with bank accounts started using digital payments online more because of the risk of spreading diseases, government lockdowns, and other restrictions. Moreover, it is important to keep in mind that the Covid-19 pandemic has had a considerable influence on the behavior of society with regard to the allocation of financial resources. Several studies have investigated how the Covid-19 pandemic has affected people's lives (Dębski et al., 2021; Kolosok & Jakubowska, 2020; Tomcikova et al., 2021) on a day-to-day basis, countries' economic indicators of growth (N. Liu et al., 2021; Mishenina et al., 2021; Tiutiunyk et al., 2021), social issues (Kadar & Reicher, 2020; Stefan et al., 2020), and the financial aspects of development (Hinrichs & Bundtzen, 2021; Pardal et al., 2020).

Limitations of Digital Payments

Digital payments have transformed the way financial transactions are conducted, making it easier and faster to send and receive money. However, it is important to consider several limitations of digital payments, including issues of access, the risk of fraud and security breaches, associated transaction fees, and the potential for exclusion.

One of the primary limitations is the issue of access (Di. Gregorio et al., 2005; Ferrari, 2022). While digital payments are becoming increasingly popular, there are still many individuals and communities that lack the necessary infrastructure to access these payment methods. This is particularly true in low-income or rural areas, where access to reliable internet or mobile networks may be limited. As a result, digital payments may not be a viable option for everyone.

Another limitation is the risk of fraud and security breaches (Chang et al., 2022). Digital payments can be vulnerable to cyberattacks and data breaches (Ferrari, 2022), which can compromise personal and financial information. This risk can be particularly high in developing countries, where cybersecurity measures may not be as robust as in developed nations.

Moreover, digital payments are often subject to transaction fees and other charges (Ong & Chong, 2022), which can add up and make them less affordable for some individuals or small businesses. Additionally, digital payment systems may not always be compatible with one another, creating barriers to seamless transactions between different platforms.

Finally, there is a risk of exclusion for those who are not comfortable with or do not have the necessary skills to use digital payment systems. This can particularly impact older adults or those who have limited experience with technology, as well as those who may have disabilities or other impairments that make it difficult to navigate digital payment platforms (Ferrari, 2022; Lo Prete, 2022).

In summary, while digital payments offer many benefits, including convenience and speed, there are several limitations that need to be considered. Addressing these limitations will be crucial to ensuring that digital payments are inclusive and accessible to everyone and can be used effectively to promote financial inclusion and economic growth.

Digital Payments Channels

Digital payments are conducted through a variety of electronic channels, such as the internet, mobile devices, or electronic point-of-sale (POS) terminals. These channels allow for the transfer of funds from one account to another without the need for physical cash or checks. Some of the most common methods of digital payments include:

1. **Online Banking:** This method involves using an online banking platform to transfer funds from one bank account to another. Online banking platforms typically offer a variety of features, such as bill pay, account monitoring, and transaction history (Gupta et al., 2022).
2. **Mobile Payments:** Mobile payments involve using a mobile device, such as a smartphone or tablet, to make payments. This can be done through a mobile app, such as Apple Pay or Google Pay, or by scanning a QR code or using Near Field Communication (NFC) technology (T. Liu et al., 2020).
3. **E-Wallets:** E-wallets, also known as digital wallets, are virtual wallets that allow individuals to store and manage their payment information in one place. This information can then be used to

make payments through a variety of channels, including online shopping, in-store purchases, and peer-to-peer (P2P) payments (Di. Gregorio et al., 2005; Kala Kamdjoug et al., 2021).

4. **Electronic Point-of-Sale (POS) Terminals:** POS terminals are electronic devices that allow merchants to accept payments from customers using credit cards, debit cards, or other electronic payment methods. These devices are typically found in retail stores, restaurants, and other businesses (Ong & Chong, 2022).
5. **SMS Banking:** SMS banking is a form of mobile banking (Sardana & Singhania, 2018) that allows users to perform financial transactions via text message on their mobile devices. SMS banking can be used to initiate some types of financial transactions, such as transferring funds between accounts or paying bills.
6. **ATM Fund Transfer:** ATM fund transfer is a type of digital payment, as it enables the transfer of funds electronically between bank accounts without the need for physical cash. While it involves a physical device (the ATM), customers can initiate transfers between their own accounts or to another recipient's account by inserting their debit or ATM card into the machine, entering their PIN and following the prompts (Sardana & Singhania, 2018). The transfer is processed electronically, and while it is not as instant as some other forms of digital payments, such as mobile payments or online banking transfers, it is still a convenient way to transfer funds electronically, especially for customers who prefer to use physical machines rather than digital devices.

METHODOLOGY

This study aims to identify the social and economic implications of digital payments on EMDEs. To achieve this aim, a literature review on the effects of digital payments has been carried out. Research articles and books that have a clear focus on the impacts of digital payments on the social and economic life of people and governments are sought after being based on keywords such as "digital payments", "impacts of digital payments", "positive impacts of digital payments", "negative impacts of digital payments", "good governance", "digital payments and social welfare schemes", "social and economic impacts of digital payments", using online databases like Web of Science, ScienceDirect and Google Scholar. Although they are few in number, they have been developed based on a variety of theoretical viewpoints and empirical approaches to provide methods and checklists, as well as to assist with impact identification and recommendations. This makes it possible to find some frameworks and case studies in the published research that are explicitly focused on identifying digital payments' impacts on people's daily lives and how governments deliver their services. After that, a content analysis of the chosen articles is carried out in order to draw attention to the various kinds of impacts that digital payments have had on EMDEs that have been stated by the authors. This allows elaborating, in a final step, a synthesis by proposing a list of impacts and their categories in terms of positive and negative. Finally, it leads to the proposition of solutions and recommendations for developing countries about implementing digital payments and their benefits on their social and economic aspects.

IMPACTS OF DIGITAL PAYMENTS

The impacts of digital payments in almost every aspect of day-to-day life. It is even more striking in developing economies as it holds the potential to transform the socio-economic landscape of such counties (Natile, 2020). Figure 1, derived from the Findex database, illustrates a discernible upward trend of digital inclusion that coincides with the proliferation of digital payments. This trend is observable in other developing regions of the world where the increasing mobile penetration rate is leading to greater financial access. A report published by the Central Bank of India, as demonstrated in Figure 2, reveals a decrease of 3.5% in the utilization of banknotes in comparison to projections, despite the country's expanding economy. In contrast, the same period saw a remarkable 30% growth in retail digital payments.

Figure 1. Digital inclusion and digital payment
Source: The World Bank (2021)

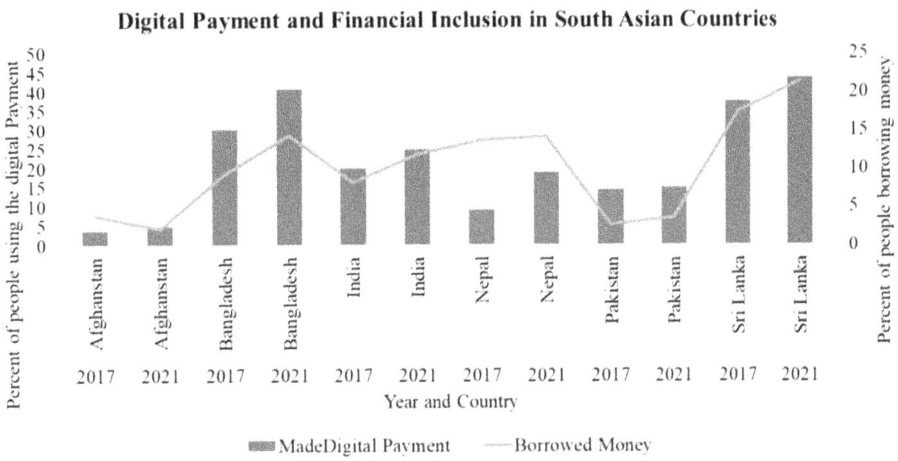

Figure 2. Notes in circulation in India
Source: Reserve Bank of India (2020)

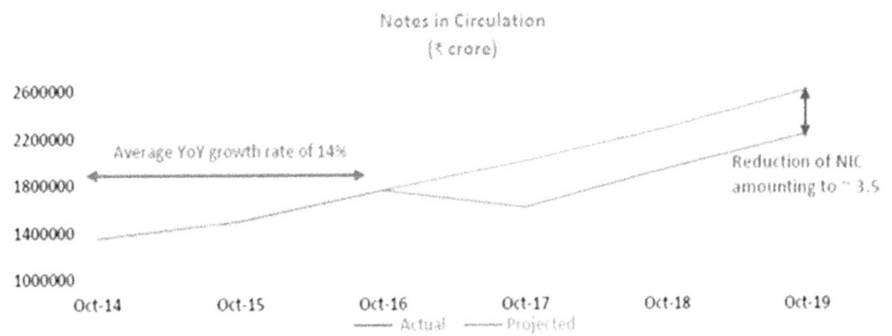

The rising adoption of digital payments can be attributed to its evident advantages, such as simplicity, convenience, speed, and security, as indicated by the analysis presented in Figure 3 of the Cambodia Investment Review. According to a report by Deloitte, digital payments can reduce payment processing time by 75% (Chaudhuri et al., 2022). Furthermore, McKinsey's study reveals that digital payment adoption is thriving in new and innovative businesses, which is reflected in Figure 4 that highlights social media, ride-hailing platforms, and e-commerce as prime growth areas for payment platforms. The COVID-19 pandemic has also played a significant role in accelerating the adoption of digital payments. Figure 5 shows that in Rwanda, there was a surge of over 250% in digital payment subscribers immediately after the COVID-19 lockdown was imposed.

Figure 3. Reasons for choosing digital payment
Source: White (2023)

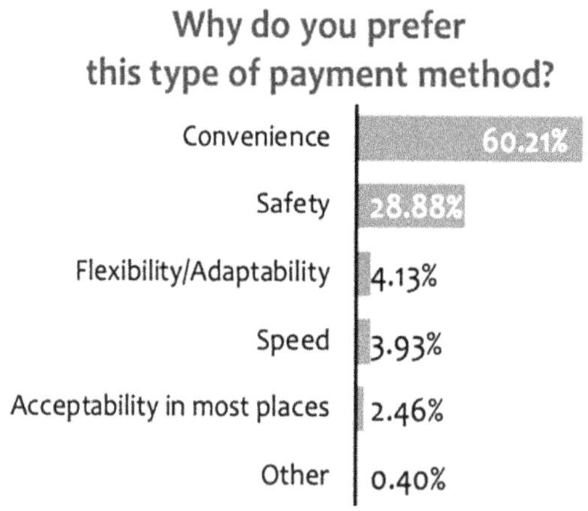

Figure 4. User engagement vs. potential payment value
Source: Chaudhuri et al. (2022)

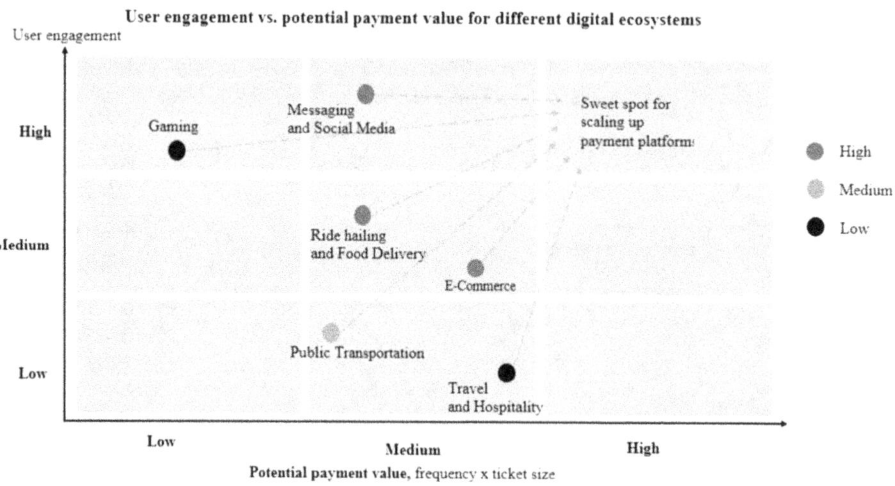

Figure 5. COVID-19 boosted digital payment
Source: Carboni and Bester (2020)

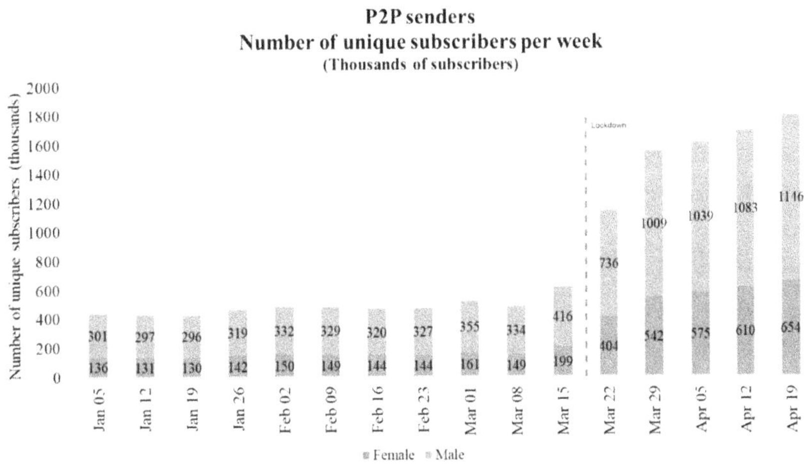

This study has tried to collect, classify, and understand the length and breadth of those impacts. Broadly, the consequences of digital payments can be classified as positive and negative, as depicted in Figure 6. The positive consequences are obvious and abundant, so governments and organizations have invested significant efforts to digitalize payments and financial transactions (Dziatkovskii et al., 2021)

Figure 6. Impacts of digital payments on socio-economic factors in emerging market and developing economies
Source: Author

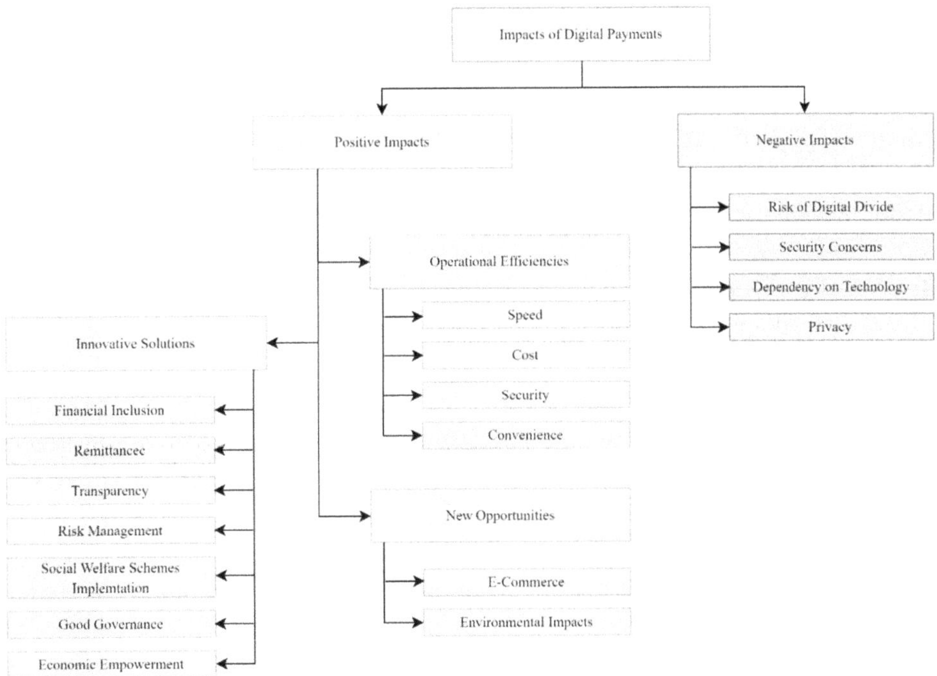

to the maximum possible. Digital payments improve individuals' local and private motives, like faster, secure, and easier payments (Putra et al., 2022) to the larger public interests like social inclusion, good governance, transparency, and innovation. While the fruits of digital payments are promising, their hind side should be carefully understood and taken care of. Cybersecurity is the biggest fear among digital payment critics (Kholiavko et al., 2021). Besides, there is a good chance of having a segment of left-behind people (van Dijk & Hacker, 2011) who are not yet ready to adopt these modern payment technologies. And this second hazard can jeopardize the situation more in weaker economies if not handled on time. This chapter will discuss both positive and negative impacts in the following sections in more detail.

Positive Impacts of Digital Payments

This study has grouped the multitude of digital payment benefits into three major categories - operational efficiencies, innovative solutions, and new opportunities. The first one is related to all different sorts of outcomes that are related to the efficiencies in the existing process that is introduced by digital payment innovations. The efficiencies came from reduced cost, increased speed, a better sense of security and convenience, better integrations between businesses, etc. "Innovative solutions" encompass the different challenging solutions that were almost impossible to resolve before the advent of digital payments. With digital payments, it is possible to access, trace and track every penny spent. It enables the government and agencies to enforce transparency, good governance, and control of money-related crimes. Many loopholes created in the cash-based operational systems are closed with digital payments. Finally, a new bunch of opportunities flourishes with digital payments that would not exist before. There is a slight difference between this and the "Innovative solution". The latter is linked to the existing challenges that desperately needed a solution and helped larger-scale economies. The former is more like new value creations as new capabilities emerge.

Operational Efficiencies

Operational efficiencies encompass a broad range of improvements in activities conducted to run an entity (Hult et al., 2008). The entity can be government, business houses, organizations, households and even individuals. Improvements in activities can be in many dimensions. They bring tangible or intangible benefits to those entities. Some of such dimensions and the underlying positive effects are discussed in the following sections.

- **Speed:** Digital payments introduce time-saving (Taylor, 2016) in many places. The most intuitive is the freedom from counting and reconciling cash. Counting cash is very mundane, error-prone, and time-consuming at all levels. Besides counting, it removes the time and effort of cash management, like recycling and transporting cash. In short, all the overheads of cash are eliminated. There is a one-time time investment on getting the banking or fintech app and occasional maintenance, but time-saving from using apps for transactions is many folds more (Al-Okaily et al., 2020). Beyond that, integrations between the different systems have facilitated faster business across the globe. Without digital payments, paying someone at a far distance was a difficult job that would take days, if not months, with an additional surcharge (Beine et al., 2012). In developing countries, people spend even more time paying and receiving money as their means of transportation are not readily available. Digital payments have the potential to revolutionize social life as people spend more time doing productive work rather than spending hours and days commuting to pay and get paid. This time saving may look smaller on an individual level but is significant on a national scale.

- **Cost:** Cost is an important metric of "efficiency" to measure the optimality of an action. Digital payments are exceedingly optimal compared to cash. The cost of printing cash is high (Al-Okaily et al., 2020). The cost of securing cash is equally big; be it institutions or individuals, they spend a significant amount protecting the cash from different forms of natural or human threats (Taylor, 2016). Additionally, the cost of doing transactions with cash is higher too. It involves employing staff and machines to count, space to store, resources to transport, etc. These overheads are non-existent in the case of digital payments. Businesses and organizations motivate people to do online payments for these benefits as they save substantial amounts from operational costs, which adds to their profitability and hence longevity of the firm (Humphrey & Hunt, 2013). Emerging economies can organize their business model to go cashless and thrive because they skip a significant cost that would not attract extra revenue. Governments can save budgets for better development projects. The saved budget may be insignificant to developed nations but important resources for developing countries.
- **Security:** Though cybersecurity concerns on digital payment mechanisms, it provides security from the rest of the threats that cash has. All the insecurities against a physical loss like fire, flood, and theft will be eliminated as money is now stored in a remote server secured by international standards. Physical threats like fire, flood, and theft are more prevalent in weaker economies (Bonfiglio et al., 2021), and hence people can soon have a sense of security on digital payment systems than cash. Even for institutions, the investment in security personnel, technologies and assets like vaults, sirens, and cameras becomes lesser. Further, going digital is a creative way to solve the threat of counterfeit cash, a solution at the root. Counterfeit cash exists because cash exists. If society becomes cashless more, counterfeit cash will automatically become extinct. In fact, digital payments safeguard consumers from being robbed or losing money, as well as avoiding the burden of continually carrying a wallet (Cerulus & Contiguglia, 2018). Developing countries should focus on investing in digital payments as they grow their economy. It helps them save spending on physical security measures at the government level and remain safer in case of any form of physical calamities they may face.
- **Convenience:** The operational efficiency mentioned above is objective and can be measured directly. Beyond these, there is one more positive outcome of digital payments, which is subjective in nature. Convenience is subjective in the sense that different people consider the same thing of different convenience (Taylor, 2016), but digital payments generally free people from doing many things just to pay and get paid. Having a bank app is equivalent to having all the money in pocket, and it gives freedom to spend. It is actually carrying a bank in the pocket, which can be accessed almost anytime. People are no more forced to walk to banks or even ATMs. Carrying all those money in cash and doing transactions would be more hectic. One should not worry about how much money is left in the pocket before initiating a transaction. There is no need to reconcile the balance again and again by counting. The transaction history is readily available to recall and reconcile if required. Digital payments may hold the opportunity to foster consumer spending (Stofkova et al., 2022), which is better for healthier economies. A previous study done in Thailand shows that a mobile payment service named "Promptpay" seen a massive growth since its beginning (R. Kumar et al., 2021) as shown in Figure 7.

Figure 7. Promptpay transactions
Source: R. Kumar et al. (2021)

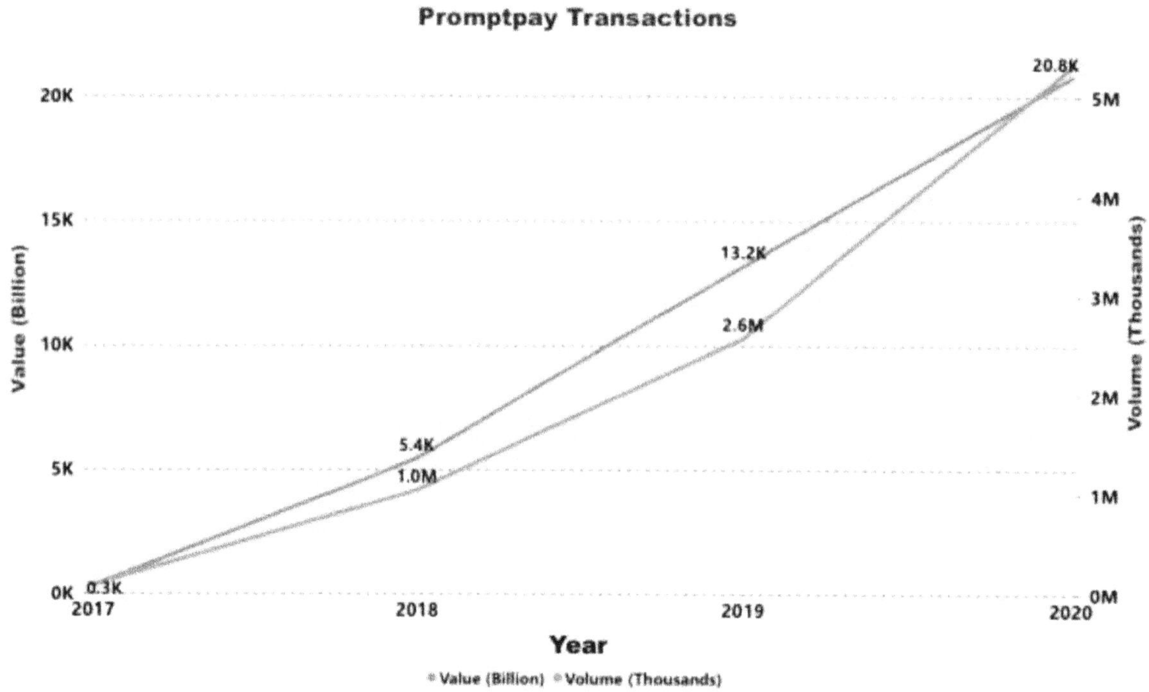

Innovative Solutions

Technologies have enabled mankind to achieve the unachievable. Digital payment is one such technology that holds immense potential to eliminate societal problems that have prevailed for a long. The machine power of computing humongous data, tracing back to the source, integrating different systems, and having round-the-clock availability has cured the government's and people's headaches. Some of the innovative solutions that could solve society's bigger problems and help transform the socio-economic dimension of developing countries are discussed in the following sections.

- **Financial Inclusion:** Efforts have been made around the globe to reach the unreached and include the excluded (Suri, 2017). The world is hyperconnected with higher Internet and mobile device penetration. Financial institutions can now serve customers at a distance through their apps and websites. Almost all the activities, including account creation and monetary transactions, can be done online. This opens financial services to greater numbers of people. The government and other non-governmental programs can touch them through these apps (Arner et al., 2020). They will no longer be excluded from opportunities to participate in financial activities. Regulators will have better information and access to these marginalized people and connect more often through established digital payment channels.
- **Remittance:** Remittance was a time-consuming, expensive, and highly sensitive job (Beine et al., 2012). In developing economies, remittance is more frequent and relevant as people migrate for employment and send money back home. When a few larger players controlled the remit-

tance, the cost was high, whereas the process was time-consuming and hectic (Suri, 2017). But with well-integrated financial systems, remittance has become almost instant and very cheap. This is very important in emerging markets as it empowers people's spending. People can do more with this ease and freedom of transferring money easily, strengthening the backbone of the developing economies.

- **Transparency:** Going cashless is synonymous with every transaction recorded digitally. The beauty of electronic data records is that they can be easily stored, cleaned, searched, and used for further analysis (Powell & Buchan, 2005). This accessibility to past records provides proof of activities and enhances the system's transparency. The loopholes in taxation can be closed as the income and expenditure are more transparent with electronic payments, hence electronic records (Setor et al., 2021b). Intelligent systems can sniff the data more comprehensively yet efficiently, fostering transparency and fairness in the systems. The least developed countries are vulnerable to irregularities in financial matters as the government is weaker (Bonfiglio et al., 2021). Hence, evil money can function well behind the curtain in such an environment, which further crumbles down the government and the majority of people. But with the advent of digital payments, the cash-based traditional system can be cut down to a larger scale, forcing everyone, especially firms and businesses, to adopt digital payments. This solves many transparency-related issues and strengthens emerging markets' socioeconomic status.
- **Risk Management:** Fiat money comes with different extrinsic risks. The risk from fire, theft and natural calamities are some low nobility ordinary threats covered above. People may face such issues in their day-to-day life, and digital payments circumvent many such threats. But beyond that, other sophisticated acts tamper the financial security measures and jeopardize the financial systems. Fraudulent transactions, counterfeit money, money laundering, tax evasion and black money from other different sources are threats not just at an individual level but to the whole economy (Amiram et al., 2018). In a cashless or less cash society, these problems get solved at the root because the regulators have access to every bit of money, who owns it, and trace it back to sources. But in a fiat money-based system, these loopholes will persist. Tax evasion is a huge issue in lesser developed nations; law enforcement is weaker, which undermines the nation's development even more (Bonfiglio et al., 2021). Equally excruciating is the issue of black money and the business of illegal things like drugs, human trafficking and so on (Gainsbury & Blaszczynski, 2020). The cash-based system is the fertile ground for these crimes, as tracking and tracing back is next to impossible. And the impacts of these activities are insane. With digital payments, a significant portion of these risks can be mitigated, saving developing countries from unwanted perils.
- **Social Welfare Schemes Implementation:** One feature of poor economies is the huge gap between rich and poor people (Berglof & Bolton, 2002). And the latter depends heavily on external support, especially from the government. Sometimes, this dependency is on basic living requirements like food and shelter. Government and organizations release funds through welfare programs to uplift such communities and people. These welfare programs come in different shapes and sizes. Some of them are the direct distribution of money through different allowances (Klapper & Singer, 2017). The distribution of fiat money through physical logistics is vulnerable to irregularities and expensive. With digital payments, government organizations can ensure that the right person gets the right amount at the right time with very little management and operational overheads. Ideally, the implementation of such projects is just a few clicks away, where people

can access digital payment. This is an efficient and cost-effective way to implement social welfare schemes that pay the target group of people.

- **Good Governance:** Digital payments enhance transparency. Transparency closes the loopholes in public service administrations. Studies show that there has been a significant cut in corruption with digital payments (Setor et al., 2021c). As government discourages cash in government-related affairs, civil service becomes faster and corruption free; faster because the necessity of filling the different payment forms and standing up on the payment line is eliminated. Besides these direct benefits, the government saves substantial expenses on money management that it would incur otherwise. This is saved public money that can be utilized for other projects to uplift society. In poor economies where resources are scarce, even this saving is significant.
- **Economic Empowerment:** Development organizations, including the government, invest intensive efforts in empowering people. Economic empowerment covers activities like providing skills and resources to make people economically productive and sustainable (Purwanti et al., 2020). With the digitalization of payments, distributing the fund and monitoring their usage is direct benefit governments can leverage for developing their people. They can better access people's financial behavior and design and develop plans for their development. On the people's side, money sitting in the banks appearing on the mobile screen is beneficial as at least a tiny interest will add on over time. Besides, Fintech companies, including banks, will proactively create investment products and motivate people to be more financially productive (Stofkova et al., 2022). This is better to mobilize the economy, empower people and develop emerging markets. Additionally, people will have more financial sense through the fintech apps as they can apply for loans, they are eligible for, invest in financial products like mutual funds and shares, buy insurance for their projects and themselves (Akter et al., 2021) and so on. All of these combined helps to push the economic empowerment level of people to higher elevations.
- **Environmental Impacts:** The carbon footprint of the fiat money system is higher than digital payment systems (Rana et al., 2019). And this is obvious because fiat money goes through a rigorous process of sourcing material and processing for printing. The logistics of money creation, usage and destruction are not eco-friendly. Money is more of a concept than material, proof of ownership of value. It was created to facilitate transactions in a trustworthy way when digital means did not exist. The current paper-based money is an economical and efficient transformation of the metal, stone and bone-based currencies that existed in old times (Angel, 2017). Now countries can reduce their carbon footprint by encouraging digital payments. The reason to switch to digital money is even stronger in weaker economies as they outsource money printing to countries with more sophisticated technologies. The logistics of money are even higher for them. The cost of owning fiat money is more for developing countries. Hence, they can opt for digital money to save nature and themselves.

New Opportunities

"New opportunities" can be easily confused with "innovative solutions" discussed above. But the fundamental difference between the two is that "innovative solutions" came as solutions to the problems that have existed in societies for a long time. The root cause of those problems was the inherent nature of a cash-based economy. Digital payment is one innovative solution that acted as a solution to all these that remain unsolved. On the other hand, "new opportunities" are another class of solutions created after the advent of digital payments, as entrepreneurs saw an immense pool of opportunities beneath it. The following section attempts to shed some light on those new opportunities.

- **E-Commerce:** Remotely buying and selling goods and services involves digitalizing a few essential components. Payments are one of them. Money sent physically using any delivery means carries more risks, and people are hesitant to do so (Ong & Chong, 2022). But digital payments are safer and can be traced back to resolve in case of disputes. Ecommerce has flourished much more after the advent of digital payments than just after the advent of web technologies. The proliferation of different online marketplaces of physical, digital, and logical things can largely be attributed to the availability of digital payments. Social media websites like Facebook, Instagram and Twitter were used mostly for entertainment and socialization, but an increasing trend of exchange of goods and services is seen there as well (Ferrell & Ferrell, 2012). Since remote payment has become easier, an immense opportunity to conduct business online has sprouted, and people are taking advantage of it. Online markets hold larger potential and promise to emerging markets where the physical environment is not well set up. Ecommerce can be a dominant and transforming factor for emerging markets in such economies.
- **Innovative Financial Products:** Digital payments have created humongous data on human behavior with money, buying, and other financial patterns (Stofkova et al., 2022). This has given rise to the creation of products that never existed before. The most common of them is the digital wallet, which does much more functionality than just a wallet. They facilitate basic functionalities like topping up other wallets and internet-based services like Internet, telecom services, games, etc. Besides, they partner with other companies to sell products through their platforms, like insurance, travel tickets, and other products. The wallet industry has grown so big that some are equal to or bigger than banks (Lu, 2018). Even more innovative ideas have materialized into new kinds of companies that could not be imagined before, like- branchless banks, digital investment products, online lending, innovative credit scoring and lending, insuretech, smoother global payments and so on (Du et al., 2020). Emerging markets are fertile ground for these products as there is a non-existent or negligible cost of migration as people are still far from access to the traditional form of financial products. Digital financial measures bridge the gap between the people and the financial services helping emerging economies to thrive irrespective of their weaker physical infrastructure.

Negative Impacts of Digital Payments

Amid a lot of potential and promises, digital payments are not flourishing as much as expected. Some basic preliminaries can get overlooked so that digital payment projects can stall (Leong et al., 2021). When technologies are transferred from the first world to the third work, a few basic criteria must be checked and ensured that the new market can accept these payment technologies. Overlooking these factors can negatively affect payment digitalization in emerging economies. Some of these factors are discussed in the following section.

- **Risk of Digital Divide:** Lack of readiness among people can divide the people into two groups – one who can access the technology to use the innovative digital payment systems and those who cannot still access it, despite the availability of such services. This will leave a group of people behind (Suri, 2017), causing a backlash from such groups and making further digital penetration harder. Policymakers must carefully take decisions related to these so that the unserved don't get pushed out to the edge even more. And they may hesitate to introduce digital payments in the interest of such groups as they have political repercussions later. But resisting digital payments has negative consequences as a society will suffer from the weakness and loopholes in the traditional cash-based system.

- **Security Concerns:** Digital payments successfully defend almost all physical security threats by replacing fiat money with digital money. Digital money is resilient to all physical threats like fire, flood, robbery etc. But this form of innovative money is subject to the threat of innovative crimes using equally or even higher intelligence (Milian et al., 2019). These cybersecurity incidents cause more fear among common people as it is beyond their comprehension and hinders their trust in digital payments. This different and complex security concern is the undesirable byproduct of the digital payment system that people must get over.
- **Dependency on Technology:** With a fiat money-based system, people struggle with the problem inherent to fiat money. With digital payment, people will struggle with the problems inherent in digital technology (Di. Gregorio et al., 2005). The need to have a working digital device and Internet is one of the basic requirements. Losing a phone can cost much more than the actual market price of the device. Person, losing it suffers breach from almost all the systems like communications, banks, and other payment mechanisms. Digital payment comes with a dependency on the device.
- **Privacy:** Digital payments have promising benefits from analytics as they can be utilized to analyze the data and pull insights that were never possible. But being able to track and analyze these data (Rodriguez-Carrion et al., 2015) underpin a strong chance of data being misused. Financial transactions are very sensitive data, and the impact of their compromise can be higher (Milian et al., 2019). Due to the nature of fiat money, traditional transactions are less susceptible to this threat, but digital payments are prone to privacy breaches.

CONCLUSION

This chapter aims to assess the impacts of digital payments on socio-economic factors in EMDEs. The authors have discussed the positive and negative impacts of digital payments in detail and highlighted some of the recommendations that government and policymakers can take to get benefitted from the positive impacts, such as operational efficiencies, innovative solutions, and new opportunities. At the same time, they should also pay attention to the negative impacts to mitigate any risk.

Operational efficiencies range from time savings to cost savings in doing transactions. Digital payments not only free people from the burden of cash management but also from buying security for the cash in the form of costly vaults and security personnel. Without digital payments, the world would be much slower than it is today. Beyond the efficiencies, digital payments have democratized financial access even more, solving the conundrum of social inclusion and corruption. The innovativeness of digital payment has empowered and enabled regulators to track down every penny exchanged and every person excluded/included from the system. This generally remained impractical so far. Furthermore, digital payments create opportunities that did not prevail before. Fintech companies like e-wallets, digital banks, and online investment portals/apps have emerged, creating, and sharing entirely new values. On the other hand, cyber security threats that hurt public trust and morale and fear of workforce replacement are major negative impacts. Additionally, the lack of readiness among the people to use digital payments may widen the digital divide between the served and the unserved.

The available research implies that governments should enact regulations that restrict cash transactions above a certain threshold level. Additionally, central banks ought to make a serious effort to cut down on high-denomination currencies. It is because these are not frequently used in legal transactions (Singh & Bhattacharya, 2017). The authors would like to stress that cutting back on the number of large denomination notes in circulation could be a creative, inexpensive, and easily implemented strategy for combating corruption. To combat money laundering and tax evasion, several governments are encouraging a transition to digital services, which they believe will increase competition in financial services. India is exploring alternatives to the country's long-standing reliance on cash transactions. Some high-denomination bank notes were taken out of circulation by the government a few years ago. For example, Narendra Modi, the prime minister of India, established numerous cashless townships where using cash and coins is frowned upon (Jenkins, 2018).

SOLUTIONS AND RECOMMENDATIONS

Despite the overall positive impact of digital payments on the socio-economic context, their potential negative impact cannot be ignored as it can significantly undermine their success. This study recommends five key areas to address these challenges. Firstly, the government should prioritize financial education to increase awareness and understanding of digital payments among citizens. This entails collaboration between central banks, commercial banks, and payment service providers to provide information in local languages and through government initiatives.

Secondly, building trust is crucial for the successful implementation of digital payments. Trust can be fostered through transparent and safe practices and positive communication. Institutions must also enhance their visibility and accessibility to increase consumer confidence. Thirdly, regulators and financial players should focus on establishing necessary infrastructural requirements, such as affordable and reliable internet connectivity, as digital payments are largely dependent on internet connectivity. Fourthly, financial service providers must reduce the barriers to entry for citizens in the fintech industry to expand financial inclusion. This includes encouraging the inclusion of small businesses in digital payment networks and rethinking bank agents' networks that primarily rely on cash payments.

Lastly, policy-makers should play a critical role in introducing new monetary policies that limit cash transactions to curb corruption, money laundering, and tax evasion. For example, governments could limit cash-based transactions to 10% of the total transaction amount to encourage the adoption of digital payments over cash transactions. In EMDEs, there is a positive correlation between corruption and cash holdings, which highlights the importance of such policies.

REFERENCES

Akter, S., Mohiuddin Babu, M., Hossain, M. A., & Hani, U. (2021). How does value co-creation transform quality of life at the bottom of the pyramid? *Journal of Marketing Management*, *37*(9–10), 962–992. doi:10.1080/0267257X.2021.1919745

Al-Okaily, M., Lutfi, A., Alsaad, A., Taamneh, A., & Alsyouf, A. (2020). The Determinants of Digital Payment Systems' Acceptance under Cultural Orientation Differences: The Case of Uncertainty Avoidance. *Technology in Society*, *63*. Advance online publication. doi:10.1016/J.TECHSOC.2020.101367

Ali, B. J., & Anwar, G. (2021). Factors Influencing the Citizens' Acceptance of Electronic Government. *Development*, *5*, 1.

Ali, R., Barrdear, J., Clews, R., & Southgate, J. (2014, Q3). Innovations in payment technologies and the emergence of digital currencies. *Bank of England Quarterly Bulletin*.

Alkhowaiter, W. A. (2020). Digital payment and banking adoption research in Gulf countries: A systematic literature review. *International Journal of Information Management*, *53*, 102102. doi:10.1016/J.IJINFOMGT.2020.102102

Allen, F., Demirguc-Kunt, A., Klapper, L., & Martinez Peria, M. S. (2016). The foundations of financial inclusion: Understanding ownership and use of formal accounts. *Journal of Financial Intermediation*, *27*, 1–30. doi:10.1016/J.JFI.2015.12.003

Amiram, D., Bozanic, Z., Cox, J. D., Dupont, Q., Karpoff, J. M., & Sloan, R. (2018). Financial reporting fraud and other forms of misconduct: A multidisciplinary review of the literature. *Review of Accounting Studies*, *23*(2), 732–783. doi:10.1007/S11142-017-9435-X

Angel, J. J. (2017). The Evolution of Money. By David Orrell and Roman Chlupatý. New York: Columbia University Press, 2016. x + 309 pp. Figures, notes, bibliography, index. Cloth, $35.00. ISBN: 978-0-231-17372-8. *Business History Review*, *91*(2), 397–399. doi:10.1017/S0007680517000800

Arner, D. W., Buckley, R. P., Zetzsche, D. A., & Veidt, R. (2020). Sustainability, FinTech and Financial Inclusion. *European Business Organization Law Review*, *21*(1), 7–35. doi:10.1007/S40804-020-00183-Y

Aurazo, J., & Vega, M. (2021). Why people use digital payments: Evidence from micro data in Peru. *Latin American Journal of Central Banking*, *2*(4), 100044. doi:10.1016/J.LATCB.2021.100044

Balakrishnan, V., & Shuib, N. L. M. (2021). Drivers and inhibitors for digital payment adoption using the Cashless Society Readiness-Adoption model in Malaysia. *Technology in Society*, *65*, 101554. doi:10.1016/J.TECHSOC.2021.101554

Beine, M., Lodigiani, E., & Vermeulen, R. (2012). Remittances and financial openness. *Regional Science and Urban Economics*, *42*(5), 844–857. doi:10.1016/J.REGSCIURBECO.2011.12.005

Berglof, E., & Bolton, P. (2002). The great divide and beyond: Financial architecture in transition. *The Journal of Economic Perspectives*, *16*(1), 77–100. doi:10.1257/0895330027120

Bisma, R., Puspita, Y., & Sulistiyani, E. (2020). Technology Compatibility Factors in the Implementation of the Ovo Digital Payment Application. *International Joint Conference on Science and Engineering (IJCSE 2020)*, 146–151.

Bonfiglio, A., Coderoni, S., Esposti, R., & Baldoni, E. (2021). The role of rurality in determining the economy-wide impacts of a natural disaster. *Economic Systems Research*, *33*(4), 446–469. doi:10.1080/09535314.2020.1814206

Brühl, V. (2020). Libra—A differentiated view on facebook's virtual currency project. *Inter Economics*, *55*(1), 54–61.

Carboni, I., & Bester, H. (2020). *When Digital Payment Goes Viral: Lessons from COVID-19s Impact on Mobile Money in Rwanda*. Academic Press.

Cerulus, L., & Contiguglia, C. (2018, August 14). *Central bankers warn of chaos in a cashless society*. https://www.politico.eu/article/central-bankers-fear-cybersecurity-chaos-in-a-cashless-society/

Chang, V., Doan, L. M. T., di Stefano, A., Sun, Z., & Fortino, G. (2022). Digital payment fraud detection methods in digital ages and Industry 4.0. *Computers & Electrical Engineering*, *100*, 107734. doi:10.1016/J.COMPELECENG.2022.107734

Chaudhuri, R., Carolyne, G., Tayar, G., & Williams, E. (2022). *Sustaining digital payments growth: Winning models in emerging markets*. Academic Press.

Chaveesuk, S., Khalid, B., & Chaiyasoonthorn, W. (2021). Digital payment system innovations: A marketing perspective on intention and actual use in the retail sector. *Innovative Marketing*, *17*(3), 109.

Chen, R., Yamaka, W., & Osathanunkul, R. (2019). Determinants of non-cash payments in Asian countries. *Journal of Physics: Conference Series*, *1324*(1), 012103.

Chiu, J., & Wong, T.-N. (2021). Payments on digital platforms: Resiliency, interoperability and welfare. *Journal of Economic Dynamics & Control*, *104173*. Advance online publication. doi:10.1016/J.JEDC.2021.104173

Dębski, M., Borkowska-Niszczota, M., & Andrzejczyk, R. (2021). Tourist Accommodation Establishments during the Pandemic – Consequences and Aid Report on a Survey among Polish Micro-enterprises Offering Accommodation Services. *Journal of Intercultural Management*, *13*(1), 1–25. doi:10.2478/joim-2021-0001

Di. Gregorio, D., Kassicieh, S. K., & de Gouvea Neto, R. (2005). Drivers of e-business activity in developed and emerging markets. *IEEE Transactions on Engineering Management*, *52*(2), 155–166. doi:10.1109/TEM.2005.844464

Du, M., Chen, Q., Xiao, J., Yang, H., & Ma, X. (2020). Supply Chain Finance Innovation Using Blockchain. *IEEE Transactions on Engineering Management*, *67*(4), 1045–1058. doi:10.1109/TEM.2020.2971858

Dziatkovskii, A., Hryneuski, U., Dudov, A., & Krylova, A. (2021). The economic impact of digitalization and the creation of digital products on the development of the state. *Economic Annals-XXI*, *193*(9–10), 4–14. doi:10.21003/EA.V193-01

Effah, J. (2016). Institutional effects on e-payment entrepreneurship in a developing country: Enablers and constraints. *Information Technology for Development*, *22*(2), 205–219.

Fabris, N. (2019). Cashless Society - The Future of Money or a Utopia? *Journal of Central Banking Theory and Practice*, *8*(1), 53–66. doi:10.2478/jcbtp-2019-0003

Ferrari, M. V. (2022). The platformisation of digital payments: The fabrication of consumer interest in the EU FinTech agenda. *Computer Law & Security Review*, *45*, 105687. doi:10.1016/J.CLSR.2022.105687

Ferrell, L., & Ferrell, O. C. (2012). Redirecting direct selling: High-touch embraces high-tech. *Business Horizons*, *55*(3), 273–281. doi:10.1016/J.BUSHOR.2012.01.004

Frączek, B., & Urbanek, A. (2021). Financial inclusion as an important factor influencing digital payments in passenger transport: A case study of EU countries. *Research in Transportation Business & Management*, *41*, 100691. doi:10.1016/J.RTBM.2021.100691

Gainsbury, S. M., & Blaszczynski, A. (2020). Digital gambling payment methods: Harm minimization policy considerations. *Gaming Law Review*, *24*(7), 466–472. doi:10.1089/GLR2.2020.0015

Gupta, S., Kiran, R., & Sharma, R. K. (2022). Validating the role of digital payment mode as a new driver of online shopping: A modified UTAUT2 model. *Journal of Public Affairs*, *22*(2), e2434.

Hidayanto, A. N., Hidayat, L. S., Sandhyaduhita, P. I., & Handayani, P. W. (2015). Examining the relationship of payment system characteristics and behavioural intention in e-payment adoption: A case of Indonesia. *International Journal of Business Information Systems*, *19*(1), 58–86.

Hinrichs, G., & Bundtzen, H. (2021). Impact of COVID-19 on personal insurance sales – Evidence from Germany. *Financial Markets. Institutions and Risks*, *5*(1), 80–86. doi:10.21272/fmir.5(1).80-86.2021

Howcroft, J. B., & Lavis, J. (1987). Evolution of the payment systems of London clearing banks. *Service Industries Journal*, *7*(2), 176–194.

Hult, G. T. M., Ketchen, D. J., Griffith, D. A., Chabowski, B. R., Hamman, M. K., Dykes, B. J., Pollitte, W. A., & Cavusgil, S. T. (2008). An assessment of the measurement of performance in international business research. *Journal of International Business Studies, 39*(6), 1064–1080. https://doi.org/ doi:10.1057/PALGRAVE.JIBS.8400398

Humphrey, D. B., & Hunt, R. (2013). Cost savings from check 21 electronic payment legislation. *Journal of Money, Credit and Banking*, *45*(7), 1415–1429. doi:10.1111/JMCB.12057

Jenkins, P. (2018, May 10). *We don't take cash': is this the future of money?* Financial Times. https://www.ft.com/content/9fc55dda-5316-11e8-b24e-cad6aa67e23e

Kadar, B., & Reicher, R. Z. (2020). Innovations in Health Care Management: The Effect of the Pandemic on the Labour Market Change. *Marketing and Management of Innovations*, *4*, 120–130. doi:10.21272/mmi.2020.4-09

Kala Kamdjoug, J. R., Wamba-Taguimdje, S. L., Wamba, S. F., & Kake, I. B. e. (2021). Determining factors and impacts of the intention to adopt mobile banking app in Cameroon: Case of SARA by afriland First Bank. *Journal of Retailing and Consumer Services*, *61*. Advance online publication. doi:10.1016/J.JRETCONSER.2021.102509

Kholiavko, N., Popelo, O., & Tulchynska, S. (2021). Priority directions of increasing the adaptivity of universities to the conditions of the digital economy. *Revista Tempos e Espaços Em Educação*, *14*(33), e16383–e16383. doi:10.20952/REVTEE.V14I33.16383

Klapper, L., & Singer, D. (2017). The opportunities and challenges of digitizing government-to- person payments. *The World Bank Research Observer*, *32*(2), 211–226. doi:10.1093/WBRO/LKX003

Kolosok, S., & Jakubowska, A. (2020). COVID-19 And Public Health Administration: Trends And Prospects. *Health Economics and Management Review*, *1*(1), 69–75. doi:10.21272/hem.2020.1-06

Kumar, P., & Chaubey, D. S. (2017). Demonetization and its impact on adoption of digital payment: Opportunities, issues and challenges. *Abhinav National Monthly Refereed Journal of Research in Commerce & Management*, *6*(6), 15.

Kumar, R., Shrestha, M., & Badir, Y. (2021). *Digital transformation of financial institutions and its impact on their profitability*. Korea Advanced Institute of Science and Technology.

Leong, C. M., Tan, K. L., Puah, C. H., & Chong, S. M. (2021). Predicting mobile network operators users m-payment intention. *European Business Review*, *33*(1). Advance online publication. doi:10.1108/EBR-10-2019-0263

Liu, N., Xu, Z., & Skare, M. (2021). The research on COVID-19 and economy from 2019 to 2020: Analysis from the perspective of bibliometrics. *Oeconomia Copernicana*, *12*(2), 217–268.

Liu, T., Pan, B., & Yin, Z. (2020). *Pandemic, Mobile Payment, and Household Consumption: Micro-Evidence from China*. https://doi.org/ doi:10.1080/1540496X.2020.1788539

Lo Prete, A. (2022). Digital and financial literacy as determinants of digital payments and personal finance. *Economics Letters*, *213*, 110378. doi:10.1016/J.ECONLET.2022.110378

Lu, L. (2018). *How A Little Ant Challenges Giant Banks? The Rise of Ant Financial (Alipay)'s Fintech Empire and Relevant Regulatory Concerns*. Academic Press.

Milian, E. Z., Spinola, M. de M., & de Carvalho, M. M. (2019). Fintechs: A literature review and research agenda. *Electronic Commerce Research and Applications*, *34*. Advance online publication. doi:10.1016/J.ELERAP.2019.100833

Mills, G. M. (2022, January 15). *Exploring The Growing List Of Countries That Indicate…*. https://www.koparunescape2gold.com/exploring-the-growing-list-of-countries-that-indicate/

Mishenina, H., Kirichenko, D., & Puzemsky, V. (2021). COVID-19 impact on the company's development: A case of UNIT.City. *Health Economics and Management Review*, *2*(2), 58–70. doi:10.21272/hem.2021.2-06

Mittal, D., & Agrawal, S. R. (2022). Determining banking service attributes from online reviews: Text mining and sentiment analysis. *International Journal of Bank Marketing*, *40*(3), 558–577. doi:10.1108/IJBM-08-2021-0380

Natile, S. (2020). Digital Finance Inclusion and the Mobile Money "Social" Enterprise. *Historical Social Research. Historische Sozialforschung*, *45*(3), 74–94.

Ngamije, J. (2021). The impact of Internet use during COVID-19 lockdown in Rwanda: a potential public health threat. Journal of Addictive Diseases, 39(3), 417–420. https://doi.org/ doi:10.1080/10550887.2021.1882649

Ong, H. B., & Chong, L. L. (2022). The effect of cashless payments on the internet and mobile banking. *Journal of Financial Services Marketing*. Advance online publication. doi:10.1057/S41264-022-00145-0

Pardal, P., Dias, R., Šuleř, P., Teixeira, N., & Krulický, T. (2020). Integration in Central European capital markets in the context of the global COVID-19 pandemic. *Equilibrium: Quarterly Journal of Economics and Economic Policy*, *15*(4), 627–650.

Pazarbasioglu, C., & Mora, A. G. (2020). *Expanding digital financial services can help developing economies cope with crisis now and boost growth later. World BankVoices* Blog.

Powell, J., & Buchan, I. (2005). Electronic health records should support clinical research. *Journal of Medical Internet Research*, *7*(1). Advance online publication. doi:10.2196/JMIR.7.1.E4

Purwanti, P., Susilo, E., & Indrayani, E. (2020). Business empowerment program and household economic welfare: Lesson from Indonesia. *Journal of Asian Finance. Economics and Business*, *7*(1), 313–320. doi:10.13106/JAFEB.2020.VOL7.NO1.313

Putra, R. L., Setiawan, M., Hussein, A. S., & Yuniarinto, A. (2022). Perceived Digital Value Toward Continuous Intention to Use Among Mobile Payment Users During Pandemic Outbreak. *Frontiers in Psychology*, *0*, 1995. doi:10.3389/FPSYG.2022.892821

Rana, R. L., Giungato, P., Tarabella, A., & Tricase, C. (2019). Blockchain applications and sustainability issues. *Amfiteatru Economic, 21*(13), 669. https://doi.org/ doi:10.24818/EA/2019/S13/861

Reserve Bank of India. (2020). *Annual Report 2020*. Author.

Rodriguez-Carrion, A., Rebollo-Monedero, D., Forné, J., Campo, C., Garcia-Rubio, C., Parra-Arnau, J., & Das, S. K. (2015). Entropy-based privacy against profiling of user mobility. *Entropy (Basel, Switzerland)*, *17*(6), 3913–3946. doi:10.3390/E17063913

Sahu, G. P., & Singh, N. K. (2018). Identifying Critical Success Factor (CSFs) for the adoption of digital payment systems: A study of Indian national banks. *Emerging Markets from a Multidisciplinary Perspective: Challenges, Opportunities and Research Agenda*, 61–73.

Sardana, V., & Singhania, S. (2018). Digital technology in the realm of banking: A review of literature. *International Journal of Research in Finance and Management*, *1*(2), 28–32.

Setor, T. K., Senyo, P. K., & Addo, A. (2021a. Do digital payment transactions reduce corruption? Evidence from developing countries. *Telematics and Informatics*, *60*, 101577. doi:10.1016/J.TELE.2021.101577

Shahzad, S. J. H., Anas, M., & Bouri, E. (2022). Price explosiveness in cryptocurrencies and Elon Musk's tweets. *Finance Research Letters*, *47*, 102695. doi:10.1016/J.FRL.2022.102695

Singh, S. K., & Bhattacharya, K. (2017). Does easy availability of cash affect corruption? Evidence from a panel of countries. *Economic Systems*, *41*(2), 236–247. doi:10.1016/J.ECOSYS.2016.06.002

Sivathanu, B. (2019). Adoption of digital payment systems in the era of demonetization in India: An empirical study. *Journal of Science and Technology Policy Management*, *10*(1), 143–171.

Stefan, G., Coca, O., Creanga, D. E., Mursa, G. C., & Mihai, C. (2020). The impact of the crisis generated by covid-19 on the population concerns. A comparative study at the level of the European Union. *Transformations in Business & Economics*, 19.

Stofkova, K. R., Laitkep, D., & Stofkova, Z. (2022). Shopping Behavior in the Context of the Digital Economy. *Journal of Risk and Financial Management*, *15*(2). Advance online publication. doi:10.3390/JRFM15020039

Suri, T. (2017). Mobile money. *Annual Review of Economics*, *9*, 497–520. doi:10.1146/ANNUREV-ECONOMICS-063016-103638

Suyunchaliyeva, M. M., Nautiyal, R., Shaikh, A. A., & Sharma, R. (2021). *The Use of Mobile Payment Systems in Post-COVID-19 Economic Recovery: Primary Research on an Emerging Market for Experience Goods*. https://doi.org/ doi:10.3390/su132413511

Taylor, E. (2016). Mobile payment technologies in retail: A review of potential benefits and risks. *International Journal of Retail & Distribution Management*, *44*(2), 159–177. doi:10.1108/IJRDM-05-2015-0065

The World Bank. (2021). *The Global Findex Database 2021*. Author.

Tiutiunyk, I., Humenna, Y., & Flaumer, A. (2021). COVID-19 Impact on Business Sector Activity in the EU Countries: Digital Issues. *Health Economics and Management Review*, *1*, 54–66. doi:10.21272/hem.2021.1

Tomcikova, L., Svetozarovova, N., & Coculova, J. (2021). Challenges and priorities in talent management during the global pandemic caused by COVID-19. *Marketing and Management of Innovations*, *5*(2), 94–103. doi:10.21272/mmi.2021.2-08

Tronnier, F., Harborth, D., & Hamm, P. (2022). Investigating privacy concerns and trust in the digital Euro in Germany. *Electronic Commerce Research and Applications*, *53*, 101158. doi:10.1016/J.ELERAP.2022.101158

van Dijk, J., & Hacker, K. (2011). *The Digital Divide as a Complex and Dynamic Phenomenon*. https://doi.org/ doi:10.1080/01972240309487

Varshney, D., Kumar, A., Mishra, A. K., Rashid, S., & Joshi, P. K. (2021). India's COVID-19 social assistance package and its impact on the agriculture sector. *Agricultural Systems*, *189*, 103049. doi:10.1016/J.AGSY.2021.103049

Verkijika, S. F. (2018). Factors influencing the adoption of mobile commerce applications in Cameroon. *Telematics and Informatics*, *35*(6), 1665–1674. doi:10.1016/J.TELE.2018.04.012

Vinitha, K., & Vasantha, S. (2017). Influence of demographic variables on usage of e-payment system. *Int J Mech Eng Technol*, *8*, 265–276.

White, H. (2023). *PROFITENCE 2022 E-commerce Report: Banking & Online Payment Gateways*. Academic Press.

Yang, S., Lu, Y., Gupta, S., Cao, Y., & Zhang, R. (2012). Mobile payment services adoption across time: An empirical study of the effects of behavioral beliefs, social influences, and personal traits. *Computers in Human Behavior*, *28*(1), 129–142. doi:10.1016/J.CHB.2011.08.019

ADDITIONAL READING

Ali, R., Barrdear, J., Clews, R., & Southgate, J. (2014, Q3). Innovations in payment technologies and the emergence of digital currencies. *Bank of England Quarterly Bulletin*.

Allen, F., Demirguc-Kunt, A., Klapper, L., & Martinez Peria, M. S. (2016). The foundations of financial inclusion: Understanding ownership and use of formal accounts. *Journal of Financial Intermediation*, *27*, 1–30. doi:10.1016/J.JFI.2015.12.003

Balakrishnan, V., & Shuib, N. L. M. (2021). Drivers and inhibitors for digital payment adoption using the Cashless Society Readiness-Adoption model in Malaysia. *Technology in Society*, *65*, 101554. doi:10.1016/J.TECHSOC.2021.101554

Chiu, J., & Wong, T.-N. (2021). Payments on digital platforms: Resiliency, interoperability and welfare. *Journal of Economic Dynamics & Control*, *104173*. Advance online publication. doi:10.1016/J.JEDC.2021.104173

Fabris, N. (2019). Cashless Society - The Future of Money or a Utopia? *Journal of Central Banking Theory and Practice*, *8*(1), 53–66. doi:10.2478/jcbtp-2019-0003

Singh, S. K., & Bhattacharya, K. (2017). Does easy availability of cash affect corruption? Evidence from a panel of countries. *Economic Systems*, *41*(2), 236–247. doi:10.1016/J.ECOSYS.2016.06.002

Suri, T. (2017). Mobile money. *Annual Review of Economics*, *9*, 497–520. doi:10.1146/ANNUREV-ECONOMICS-063016-103638

KEY TERMS AND DEFINITIONS

Cashless Society: A system in which paying for goods or services with cash or checks is no longer the norm and is replaced using credit cards or electronic fund transfers.

Digital Divide: It describes the division between people and places with and without easy access to cutting-edge information and communication technologies. This category includes common household items such as telephones, televisions, computers, and access to the internet.

Digital Literacy: Digital literacy refers to the abilities required to live, learn, and work in a society where communication and access to information are increasingly mediated by digital technologies such as internet platforms, social media, and mobile devices.

Digital Payment: A payment method that is based on the Internet is referred to as digital payment, where several transactions can be processed concurrently in an orderly, precise, and productive manner, which increases productivity.

Economic Empowerment: Empowerment in the economic sphere refers to the capacity to make and carry out decisions that include the management of and distribution of monetary resources. It has a direct influence on the growth of the economy and vice versa. In other words, economic empowerment can be defined as the process of assisting individuals, primarily women from low-income backgrounds, in obtaining the education, training, and job-related skills they require to support themselves and their families.

Emerging Market and Developing Economies (EMDEs): Emerging economies are those of developing countries that are becoming increasingly involved in global markets as they grow. Emerging market economies are those that have some of the features of developed market economies but not all of them. These countries are categorized as emerging market economies.

Financial Inclusion: Individuals and organizations are considered to be financially included when they have access to relevant and affordable financial products and services that satisfy their requirements such as financial dealings of all kinds (transactions, payments, savings, credit, and insurance), carried out in an ethical and environmentally conscious manner.

Good Governance: The International Monetary Fund (IMF) defines governance as the process by which a nation is administered, considering economic, policy, and legal aspects. The goals of good governance include reducing corruption, including minorities' viewpoints, hearing from oppressed people during the decision-making process, and actively attending to the present and future needs of the community.

Chapter 11
Leveraging Machine Learning Techniques to Improve Learning and Recommendations Within Dairy Farms:
Towards High Milk Yields for Small-Scale Farmers

Devotha G. Nyambo
Nelson Mandela African Institution of Science and Technology, Tanzania

Glory C. Malamsha
Nelson Mandela African Institution of Science and Technology, Tanzania

Fatuma Mavura
Nelson Mandela African Institution of Science and Technology, Tanzania

ABSTRACT

Tanzania's small-scale dairy industry faces similar challenges to those of other developing nations whereby insufficient infrastructure, outdated technology, and low productivity are serious problems for higher milk yield. Tanzania urgently needs to adopt cutting-edge solutions in order to boost dairy performance. With 3500 households' secondary data and 202 households' primary data from 8 villages throughout the Kilimanjaro and Arusha regions, this chapter demonstrates the use of machine learning (ML) techniques to derive homogeneous production clusters and recommendations for more milk yield among dairy farmers. The likelihood for higher milk yield is demonstrated for various clusters with the use of support, confidence, and lift values of association rules analysis. Finally, the production clusters and recommendations are deployed through a mobile application. Recommendations for future improvement are suggested especially on further deployment of learning recommendations and development of a platform-independent mobile solution.

DOI: 10.4018/978-1-6684-6873-9.ch011

INTRODUCTION

Over 150 million farm households around the world are supported by small-scale dairy farming, which is characterized by small herds of 1-2 milking cows (Chawala et al., 2019). Small-scale farmers are most prevalent in developing nations (Chawala et al., 2019). Due to the valuable food items it produces that improve household nutrition and food security, small-scale dairying is a significant agricultural activity in many developing countries (Kingu & Ndiege, 2018). In line with an expanding population and rising per capita income, there is a substantial increase in the demand for dairy products (Taneja et al., 2019). In line with the rising demand for milk as a result of the world population's expansion to over 7 billion people, the dairy sector is a significant employer worldwide and is expanding (Gitau, 2013). The consumption of milk and dairy products is higher in industrialized countries than in developing ones, although this disparity is closing due to rising incomes, population growth, urbanization, and dietary changes (Taneja et al., 2019).

According to estimates, the number of people who consume dairy and dairy products would increase from 1.8 billion in 2009 to 4.9 billion by the year 2030 (Taneja et al., 2019). However, the development of techniques to raise agricultural and dairy sector yield has lagged behind the rate of demand growth (Taneja et al., 2019). While global milk output as a whole has increased by 32%, milk production per person has decreased by 9% (Gitau, 2013). Small-scale dairy farmers run around half of all livestock operations in Africa, yet they struggle to produce adequate amounts of milk due to lack of infrastructure and a framework that would allow them to do so (Mavura et al., 2022). In light of this, it can be concluded that global milk production has not kept up with the population growth (Gitau, 2013). New and efficient strategies are required to increase this sector's production capacity in order to meet the rising demand for food (Taneja et al., 2019).

BACKGROUND INFORMATION

Goal two of the Sustainable Development Agenda aims to eradicate hunger, establish food and nutrition security, and advance sustainable agriculture by 2030 (Liverpool-Tasie et al., 2020). To achieve this, it is necessary for small-scale farmers to participate in and gain from the rapid expansion and development of food systems (Liverpool-Tasie et al., 2020). Small-scale livestock producers have an opportunity to improve their livelihoods and become food and nutritionally secure, thanks to the global increase in the demand for and production of animal-source foods, which has been mostly concentrated in Low and Middle Income Countries (LMIC) (four to fivefold increase between 1960 and 2015) (Balehegn et al., 2020).Globally, and especially in LMIC, the demand for animal products is expanding due to population increase, urbanization, and rising affluence (Balehegn et al., 2020).Consumer demand for milk in LMIC will increase by 5.5 million tons, by the year 2050 compared to 2005/2007 (Balehegn et al., 2020). The dairy farming sub-sector has a huge potential to raise people's standards of living (SDG#3) and help end poverty (SDG#1) by promoting better nutrition through milk consumption and revenue from the sale of milk and milk-related goods (Mbilu, 2015; Mzingula, 2019).

Tanzania's livestock sector includes the dairy industry as one of its key constituents (Mzingula, 2019). In terms of the Gross Domestic Product, it accounts for nearly one-third of the 4.6% share of the cattle industry (Mzingula, 2019). Small-scale dairy farming has grown quickly in Tanzania over the past three decades, mostly as a result of its effective role in reducing poverty and bridging the gap to rising demand for milk and milk products (Chawala et al., 2019). More than 1.3 million households in Tanzania are estimated to be served by the production of dairy products (Mbilu, 2015). For the majority of farmers who are involved in farming productivity in addition to meeting the demand for dairy products, small-scale dairy farming projects are a crucial source of livelihood (Atuhaire et al., 2014). Small-scale dairy farmers dominate Tanzania dairy sector hence are important in improving milk supply to accommodate the growing milk demand (Brett, 2019). For greater output and family welfare, it is essential to increase the productivity of dairy animals in the small-scale sector (Urassa & Raphael, 2017).

Tanzania's small-scale dairy industry faces similar challenges to those of other developing nations where limited infrastructure, outdated technology, and low productivity are major factors in milk production (Kingu & Ndiege, 2018). For productivity to increase, management in the areas of feeding, breeding, and disease control need to be improved (Urassa &Raphael, 2017). Small-scale farmers make up the majority of Tanzania's dairy industry, which struggles for a number of reasons, including the fact that 97 percent of the country's dairy cattle are low-yield breeds with poor management techniques, and there are seasonal variations in forage and feed availability (Alonso et al., 2014; Brett, 2019). Small-scale farmers' lives could be improved by dairy farming, but it does not receive the same degree of development assistance as other agricultural sectors (Turiansky, 2021). Increased animal productivity and commercialization of the livestock sector are the goals of Tanzania's livestock industry, which would lead to better household food security and revenue (Chawala et al., 2019). The small-scale farmers are characterized with highly heterogeneous substructures which complicates service delivery and support (Mavura et al., 2022). Since this is the case, the right framework and substructures should be used to ensure that farmers are supplied with the necessary services, which may help to maximize their production (Alonso et al., 2014). To achieve this, disaggregation of the production systems is important for farmers to be supported based on their production homogeneity.

Machine learning is a technique that enhances system performance by using computational techniques to learn from experience (Zhou, 2021). Data is the primary type of experience in computer systems, and the goal of machine learning is to create learning algorithms that create models from data (Zhou, 2021). Data on agricultural production are generally available, but are not sufficiently utilized to provide information on tasks that are relevant to production (Cockburn, 2020). It is found that ML techniques were used to forecast data in a number of dairy farming contexts, such as milk yield or energy usage; nevertheless, larger integrated datasets are needed to improve the dependability of the generated algorithms (Cockburn, 2020). This demonstrates the opportunities that ML approaches may present for the dairy industry (Cockburn, 2020).

This chapter presents a Machine Learning technique to form farmers homogenous groups (Nyambo et al., 2019), referred to as production clusters; an approach to provide recommendations for higher milk yield based on association rules mining; and a deployment of the solution into a farmer-centric mobile application.

MAIN FOCUS OF THE CHAPTER

The demand of milk production is increasing but the production from small-scale farming systems is not keeping up with the demand. Small-scale dairy farmers in Tanzania have problems such as low-yield breeds, poor management practices and seasonal fluctuations of feeds (C.I. Brett, 2019). There is low milk production and high demand of milk supply in Tanzania. Milk demand is rising sharply as the growth of human population at the rate of 3.3% per year and 7% per year in economic growth (Kurwijila et al., 2012). These challenges are largely aggravated by the lack of homogenous groupings where service delivery and support can be given to farmers. Since efficient classification can educate extension services that support agricultural development, farm typologies can aid in the generation of context-specific improvement solutions (Ahikiriza et al., 2021). As such, the establishment of better dairy farming managing practices and extension provisions can be effective if particular restraints are recognized for each farm classification (Nyambo et al., 2019). Due to the pertinent characteristics of farmers based on management practices, there are heterogeneous groups that complicate service provision, knowledge exchange, and technology dissemination, particularly for those who intend to maximize productivity and profitability (Nyambo et al., 2019). When smallholder producers work together, they learn new abilities and are better able to handle difficulties jointly. In addition, farmers' knowledge sharing is limited with respect to structures and inadequate knowledge on key production characteristics among them. This chapter details how Machine Learning can be used in formation of the homogeneous groups, characterize and render a peer-to-peer learning approach which can be used by farmers to learn and share knowledge among themselves.

The Tanzania's dairy industry contributes only 1.5% of the total GDP compared to Rwanda and Kenya (6% contribution to GDP) because of low investments in the sector. Application of technology to solve various problems in the dairy sector is highly needed in Tanzania to increase the dairy performance (Njuguna, 2021). Farm groups created using machine learning were therefore, used to develop a network among famers to help farmers increase milk yield by adapting better management strategies from successful farmers within their groups (Nyambo et al., 2020).

METHODOLOGY

The study adopted a quantitative approach where Machine Learning (ML) techniques were used to achieve the stated objectives. A total of 3500 small-scale dairy households were involved in a baseline data collection under the PEARL[1] project in 2016, this was used as a secondary data and was complemented with additional primary data that was collected in 8 villages in Kilimanjaro and Arusha regions, where 202 households were involved. Various ML techniques were used in data preparation that also included removal of location effect so as to achieve a universal dataset to be used in ML models. Unsupervised Learning Algorithms including clustering and association rules mining were applied in this study.

Understanding Various Production Clusters in the Dairy Industry by Using Machine Learning Techniques

The diversity of small-scale dairy farming systems makes it more difficult to provide services, share information, and spread new technology, particularly those required to increase productivity and profitability. Clustering can be helpful in a variety of exploratory pattern-analysis, grouping, decision-making, and machine learning scenarios (Gelbard et al., 2007). It is vital to identify groups of farmers who engage in comparable management activities in order to create homogeneous groups within which interventions can be implemented (Nyambo, 2020). Six clusters were identified in Tanzania using the Elbow method as a determinant of appropriate number of clusters with minimum within sum of square differences (Nyambo, 2020). The Self-Organizing Maps (Kohonen algorithm) and the K-means were applied for a comparative assessment. In order to achieve maximum distances between the various groups and minimum distances within each group, cluster evaluation metrics based on Euclidian distances were used (Gelbard et al., 2007).

Understanding How Machine Learning Can Be Used in Building Recommendations on How Farmers Can Increase Daily Milk Yield

Pattern and association rules mining were done to uncover relationships among farm practices in relation to milk yield. Association rule mining is a technique in descriptive data mining where characteristics of a large dataset are obtained (Slimani & Lazzez, 2014). Association rule mining is very important as it helped the researcher to identity how farm practices in various farms are linked to milk yield. This involved the identification of high, medium and low milk producing clusters using production features performance. From the six clusters identified, three were purposively chosen for association rules mining. The chosen clusters represented farmers with high (14.45 ± 5.12), medium (11.08 ± 4.29), and low (9.15 ± 3.25), milk yield with commercial orientation (Mavura et al., 2022). Cluster one was the high producers, cluster five was the medium producers and cluster four contained the low milk producers (Mavura et al., 2022).

From frequent patterns analysis, association rules were developed. Rules were mined from the three clusters and evaluation metrices based on support, confidence and lift were used to confirm strong rules. The aim of the rules is to find the link between farm practices and milk yield so as to improve the farm practices of the farmers. The measure of support is how often or frequent the particular items appear in a mined database (Hussein et al., 2015). Confidence is the absolute or probability based number of times the if-then statements mined are found to be true (John et al., 2016). Lift is an indicator of how strong the items of the rules are when they are together than how they are apart. The measure of Lift, signifies how important a rules is with a value of 1 or above (Mourelatos et al., 2016).

Apriori algorithm was used in the mining of association rules. This involved four steps: visualizing data set, mining of the association rules, arranging rules by using lift value and visualizing rules in a table format. The following is a sample code for mining rules in clusters one for the high milk producers. The name of the data set used was Type-one. The minimum support was varied from 0.15 to 0.6 and minimum confidence was varied from 0.645 to 0.95. This variation of the support and confidence was based on the number of occurrences of the farm practices in the clusters. The lift values were observed from the highest to the lowest values and mining was made sure to obtain rules of lift above 1.0.

Sample code:

```
#1. Visualizing the dataset
View(Type_one)
#2. Mining of association rules
library(arules)
rules=apriori(Type_one,
                  parameter=list(supp=0.15,
                                 conf=0.645, minlen=2))
#3. Arranging rules using lift value
rules=sort(rules, by="lift")
#4. Visualizing rules in a table format
df_basket1 <- as(rules,"data.frame")
View(df_basket1)
```

Deployment and Validation of the Machine Learning Approaches by Using Mobile Applications

To validate the applicability of the ML techniques, resulting models were deployed in a mobile application to test for farmer profiling (auto-allocation) into relevant production clusters according to actual milk yield; and provide a data driven recommendation on best strategies to apply for higher milk yield. Development of the mobile application was done by using Android development framework. In agriculture, the importance of farmer information sharing, particularly the transmission of the most effective farming techniques motivates other dairy experts to adopt the technique to increase milk yield (Mavura et al., 2022). More emphasis should be placed on encouraging adaptability in each learner's behavior and enhancing the sharing of accomplishments (Thakur & Chander, 2018). The level of production of small-scale dairy farmers can be significantly increased by improving their understanding of new technologies and techniques (Patii et al., 2017).

Mobile Phones

take communication to a new level by linking small-scale dairy farmers, allowing them to access extension services, and attaining awareness (Thiam & Matofari, 2018). The value of social networks for farmer learning, particularly for peer-to-peer communication within farmer groups, has been demonstrated to show positive results in numerous studies (Faysse et al., 2012).

RESULTS

Identified Production Clusters in the Dairy Industry by Using Machine Learning Techniques

Self-Organizing Maps (SOM) and the K-mean clustering was employed to formulate homogeneous groups of farmers according to various production characteristics. Intra-cluster similarity and mean distance from the centroids were used to evaluate performance of the three solutions. Based on the Elbow technique, six clusters were identified. The SOM tended to have more defined clusters, despite the fact that the mean silhouette separation coefficients for K-means and SOM were not substantially different; 0.66 and 0.64, respectively (Nyambo, 2020).

No significant difference could be observed with regard to the inter-cluster adhesion between K-means and SOM. Ranking correlation was used to study the levels of household relocation for the training and testing datasets. Results indicated very high re-ranking of cluster membership between training and testing datasets. Clusters from the K-means model achieved significant prediction accuracies for both milk yield and sales (at 46% and 41%, respectively). However, the K-means clusters had lower prediction accuracy for choice of breeding method (29%). Clusters from the SOM model performed poorly on the quantitative traits but had higher probability (46%) for correctly assigning the choice of breeding method. The total variance as an effect of the clusters (from the SOM model) was 1.076 and 1.09 for milk yield and sales, respectively. Table 1 summarizes the cluster characteristics for cluster one to six.

Table 1. Cluster characteristics for Tanzania small-scale dairy farmers

Cluster	High Cluster Loadings	Low Cluster Loadings	Cluster Name
1	Vaccination frequency, frequency of watering, experience in dairy farming	Distance to buyers, total land size, area under fodder production	*Commercially oriented high production households*
2	Frequency of watering, area under fodder production, distance to breeding service providers	Area under grazing, years of schooling, sell of bulk milk	*Semi-intensive commercially oriented low production households*
3	Frequency of watering, sell of bulk milk, vaccination frequency	Frequency of visits by extension officers, distance to breeding service providers, number of milking cows	*commercially oriented and self-reliant high dairy production households*
4	Frequency of watering, vaccination frequency, area under fodder production	Area under grazing, years of schooling, sell of bulk milk	Semi-intensive commercially oriented low production households
5	Frequency of watering, liters of milk sold, vaccination frequency	Distance to markets, experience in dairy farming, total land size	*Commercially oriented medium production entrant households*
6	Distance to water sources, total cattle owned, frequency of watering	Total crop sales, distance to breeding service providers, experience in dairy farming	*Non-commercially oriented mixed crop-dairy low production entrant households*

Building Recommendations on How Farmers Can Increase Daily Milk Yield by Using Machine Learning

Feeding Practices

From the mined rules farmers based most in using only stall-feeding system for their cattle in all the clusters. This feeding practice was obtained in high milk producing cluster (one) at the support of 62% and confidence of 99% and lift of 1.29. This feeding practice was obtained in medium milk producing cluster (five) at the support of 40% and confidence of 100% and lift of 1.39. This feeding practice was obtained in low milk producing cluster (4) at the support of 74% and confidence of 99% and lift of 1.14. Other mined feeding practices include farmers do not possess land for fodder production in all the clusters. Watering frequency in cluster one is at least twice a day compared to other clusters where it is practiced once per day.

Breeding Practices

Farmers in cluster one prefers bull breeding. This breeding practice was obtained in high milk producing cluster (one) at the support of 61% and confidence of 95% and lift of 1.02. Farmers in cluster five (medium producers) prefer artificial insemination. This breeding practice was obtained in medium milk producing cluster at the support of 40% and confidence of 100% and lift of 1.39. The farmers in the low milk producing cluster prefer bull breeding. This breeding practice was obtained in cluster four at the support of 74% and confidence of 99% and lift of 1.14. Cluster one (high producers) and five (medium producers) indicated strong rules on preference of breed type/rank. The preferred breed in rank 1 was Friesian breed. This breeding practice was obtained in high milk producing cluster at the support of 22%

and confidence of 99% and lift of 3.57. This breeding practice was obtained in medium milk producing cluster at the support of 22% and confidence of 98% and lift of 3.15. There was no preferred breed in rank 1 in the low milk producing cluster. This breeding practice was obtained in cluster four at the support of 37% and confidence of 100% and lift of 2.07. The preferred breed in rank 2 was Ayrshire breed. This breeding practice was obtained in high milk producing cluster at the support of 22% and confidence of 99% and lift of 3.57. This breeding practice was obtained in medium milk producing cluster at the support of 22% and confidence of 98% and lift of 3.15. There was no preferred breed in rank 2 in the low milk producing cluster. This breeding practice was obtained in cluster four at the support of 37% and confidence of 100% and lift of 2.07. The preferred breed in rank 3 was Jersey breed. This breeding practice was obtained in high milk producing cluster at the support of 22% and confidence of 99% and lift of 3.57. This breeding practice was obtained in medium milk producing cluster at the support of 22% and confidence of 98% and lift of 3.15. There was no preferred breed in rank 3 in the low milk producing cluster. This breeding practice was obtained in cluster four at the support of 37% and confidence of 100% and lift of 2.07.

Health Practices

Under this category, various heath practices including extension visits form the extension officers and deworming frequency was examined. Frequency of visits from extension officers for most farmers in all clusters is one to nine visits. This health practice was obtained in the high milk producing cluster (one) at the support of 61% and confidence of 99% and lift of 1.29. This health practice was obtained in medium milk producing cluster (five) at the support of 40% and confidence of 97% and lift of 1.08. This health practice was obtained in low milk producing cluster (four) at the support of 73% and confidence of 96% and lift of 1.11. Other mined rules include deworming frequency and spraying frequency of the cattle.

Milk Yield

Farmers in the high milk producing cluster indicated an average milk production of (14.45 ± 5.12) liters of milk per cow. This was obtained from the farmers at the support of 25% and confidence of 75% and lift of 1.22. Farmers in the medium milk producing cluster have average milk production of (11.08 ± 4.29) liters of milk. This was obtained from the farmers at the support of 41% and confidence of 86% and lift of 1.2. Low milk producing farmers have average milk production of (9.15 ± 3.25) liters of milk. This was obtained from the farmers at the support of 27% and confidence of 68% and lift of 1.47. Table 2 shows a summary of Farm practices and milk yield of small-scale farmers in high (one), medium (five) and low (four) clusters that will help in building recommendations.

Deployment of the Machine Learning Approaches by Using Mobile Applications

In research on how farmers might boost yield, the peer-to-peer learning paradigm is rarely applied (Nyambo, 2020). Collaboration among small-scale dairy producers helps them develop new skills and cope with challenges more effectively (Nyambo et al., 2019). To achieve the intended results, farmers must engage in collaborative behavior (Mavura et al., 2022). From the produced clusters and association rules which can help farmers learn from one another and improve their milk yield, a mobile based application was implemented as an approach for deploying the solutions.

Table 2. Farm practices and milk yield of small-scale farmers

Category	Features	Clusters	Support	Confidence	Lift
Feeding practices	Only stall-feeding system	High	62%	99%	1.29
	Only stall-feeding system	Medium	40%	100%	1.39
	Only stall-feeding system	Low	74%	99%	1.14
Breeding practices	Bull breeding	High	61%	95%	1.02
	Artificial insemination	Medium	40%	100%	1.39
	Bull breeding	Low	74%	99%	1.14
	Friesian breed preferred rank 1	High	22%	99%	3.57
	Friesian breed preferred rank 1	Medium	22%	98%	3.15
	No breed preferred rank 1	Low	37%	100%	2.07
	Ayrshire breed preferred rank 2	High	22%	99%	3.57
	Ayrshire breed preferred rank 2	Medium	22%	98%	3.15
	No breed preferred rank 2	Low	37%	100%	2.07
	Jersey breed preferred rank 3	High	22%	99%	3.57
	Jersey breed preferred rank 3	Medium	22%	98%	3.15
	No breed preferred rank 3	Low	37%	100%	2.07
Health practices	One to nine extension officer visits	High	61%	99%	1.29
	One to nine extension officer visits	Medium	40%	97%	1.08
	One to nine extension officer visits	Low	73%	96%	1.11
Milk yield	Average milk production	High	23%	75%	1.22
	Average milk production	Medium	41%	86%	1.2
	Average milk production	Low	27%	68%	1.47

Consequently, the mobile-based peer-to-peer learning prototype was developed with the primary objective of increasing milk yield. It allows small-scale dairy farmers to share agricultural experiences and learn from each other (Mavura et al., 2022). Additionally, small-scale dairy farmers were automatically assigned to their respective clusters utilizing a Rule-based engine of the mobile-based peer-to-peer learning prototype (Mavura et al., 2022) as shown in Figure 1. Small-scale dairy farmers who are part of these production clusters exchange knowledge and expertise about farming-related difficulties and receive prompt assistance from the system's extension staff (Mavura et al., 2022).

DISCUSSION

This study obtained various findings that have a variety of practical significances for the dairy sector. They provide information to small-scale dairy producers and service providers (extension officers). The following are some of the most significant discoveries.

Figure 1. Conceptual framework
Source: Mavura et al. (2022)

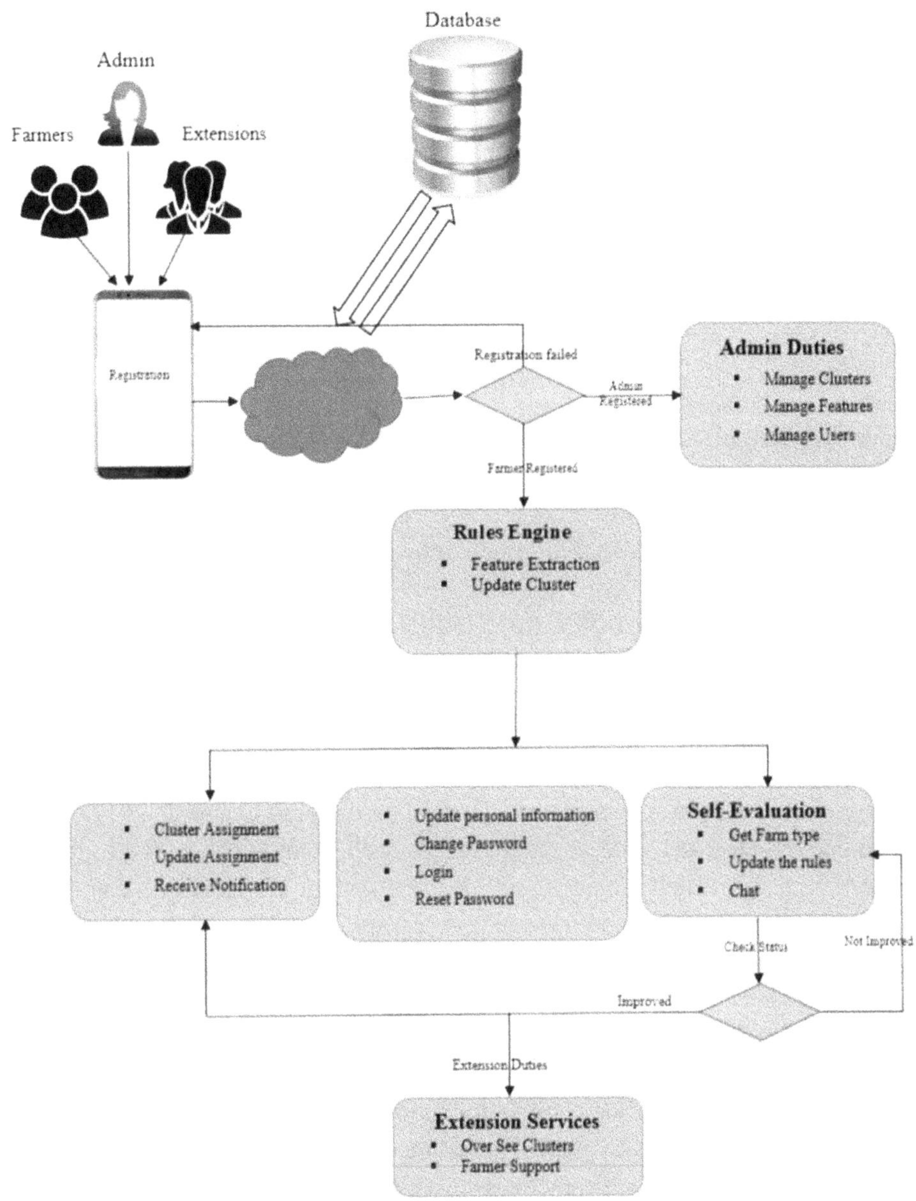

Small-Scale Dairy Farmers' Characterization for Easy Interventions and Farming Management

Six (6) clusters of small-scale dairy farmers were identified, and each cluster differs from the others in a number of ways. Despite the fact that unsupervised learning models have a poor consistency and are quite unpredictable, they have been used to describe small-scale farmers (Gelbard et al., 2007). This study assessed the effectiveness of three popular clustering techniques for agricultural households: K-means, and SOM (Nyambo et al., 2019). It is suggested to use a set of validation criteria to judge how reliable the defined clusters are, this method is rarely applied to similar investigations (Nyambo et al., 2019). Common hierarchical and nonhierarchical clustering methods have been used to describe small-scale farming systems in Africa (Nyambo et al., 2019). Work done by (Dossa et al., 2011; Kuivanen, Alvarez, et al., 2016; Kuivanen, Michalscheck, et al., 2016)utilized the ward and K-means methods to define clusters for small-scale households. To validate cluster-based characterization in addition to machine learning methodologies, it is strongly advised to leverage expert knowledge (Kuivanen, Alvarez, et al., 2016; Kuivanen, Michalscheck, et al., 2016). In several research, a participatory technique has been employed to accurately determine the types of farms by drawing on local knowledge (Nyambo et al., 2019). Additionally, complicated clustering methods have been investigated in the examination of various small-scale clusters, as done by (Galluzzo, 2015; Paas & Groot, 2017; Salasya & Stoorvogel, 2010). These studies, in turn, demonstrate the application of fuzzy clustering, neural networks, and naive Bayes algorithms. A farm may belong to more than one cluster or none at all, despite the fact that all clustering categorizes farmers into specific types, this is achieved through fuzzy clustering (Nyambo et al., 2019). It is necessary to incorporate the small-scale farmer study conducted by (Goswami et al., 2014) into the creation of predictive clusters. As such, evolvement of farmers in the homogeneous groups can be predicted because the clusters' stabilities are known.

Recommender System for Small-Scale Dairy Farmers

Association rules were mined in the relevant clusters to identify the farm practices in each cluster. Farm practices included feeding, health and breeding practices that farmers used in their dairy farms. Purchasing of feeds for cattle lead to low supply of fodder to the cattle hence low milk production. This is especially due to poverty or dry season hence less feeds in market (Lukuyu et al., 2017). Animals should have quality and enough feed and water to produce milk well (Kim et al., 2011). In feeding practices most farmers have been identified to practice stall feeding system for their cattle but do not have area for fodder production. Area for fodder production is necessary in order to facilitate for feeds throughout the year for cattle and increase milk production. Artificial insemination favors the introduction of breeds with favorable traits such as milk production and improved beef cattle (Berry et al., 2016). In breeding practices only medium producers in Tanzania are using artificial insemination method hence encouraging future improvement of milk production. The higher and low milk producers are still using bull breeding method which may not favor the increase of milk production. Milk production in cows is good if they are kept in clean and comfortable places to graze and rest hence comfortable healthy cows have increased milk production (Toledo, 2018). In health practices most farmers in all clusters have frequent visits of one to nine in a year which means the farmers are aware of cattle health. Although this frequency does not cover all months in a year hence a recommender will be important in giving recommendations to assist the farmers in their dairy farms. A dairy cow has an average milk production of 30 liters per day (Dunn et al., 2014). In Tanzania milk yield the best cow produce an average of (14.45 ± 5.12) liters of milk for most farmers in high milk producing cluster. The milk production in medium and low milking clusters is lower in (11.08 ± 4.29) liters and (9.15 ± 3.25) liters respectively. The average milk improvement is needed so as to increase the quantity and quality of the milk produced by the cows in high, medium and low clusters and maintenance required for high producers. Recommendations on how to improve the farm practices and maintain good farm practices in each cluster in order to increase the milk yield will be given based on the identified outcome in the mined rules. The available information obtained using association mining is significant especially on describing the differentials among farmers within and across production clusters.

Peer-to-Peer Learning for Knowledge and Experience Sharing Between Small-Scale Dairy Farmers

With the help of this discovery, small-scale dairy farmers are able to chat among themselves inside their clusters in order to increase milk production and share their knowledge and experience (Mavura et al., 2022), which is in line with the research by (Nyambo, 2020). Peer interactions have been found to have positive significances, including extending knowledge and acquiring experience (Akpan & Okoro, 2020) stating that interaction with other people, the physical and non-physical environment, and other environments leads to learning and experience. (Tran, 2013) Describe how learning occurs in a social setting where people observe one another and pick up knowledge, customs, skills, strategies, and beliefs. According to (Thakur & Chander, 2018), peer-to-peer learning also aids in bridging the gap between extension officers and small-scale dairy farmers.

FUTURE RESEARCH DIRECTIONS

Future work is entailed in extending the mobile application to provide learning recommendations to the farmers. Recommendations to the farmers will be provided in terms of feeding, breeding, and health in order to increase their milk production based on relevant practices. Improvement to the mobile application framework from android to Flutter so it can be used by different mobile operating systems.

CONCLUSION

It has been shown that, application of technologies such as Machine Learning in grouping farmers based on similar characteristics help farmers to learn from the best milk producers in the same production cluster. Deployment of such models into mobile applications simplifies farmers allocation into various homogeneous groups. These groups may help in dissemination of information and knowledge among farmers with similar characteristics and extension officers.

ACKNOWLEDGMENT

The following agencies are acknowledged with gratitude by the authors: (i) International Development Research Center (IDRC) and Swedish International Development Cooperation Agency are scholarship sponsors (SIDA) (ii) Africa's Artificial Intelligence for Development (AI4D) fellowship programme; (iii) Manager of the Africa Center for Technology Studies scholarship fund (ACTS).

REFERENCES

Akpan, Blessing, & Okoro. (2020). Social constructivism: Implications on teaching and learning. *British Journal of Education*.

Alonso, S., Toye, P. G., Msalya, G., Grace, D., & Unger, F. (2014). *Smallholder dairy farming in Tanzania: Farming practices, animal health and public health challenges and opportunities*. Academic Press.

Atuhaire, A. M., Mugerwa, S., Kabirizi, J., Okello, S., & Kabi, F. (2014). Production characteristics of smallholder dairy farming in the Lake Victoria agro-ecological zone, Uganda. *Frontiers in Science*, *4*(1), 12–19.

Balehegn, M., Duncan, A., Tolera, A., Ayantunde, A. A., Issa, S., Karimou, M., Zampaligré, N., André, K., Gnanda, I., Varijakshapanicker, P., Kebreab, E., Dubeux, J., Boote, K., Minta, M., Feyissa, F., & Adesogan, A. T. (2020). Improving adoption of technologies and interventions for increasing supply of quality livestock feed in low-and middle-income countries. *Global Food Security*, *26*, 100372. doi:10.1016/j.gfs.2020.100372 PMID:33324534

Berry, D., Friggens, N., Lucy, M., & Roche, J. (2016). Milk production and fertility in cattle. *Annual Review of Animal Biosciences*, *4*(1), 269–290. doi:10.1146/annurev-animal-021815-111406 PMID:26526546

Brett, C. I. (2019). *A new way to boost smallholder dairy productivity in Tanzania*. World Bank. https://blogs.worldbank.org/voices/new-way-boost-smallholder-dairy-productivity-tanzania

Brett, C. I. (2019). *A new way to boost smallholder dairy productivity in Tanzania*. https://blogs.worldbank.org/voices/new-way-boost-smallholder-dairy-productivity-tanzania

Chawala, A., Banos, G., Peters, A., & Chagunda, M. (2019). Farmer-preferred traits in smallholder dairy farming systems in Tanzania. *Tropical Animal Health and Production*, *51*(6), 1337–1344. doi:10.100711250-018-01796-9 PMID:30715656

Cockburn, M. (2020). Application and prospective discussion of machine learning for the management of dairy farms. *Animals (Basel)*, *10*(9), 1690. doi:10.3390/ani10091690 PMID:32962078

Dossa, L. H., Abdulkadir, A., Amadou, H., Sangare, S., & Schlecht, E. (2011). Exploring the diversity of urban and peri-urban agricultural systems in Sudano-Sahelian West Africa: An attempt towards a regional typology. *Landscape and Urban Planning*, *102*(3), 197–206. doi:10.1016/j.landurbplan.2011.04.005

Dunn, R. J., Mead, N. E., Willett, K. M., & Parker, D. E. (2014). Analysis of heat stress in UK dairy cattle and impact on milk yields. *Environmental Research Letters*, *9*(6), 064006. doi:10.1088/1748-9326/9/6/064006

Fatima, M., & Pasha, M. (2017). Survey of machine learning algorithms for disease diagnostic. *Journal of Intelligent Learning Systems and Applications*, *9*(01), 1–16. doi:10.4236/jilsa.2017.91001

Fatuma Mavura, Mkoba, & Nyambo. (2022). Rule-Based Engine for Automatic Allocation of Smallholder Dairy Producers in Pre-Identified Production Clusters. *The Scientific World Journal*.

Faysse, N., Sraïri, M. T., & Errahj, M. (2012). Local farmers' organisations: A space for peer-to-peer learning? The case of milk collection cooperatives in Morocco. *Journal of Agricultural Education and Extension, 18*(3), 285–299. doi:10.1080/1389224X.2012.670053

Galluzzo, N. (2015). Technical and economic efficiency analysis on Italian smallholder family farms using Farm Accountancy Data Network dataset. *Studies in Agricultural Economics (Budapest), 117*(1), 35–42. doi:10.7896/j.1501

Gelbard, R., Goldman, O., & Spiegler, I. (2007). Investigating diversity of clustering methods: An empirical comparison. *Data & Knowledge Engineering, 63*(1), 155–166. doi:10.1016/j.datak.2007.01.002

Gitau, K. J. (2013). *Factors influencing milk production among small scale dairy farmers in Mirangine in Nyandarua county and Mauche in Nakuru county*. University of Nairobi.

Goswami, R., Chatterjee, S., & Prasad, B. (2014). Farm types and their economic characterization in complex agro-ecosystems for informed extension intervention: Study from coastal West Bengal, India. *Agricultural and Food Economics, 2*(1), 1–24. doi:10.118640100-014-0005-2

Hussein, N., Alashqur, A., & Sowan, B. (2015). Using the interestingness measure lift to generate association rules. *Journal of Advanced Computer Science & Technology, 4*(1), 156. doi:10.14419/jacst.v4i1.4398

John, S. N., Anele, C., Kennedy, O. O., Olajide, F., & Kennedy, C. G. (2016). Realtime fraud detection in the banking sector using data mining techniques/algorithm. *2016 International Conference on Computational Science and Computational Intelligence (CSCI)*.

Kim, M.-K., Jeong, S.-G., Oh, M.-H., Kim, D.-H., Son, Y.-S., & Ham, J.-S. (2011). Guide to Good Dairy Farming Practice. *Journal of Dairy Science and Biotechnology, 29*(2), 75–80.

Kingu, D., & Ndiege, B. O. (2018). Empowering Small Scale Dairy Farmers Through The Cooperatives Model. *Journal of Co-operative and Business Studies, 2*(1), 1–12.

Kuivanen, K., Alvarez, S., Michalscheck, M., Adjei-Nsiah, S., Descheemaeker, K., Mellon-Bedi, S., & Groot, J. C. (2016). Characterising the diversity of smallholder farming systems and their constraints and opportunities for innovation: A case study from the Northern Region, Ghana. *NJAS Wageningen Journal of Life Sciences, 78*(1), 153–166. doi:10.1016/j.njas.2016.04.003

Kuivanen, K., Michalscheck, M., Descheemaeker, K., Adjei-Nsiah, S., Mellon-Bedi, S., Groot, J. C., & Alvarez, S. (2016). A comparison of statistical and participatory clustering of smallholder farming systems–A case study in Northern Ghana. *Journal of Rural Studies, 45*, 184–198. doi:10.1016/j.jrurstud.2016.03.015

Kurwijila, L. R., Omore, A., & Delia, G. (2012). *The Tanzania Dairy Industry*. Academic Press.

Liverpool-Tasie, L. S. O., Wineman, A., Young, S., Tambo, J., Vargas, C., Reardon, T., Adjognon, G. S., Porciello, J., Gathoni, N., Bizikova, L., Galiè, A., & Celestin, A. (2020). A scoping review of market links between value chain actors and small-scale producers in developing regions. *Nature Sustainability, 3*(10), 799–808. doi:10.103841893-020-00621-2

Lukuyu, M. N., Njehu, A., Mwilawa, A., Lukuyu, B. A., Omore, A. O., & Rao, E. (2017). *The role of fodder markets in meeting the year-round forage requirements of smallholder dairy farmers in Tanzania*. Livestock Brief.

Mavura, F., Pandhare, S. M., Mkoba, E., & Nyambo, D. G. (2022). Rule-Based Engine for Automatic Allocation of Smallholder Dairy Producers in Preidentified Production Clusters. *TheScientificWorld-Journal, 2022*, 2022. doi:10.1155/2022/6944151 PMID:35874847

Mbilu, A. P. (2015). *Smallholder dairy farmers' technical efficiency in milk production: case of EPINAV dairy project in Njombe District*. Sokoine University of Agriculture.

Mourelatos, E., Tzagarakis, M., & Dimara, E. (2016). A review of online crowdsourcing platforms. *South-Eastern Europe Journal of Economics, 14*(1).

Mzingula, E. P. (2019). Socio-economic impacts of smallholder dairy cattle farming on livelihood in Sunga Ward of Lushoto District, Tanzania. *International Journal of Economics and Management, 1*(2), 41–49.

Njuguna, C. (2021). *Upgrading Tanzania's dairy value chain to unlock its productivity potential*. https://www.ilri.org/news/upgrading-tanzania%E2%80%99s-dairy-value-chain-unlock-its-productivity-potential

Nyambo, D. G. (2020). *Use of agent–based models in characterizing farm types and evolvement in smallholder dairy systems*. NM-AIST.

Nyambo, D. G., Luhanga, E. T., & Yonah, Z. O. (2019). Characteristics of smallholder dairy farms by association rules mining based on apriori algorithm. *International Journal of Society Systems Science, 11*(2), 100–116. doi:10.1504/IJSSS.2019.100101

Nyambo, D. G., Luhanga, E. T., Yonah, Z. O., & Mujibi, F. D. (2019). Application of multiple unsupervised models to validate clusters robustness in characterizing smallholder dairy farmers. *TheScientific-WorldJournal, 2019*, 2019. doi:10.1155/2019/1020521 PMID:30718979

Nyambo, D. G., Luhanga, E. T., Yonah, Z. O., Mujibi, F. D. N., & Clemen, T. (2020). Leveraging peer-to-peer farmerlearning to facilitate better strategies in smallholder dairy husbandry. *Adaptive Behavior*, 1–11.

Paas, W., & Groot, J. C. (2017). Creating adaptive farm typologies using Naive Bayesian classification. *Information Processing in Agriculture, 4*(3), 220–227. doi:10.1016/j.inpa.2017.05.005

Patii, U., Saxena, P., & Sidnal, N. (2017). Peer-to-peer knowledge sharing platform for farmers with auto-recommendation feature. *2017 International Conference On Smart Technologies For Smart Nation (SmartTechCon)*.

Salasya, B., & Stoorvogel, J. (2010). Fuzzy classification for farm household characterization. *Outlook on Agriculture, 39*(1), 57–63.

Slimani, T., & Lazzez, A. (2014). *Efficient analysis of pattern and association rule mining approaches*. arXiv preprint arXiv:1402.2892.

Taneja, M., Jalodia, N., Malone, P., Byabazaire, J., Davy, A., & Olariu, C. (2019). Connected cows: Utilizing fog and cloud analytics toward data-driven decisions for smart dairy farming. *IEEE Internet of Things Magazine, 2*(4), 32–37. doi:10.1109/IOTM.0001.1900045

Thakur, D., & Chander, M. (2018). Use of social media in agricultural extension: Some evidences from India. *International Journal of Science, Environment and Technology*, *7*(4), 1334–1346.

Thiam, S. M. b., & Matofari, J. W. (2018). The Role of Information and Communication Sharing Pathway in Improving Peri-Urban Dairy System of Bamako, Mali. *American Journal of Science. Engineering and Technology*, *3*(1), 21.

Toledo, I. (2018). Are Cows Comfortable in Modern Dairy Facilities? AN349, 12/2018. *EDIS, 2018*(6).

Tran, V. D. (2013). Theoretical Perspectives Underlying the Application of Cooperative Learning in Classrooms. *International Journal of Higher Education*, *2*(4), 101–115. doi:10.5430/ijhe.v2n4p101

Turiansky, E. J. Q. A. (2021). *Unlocking the Dairy Sector's Potential for Smallholder Farmers*. Mathematica. https://www.mathematica.org/blogs/unlocking-the-dairy-sectors-potential-for-smallholder-farmers

Urassa, J., & Raphael, E. (2017). *The contribution of small scale dairy farming to community welfare: A case study of Morogoro Municipality*. Academic Press.

Zhou, Z.-H. (2021). *Machine learning*. Springer Nature. doi:10.1007/978-981-15-1967-3

KEY TERMS AND DEFINITIONS

Breeding Practices: A selection of animal reproduction techniques that dairy farmers employ for the majority of cattle calving.

Confidence: Is a probability of occurrence of an association rule indicating the relationship between the antecedent and consequent.

Dairy Farming: A dedicated process for raising cattle specifically for the goal of producing milk from hybrid or exotic breeds of cattle.

Dairy Production Clusters: A group of dairy farmers that have been identified as using comparable methods, carrying out comparable farm management tasks, and producing comparable results or yields.

Homogenous Groups: A collection of entities that can be objectively distinguished from the other entities and share a common behavior or set of behaviors.

Inter-Cluster Separation: Demonstrates the average distance between the cluster centroids of two or more groups and serves as a gauge of how heterogeneous two groups are.

Intra-Cluster Similarity: Is a metric for group homogeneity that shows how far apart on average entities are from the cluster's Centre.

Lift: Is a measure of an association rule's interestingness indicating the strength of items in a rule when they appear together rather than when they are apart.

Machine Learning: A collection of methods and tools for creating software programmes that can analyses previous data and make precise predictions about the future.

Peer-to-Peer Learning: A strategy that enables entities with comparable characteristics and patterns of behavior to share information and knowledge with the aim of enhancing performance.

Recommender System: A data-driven model that has been implemented as an information system to offer recommendations for best practices that could lead to increased yields.

Small-Scale Farmers: A person who practices agriculture (crop or/and livestock keeping) in a relatively small area of land, normally less than 2 acres.

Supervised Learning: A subfield of machine learning that builds and trains models that can reliably predict and generalize well to new datasets using labelled data.

Support: Number of instances of an attribute value in the dataset.

Unsupervised Learning: A subfield of machine learning that looks for patterns and untapped information in unlabeled datasets.

ENDNOTE

1 Program for Emerging Agricultural Research Leaders.

Chapter 12
Someone Like Us:
Anthropomorphism in the Consumer Behavior in the Scope of Emerging Countries

Ece Özer Çizer
https://orcid.org/0000-0002-8597-2073
Yıldız Technical University, Turkey

ABSTRACT

This study analyzes the development of anthropomorphism research in consumer behavior over the last three decades, with a particular focus on emerging countries. A dataset of 475 articles was collected from the Web of Science database, using the keywords "anthropomorph" and "consum*". The study includes graphics related to annual scientific production, corresponding author's country, most cited countries, most relevant sources, word cloud, word tree, trend topics, and thematic map, revealing the visualization technique. The meta-analysis aims to create a comprehensive framework for articles on anthropomorphism in consumer behavior published in the last 30 years, with a specific focus on emerging countries. The study will examine the anthropomorphism studies carried out in these countries separately and make suggestions for anthropomorphism applications that can be applied in consumer behavior in emerging countries, comparing the general findings to those from emerging countries.*

INTRODUCTION

Artificial intelligence (AI) has become a major disruptor in emerging and developing countries, and one of the ways in which it is impacting these countries is through the development of anthropomorphic features (McDuie-Ra and Gulson, 2020). Anthropomorphism refers to the attribution of human-like characteristics and behaviors to machines, such as intelligent digital assistants and chatbots like Siri, Alexa, and Google Assistant (Abercrombie et al., 2021). The use of AI and anthropomorphism in developing countries has both positive and negative impacts (Blut et al., 2021). On the positive side, AI can help optimize supply chains, reduce energy consumption, and improve the quality of healthcare services (Dash,

DOI: 10.4018/978-1-6684-6873-9.ch012

2019). For example, AI can help medical professionals diagnose diseases more accurately and provide personalized treatment plans. It can also improve patient outcomes by monitoring and predicting health risks (Yeasmin, 2019; Omary et al., 2009). However, there are also concerns about job displacement due to the automation of certain tasks by AI. There is a need for skilled workers to design, build, and operate AI systems. Additionally, there are ethical concerns such as data privacy, bias, and transparency that must be addressed through the development of regulations and guidelines (Martin et al., 2022).

To guide future studies on the use of AI and anthropomorphism in developing countries, it is important to systematically classify studies on this subject. This will help identify the most studied topics, most cited authors, and trending topics by year. This information can help policymakers and business leaders make informed decisions about investing in education and skills development, developing regulations and guidelines, and making technology accessible to all to maximize benefits and reduce challenges. It is crucial that policymakers and business leaders take a proactive approach to AI and anthropomorphism in developing countries. This means investing in education and skills development to ensure that workers have the skills needed to design, build, and operate AI systems. It also means developing regulations and guidelines that address ethical concerns and ensure that AI is used for the benefit of society as a whole. Finally, it means making technology accessible to all, regardless of socio-economic status, to ensure that the benefits of AI are available to everyone.

BACKGROUND

Anthropomorphism

Anthropomorphism is a concept that refers to the attribution of human-like characteristics to non-human beings by humans (Milton, 2020). Studies conducted to measure people's perceptions of animals and non-human beings show that people easily attribute humanoid characteristics to non-human beings. In practice, it is seen that anthropomorphic studies are frequently made by engineers, designers, and programmers (Whitson, 2018; Waytz et. al., 2010). Products such as the world-renowned Honda Asimo Robot, Ameca by Engineered Arts, and Sophia by Hanson Robotics are some of the anthropomorphic works that mimic the human form. Anthropomorphism is also frequently used in the field of marketing and advertising (Laksmidewi et. al., 2017). Making non-living characters talk like human beings makes it easier for consumers to be convinced of the character. Some brands such as Michelin (Michelin Man), The Walt Disney Company (Mickey Mouse), and Monopoly (Rich Uncle Pennybags) appeal to consumers by humanizing their logos and mascots.

Anthropomorphism, which expresses human-like features exhibited by non-human beings, plays an important role in the effectiveness of artificial intelligence artifacts, greatly affecting the user experience during human-AI interaction (Yuan & Dennis, 2019). Because of the essential role of AI anthropomorphism in human-AI interaction, it is important to identify the antecedents that influence perceived anthropomorphism. When the studies on artificial intelligence and anthropomorphism in the literature are examined, it is seen that the humanoid features attributed to artificial intelligence are examined under 3 headings. The first of these is human images (human figures), the second is human identity features (human names, identities), and the third is human speech (imitating human language) (Cheng et. al., 2022; Go & Sundar, 2019).

The use of anthropomorphic features in technological innovations enables consumers to perceive technology as a real person, and this leads to increased trust in technology (Ameen et. al., 2021). According to studies in the literature, two main features of an anthropomorphic technology influence increased consumer confidence in the technology (Pitardi & Marriott, 2021). The first of these is humanlike visual design and behavior, while the other is human imitation ability (Sowmiya et. al., 2022). Faced with technology with visible anthropomorphic features, a consumer automatically expects it to look, act, and communicate like a human. If these parameters are realistic enough and quite close to real human characteristics, consumer confidence in this particular technology will increase (Adam et. al., 2021). Besides, anthropomorphic technology evokes negative consumer emotions if it mimics a human's behavior and appearance quite similarly but well enough. This causes it to refuse to interact with this technology and significantly reduces trust in it (Crolic et. al., 2022). Another factor that increases consumer confidence in anthropomorphic technology is its ability to conform to the social norms and rules of human communication. Previous research has shown that consumers trust anthropomorphic technologies more if these technologies are polite and follow social etiquette. On the other hand, if technology is rude or not polite enough in communication, it automatically reduces trust between customers (Foehr & Germelmann, 2020; Pfeuffer et., al., 2019; Pak et. al., 2014). As a result, behavioral characteristics of an anthropomorphic technology such as etiquette and courtesy significantly affect the positive perception of the consumer towards the technology and increase their trust in it (Sitorus & Yustisia, 2018).

Strategic decisions about anthropomorphism can create positive connotations in the minds of consumers as well as create negative connotations. The ability of anthropomorphic technologies to mimic human emotions, thoughts and behaviors makes consumers feel like they are dealing with something truly "live" and can lead to consumer fear of technological intelligence. Thus, the fact that an anthropomorphic technology looks and behaves very realistically creates a major barrier to using the technology and ultimately has a negative impact on the consumer's willingness to trust it. For example, one of the authors' previous studies gives an example of a high level of human-likeness of robots in medical counseling, making patients feel uncomfortable because they find robots too realistic and are embarrassed to talk about their medical problems, and would prefer a more machine-like robot. In the study of Liu and Tao (2022), the positive effect of anthropomorphism on trust in smart health services was investigated. One of the findings of the study was that attribution of human identity features to smart health services adversely affected trust. According to the research, a human-like intelligent artificial intelligence system creates a feeling of discomfort in consumers and reduces trust (Weisman & Peña, 2021). In another study in the literature, how an artificial intelligence system that imitates human speech is perceived by consumers was examined. According to the results of the study, it has been determined that humanization negatively affects consumers' trust in voice artificial intelligence (Hu et al. 2021).

Anthropomorphism can occur in 4 different ways (DiSalvo et al., 2005):

- **Structural Anthropomorphic Form (Structural):** Structural anthropomorphic form is the material imitation of the structure and functioning of the human body. Shapes, volumes, mechanisms, or assemblies that mimic the human body in appearance or function are evidence of structural anthropomorphic form.
- **Gesture-Based Anthropomorphic Form (Gestural):** This anthropomorphic form is about imitating how people communicate with each other through their bodies, focusing on human behav-

ior. The use of movements and postures, the elements of human behavior, to express any meaning, intention, or direction can be an example of the gesture-based anthropomorphic form.

- **Character-Based Anthropomorphic Form (Character):** This form is more about imitating people's personality traits, social roles, and functions in any context. The reflection of the characteristics and habits that reveal who people are inanimate objects is proof that this form works.
- **Awareness-Based Anthropomorphic Style (Aware):** This form is based on the principle of imitating people's thinking and questioning abilities. Today's robotic and artificial intelligence applications can be given as examples of awareness-based anthropomorphic forms. Traces of the increasing anthropomorphization trend in the field of marketing; It is possible to apply human names to products, as in Amazon's Alexa example, in attributing gender to the product and creating a voice and accent compatible with this gender, as in the case of Apple Siri, and in applications of equipping it with human-like physical features such as in the example of Michelin Man (MacInnis and Folkes, 2017). In this sense; While Alexa and Siri examples reflect anthropomorphic forms based on character and awareness, it can be said that Michelin Man has a structural and gesture-based anthropomorphic form.

Anthropomorphism for Service Robots

Service robots are robots that interact with customers and aim to serve customers. Service robots have started to be used frequently, especially after the Covid-19 pandemic, both to reduce costs and to provide a contactless service environment. Service robots used in various sectors, especially in the accommodation sector, use artificial intelligence in their systems. Service robots with artificial intelligence are self-learning and can also make their own decisions based on their previous experience. Intelligent service robots, which have a high intellectual capacity, are also loaded with human features that will enable them to look and behave like service personnel during their interactions with humans. Service robots, who are exposed to active learning during their duties, can interact with customers socially and emotionally in addition to the tasks assigned to them.

In the literature on the adoption of service robots, the importance of the social and emotional dimension of the interaction between customers and service robots has been emphasized. According to the service acceptance model, in addition to variables such as perceived ease of use and perceived usefulness, the social and emotional relationships they establish with service robots have a significant degree of impact when customers adopt service robots (Wirtz et al., 2018). The stronger the social and emotional relationships, the closer the interaction between service robots and customers will be to real communication. These social and emotional elements of service robots distinguish them from classical autonomous machines (self-service kiosks).

Service robots are increasingly being adopted by the hospitality industry, especially for service encounters, to improve the guest experience, reduce labor costs, and help create a contactless system since the pandemic. Hotels like Marriott and Sheraton use service robots such as luggage robots and room service robots in certain locations in the US. For example, the Sheraton in Los Angeles uses its robot to accompany guests, carry luggage, and deliver food. Incheon airport in South Korea uses escort robots to answer questions and provide directions at the airport and entertain children at airports. Some hotel chains in Japan and China have opened fully automated hotels with only service robot employees. Although service robots increase productivity in businesses, both customers and practitioners are concerned about malfunctions and the lack of human interaction that may occur in robots (Seo, 2022).

Although the benefits of the use of service robots seem to be quite high, studies are being carried out to better understand how the operation of the application takes place. Especially in the studies carried out in the accommodation sector, the role of service robots in this sector has been investigated. The research, it is aimed to determine the antecedents that are effective in the adoption of service robots by the consumer. According to the results of the studies, it was understood that some consumer-related features also affect the adoption of service robots. For example, the higher the customer innovativeness, the higher the perception of robot restaurants and the higher their intention to visit. Another finding revealed in studies is that consumers' attitudes and expectations toward service robots affect their willingness to pay in parallel (Ivanov and Webster 2021). It has been found that some of the main features of service robots that affect consumer adoption are the robot's aesthetics, design, interface, and language use (Wirtz et al., 2018). Bartneck et al. (2009), it is emphasized that humanoid robots have five different dimensions. According to this study, anthropomorphism, vitality, likability, perceived intelligence, and perceived security constitute the five dimensions of humanoid robots. Among these dimensions, likability is a critical factor influencing consumer perception of service robots.

Uncanny valley theory is a theory that is widely used in the field of interaction between humans and robots. The theory is generally based on understanding how people understand objects with humanoid features (Mori, 1970). This theory has been used especially in studies conducted in the service sector to explain how customers respond to humanoid robots (Yu and Ngan, 2019). According to the theory, consumers perceive anthropomorphized products positively only up to a certain level of anthropomorphism, and when the products are perceived as very real, their perceptions turn negative, which is called the "uncanny valley". While consumers may enjoy interacting with service robots when they are perceived as more likely to be a machine, they will be embarrassed if the robots are perceived as too humanlike.

Anthropomorphism refers to the attribution of human characteristics and emotions to inanimate objects (Epley et al., 2007). The level of anthropomorphism has been discussed as a key factor in consumers' adoption of service robots (Bartneck et al., 2020). Studies in the literature have found that high levels of anthropomorphism lead to familiarity, engagement, and positive evaluations from customers (Gursoy et al., 2019). When people perceive the robot as more human-like, customers are more likely to be satisfied with the service, and this varies according to contextual factors (Seo, 2022).

Anthropomorphism for Brands and Mascots

Anthropomorphism is a phenomenon that has an application area as a brand strategy. In today's world marketers; It tries to transform products/services, brands, or companies into relationship partners for consumers by giving them human characteristics. The results of the research conducted by Castelli et al., (2002) reveal that the nerve areas in the brain that are activated during anthropomorphic thoughts about inanimate objects and those that are activated when making a certain judgment about people are the same. In other words, when people develop thoughts about anthropomorphic inanimate objects (eg branded products/services), they evaluate them just like humans. When consumers believe that certain products have human-like characteristics, they like these products more (Aggarwal & McGill, 2012) and avoid changing the products in question (Chandler & Schwarz, 2010). Marketers who set off from this consumer reality; It carries out its anthropomorphism approach mostly through brand characters, mascots, and brand spokespersons. Because; consumers perceive brand characters as figures with whom they can identify, associate themselves with their personality traits, and find themselves in their stories.

The association of brand identity with certain characteristics through the humanization of inanimate objects such as mascots; is put forward as one of the ways to differentiate from the competition and to create a strong brand value. Consumers attribute certain personality traits to brands (Aaker, 2016), perceive brands as characters (Plummer, 2000), and when appropriate, accept the brand's point of view as their own (Blackston, 1993). From this, it is not surprising that anthropomorphism is widely used in branding and brand mascot strategies. When we look at the literature on brand mascots, which is one of the main areas of use of the concept of anthropomorphism, we witness that mascots are evaluated at the intersection of anthropomorphism and brand identity. Based on the idea that anthropomorphism is based on the principle of attributing emotional, behavioral, mental, and personality traits to inanimate objects; brand mascots are also considered to be the carriers of these human characteristics that the brand wants to own, that is, the figures representing the brand identity.

Brand mascots; it is described as a basic element that visually expresses the brand through an anthropomorphic representation, an iconic indicator that imitates the brand, and a tool that provides an emotional bond between the consumer and the brand. Brand mascot is brand spokespersons who inform consumers about products, services, and brands. Phillips and Lee (2005) state that brand mascots used to promote branded products, services, or ideas are defined as brand spokespersons in the literature because they are created by the brand and only for the brand. In other words, since the branded product or service cannot speak for itself, a character is needed to undertake this task instead. This is one of the reasons why brand mascots were chosen as spokespersons (Pairoa and Arunrangsiwed, 2016)

The use of brand mascots has different importance in terms of both the brand, the consumer, and the advertisement. When the mascot is associated with a branded product or service, it now becomes the symbol of that brand. This also contributes to brand recall. An effective brand mascot increases brand awareness and creates an emotional bond between the consumer and the brand, thus distinguishing the brand from the competition (Patterson, 2013). Besides all these; Mascots as brand characters increase the strength of corporate identity as they positively affect the brand image (Yadav et al., 2015). When evaluated in terms of consumers, it is emphasized that brand mascots provide an emotional appeal. While people are distant from being a fan of a product or service, it is easier to feel close to humanized objects such as brand mascots (Pairoa & Arunrangsiwed, 2016). The fact that the two-dimensional logo, which is one of the visual identity elements of the brand, turns into three-dimensional over the mascot and the mascot makes the advertisement more attractive by increasing the visual appeal, shows the advantages of the brand mascot in terms of advertising. Using a brand mascot in an advertisement not only increases the perception of sincerity but also makes the viewing experience more enjoyable. Thus, it becomes easier to connect the advertisement with potential consumers. In this respect, mascots have an important contribution to making advertisements more personal, authentic, reliable, entertaining, and attractive (Yadav et al., 2015).

Anthropomorphism in the Emerging Countries

In recent years, the concept of anthropomorphism has become increasingly relevant in the context of artificial intelligence (AI), particularly in developing countries (Peleau et al., 2021). Developing countries are increasingly turning to AI technology to address a wide range of social, economic, and environmental challenges. For example, AI-powered systems are being used to improve healthcare, enhance agricultural productivity, and facilitate disaster response (Nagaty, 2023). However, as AI becomes more prevalent in developing countries, there is a growing concern that anthropomorphism may undermine the effectiveness and reliability of these systems.

One of the key challenges associated with anthropomorphism in AI is the tendency to overestimate the capabilities of AI systems (Lockey et al., 2021). When people attribute human-like characteristics to AI, they may assume that the system has a level of intelligence, intuition, or empathy that it does not actually possess. This can lead to unrealistic expectations and a misunderstanding of what AI can actually do. For example, a medical diagnosis system may be overestimated by patients, who may believe that the system is capable of providing a diagnosis with 100% accuracy, leading to frustration when the system is unable to provide the same accuracy as a human physician (Genin and Grote, 2021). Another challenge associated with anthropomorphism in AI is the potential for biased decision-making (Benbya et al., 2021). When people attribute human-like emotions and motivations to AI, they may assume that the system is capable of making decisions in the same way that humans do. However, AI systems are only as unbiased as the data they are trained on. If the data is biased, the AI system may make biased decisions. In the context of developing countries, where data may be limited or biased due to historical or societal factors, this can be a significant concern. Finally, anthropomorphism in AI can also lead to ethical concerns (Salles et al., 2020). For example, if people perceive AI systems as having emotions or feelings, they may be more likely to anthropomorphize the system and assign it moral standing. This can lead to complex ethical questions about the responsibility of the AI system and the actions that it takes. For example, if an AI-powered vehicle is involved in an accident, who is responsible for the harm caused? The designer, the operator, or the AI system itself? To address these challenges, it is important for developers and policymakers to take a proactive approach to managing anthropomorphism in AI (Benhamou and Ferland, 2020). This may involve developing clear guidelines for the use of AI in different contexts, educating users about the capabilities and limitations of AI, and implementing safeguards to prevent biased decision-making (Marda, 2018). Additionally, there is a need for more research into the social and psychological factors that contribute to anthropomorphism in AI, particularly in the context of developing countries.

In conclusion, anthropomorphism in AI is a complex and multifaceted challenge that requires careful consideration and management. While AI has the potential to bring significant benefits to developing countries, it is important to recognize the limitations of the technology and avoid overestimating its capabilities. By taking a proactive approach to managing anthropomorphism, we can help to ensure that AI is used in a responsible and ethical manner that benefits everyone. Examples of anthropomorphism in artificial intelligence in developing countries in the Global South and all over the world are as follows:

- **Virtual Assistants With Localized Accents:** AI assistants like Siri, Alexa, and Google Assistant have become popular in many countries. However, in emerging countries, some companies have developed virtual assistants with localized accents to make them more relatable and appealing to users. For example, in India, Amazon's Alexa speaks in a Hindi accent, while Google Assistant has a Tamil and Telugu voice option (Swamy, 2022).
- **Chatbots With Human-Like Personalities:** Chatbots are becoming increasingly common in emerging countries, where they are used for customer service, healthcare, and education. Some developers have designed chatbots with human-like personalities, using anthropomorphic language and emotional cues to make them seem more engaging and empathetic. For instance, the Woebot chatbot, which provides mental health support, uses emojis and personalized messages to create a more human-like interaction with users (Rathnayaka et al., 2022).

- **Social Robots as Companions:** Social robots are designed to interact with humans in a social and emotional way. In emerging countries, they are often used as companions for children or elderly people who may be socially isolated. Some robots are designed to have anthropomorphic features, such as humanoid bodies or expressive faces, to create a more lifelike and engaging interaction. For example, the Pepper robot, which is used in schools and hospitals in some Asian countries, has a humanoid body and can dance, play games, and provide information (Wright, 2019).
- **AI-Powered Avatars for Education:** AI avatars are virtual representations of human-like figures that can interact with users in a conversational way. In emerging countries, they are being used in education to create more engaging and interactive learning experiences. Some avatars are designed to have anthropomorphic features, such as facial expressions and body language, to create a more human-like interaction. For example, the Avatar Classroom platform, which is used in some African countries, uses AI avatars to provide personalized and interactive lessons to students (Alam and Mohanty, 2022).

In summary, anthropomorphism in AI can make these technologies more relatable and engaging to users, particularly in emerging countries where people may be less familiar with these technologies. However, there is also a risk of over-attributing human qualities to AI systems, which can create unrealistic expectations and potentially harmful interactions.

METHODOLOGY

In the study, a comprehensive bibliometric analysis was made on the studies in the literature from the past to the present regarding the concept of "anthropomorphism". For analysis, articles containing the keyword the keywords "anthropomorph*" and "consum*" were searched from the Web of Science database. A total of 475 articles were reached. Bibliometric analysis was applied to the articles with the R Studio analysis program.

RESULTS

Word Cloud

In Figure 1, the 50 most repetitive words in the data set were examined. Among these words, it is seen that words such as "artificial intelligence", "brand anthropomorphism", "social presence", "robots" and "chatbots" are common words in articles.

Word Tree

In the word tree shown in Figure 2, the distribution of the frequencies of the words is given in order. In addition to the leading words in the word cloud, anthropomorphism-related words such as "service robots", "social media", "brand personality", "animal welfare" and "brand love"are frequently discussed in the literature.

Figure 1. Word cloud

Figure 2. Word tree

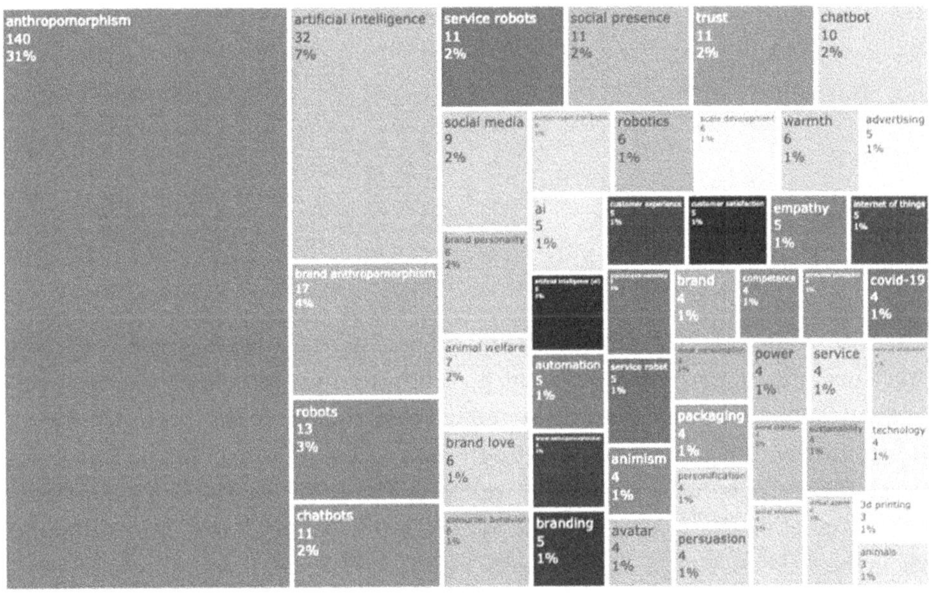

Trend Topics

Since 2000, studies on anthropomorphism in consumer behavior have been carried out in the literature. In Figure 3, the distribution of the trending topics in the last 22 years is given. During the first two-year period, “anthropomorphic” concept was discussed. Between 2008-2018 it is seen that the concepts of “avatar”, “zoomorphism”, “branding”, “brand loyalty”, “personification”, “humanoid robot”, “animals”, “social exclusion”, “advertising”, “automation”, “brand anthropomorphism”, and “anthropomorphization” have come to the fore. After the 2018 “customer experience”, “self-service technologies”, “artificial intelligence”, “trust”, “social presence” and “service robots” topics gain popularity.

Figure 3. Trend topics

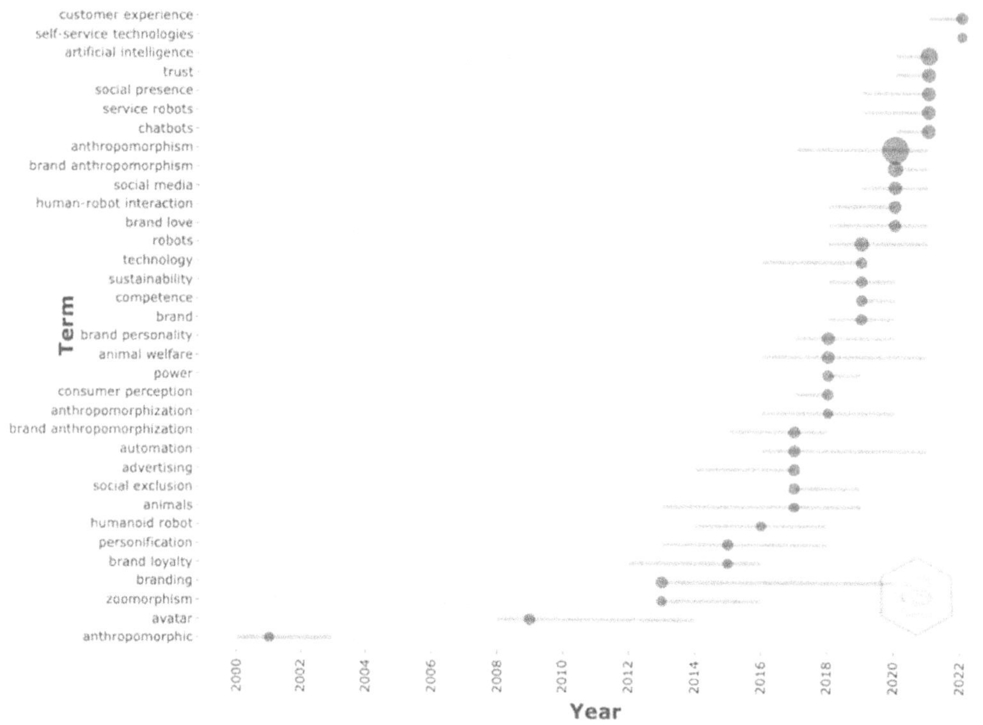

Thematic Map

The thematic map of the anthropomorphism in consumer behavior is given in Figure 4. While examining the thematic maps of the works of a certain period, the motor themes show the most important and developed main fields of study related to that period. It is seen that the most intense topics in the studies within the scope of anthropomorphism in consumer behavior are "artifical intelligence" and "service robot". "Warmth" and "competence" topics are located between the all themes. Further studies on these subjects will enable them to be among the motor themes. When the niche themes in the field are examined, it is seen that the subjects of "eleboration likelihood model" and "involment"; "internet of things" and "assemblage theory"; "social exclusion" and "belonging" are studied. It is observed that these subjects have strong ties among themselves and differ from other subjects. "Animal welfare" and "empathy" are included in the emerging and declining subjects of the thematic map. "Brand anthropomorhism" and "social media"; "artificial intelligence" and "robots"; "anthropomorphism" and "chatbots" topics are included in the basic themes and are used in conjunction with each other.

Most Cited Countries

According to Figure 5, it is seen that the most cited publications in studies on anthropomorphism in consumer behavior are presented by authors from USA, Canada, Netherlands and China, respectively.

Figure 4. Thematic map

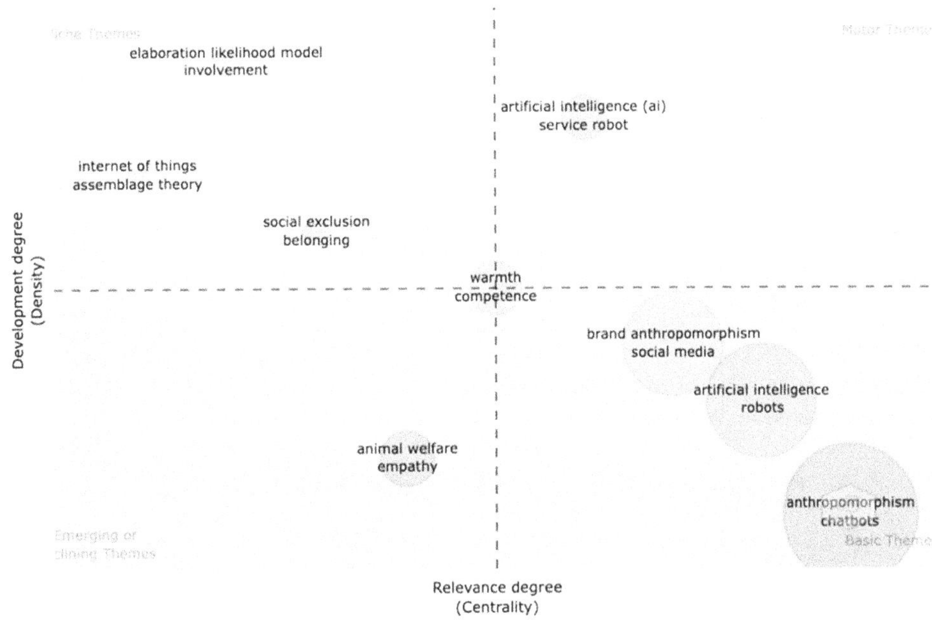

Figure 5. Most-cited countries

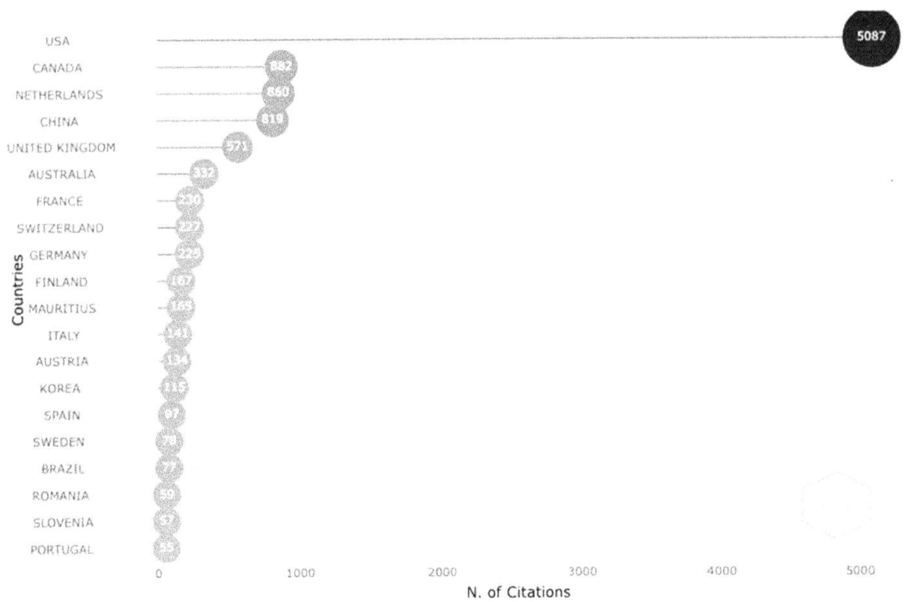

Annual Scientific Production

In Figure 6, it is seen that the first studies on anthropomorphism in consumer behavior were put forward in 1991. In addition, the number of studies increased rapidly starting from 2015 and reaching the highest level in 2021.

Figure 6. Annual scientific production

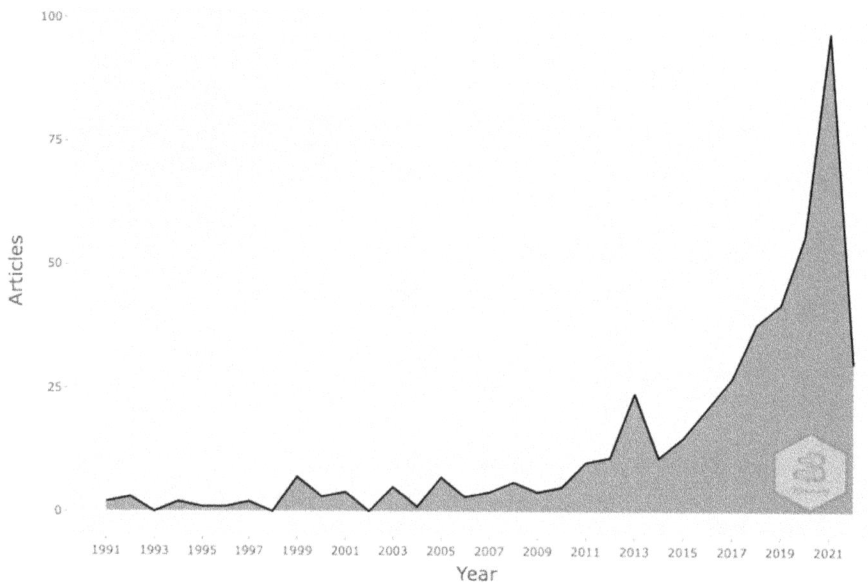

Corresponding Author's Country

The countries of the responsible authors for the publications were examined and shown in Figure 7. According to Figure 7, it is seen that the country with the most publications is the United States of America. The United States is followed by China, the United Kingdom, and Australia, respectively. While the

Figure 7. Corresponding author's country

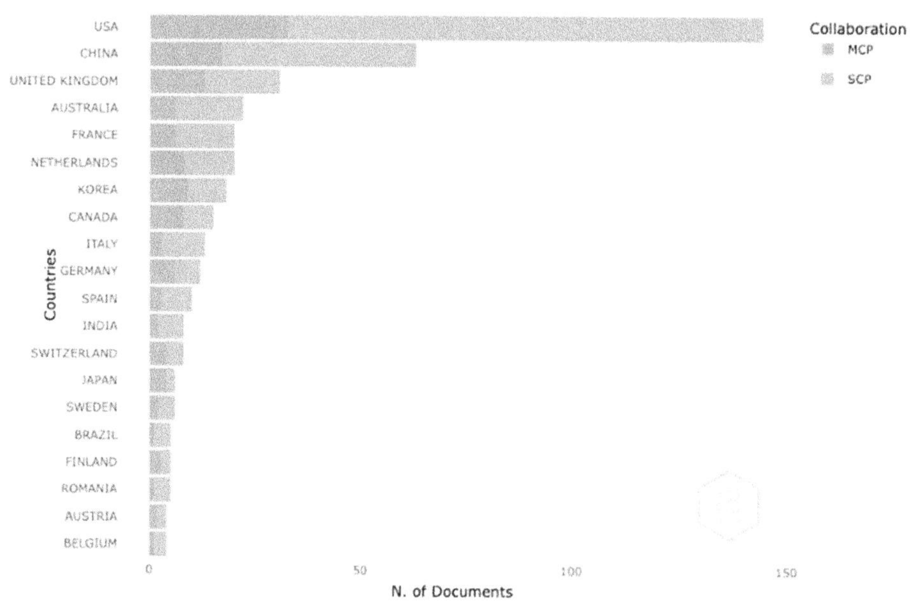

green colors in the table show that the broadcasts are made in a single country, the orange-colored parts indicate the number of broadcasts from multiple countries.

Most Relevant Sources

The most preferred journals were searched to publish studies on anthropomorphism in consumer behavior. According to the most relevant sources table in Figure 8, “Journal of Consumer Research”, “Journal of Business Research”, “Psychology & Marketing” and “Journal of Marketing Management” are the most popular scientific journals, respectively.

Figure 8. Most-relevant sources

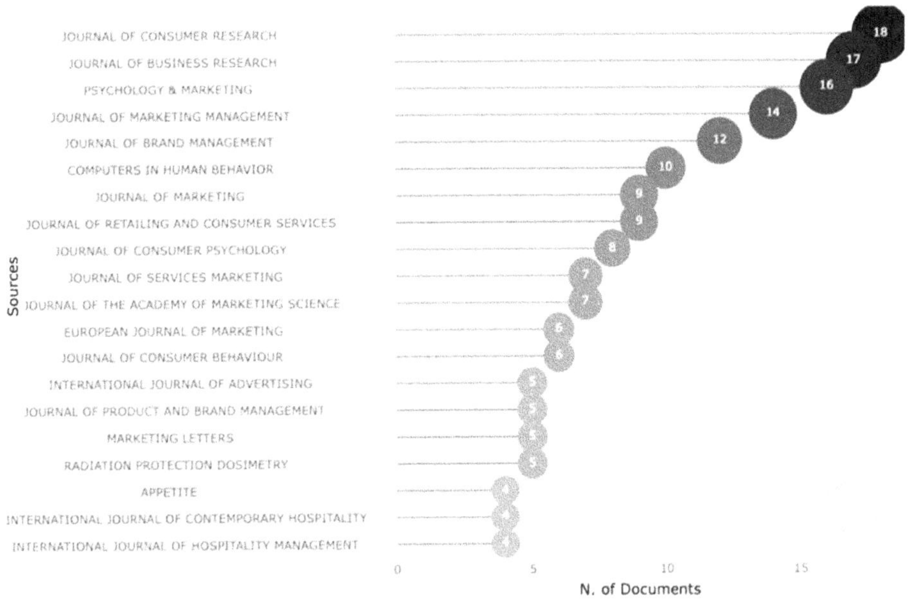

Country Scientific Production Map

Information on the distribution by countries is provided in Figure 9. The abundance of publications is indicated by the blue color in Figure 9, while the absence of publications is shown by the gray colors. Figure 9 shows USA is the most productive country.

Emerging Countries Scientific Production

The number of publications by country is provided in Table 1. For the comparison between developing and other countries, the list of 137 developing countries based on ISI (2022) was used, and these countries are highlighted in green in Table 1. It was found that publications on anthropomorphism in consumer behavior were produced in 21 developing countries, demonstrating that research in this area

Figure 9. Country scientific production map

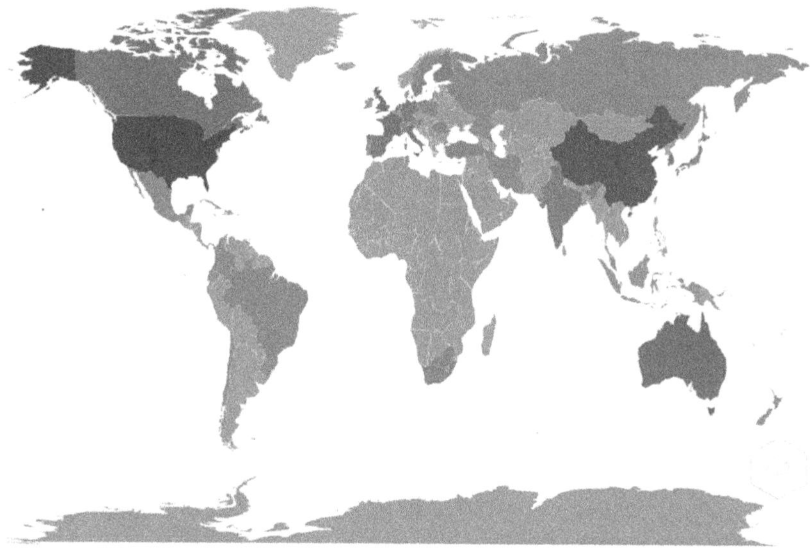

is contributed to by both developed and developing countries. Among the developing countries, China has the highest number of publications, followed by India, South Africa, and Brazil.

DISCUSSION

The Comparison Anthropomorphism: AI in the Emerging Countries and Developed Countries

Anthropomorphism-AI is a term used to describe the attribution of human-like qualities or characteristics to artificial intelligence systems. The phenomenon is becoming increasingly prevalent in both developed and emerging countries. However, the way it is manifested in each context differs. In developed countries, anthropomorphism-AI is often found in popular media and entertainment. AI characters are frequently portrayed as having human-like personalities, emotions, and behaviors. For instance, the movie "Her" portrays an AI character named Samantha who has a complex emotional life and is capable of having a romantic relationship with the protagonist. Virtual assistants like Siri and Alexa are also given personalities and voices to make them more relatable to users. On the other hand, in emerging countries, anthropomorphism-AI is being used to solve practical problems. For example, in China, AI chatbots are increasingly used to provide emotional support and counseling to individuals who do not have access to human therapists. These chatbots are designed to be empathetic and understanding, and users often report feeling a sense of connection with them.

Table 1. Country scientific production

No	Region	Freq	No	Region	Freq
1	USA	383	28	RUSSIA	6
2	CHINA	149	29	MALAYSIA	5
3	UK	55	30	PORTUGAL	5
4	AUSTRALIA	53	31	CHILE	4
5	FRANCE	49	32	DENMARK	4
6	NETHERLANDS	43	33	ECUADOR	4
7	CANADA	40	34	INDONESIA	4
8	SOUTH KOREA	35	35	IRELAND	4
9	ITALY	29	36	SINGAPORE	4
10	GERMANY	23	37	MALTA	3
11	SPAIN	23	38	SLOVENIA	3
12	INDIA	20	39	ISRAEL	2
13	FINLAND	16	40	SERBIA	2
14	JAPAN	15	41	TUNISIA	2
15	AUSTRIA	12	42	CZECH REPUBLIC	1
16	SOUTH AFRICA	12	43	GREECE	1
17	SWEDEN	11	44	GUATEMALA	1
18	SWITZERLAND	10	45	HUNGARY	1
19	BRAZIL	8	46	LEBANON	1
20	ROMANIA	8	47	LUXEMBOURG	1
21	TURKEY	8	48	MAURITIUS	1
22	BELGIUM	7	49	PAKISTAN	1
23	MEXICO	7	50	PERU	1
24	POLAND	7	51	QATAR	1
25	COLOMBIA	6	52	SAUDI ARABIA	1
26	IRAN	6	53	VENEZUELA	1
27	NEW ZEALAND	6			

In total, anthropomorphism-AI is a trend that is present in both developed and emerging countries. However, the way it is manifested in each context differs, with developed countries emphasizing its use in popular media and entertainment, while emerging countries use it to solve practical problems.

The Examples of Anthropomorphism-AI in the Emerging Countries

In Figure 1, Anthropomorphism-AI samples from the country where the most studies were conducted (China) and the following five countries are given, starting from the developing countries in the "Emerging Countries Scientific Production" table. Below are some examples of anthropomorphism in AI from emerging countries that aim to solve practical problems. These examples:

China

XiaoIce: XiaoIce is an AI chatbot developed by Microsoft for the Chinese market. The chatbot is designed to simulate human-like conversations with users and is often described as having a "personality" due to its ability to understand emotions and engage in social interactions (Shum et al., 2018).

Jia Jia: Jia Jia is a humanoid robot developed by the University of Science and Technology of China. The robot is designed to look and act like a human, with the ability to make facial expressions, hold conversations, and interact with its environment (Cebo, 2020).

Xinhua News Agency's AI News Anchor: In 2018, China's Xinhua News Agency introduced an AI news anchor that was designed to look and sound like a human news anchor. The AI anchor was created using advanced machine learning algorithms that analyzed the facial movements, voice, and delivery style of a human anchor to create a realistic digital avatar (Gal, 2019).

Baidu's Duer: Baidu's Duer is an AI assistant that can be integrated into a variety of devices, including smart speakers, smartphones, and home appliances. The assistant is designed to be conversational and is often anthropomorphized in marketing materials as a friendly, helpful character that can understand and respond to users' needs (Song et al., 2022).

India

Mitra: Mitra is a humanoid robot developed by Indian startup Invento Robotics. The robot is designed to interact with humans in public spaces such as malls, airports, and hospitals. Mitra is anthropomorphized in its design and behavior, with a friendly and approachable appearance and the ability to understand and respond to natural language commands (Meghani, 2020).

Haptik: Haptik is an AI-powered chatbot developed by an Indian startup of the same name. The chatbot is designed to provide personalized assistance to users for a variety of tasks, including booking travel, ordering food, and paying bills. Haptik is anthropomorphized in its marketing materials, with a friendly and approachable persona designed to appeal to users (Majid and Lakshmi, 2022).

Niki.ai: Niki.ai is an AI-powered personal shopping assistant developed by Indian startup Niki.ai. The assistant is designed to help users with online shopping, with the ability to understand natural language commands and make personalized recommendations based on user preferences. Niki.ai is anthropomorphized in its marketing materials, with a friendly and approachable persona that aims to make users feel more comfortable interacting with the assistant (Achary, 2021).

JioSaavn: JioSaavn is an Indian music streaming service that uses AI to personalize the listening experience for users. The service uses machine learning algorithms to analyze user behavior and make recommendations based on their listening history and preferences. JioSaavn is anthropomorphized in its marketing materials, with a friendly and approachable persona designed to appeal to users (Dabholkar et al., 2021).

Wysa: Wysa is an AI-powered mental health chatbot developed by Indian startup Touchkin. The chatbot is designed to provide emotional support and therapy to users, with the ability to understand natural language commands and provide personalized recommendations. Wysa is anthropomorphized in its design and behavior, with a friendly and empathetic persona designed to make users feel more comfortable sharing their feelings and experiences (Paul et al., 2018).

South Africa

Pepper Robot: Pepper is a humanoid robot that is designed to interact with humans using natural language processing and facial recognition technology. The robot is used in various industries in South Africa, including hospitality, retail, and healthcare (Gardecki and Podpora, 2017).

Kudi: Kudi is an AI-powered chatbot that helps users to manage their finances through messaging apps like WhatsApp and Facebook Messenger. The chatbot uses natural language processing to understand user queries and responds with helpful advice (Ade-Ibijola and Okonkwo, 2023).

ReKindle Learning: ReKindle Learning is an AI-powered platform that delivers personalized learning experiences to students in South Africa. The platform uses machine learning algorithms to adapt to each student's individual learning style and pace (Wernick, 2016).

Aerobotics: Aerobotics is an AI-powered platform that helps farmers to monitor their crops and identify potential issues. The platform uses machine learning algorithms to analyze drone imagery and provide insights to farmers, helping them to make data-driven decisions (Sampene et al., 2022).

Brazil

Laura: Laura is an AI-powered virtual assistant developed by Brazilian startup Laura. The assistant is designed to help healthcare professionals manage patient care, with the ability to analyze medical records and make personalized recommendations. Laura is anthropomorphized in its marketing materials, with a friendly and approachable persona that aims to make healthcare professionals feel more comfortable interacting with the assistant (Nair, 2022).

Sophie: Sophie is an AI-powered chatbot developed by Brazilian startup Crebito. The chatbot is designed to provide personalized financial advice and investment recommendations to users, with the ability to understand natural language commands and make personalized recommendations. Sophie is anthropomorphized in its design and behavior, with a friendly and approachable persona that aims to make users feel more comfortable interacting with the assistant (Reindly, 2020).

Olly: Olly is an AI-powered personal assistant developed by Brazilian startup Olly. The assistant is designed to help users with a variety of tasks, including scheduling appointments, making reservations, and ordering food. Olly is anthropomorphized in its marketing materials, with a friendly and approachable persona that aims to make users feel more comfortable interacting with the assistant (Bosse et al., 2023).

ELSA: ELSA is an AI-powered language learning app developed by Brazilian startup ELSA. The app is designed to help users improve their English pronunciation and speaking skills, with the ability to analyze user speech and provide personalized feedback. ELSA is anthropomorphized in its marketing materials, with a friendly and approachable persona that aims to make users feel more comfortable using the app (Kholis, 2021).

Romania

Robo-C: Robo-C is a humanoid robot designed by a Romanian company, RoboTech. It can recognize and respond to human voice and gestures and is used in various industries, including hospitality, education, and entertainment (Aymerich-Franch and Ferrer, 2021).

UiPath: UiPath is a Romanian software company that develops robotic process automation (RPA) software. Their software robots can automate routine tasks in various industries, including banking, healthcare, and manufacturing (Dobrica, 2022).

Turkey

Akıncı 4: Akıncı-4, designed as a humanoid robot, has 37 articulation points by the Turkish company, AKINROBOTICS. Akıncı-4, which works entirely with domestic software and speaks three languages, can speak with artificial intelligence and image processing software, can see in 3D, recognize people, interpret the information it has learned and can analyze age and gender. Akıncı-4, with its deep learning feature, can be programmed to work in different sectors (Özekinci, 2018).

Mini Ada: Social Robot Mini ADA is produced by AKINROBOTICS, which carries out production, software, and robot studies. Mini Ada can take part in many areas such as airports, bus stations, centers, shopping malls, stores, educational institutions, fairs, concerts, openings, and celebration organizations (Akinrobotics, 2023).

Cere: Cere is an artificial intelligence supported application developed by Cerebrum Tech, a technology company based in Turkey. Cere has the ability to chat with users both verbally and in written form. Equipped with deep learning-based language models, the application allows users to suggest music according to their mood, summarize news topics, and provide information on many topics from food to fashion, health to sports. Cere's development has included the use of advanced artificial intelligence techniques, including empathetic design principles, resulting in a unique mobile application that stands out in its category (Sırt, 2023).

CONCLUSION

Destructive innovations have destroyed sectors that cannot keep up with the times and accelerated the formation of new sectors. In order to be a long-lasting business and to make successful marketing decisions, it is important to get rid of marketing myopia and take innovative steps. Disruptive technologies such as the internet of things, big data analytics, blockchain, and artificial intelligence have changed the way both industries and businesses work. Artificial intelligence, which is one of the latest destructive innovations, has started to be used in many fields, especially in production, the health sector, agriculture, logistics, and marketing. While developing systems based on artificial intelligence, these systems are expected to be user-friendly and communicate with consumers correctly. Various research is carried out in order to increase artificial intelligence and consumer interaction. One of the subjects studied on increasing consumer-artificial intelligence interaction is anthropomorphism. When humanoid features are attributed to artificial intelligence systems, the effects of this on consumer behavior have been examined in the literature. Within the scope of this study, it is important to determine the topics that are the most popular in the literature, have lost their popularity or the number of studies on them is increasing, in terms of determining the fields that are important both academically and sectorally.

In the study, 475 articles containing the keywords "anthropomorph*" and "consum*" were selected from the Web of Science database. Selected articles were analyzed with the help of the R program. Analysis results were visualized and included in the study. Although it is seen that the concepts of "artificial intelligence", "robots" and "chatbots" are frequently used in studies in the direction of the findings obtained, it is also seen that there are studies on "customer experience", "self-service technologies" and "trust", which have increased in importance in recent years. In addition, when the engine themes of the thematic map are examined, it is seen that some frequently studied topics such as "artificial intelligence-service robot" are clustered together. According to the findings of the study, it has been revealed that the country that contributes the most to the literature and receives the most references in the United States of America, and the journal with the most publications on the subject is the "Journal of Consumer Research".

The study's findings have provided valuable insights and recommendations for future research in the same field. To address gaps in the literature and contribute to it, it is suggested that future studies should focus on more current subjects. One area of research that has gained significant global importance is trust-based research, specifically in the context of artificial intelligence and marketing. As AI systems continue to develop and become more human-like, consumers' trust levels in such technology are changing. Therefore, further research is necessary to better understand the relationship between trust and AI. Another area that requires more research is customer experience and self-service technologies. As AI continues to be utilized more extensively in the service sector, anthropomorphic robots and digital systems are becoming increasingly common. As such, it is essential to study how these technologies impact the customer experience and how they can be optimized for optimal outcomes. Additionally, unmanned hotels and service machines are on the rise, and studying their implications on the service sector is necessary. The researchers emphasize the importance of conducting studies on these topics and proposing regulations to address any issues that arise. Such studies will contribute to the academic discourse while providing valuable insights into how technology can enhance the customer experience and build trust with customers.

REFERENCES

Aaker, D., & Aaker, J. L. (2016). What are your signature stories? *California Management Review*, *58*(3), 49–65. doi:10.1525/cmr.2016.58.3.49

Abercrombie, G., Curry, A. C., Pandya, M., & Rieser, V. (2021). Alexa, Google, Siri: What are your pronouns? Gender and anthropomorphism in the design and perception of conversational assistants. doi:10.18653/v1/2021.gebnlp-1.4

Achary, R. (2021). Artificial Intelligence Transforming Indian Banking Sector. *International Journal of Economics and Management Systems, 6*.

Adam, M., Wessel, M., & Benlian, A. (2021). AI-based chatbots in customer service and their effects on user compliance. *Electronic Markets*, *31*(2), 427–445. doi:10.100712525-020-00414-7

Ade-Ibijola, A., & Okonkwo, C. (2023). Artificial Intelligence in Africa: Emerging Challenges. In *Responsible AI in Africa: Challenges and Opportunities* (pp. 101–117). Springer International Publishing. doi:10.1007/978-3-031-08215-3_5

Aggarwal, P., & McGill, A. L. (2012). When brands seem human, do humans act likc brands? Automatic behavioral priming effects of brand anthropomorphism. *The Journal of Consumer Research*, *39*(2), 307–323. doi:10.1086/662614

Akınrobotics. (2023). AkınRobotics. *Mini Ada 3*. Retrieved on 12.04.2023 from https://www.akinrobotics.com/sosyal-robot-mini-ada-3

Alam, A., & Mohanty, A. (2022). Metaverse and Posthuman Animated Avatars for Teaching-Learning Process: Interperception in Virtual Universe for Educational Transformation. In *International Conference on Innovations in Intelligent Computing and Communications* (pp. 47-61). Springer. 10.1007/978-3-031-23233-6_4

Ameen, N., Tarhini, A., Reppel, A., & Anand, A. (2021). Customer experiences in the age of artificial intelligence. *Computers in Human Behavior*, *114*, 106548. doi:10.1016/j.chb.2020.106548 PMID:32905175

Aymerich-Franch, L., & Ferrer, I. (2021). Socially assistive robots' deployment in healthcare settings: a global perspective. arXiv preprint arXiv:2110.07404.

Bartneck, C., & Keijsers, M. (2020). The morality of abusing a robot. *Paladyn : Journal of Behavioral Robotics*, *11*(1), 271–283. doi:10.1515/pjbr-2020-0017

Bartneck, C., Kulić, D., Croft, E., & Zoghbi, S. (2009). Measurement instruments for the anthropomorphism, animacy, likeability, perceived intelligence, and perceived safety of robots. *International Journal of Social Robotics*, *1*(1), 71–81. doi:10.100712369-008-0001-3

Benbya, H., Pachidi, S., & Jarvenpaa, S. (2021). Special issue editorial: Artificial intelligence in organizations: Implications for information systems research. *Journal of the Association for Information Systems*, *22*(2), 10. doi:10.17705/1jais.00662

Benhamou, Y., & Ferland, J. (2020). (Forthcoming). Artificial Intelligence & Damages: Assessing Liability and Calculating the Damages. *Leading Legal Disruption: Artificial Intelligence and a Toolkit for Lawyers and the Law*.

Benlian, A., Klumpe, J., & Hinz, O. (2020). Mitigating the intrusive effects of smart home assistants by using anthropomorphic design features: A multimethod investigation. *Information Systems Journal*, *30*(6), 1010–1042. doi:10.1111/isj.12243

Blackston, M. (1993). Beyond brand personality: building brand relationships. *Brand equity and advertising: Advertising's role in building strong brands*, 113-124.

Blut, M., Wang, C., Wünderlich, N. V., & Brock, C. (2021). Understanding anthropomorphism in service provision: A meta-analysis of physical robots, chatbots, and other AI. *Journal of the Academy of Marketing Science*, *49*(4), 632–658. doi:10.100711747-020-00762-y

Bosse, D., Thompson, S., & Ekman, P. (2023). In consilium apparatus: Artificial intelligence, stakeholder reciprocity, and firm performance. *Journal of Business Research*, *155*, 113402. doi:10.1016/j.jbusres.2022.113402

Castelli, F., Frith, C., Happé, F., & Frith, U. (2002). Autism, Asperger syndrome and brain mechanisms for the attribution of mental states to animated shapes. *Brain*, *125*(8), 1839–1849. doi:10.1093/brain/awf189 PMID:12135974

Cebo, P. (2020). Artificial Intelligence In Humanoid Robots. *Conference Paper: Online International Conference on Humanoids*.

Chandler, J., & Schwarz, N. (2010). Use does not wear ragged the fabric of friendship: Thinking of objects as alive makes people less willing to replace them. *Journal of Consumer Psychology*, *20*(2), 138–145. doi:10.1016/j.jcps.2009.12.008

Cheng, X., Zhang, X., Cohen, J., & Mou, J. (2022). Human vs. AI: Understanding the impact of anthropomorphism on consumer response to chatbots from the perspective of trust and relationship norms. *Information Processing & Management*, *59*(3), 102940. doi:10.1016/j.ipm.2022.102940

Crolic, C., Thomaz, F., Hadi, R., & Stephen, A. T. (2022). Blame the bot: Anthropomorphism and anger in customer–chatbot interactions. *Journal of Marketing*, *86*(1), 132–148. doi:10.1177/00222429211045687

Dabholkar, A., Kakarla, S., & Saha, D. (2021). Looney tunes: Exposing the lack of DRM protection in indian music streaming services. arXiv preprint arXiv:2103.16360.

Dash, R., McMurtrey, M., Rebman, C., & Kar, U. K. (2019). Application of artificial intelligence in automation of supply chain management. *Journal of Strategic Innovation and Sustainability*, *14*(3), 43–53.

DiSalvo, C., Gemperle, F., & Forlizzi, J. (2005). *Imitating the human form: Four kinds of anthropomorphic form.* Unpublished manuscript.

Dobrica, L. (2022). Robotic process automation platform UiPath. *Communications of the ACM*, *65*(4), 42–43. doi:10.1145/3511667

Epley, N., Waytz, A., & Cacioppo, J. T. (2007). On seeing human: A three-factor theory of anthropomorphism. *Psychological Review*, *114*(4), 864–886. doi:10.1037/0033-295X.114.4.864 PMID:17907867

Fan, A., Wu, L. L., & Mattila, A. S. (2016). Does anthropomorphism influence customers' switching intentions in the self-service technology failure context? *Journal of Services Marketing*, *30*(7), 713–723. doi:10.1108/JSM-07-2015-0225

Festerling, J., & Siraj, I. (2021). Anthropomorphizing Technology: A Conceptual Review of Anthropomorphism Research and How it Relates to Children's Engagements with Digital Voice Assistants. *Integrative Psychological & Behavioral Science*, 1–30. PMID:34811705

Foehr, J., & Germelmann, C. C. (2020). Alexa, can I trust you? Exploring consumer paths to trust in smart voice-interaction technologies. *Journal of the Association for Consumer Research*, *5*(2), 181–205. doi:10.1086/707731

Gal, D. (2019). *Perspectives and approaches in AI ethics: East Asia. Oxford Handbook of Ethics of Artificial Intelligence*. Oxford University Press.

Gardecki, A., & Podpora, M. (2017). Experience from the operation of the Pepper humanoid robots. In 2017 Progress in Applied Electrical Engineering (PAEE) (pp. 1-6). IEEE. doi:10.1109/PAEE.2017.8008994

Genin, K., & Grote, T. (2021). Randomized controlled trials in medical AI: A methodological critique. *Philosophy of Medicine*, *2*(1), 1–15. doi:10.5195/pom.2021.27

Go, E., & Sundar, S. S. (2019). Humanizing chatbots: The effects of visual, identity and conversational cues on humanness perceptions. *Computers in Human Behavior*, *97*, 304–316. doi:10.1016/j.chb.2019.01.020

Gursoy, D., Chi, O. H., Lu, L., & Nunkoo, R. (2019). Consumers acceptance of artificially intelligent (AI) device use in service delivery. *International Journal of Information Management*, *49*, 157–169. doi:10.1016/j.ijinfomgt.2019.03.008

ISI. (2022). *Developing Countries.* Retrieved 9 August, 2022 from https://www.isi-web.org/resources/developing-countries

Ivanov, S., & Webster, C. (2021). Willingness-to-pay for robot-delivered tourism and hospitality services–an exploratory study. *International Journal of Contemporary Hospitality Management*, *33*(11), 3926–3955. doi:10.1108/IJCHM-09-2020-1078

J. R. (2018). Voodoo software and boundary objects in game development: How developers collaborate and conflict with game engines and art tools. *New Media & Society, 20*(7), 2315-2332.

Kholis, A. (2021). Elsa speak app: automatic speech recognition (ASR) for supplementing English pronunciation skills. *Pedagogy: Journal of English Language Teaching, 9*(1), 1-14.

Laksmidewi, D., Susianto, H., & Afiff, A. Z. (2017). Anthropomorphism in Advertising: The Effect of Anthropomorphiic Product Demonstration on Consumer Purchase Intention. Asian Academy of Management Journal, 22(1).

Letheren, K., Jetten, J., Roberts, J., & Donovan, J. (2021). Robots should be seen and not heard… sometimes: Anthropomorphism and AI service robot interactions. *Psychology and Marketing*, *38*(12), 2393–2406. doi:10.1002/mar.21575

Liu, K., & Tao, D. (2022). The roles of trust, personalization, loss of privacy, and anthropomorphism in public acceptance of smart healthcare services. *Computers in Human Behavior*, *127*, 107026. doi:10.1016/j.chb.2021.107026

Lockey, S., Gillespie, N., Holm, D., & Someh, I. A. (2021). *A review of trust in artificial intelligence: Challenges, vulnerabilities and future directions*. Academic Press.

MacInnis, D. J., & Folkes, V. S. (2017). Humanizing brands: When brands seem to be like me, part of me, and in a relationship with me. *Journal of Consumer Psychology*, *27*(3), 355–374. doi:10.1016/j.jcps.2016.12.003

Majid, I., & Lakshmi, Y. V. (2022). An Analysis of Artificial Intelligence Initiatives and Programmes in India. In *Convergence of Deep Learning and Artificial Intelligence in Internet of Things* (pp. 281–292). CRC Press. doi:10.1201/9781003355960-19

Marda, V. (2018). Artificial intelligence policy in India: A framework for engaging the limits of data-driven decision-making. *Philosophical Transactions - Royal Society. Mathematical, Physical, and Engineering Sciences*, *376*(2133), 20180087. doi:10.1098/rsta.2018.0087 PMID:30323001

Martin, C., DeStefano, K., Haran, H., Zink, S., Dai, J., Ahmed, D., Razzak, A., Lin, K., Kogler, A., Waller, J., Kazmi, K., & Umair, M. (2022). The ethical considerations including inclusion and biases, data protection, and proper implementation among AI in radiology and potential implications. *Intelligence-Based Medicine*, *6*, 100073. doi:10.1016/j.ibmed.2022.100073

McDuie-Ra, D., & Gulson, K. (2020). The backroads of AI: The uneven geographies of artificial intelligence and development. *Area, 52*(3), 626–633. doi:10.1111/area.12602

Meghani, K. (2020). Use of artificial intelligence and Blockchain in banking sector: A study of scheduled commercial banks in India. Use of Artificial Intelligence and Blockchain in Banking Sector: A Study of Scheduled Commercial Banks in India, Kishore Meghani. *Indian Journal of Applied Research*, 10.

Milton, K. (2020). Anthropomorphism or egomorphism? The perception of non-human persons by human ones. In *Animals in person* (pp. 255–271). Routledge. doi:10.4324/9781003135883-13

Mori, M. (1970). The uncanny valley: The original essay by Masahiro Mori. *IEEE Spectrum.*

Nagaty, K. A. (2023). IoT Commercial and Industrial Applications and AI-Powered IoT. In *Frontiers of Quality Electronic Design (QED) AI, IoT and Hardware Security* (pp. 465–500). Springer International Publishing. doi:10.1007/978-3-031-16344-9_12

Nair, P. (2022). Health Technologies and Innovations to Effectively Respond to the Covid-19 Pandemic. *Frontiers in Digital Health, 4*, 15. doi:10.3389/fdgth.2022.849652 PMID:35237764

Omary, Z., Lupiana, D., Mtenzi, F., & Wu, B. (2009). Challenges to E-healthcare adoption in developing countries: A case study of Tanzania. In *2009 First International Conference on Networked Digital Technologies* (pp. 201-209). IEEE. 10.1109/NDT.2009.5272067

Özekinci, E. (2018). *Anadolu Ajansı, Adım atan robot 'Akıncı-4' görücüye çıktı.* Retrieved on 12.04.2023 from https://www.aa.com.tr/tr/bilim-teknoloji/adim-atan-robot-akinci-4-gorucuye-cikti/1276507

Pairoa, I., & Arunrangsiwed, P. (2016). The effect of brand mascots on consumers' purchasing behaviors. *International Journal of Economics and Management Engineering, 10*(5), 1702–1705.

Pak, R., McLaughlin, A. C., & Bass, B. (2014). A multi-level analysis of the effects of age and gender stereotypes on trust in anthropomorphic technology by younger and older adults. *Ergonomics, 57*(9), 1277–1289. doi:10.1080/00140139.2014.928750 PMID:24935771

Patterson, A., Khogeer, Y., & Hodgson, J. (2013). How to create an influential anthropomorphic mascot: Literary musings on marketing, make-believe, and meerkats. *Journal of Marketing Management, 29*(1-2), 69–85. doi:10.1080/0267257X.2012.759992

Paul, Y., Hickok, E., Sinha, A., Tiwari, U., Mohandas, S., Ray, S., & Bidare, P. M. (2018). *Artificial intelligence in the healthcare industry in India.* The Centre for Internet and Society.

Pelau, C., Dabija, D. C., & Ene, I. (2021). What makes an AI device human-like? The role of interaction quality, empathy and perceived psychological anthropomorphic characteristics in the acceptance of artificial intelligence in the service industry. *Computers in Human Behavior, 122*, 106855. doi:10.1016/j.chb.2021.106855

Pelau, C., Dabija, D. C., & Ene, I. (2021). What makes an AI device human-like? The role of interaction quality, empathy and perceived psychological anthropomorphic characteristics in the acceptance of artificial intelligence in the service industry. *Computers in Human Behavior, 122*, 106855. doi:10.1016/j.chb.2021.106855

Pfeuffer, N., Benlian, A., Gimpel, H., & Hinz, O. (2019). Anthropomorphic information systems. *Business & Information Systems Engineering*, *61*(4), 523–533. doi:10.100712599-019-00599-y

Phillips, B., & Lee, W. N. (2005). Interactive animation: Exploring spokes-characters on the internet. *Journal of Current Issues and Research in Advertising*, *27*(1), 1–17. doi:10.1080/10641734.2005.10505170

Pitardi, V., & Marriott, H. R. (2021). Alexa, she's not human but… Unveiling the drivers of consumers' trust in voice-based artificial intelligence. *Psychology and Marketing*, *38*(4), 626–642. doi:10.1002/mar.21457

Plummer, J. T. (2000). How personality makes a difference. *Journal of Advertising Research*, *40*(6), 79–83. doi:10.2501/JAR-40-6-79-83

Rathnayaka, P., Mills, N., Burnett, D., De Silva, D., Alahakoon, D., & Gray, R. (2022). A mental health chatbot with cognitive skills for personalised behavioural activation and remote health monitoring. *Sensors (Basel)*, *22*(10), 3653. doi:10.339022103653 PMID:35632061

Reinly, J. C. (2020). *Look out Alexa, Southfield-based IT firm bets future on 'Sophie'.* Retrieved on 12.04.2023 from https://www.freep.com/story/money/business/2020/02/15/southfield-stefanini-michigan-sophie/4759791002/

Salles, A., Evers, K., & Farisco, M. (2020). Anthropomorphism in AI. *AJOB Neuroscience*, *11*(2), 88–95. doi:10.1080/21507740.2020.1740350 PMID:32228388

Sampene, A. K., Agyeman, F. O., Robert, B., & Wiredu, J. (2022). Artificial Intelligence as a Path Way to Africa's TransformationS. *Artificial Intelligence*, *9*(1).

Seo, S. (2022). When Female (Male) Robot Is Talking To Me: Effect of service robots' gender and anthropomorphism on customer satisfaction. *International Journal of Hospitality Management*, *102*, 103166. doi:10.1016/j.ijhm.2022.103166

Severson, R. L., & Woodard, S. R. (2018). Imagining others' minds: The positive relation between children's role play and anthropomorphism. *Frontiers in Psychology*, *9*, 2140. doi:10.3389/fpsyg.2018.02140 PMID:30483176

Shum, H. Y., He, X. D., & Li, D. (2018). From Eliza to XiaoIce: Challenges and opportunities with social chatbots. *Frontiers of Information Technology & Electronic Engineering*, *19*(1), 10–26. doi:10.1631/FITEE.1700826

Singh, D., Bajpai, N., & Kulshreshtha, K. (2021). The effect of brand anthropomorphism on customers' behaviour towards the indian hypermarket brands. *Journal of Creative Communications*, *16*(3), 266–284. doi:10.1177/09732586211002104

Singh, U. S., Singh, N., Gulati, K., Bhasin, N. K., & Sreejith, P. M. (2022). A study on the revolution of consumer relationships as a combination of human interactions and digital transformations. *Materials Today: Proceedings*, *51*, 460–464. doi:10.1016/j.matpr.2021.05.578

Sırt, T. (2023). *Meet Cere: Türkiye's first AI-powered mobile chatbot*. Retrieved on 12.04.2023 from https://www.dailysabah.com/business/tech/meet-cere-turkiyes-first-ai-powered-mobile-chatbot

Sitorus, T., & Yustisia, M. (2018). The influence of service quality and customer trust toward customer loyalty: The role of customer satisfaction. *International Journal of Qualitative Research, 12*(3), 639.

Song, X., Xu, B., & Zhao, Z. (2022). Can people experience romantic love for artificial intelligence? An empirical study of intelligent assistants. *Information & Management, 59*(2), 103595. doi:10.1016/j.im.2022.103595

Sowmiya, S., Ramachandran, M., Chinnasamy, S., Prasanth, V., & Sriram, S. (2022). A Study on Humanoid Robots and Its Psychological Evaluation. *Design. Modelling and Fabrication of Advanced Robots, 1*(1), 48–54. doi:10.46632/dmfar/1/1/8

Swamy, M. (2022). Speech Enhancement, Databases, Features and Classifiers in Automatic Speech Recognition. *RE:view.*

Waytz, A., Cacioppo, J., & Epley, N. (2010). Who sees human? The stability and importance of individual differences in anthropomorphism. *Perspectives on Psychological Science, 5*(3), 219–232. doi:10.1177/1745691610369336 PMID:24839457

Weisman, W. D., & Peña, J. F. (2021). Face the uncanny: The effects of doppelganger talking head avatars on affect-based trust toward artificial intelligence technology are mediated by uncanny valley perceptions. *Cyberpsychology, Behavior, and Social Networking, 24*(3), 182–187. doi:10.1089/cyber.2020.0175 PMID:33646048

Wernick, D. (2016). Innovation in Africa: A view from the peaks and hilltops of a spiky continent. *Innovation in Emerging Markets*, 121-139.

Wirtz, J., Patterson, P. G., Kunz, W. H., Gruber, T., Lu, V. N., Paluch, S., & Martins, A. (2018). Brave new world: Service robots in the frontline. *Journal of Service Management, 29*(5), 907–931. doi:10.1108/JOSM-04-2018-0119

Wright, J. (2019). Robots vs migrants? Reconfiguring the future of Japanese institutional eldercare. *Critical Asian Studies, 51*(3), 331–354. doi:10.1080/14672715.2019.1612765

Yadav, P., Bisoyi, D., & Chakrabati, D. (2015). Anthropomorphic Brand Mascot Serve as the vehicle: To quickly remind customers who you are and what you stand for in Indian Cultural context. *International Scientific Research and Experimental Development*, 1814-1818.

Yeasmin, S. (2019). Benefits of artificial intelligence in medicine. In *2019 2nd International Conference on Computer Applications & Information Security (ICCAIS)* (pp. 1-6). IEEE. 10.1109/CAIS.2019.8769557

Yu, C. E., & Ngan, H. F. B. (2019). The power of head tilts: Gender and cultural differences of perceived human vs human-like robot smile in service. *Tourism Review, 74*(3), 428–442. doi:10.1108/TR-07-2018-0097

Yuan, L., & Dennis, A. R. (2019). Acting like humans? Anthropomorphism and consumer's willingness to pay in electronic commerce. *Journal of Management Information Systems, 36*(2), 450–477. doi:10.1080/07421222.2019.1598691

KEY TERMS AND DEFINITIONS

AI-Powered Avatars: AI-powered avatars are digital representations of humans that are animated by artificial intelligence. They can be used in educational settings to provide personalized learning experiences, such as virtual tutors or language teachers.

Anthropomorphism: Anthropomorphism is the attribution of human characteristics, behaviors, or emotions to non-human entities such as animals, objects, or natural phenomena.

Artificial Intelligence: Artificial Intelligence (AI) refers to the simulation of human intelligence in machines that are programmed to perform tasks that typically require human cognition, such as learning, problem solving, and decision making.

Chatbots: Chatbots are AI-powered computer programs that can simulate conversation with human users through natural language processing. They can be used for various purposes, such as customer service, information retrieval, and entertainment.

Social Robots: Social robots are AI-powered machines that are designed to interact with humans in a social way, typically with the goal of providing companionship or emotional support. They can be used in a variety of settings, such as nursing homes, schools, and homes.

Virtual Assistant: A virtual assistant is an AI-powered software program that can perform tasks or provide information for users via text or voice commands. Examples of virtual assistants include Apple's Siri, Amazon's Alexa, and Google Assistant.

Chapter 13
Digitalization of the Tanzania's Tourism Industry:
A Marketing Perspective

Dennis M. Lupiana
Institute of Finance Management, Tanzania

ABSTRACT

In Tanzania the tourism industry is one of the main contributors to the economy. Despite the steady increase in tourists after the COVID-19 pandemic, the industry's performance is low compared to the unique and abundant tourism resources with which the country is endowed. Tanzania is ranked 1st in Africa and 12th worldwide on the quality of its nature-based resources and 32nd in Africa on its cultural resources. Yet the country holds 5th place in Sub-Saharan Africa. This is due to several factors, and the low integration of digital solutions is one of them. In order to improve the performance, the chapter identifies areas in the customer journey that can benefit from digitalization and proposes relevant interventions. The challenges include underutilization of user-generated content, limited internet access, the dominance of traditional marketing practices, inadequate planning services, and limited access to local businesses. The proposed interventions include the development of an interactive web portal and e-tourism stickers and the inclusion of planning features in a tourism portal.

INTRODUCTION

Tourism industry plays a key role in Tanzania's economy and the wellbeing of its people. In 2019, the industry contribution to GDP was 10.6%, i.e., USD 2.6 billion. Due to COVID-19 pandemic, however, the contribution fell to 5.3% in 2020. Since 2021 the industry has started to recover, recording an increase of contribution from 5.3% to 5.7%. This is attributed by the increase of tourists in the destination, raising the number of tourists from 922,692 in 2021 to 1,454,920 in 2022 post COVID-19 pandemic. This is due to a tremendous efforts the government has put forward to ensure the country's naturals resources and cultural heritages contribute significantly to the economy of the country. Among the efforts, is the establishment of Safari Channel, an exclusive TV channel for showcasing the destination, improved col-

DOI: 10.4018/978-1-6684-6873-9.ch013

laborations with foreign journalists and bloggers and establishment of destination rebranding committee that came up with renewed brand and tagline "*Tanzania Unforgettable*". Nonetheless, many credits are to The Royal Tour documentary by Her Excellency, Hon. Dr. Samia Suluhu Hassan, the first female President of the United Republic of Tanzania. The documentary has to a great deal created awareness on the tourism industry in Tanzania.

With a population of more than 60 million, Tanzania has low crime rate and a relatively stable political environment. Tanzania is blessed with abundant natural and cultural resources. Tanzania harbors the highest permanently snow-capped freestanding mountain in Africa (i.e. Mountain Kilimanjaro), the largest intact volcanic caldera on Earth (i.e. Ngorongoro Crater) and the massive annual migration of wildebeest and zebra in Serengeti National Park in the mainland. In Zanzibar, Tanzania is blessed with historic buildings, exotic beaches and parks and games, and unique and organic spices. World Economic Forum (2022) ranked Tanzania 1st in Africa and 12th globally on the quality of its nature-based tourism resources as well as 32nd in Africa on its cultural resources. Yet, Tanzania holds 5th place in Sub-Saharan Africa, behind Mauritius, South Africa, Botswana and Kenya. This clearly shows that something has to be done for the country to claim its position and achieve its target of reaching 5 million tourists by 2025.

Saner and colleagues (2019) propose four intervention pillars (political, economical, social and environmental) that any national tourism development plant should address. Specifically, this chapter contributes to social and economical intervention pillars. Within the framework of the social intervention pillar, the chapter proposes to build capacity of marketing personnel in the tourism industry to align with digital marketing strategies. As for the economic intervention pillar, the chapter proposes interventions to increase collaborations and partnerships among and beyond tourism stakeholders, and availability and access to "engaging tourism content", and improve business environment. Nevertheless, interventions proposed in this chapter are purely geared to increase ICT readiness in the industry. In particular, the interventions are geared to increase usage of digital platforms in the tourism industry, which according to the World Economic Forum (WEF) are crucial for determining destination's competitiveness globally.

DIGITALIZATION OF THE INDUSTRY

In the wake of information and digital era, countries have been striving to evolve their convectional economies to digital economies. Like many other countries, Tanzania has also started the journey to digital economy (World Bank 2021). Bukht and Heeks (2017) define digital economy as an economy driven by digital technologies and their innovative business models. In one aspect of the digital economy, governments strive to improve service delivery through digital solutions. In another aspect, governments strive to take advantage of digital solutions to build favorable business environment and encourage business diversifications. Either way, however, it is evident that digital technologies play an important role in realizing the digital economy thus enabling businesses in different sectors to become competitive and economic viable.

Globally, contribution of the tourism industry is huge in countries' economies. Consequently, integration of digital technologies in the tourism industry has attracted increasing academic interest. Bănescu and colleagues (2021), for instance, provide a systematic review of the impact of digitalization in European countries. They observed a shift on trading tourism products from physical to virtual. On Internet usage, they noted tourists use the Internet to find information about tourist destinations and for planning and booking their trips. Kumar and Shekhar (2020) evaluate how different players in tourism value chain are affected by digitalization. World Tourism Organization (UNWTO) and an Asian Development Bank (2021) jointly emphasize on applying the concept of "Big Data" to manage destinations and better understand changes in consumer behavior so as to promptly devise recovery strategies. Natocheeva and colleagues (2020) emphasized digital marketing and the use of Internet of Thinks (IoT) in analyzing tourist preferences. Although a handful of researchers (Cai & McKenna 2023; Egger *et al.* 2020; Li *et al.* 2020) are advocating for Digital-Free Tourism (DFT), the concept is far from the reality.

Digital solutions have become key ingredients to a success of any business. The solutions are crucial for businesses to access and advertise to new markets, improve efficiency and gain insights into consumer needs (WEF 2022). All these come with a reward to a business i.e. an increase in competitive edge and financial muscles. WEF (2017, p. 6), for instance, have shown a strong linkage between a destination's ICT readiness and a volume of spending by international tourists. As shown in the graph, Figure 1, the higher the score on ICT readiness, the higher and the denser the bubbles are thus implying an increase of volume and value of spending of international tourists. Despite the benefits of digital solutions, currently investments in digital transformations in the industry are patchy i.e. only undertaken by tourism operators with financial muscles. As Tanzania embarks on the journey to digital economy, digitalization of the industry in Tanzania becomes important.

Figure 1. Correlation between ICT readiness and tourist spending
Source: WEF (2017)

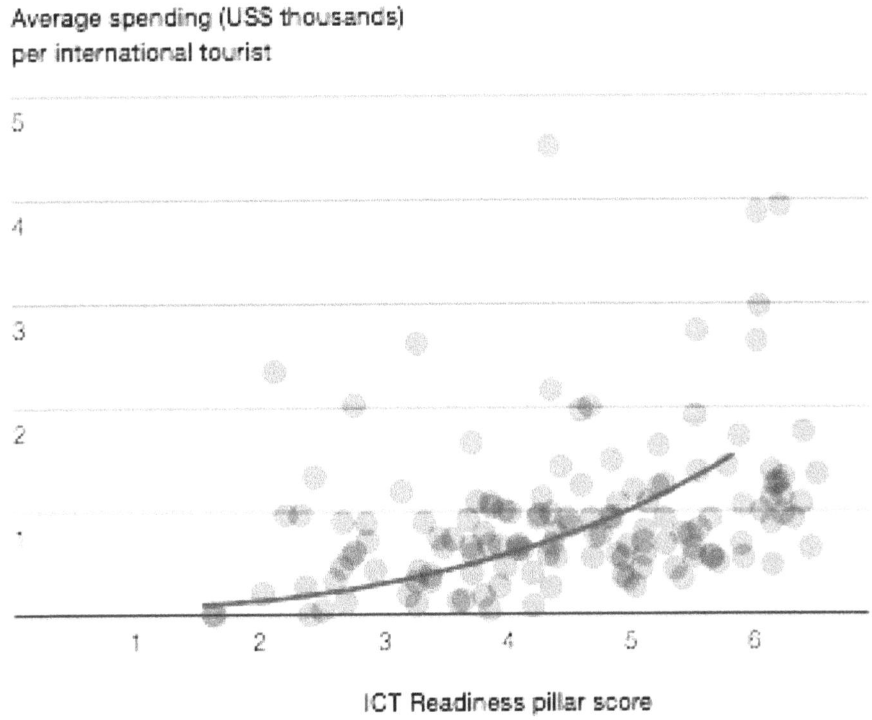

As of 2021, competiveness of the tourism industry in Tanzania is ranked at 81st place in the world by the WEF, refer to Figure 2. This is an improvement from 2019, which the industry was ranked 86th. Despite of having many of the world's renowned tourist attractions, Tanzania still claimed the 5th place in Sub-Saharan Africa. As shown in Figure 3, the 1st place is claimed by Mauritius, followed by South Africa, Botswana and then Kenya on the 4th place.

As shown in Figure 4, computation of the index is guided by 5 sub-indexes with a total of 17 pillars and 112 indicators. Nevertheless, this chapter focuses on the "ICT Readiness" pillar, which according to

Figure 2. Tanzania's travel and tourism competitiveness ranks in the globe
Source: WEF (2022)

Travel & Tourism Competitiveness Edition	2019	2021
Rank	86/117	81/117
Score	3.5	3.6

Figure 3. Tanzania's travel and tourism competitiveness rank in Sub-Saharan Africa
Source: WEF (2022)

Rank	Economy		Value	Score (1-7 best)	Dist. from Highest
62	Mauritius	(i)	4.0	4.0	
68	South Africa	(i)	3.8	3.8	
76	Botswana	(i)	3.7	3.7	
78	Kenya	(i)	3.6	3.6	
81	Tanzania	(i)	3.6	3.6	

Figure 4. Metrics for computing travel and tourism competitiveness index

WEF is increasingly becoming important. Specifically, the pillar measures the development and usage of ICT infrastructure and digital solutions in the industry.

As shown in Figure 5, the "ICT Readiness" pillar is measured by using 8 indicators. Nevertheless, since most of the indicators are broader, this chapter focuses on 3 indicators that assess usage of digital platforms in the industry, i.e., use of digital platforms for financial services, and provision of transportation, accommodation and leisure activities. On platforms for financial services, this chapter focuses only on payment aspect.

Figure 5. Indicators for measuring "ICT readiness"
Source: WEF (2022)

As mentioned by Bradić-Martinović and Miletić (2017), the tourism industry is highly fragmented. It consists various actors including suppliers and service providers of tourist attractions, hotels, restaurants, transportation, and cultural and entertainment facilities that are geographically far apart but form a part of the same value-chain. Acknowledging this diverse and complex nature of the industry, the chapter provides an analysis of each actor involved in a customer journey.

RESEARCH METHODOLOGY

Data was collected through desk research, interview, and survey methods. Desk research was used to gather data from relevant reports and websites of relevant tourism actors. Both face-to-face and phone interviews were used to gather data from key experts and tourism actors. A set of questionnaires, with open-ended questions, for domestic and inbound tourists was used to ascertain their challenges and frustrations. The researcher took advantage of the Swahili International Tourism Expo (SIITE) event to get access to different actors of the industry in one place. Due to time constraint, however, other tourism actors needed to be followed in their offices and some had to be scheduled for phone interviews. The snowball sampling technique was used to determine experts to be interviewed. In distributing questionnaires to tourists, the random sampling technique was used. Experts interviewed are from the ministry responsible for tourism, Tanzania Tourist Board (TTB), and authorities, associations and consortiums of tourism players including Ngorongoro Conservation Area Authority (NCCA), Tanzania Wildlife Management Authority (TAWA), Tanzania Forest Services Agency (TFS), Tourism Confederation of Tanzania (TCT), Tanzania Association of Tour Operators (TASOTO) and Tanzania Tour Guides Association (TTGA).

THE STATUS QUO OF THE INDUSTRY IN TANZANIA

This section provides findings of a study conducted in a tourism industry in Tanzania. Since the focus of the chapter is on digitalization, the analysis is limited to tourism aspects relevant to digitalization. In particular, the chapter focuses on aspects of the customer journey in tourism industry that are supported or have a potential of being supported by digital solutions.

Lack of Engaging Content

Video is a powerful media for communicating a positive and welcoming experience of the destination compared to texts and images. If are well prepared, videos are personal, emotive and persuasive. Nevertheless, producing a quality video requires a skilled personnel and sophisticated equipment, which in many cases are expensive. As such, only a few tourism players can afford. Nevertheless, tourism players are not mandated to produce videos of existing attractions. When tourism players with financial muscles produce videos, in many cases, they focus on attractions that fall within their business lines.

As such, texts and images remain dominant marketing and promotion materials of a majority of tourism players in Tanzania. These media of communication are not as effective as videos on stimulating people's curiosity and subsequently their desires to visit the destination. The media requires a potential visitor to create his/her mental image of the destination, which might be wrong. In the contrary, videos put a visitor into the very center of endeavors he/she sees.

Even when *engaging* content exists, content sharing among players is very little or not occurring at all. In many cases, TTB occasionally receives content from owners of tourism products and services and other tourism players. This content, however, moves in one direction (i.e. from tourism players to TTB) and is not coordinated. There is no formal approach of sharing the content and therefore currently it is shared in an ad hoc manner. As such, fact checking has always been difficult to do and therefore has not always been done.

Underutilization of User-Generated Content

Visitors find information about a destination from other visitors more credible than information provided by destination management organizations or tour operators. In marketing terms this is called Word-of-Mouth (WOM) and specifically electronic WOM (eWOM) (Henning-Thurau et al., 2004). eWOM is playing a critical role in marketing, especially in the tourism industry. Thus, getting visitors' feedback and effectively using the feedback to market the destination is important. Nevertheless, the majority of tourism players do not have web presence and those who have are inadequately using them. TTB offers online services for visitors to write their feedback and testimonials, and upload their holiday pictures and videos after their trips in Tanzania. The content gathered, however, is not included on their web portal and not shared to other players. Although the majority of visitors use TripAdvisor to write their reviews and rate destinations, tourism players do not use the reviews and ratings.

Inadequate Content Dissemination Approaches

The current dominating approach for disseminating information about tourist attractions is through distributing brochures and displaying printed materials (such as posters and banners) in embassies, hotels and events (such as trade fairs and roadshows). In events, a marketing officer normally complements printed materials for the purpose of providing more information about the attractions. The approach is limited to a handful of people who physically visits the events and/or embassies. Nonetheless, the approach is not effectively utilized as most of hotels and lodges in tourism regions are quiet about existing attractions and other relevant activities within and nearby the regions.

To complement the approach, a few tourism players utilize the digital space. TTB, for instance, has a dedicated web portal and utilize social media sites (such as Facebook, Twitter, YouTube, Instagram and Flickr) for reaching online community. Nevertheless, a majority of players are not taking full advantage of the space. The players, for instance, are not using existing high profile intermediary sites (such as Expedia, Travelocity, World Travel Guide, Concierge, and Rough Guide), influential bloggers, search engine marketing services and newswire services and neither advertise on TV channels in source markets nor use email promotions to massively disseminate tourism information about the destination.

Limited Internet Access to Inbound Tourists

Access to reliable Internet is vital to inbound tourists for communication purpose and discovery of the destination and subsequently experiencing the destination positively. Except for a few proportional of inbound tourists who use roaming service, the majorities do not have access to telephone or Internet. Thus inbound tourists are disconnected most of the time during their visits except for a brief Internet access when at the airports or in their hotels. Nevertheless, not all accommodations offer Internet service and the majority of those that offer, their services are unreliable. Travel agencies, and owners and/or caretakers of tourist attractions do not feel that they are required to offer Internet service to their customers. As such, only a handful of travel agencies offer Internet access in their vehicles.

Dominance of Traditional Marketing Practices

At the onset of technological advances and superior Internet technologies, people have changed the way they shop and buy things and therefore the "offline" marketing is not effective anymore. This provides newer avenues for reaching out target audiences by using digital channels or what is known as *digital marketing*. Chaffew and Ellis-Chadwick (2019) define digital marketing as a means of carrying out marketing endeavors and achieving their objectives through digital media, data and technology. As mentioned previously, only a handful of tourism players have social media accounts. In many cases, behind these accounts are marketing officers with little or no knowledge of digital marketing. The personnel, for instance, an only broadcast posts to followers rather than *engaging* them in relevant conversations about products and services. The personnel also do not make use of marketing features of the social media platforms.

Digital marketing is not only about having web portals and accounts in social media platforms; it is about *connecting* and *engaging* with potential consumers. Thus behind web portals and social media accounts of tourism players there should be vibrant marketing teams that are well trained to effectively utilize digital channels. The teams, among others, should take advantage of paid features of social media platforms to increase reachability of their posts. The teams should be able to use digital solutions to manage digital campaigns. The teams should also know how and when campaigns can be delivered effectively to target audience and how their impacts can effectively be measured. The teams should also be constantly aware of what is *said* on the Internet about the destination and respond positively.

Inadequate Planning Facilities

Only a handful of the tourism players with websites have online planning feature. Nevertheless, the websites limit potential visitors to services and products offered by the players or their affiliations. As such, the websites provide a limited view of products and services available in Tanzania. TTB's web portal provides planning feature to assist potential visitors when planning a trip. The portal, however, is not interactive enough to assist visitors to successfully plan their trips. The portal requires planners to have a prior knowledge of a destination. The portal, for instance, requires visitors to know destinations they want to visit and activities offered by the destinations. As such, the portal may mislead planners to specify activities and services that are not offered in destinations.

TTB does not offer any tourism product or service and therefore her web portal offers no booking facility. Instead, the portal provides links to websites of other players. The majority of the players, however, do not have their businesses online and therefore the TTB's portal provides links to only a handful of them. Nevertheless, the websites either do not have online payment facilities or support only foreign payment cards, which the majority of domestic visitors do not have. The NCAA's portal and the portals of all national parks, for instance, do not have online facilities to enable visitors to book for available tourism services and activities. Serena hotels, which their information is provided on the TTB's portal, accepts only MasterCard, Visa and AmericaExpress.

Limited Access to Local Businesses and Services

Most local businesses do not have web presence and therefore are not easily accessible by visitors. Even if a visitor is a meat lover, he would not be able to know if few yards from his hotel there is a best "nyama choma" business if such business does not have a website. Visitors may get such information, although not guaranteed, from sites such as TripAdvisor, Trivago and Expedia and use Google map to reach the destinations. If such information is available, however, much effort is required to access it. This might be a "walk-in a park" for millennial but a nightmare for generation X.

Tour guides interact directly with tourists and spend a significant amount of time with them. Tour guides tell visitors stories behind the beauties of the destination and therefore play a pertinent role in promoting the destination. It is through tour guides that visitors get to know the destination better and therefore meet or exceeding their expectations. Currently, however, visitors' access to tour guides is limited. Unless a visitor plans his/her trip through a tour operator, the visitor may not have access to a tour guide even when in need. Access to freelance tour guides is very limited because their information is not online and there is no an online service to enable visitors to link them with tour guides.

PROPOSED INTERVENTIONS

Content Generation

- Improve Sharing of Digital Tourism Content: A handful of tourism players create digital tourism content for promotional purposes. This content is currently not shared among tourism players and therefore making it more expensive to advertise the destination. On the other hand, with pervasiveness of Smartphone, built with high quality cameras, almost everyone is a photographer and video cameraman. Thus, there is an untapped content that if accessible can boost the efforts of marketing the destination. To make such content accessible and enable sharing of content among tourism players, an online content sharing platform shall be developed. In addition, picture and video contests shall be prepared to attract more content from individuals.
- Improve Quality of Digital Tourism Content: Content represents a destination and therefore how such content is represented significantly influences visitors. As content generators increases, there must be moderation on how content is generated and packaged. To increase control on how content is generated and packaged, a guideline for creating high quality tourism digital content shall be developed. In addition, a technical committee to oversee creation, packaging and usage of digital tourism content shall be established. Tourism players should also find a best way to utilize Tanzania Broadcasting Corporation's (TBC) expertise and equipment to produce *engaging* content about the industry.
- Leverage User-Generated Content: Visitors generate hundreds of pieces of content, emulating their experiences during their visits, and post them online. This content can be in a text, picture, video, or audio format, posted on visitors' blogs, websites, social media accounts, or other online channels like TripAdvisor. Since visitors believe more in information about the destination from visitors with first-hand experience, relevant user-generated content is vital in the destination's marketing efforts. This can be done by effectively utilizing some of the most popular travel websites such as TripAdvisor, Airbnb and Booking.com.

Content Dissemination

- Improve Access to Tourism Content: With the right information, anyone can be a tourist and therefore it is vital to use proper channels to disseminate information about a destination. This can be achieved through encouraging tourism players to develop or improve their websites, and developing websites specifically for source markets. Tourism content can also be disseminated through digital channels such as social media accounts and websites of media companies, ministries, government agencies and embassies. Another powerful approach is to create and disseminate e-newsletters. As demonstrated by "The Royal Tour" documentary, starred by her Excellency, Hon. Dr. Samia Suluhu Hassan, the first female President of the Republican of Tanzania, partnering and collaborating with film and movie producers is another powerful method to market the destination. This can go beyond film and movie producers to video game developers. Locally, tourism information can be disseminated through radio and TV stations, such as Safari channel of TBC. To increase the number of viewers of the Safari channel, a dedicated and an interactive web portal and a mobile app shall be developed. This is particular important in transforming youths' perceptions towards tourism.

- Increase Reliability of Tourism Information: To a large extent, inbound tourists depend on information of tourist attractions from tour operators. In many cases, however, this information is biased (i.e., limited to products and services offered by operators) and not always reliable (i.e., sources cannot always be verified). Thus, a reliable alternative source of information that provides unbiased and a holistic view of the industry is requisite. This can be achieved by developing a dedicated, content rich and interactive tourism web portal, utilizing the domain name www.tz-unforgetable.com to align with and complement the existing rebranding efforts. The portal shall be rich of engaging content of tourist attractions across the country, without favoring a particular type of tourism. The portal, among other features, should have an innovative "get-a-brochure" feature that utilizes content of the portal to create e- brochures (using different layouts) and allow visitors to download none editable format of the brochures.
- Improve Internet Access to Inbound Tourists: In this era, access to information is greatly depending on access to the Internet. Thus for accumulated digital content of tourism to be well consumed and for local businesses with web presence to be widely accessible, an inbound tourist requires access to a reliable Internet right after arriving to an airport in a destination and throughout his/her visit. To accomplish this, the ministries responsible for tourism and information technology should work closely with relevant stakeholders to improve Internet accessibility in airports, accommodations and tour vehicles. Efforts should also be put forward to enable inbound tourists to easily get SIM cards capable of connecting to high-speed broadband Internet connection.
- Improve Access to Digital Content of Tourism: Having the content and empowering tourists with reliable Internet is not enough to make the content accessible. Tourists need to know, effortlessly, where they can get reliable and complete information about tourism in the country. This can be accomplished by creating and distributing *e-tourism stickers*, printed with visible barcode or QR code containing a link to the dedicated and interactive tourism web portal described in section 4.1. Thus by scanning the code a tourist will be seamlessly redirected to the portal and interactively explore the beauty of the destination and access its vast information. This should also go in parallel with encouraging tourism players to include the barcode and QR code on their tourism promotion materials.

Marketing and Promotion

- Maximize Usage of Online Advertisement Platforms: Millions of comments are posted on social media platforms by businesses in a day and therefore the chances of a comment to be seen by the majority of the targeted audience are slim. In digital marketing terms this is called *organic search*; a phenomenon where audience naturally discovers comments i.e. without being influenced by a paid service (Kushwaha 2020). Likewise, consumers use social media platforms to praise or air their frustrations about businesses and therefore businesses need to continuously "listen" to the comments to quickly and positively respond. Creating and launching online business campaigns involves millions of money and therefore businesses need to monitor and quantify the success of these campaigns. Thus, among other efforts, marketing teams and businesses need to opt for

Pay Per Click (PPC) strategy and utilizing social media analytics to get a glimpse of consumers' perceptions of the business and to monitor ROI of online campaigns.

- Build Capacity on Digital Marketing: Marketing in digital era requires new sets of skills and therefore building capacity of marketing staff is inevitable. A number of studies have shown Internet usage has double over the past decade, implying that more people are now spending much of their time online. This trend, subsequently, has significantly affected the way people shop and buys. Thus, marketing teams in this era need to be aware of digital tactics and channels at their disposal and use them to engage their consumers. The teams need to be able to optimize Web portals and social media accounts of their businesses for search engines. They should also be able to create a compelling and visitors' focused content and improve reachability of social media posts. They should also be able to create, launch and monitor email marketing campaigns, and create and use unique and impactful social media handles and hashtags.
- Increase Collaboration With Tourism Stakeholders in Source Markets: Content disseminated through social media outlets is, in many cases, tailored to an audience regardless which country they come from. Nevertheless, such content may have high impact if it is further tailored to a source market. Such content, complemented by a proper dissemination channel, is likely to increase the number of inbound tourists. As an entry point, tourism players can collaborate with travel agencies and embassies in source markets to market the destination. This can be through developing and launching TV interactive Ads. To complement this effort, social media and blog influencers in source markets can be involved. Social media and blog influencers are "online celebrities" with expertise in specific areas, such as sports, beauty and tourism, with thousands of followers (Lou & Yuan 2019). Thus unlike WOM, content written by influencers is more reliable, because of their expertise, and the content is somehow guaranteed to be read by thousands.

Planning and Booking

- Improve Booking Facilities: Trends show people are more in favor of planning their trips themselves, i.e., without relying on tour operators. As such, efforts should also be put forward to enable potential visitors to conveniently plan and book for their visits. This can be done by encouraging and working with owners or "keepers" of tourism attractions to have web presence and support online booking. Enhancing the tourism portal previously proposed to be more interactive and able to support online booking is another viable intervention. The portal, among other features, should include an interactive map of tourist attractions by tourism categories by regions. When clicked, the map should display clickable texts, pictures and/or videos of existing tourist attractions in the region and provide a booking facility. The booking facility should accept payments through popular online payment channels and local payment channels such as Internet banking, mobile banking, and mobile money.
- Increase Access of Local Businesses to Inbound Tourists: A potential visitor needs access to local businesses prior and during his visit. Prior a visit, and particularly during planning, a visitor needs access to accommodations and transport services. A visitor would need, for instance, to book for affordable accommodations and locally available car rental services. During a visit, a tourist would need to navigate through the destination to enjoy its beauty, taste its local food and interact with local people to experience their cultural dynamics. To provide such an experience to visitors, local businesses (such as pubs, restaurants and "nyama choma" places) and information about

ongoing events in regions where tourism activities are concentrated must be readily available and accessible to visitors. As such, coordinated efforts must be put to encourage local business owners to have web presence of their businesses.

- Increase Access of Tour Guides to Inbound Tourists: A tourist wants more than a map to navigate a destination and absorb interesting historical background of whatever he encounters and see during his visit. As such, a tourist would need to have someone familiar with the region to enable him to both easily access interesting places and hear interesting stories about the places. This is the job that tour guides do best. Unfortunately, currently direct access to tour guides is very limited and ad hoc. Thus to simplify and increase access to tour guides, efforts should be put forward to develop an interactive tour guide web portal. The portal would have information of trusted tour guides located in each region where tourism activities are many. To increase confidence of tourists, the portal would take advantage of eWOW and therefore would enable tourists to express their experience with the tour guide.

BENEFITS OF THE PROPOSED INTERVENTIONS

In tourism, intermediation occurs mainly because of lack of tourism information on target destinations and unavailability of planning and booking facilities (Mensah *et al.* 2022). This is phenomenon where tourists rely on a packaged tour i.e. tour operators organize logistical issues and tourist attractions to be visited. This normally comes with a cost. As suggested by Transaction Cost Theory (Williamson 1975), each transaction comes with a "coordination" cost i.e. the cost for monitoring and managing transactions. As more actors are involved in handling a transaction, cost of services increases. In tourism context, this means the destination becomes expensive to visit. Therefore efforts to empower inbound tourists to be able to plan their visits will raise competition among tour operators and bargaining power of tourists. This will make the destination affordable and in turn increase country's revenue from the industry.

One of the challenges that prevent inbound tourists from spending much in the country, which translates to little impact the industry has to the local community, is their reliance on intermediary actors (Kazuzuru, 2014). In many cases, inbound tourists through tour operators have tight scheduled and thus have little or no time to explore places other than those prescribed in their packages. As such a local man who owns a "nyama choma" business nearby the tourists' hotel, for instance, would not be able to sell to the tourists because the cost of their meals is covered in the package. Thus, by giving inbound tourists an alternative way of planning their visits and making information of local businesses and events readily accessible to tourists, this challenge will be addressed.

Sustainability is an important aspect of any business. Due to ecological and historical nature of tourist attractions, sustainability is equally important in the tourism industry. As such, consumers need to be closely monitored so they can behave responsibly to tourist attractions (Han 2021). This is a job that can be well done by tour guides (Tătar *et al.* 2018). In this case, a local tour guide also acts as a "watchdog" of the country's tourists' attractions. The envisage tour guide web portal will increase visibility and accessibility of local tour guides. Consequently, this will discourage tourists planning to visit Tanzania from opting for alternative solutions, which in many cases are hard to be monitored.

Among the factors hindering domestic tourism, according to Mato and Mosoma (2022), is low public awareness on tourists' attractions. Increasing local content and usage of native Swahili language in websites and other promotion materials of tourism players and development of a dedicated web portal and a mobile app for "Safari" channel will increase accessibility of information about tourism in the country. This in turn will increase public awareness on tourists' attractions and the whole tourism ecosystem and potentially increase domestic tourism. Subsequently, this will help the industry to address problems associated with heavy reliance of inbound tourism (Kazuzuru, 2014) and positively shape peoples' attitude towards the environment (Bakari, 2021).

CONCLUSION

The chapter provided an analysis of the tourism industry in Tanzania with the aim of identifying challenges and providing relevant interventions. In particular, the chapter proposed interventions geared to increase integration of digital solutions into the tourism value chain. Acknowledging the diverse and complex nature of the industry, the chapter provided an analysis of each actor involved in a customer journey. Since the focus of the chapter was on digitalization, the analysis was limited to aspects of the customer journey that are supported or have a potential of being supported by digital solutions. Among the challenges the chapter outlined are lack of engaging content, underutilization of user-generated content, inadequate content dissemination approaches, limited Internet access to inbound tourists, dominance of traditional marketing practices, Inadequate planning facilities, and limited access to local business and services.

In improving quality and quantity of tourism digital content, the chapter proposed development of an online content sharing platform and launching of picture and video contests. To ensure quality and correctness of the content, the chapter proposed development of guidelines for creating tourism digital content and formulation of a technical committee to oversee creation, packaging and usage of the content. The chapter also emphasized utilization of the most popular travel websites such as TripAdvisor, Airbnb and Booking.com. To increase access to tourism digital content, the chapter underscored the importance of tourism players to develop or improve their websites. The chapter commended the role of the Royal Tour film and challenged responsible stakeholders to explore the strategy further and go beyond to work with video game developers. The chapter proposed development of a dedicated, content rich and interactive tourism web portal, utilizing the domain name www.tz-unforgetable.com to align with and complement the existing rebranding efforts.

The chapter recommended that ministries responsible with tourism and information technology to work closely with relevant stakeholders to improve Internet accessibility in airports, accommodations and tour vehicles. Efforts should also be put forward to enable inbound tourists to easily get SIM cards capable of connecting to high-speed broadband Internet connection. To enable seamless access to the dedicated tourism web portal, the chapter proposed creation and distribution of e-tourism stickers i.e. a printed sticker with a visible barcode or QR code, containing a link to the portal. The chapter underscored the importance of online advertisement platforms and specifically utilization of Pay-Per-Click (PPC) strategy and utilizing social media analytics. The chapter also emphasized capacity building on digital marketing to relevant personnel in the industry. The chapter also emphasized on collaborating with tourism stakeholders, in source markets, such as embassies and influential bloggers.

In facilitating potential tourists to plan and book for their trips by themselves, the chapter proposed enhancement of the tourism portal previously proposed to be more interactive and able to support online booking. The chapter emphasized inclusion of payments through popular online payment channels and local payment channels such as Internet banking, mobile banking and mobile money to give inbound tourists different payment options and encourage domestic tourism. The chapter also underscored the importance of local businesses to have web presence for their businesses to be accessible. The chapter also emphasized the importance of tourists' direct access to local tour guides. In addressing this, the chapter proposed development of an interactive tour guide web portal. The portal would have information of trusted tour guides located in each region where tourism activities are many. To increase confidence of tourists, the portal would take advantage of electronic word-of-mouth and therefore would enable tourists to express their experience with the tour guides.

REFERENCES

Asia Development Bank and World Tourism Organization. (2021). *Big Data for Better Tourism Policy, Management, and Sustainable Recovery from COVID-19.* https://www.adb.org/sites/default/files/publication/750966/big-data-tourism-policy-management-recovery-covid-19.pdf

Bakari, J. B. (2021). Challenges Facing Domestic Tourism Promotion – A Case of Serengeti National Park – Tanzania. *Journal of Tourism & Hospitality (Los Angeles, Calif.).*

Bănescu, C., Boboc, C., Ghiță, S., & Vasile, V. (2021, June). Tourism in Digital Era. In *Proceedings of the 7th BASIQ International Conference on New Trends in Sustainable Business and Consumption, Foggia, Italy* (pp. 3-5). Academic Press.

Bradić-Martinović, A., & Miletić, B. (2017, June). ICT readiness as a factor of competitiveness of Serbian tourism. In *Tourism International Scientific Conference Vrnjačka Banja-TISC* (*Vol. 2*, No. 1, pp. 448-469). Academic Press.

Bukht, R., & Heeks, R. (2017). Defining, conceptualising and measuring the digital economy. *Development Informatics Working Paper*, (68).

Cai, W., & McKenna, B. (2023). Power and resistance: Digital-free tourism in a connected world. *Journal of Travel Research*, *62*(2), 290–304. doi:10.1177/00472875211061208

Chaffey, D., & Ellis-Chadwick, F. (2019). Digital marketing. Academic Press.

Egger, I., Lei, S. I., & Wassler, P. (2020). Digital free tourism–An exploratory study of tourist motivations. *Tourism Management*, *79*, 104098. doi:10.1016/j.tourman.2020.104098

Han, H. (2021). Consumer behavior and environmental sustainability in tourism and hospitality: A review of theories, concepts, and latest research. *Journal of Sustainable Tourism*, *29*(7), 1021–1042. doi:10.1080/09669582.2021.1903019

Hennig-Thurau, T., Gwinner, K. P., Walsh, G., & Gremler, D. D. (2004). Electronic word-of-mouth via consumer-opinion platforms: What motivates consumers to articulate themselves on the Internet? *Journal of Interactive Marketing*, *18*(1), 38–52. doi:10.1002/dir.10073

Kazuzuru, B. (2014). History, Performance and Challenges of Tourism Industry in Tanzania. *International Journal of Business and Social Science*, *5*(11).

Kumar, S., & Shekhar. (2020). Digitalization: A strategic approach for development of tourism industry in India. *Paradigm*, *24*(1), 93–108. doi:10.1177/0971890720914111

Kushwaha, B. P. (2020). Search engine marketing a new way of marketing in digital age. *PalArch's Journal of Archaeology of Egypt/Egyptology, 17*(6), 2053-2065.

Li, J., Pearce, P. L., & Oktadiana, H. (2020). Can digital-free tourism build character strengths? *Annals of Tourism Research, 85*, 103037. doi:10.1016/j.annals.2020.103037 PMID:32905012

Lou, C., & Yuan, S. (2019). Influencer Marketing: How Message Value and Credibility Affect Consumer Trust of Branded Content on Social Media. *Journal of Interactive Advertising, 19*(1), 58–73. doi:10.1080/15252019.2018.1533501

Mato, M., & Mosoma, D. (2022). Factors Influencing Domestic Tourism in Tanzania: A Case of Arusha City. *International Journal of Engineering Business Management, 6*(4), 1–11. doi:10.22161/ijebm.6.4.1

Mensah, C., Sakyi, R., & Forson, M. A. (2022). *Destination Distribution Systems and Travel Disintermediation in Emerging Economies. In Palgrave Studies of Marketing in Emerging Economies*. Springer.

Natocheeva, N., Shayakhmetova, L., Bekkhozhaeva, A., Khamikhan, N., & Pshembayeva, D. (2020). Digital technologies as a driver for the development of the tourism industry. In *E3S Web of Conferences* (Vol. 159, p. 04002). EDP Sciences. doi:10.1051/e3sconf/202015904002

Saner, R., Yiu, L., & Filadoro, M. (2019). Tourism development in least developed countries: Challenges and opportunities. *Sustainable Tourism: Breakthroughs in Research and Practice*, 94-120.

Tătar, C. F., Herman, G. V., & Gozner, M. (2018). Tourist guides' contribution to sustainability in Romania. *Geo Journal of Tourism and Geosites, 21*(1), 282–287. doi:10.30892/gtg.21122-287

Williamson, O. E. (1975). *Markets and hierarchies: analysis and antitrust implications: a study in the economics of internal organization*. University of Illinois at Urbana-Champaign's Academy for Entrepreneurial Leadership Historical Research Reference in Entrepreneurship.

World Bank. (2021). *Project Appraisal Document on a Proposed Credit in the Amount of SDR 105.9 Million (US$150 Million Equivalent) to the United Republic of Tanzania for the Digital Tanzania Project*. https://documents1.worldbank.org/curated/en/485771622426544909/pdf/Tanzania-Digital-Tanzania-Project.pdf

World Economic Forum. (2017). *The Travel & Tourism Competitiveness Report 2017: Paving the Way for a More Sustainable and Inclusive Future*. https://www3.weforum.org/docs/WEF_TTCR_2017_web_0401.pdf

World Economic Forum. (2020). *Latin America and Caribbean Travel & Tourism Competitiveness Landscape Report: Assessing Regional Opportunities and Challenges in the Context of COVID-19*. https://www3.weforum.org/docs/ WEF_LAC_Tourism_Compet_Report_2020.pdf

World Economic Forum. (2022). *The Travel & Tourism Development Index 2021: Rebuilding for a Sustainable and Resilient Future*. https://www3.weforum.org/docs/WEF_Travel_Tourism_Development_2021.pdf

Compilation of References

Aaker, D., & Aaker, J. L. (2016). What are your signature stories? *California Management Review, 58*(3), 49–65. doi:10.1525/cmr.2016.58.3.49

Abdellatif, A., Bagian, J. P., Barajas, E. R., Cohen, M., Cousins, D., Denham, C. R., Essinger, K., Gegelashvili, G., Glenister, H., Hoffman, C., Horvath, D., Khoja, T., Klazinga, N., Lee, C. E., Letlape, T. K., Lilja, B., Manasse, H. R. Jr, Massoud, M. R., Wilson, R. M. L., ... Youngson, R. (2007). Communication During Patient Hand-Overs. *Joint Commission Journal on Quality and Patient Safety, 33*(7), 439–442. doi:10.1016/S1553-7250(07)33128-0

Abercrombie, G., Curry, A. C., Pandya, M., & Rieser, V. (2021). Alexa, Google, Siri: What are your pronouns? Gender and anthropomorphism in the design and perception of conversational assistants. doi:10.18653/v1/2021.gebnlp-1.4

Abi-Jaoude, E., Naylor, K. T., & Pignatiello, A. (2020). Smartphones, social media use, and youth mental health. *Canadian Medical Association Journal, 192*(6), E136–E141. doi:10.1503/cmaj.190434 PMID:32041697

Accenture/UJ 4IR internship programme. (2022). *4IR Internship Opportunity*. https://bit.ly/3y296nb

Achary, R. (2021). Artificial Intelligence Transforming Indian Banking Sector. *International Journal of Economics and Management Systems, 6.*

Adam, M., Wessel, M., & Benlian, A. (2021). AI-based chatbots in customer service and their effects on user compliance. *Electronic Markets, 31*(2), 427–445. doi:10.100712525-020-00414-7

Adedoyin, O. B., & Soykan, E. (2020). Covid-19 Pandemic and online learning: The challenges and opportunities. *Interactive Learning Environments*. Advance online publication. doi:0.1080/10494820.2020.1813180

Ade-Ibijola, A., & Okonkwo, C. (2023). Artificial Intelligence in Africa: Emerging Challenges. In *Responsible AI in Africa: Challenges and Opportunities* (pp. 101–117). Springer International Publishing. doi:10.1007/978-3-031-08215-3_5

Aerts, A. (2018). *The Novartis Foundation*. Academic Press.

Afolasade, A. A., & Oluyomi, S. P. (2021). *Nigeria Law Students' Perception of Online Teaching: Appraisal of COVID-19-Imposed Online Classes*. Asian Journal of Legal Education. doi:10.1177/23220058211061915

Agale, M. P. A. (2017). *Employers' perception about capabilities of persons with disabilities in the Kassena-Nankana municipality in the upper east region of Ghana* [Doctoral dissertation]. University of Education, Winneba.

Agarwal, R., Animesh, A., Prasad, K., & Smith, R. H. (2009). *Research note—Social interactions and the "digital divide": Explaining variations in internet use.* https://pubsonline.informs.org/doi/abs/10.1287/isre.1080.0194

Agarwal, S., LeFevre, A. E., Lee, J., L'engle, K., Mehl, G., Sinha, C., & Labrique, A. (2016). Guidelines for reporting of health interventions using mobile phones: Mobile health (mHealth) evidence reporting and assessment (mERA) checklist. *BMJ (Clinical Research Ed.)*, 352. doi:10.1136/bmj.i1174 PMID:26988021

Agbele, A. T., & Oyelade, E. A. (2020). Impact of COVID-19 on the Nigerian educational system: Strengths and challenges of online/virtual education. *Asian Journal of Education and Social Studies*, *13*(1), 26–35. doi:10.9734/ajess/2020/v13i130322

Aggarwal, P., & McGill, A. L. (2012). When brands seem human, do humans act like brands? Automatic behavioral priming effects of brand anthropomorphism. *The Journal of Consumer Research*, *39*(2), 307–323. doi:10.1086/662614

Agunbiade, A. (2019). *Artificial Intelligence and Law: A Nigerian Perspective*. LAP LAMBERT Academic Publishing.

ah Khan, S., Jadhav, A., et Bharadwaj, I., Rooj, M., & Shiravale, S. (2020). *Blockchain and the Identity based Encryption Scheme for High Data Security*. Paper presented at the 2020 Fourth International Conference on Computing Methodologies and Communication (ICCMC).

Aiyedun, O. T. G., Ogunode, N. J., & Aiyedun, C. T. (2021). Assessment of Virtual Learning During COVID-19 Lockdown in Nigerian Public Universities, Academicia Globe. *Inderscience Research.*, *2*(5), 159–175.

Ajadi, T. O., Salawu, I. O., & Adeoye, F. A. (2008). E-Learning and Distance Education in Nigeria. *The Turkish Online Journal of Educational Technology*, *7*(4), 7.

Ajani, F. O., Ismaila, Y. A., & Ayodele, R. O. (2021). Assessment of Library Database Utilization for Academic Activities Among Kwara State University Lecturers During Covid-19 Pandemic Period. *Journal of Applied Information Science and Technology*, *14*(2), 89–97.

Ajoke, B. S. (2022). The Place of Libraries and Information Communication Technology in Education and National Development in Nigeria. Nigeria Library Association.

Ajrun, N. (2021). Bridging the Digital Divide Affecting People with Disabilities in Malaysia. *International Journal of Disability Development and Education*, 1–13.

Akanfe, O., Valecha, R., & Rao, H. R. (2020). Assessing country-level privacy risk for digital payment systems. *Computers & Security*, *99*, 102065. doi:10.1016/j.cose.2020.102065

Akınrobotics. (2023). AkınRobotics. *Mini Ada 3*. Retrieved on 12.04.2023 from https://www.akinrobotics.com/sosyal-robot-mini-ada-3

Akkaoui, R., Hei, X., & Cheng, W. (2020). EdgeMediChain: A Hybrid Edge Blockchain-Based Framework for Health Data Exchange. *IEEE Access : Practical Innovations, Open Solutions*, *8*, 113467–113486. doi:10.1109/ACCESS.2020.3003575

Akpan, Blessing, & Okoro. (2020). Social constructivism: Implications on teaching and learning. *British Journal of Education.*

Akter, S., Mohiuddin Babu, M., Hossain, M. A., & Hani, U. (2021). How does value co-creation transform quality of life at the bottom of the pyramid? *Journal of Marketing Management*, *37*(9–10), 962–992. doi:10.1080/0267257X.2021.1919745

Alam, A., & Mohanty, A. (2022). Metaverse and Posthuman Animated Avatars for Teaching-Learning Process: Interperception in Virtual Universe for Educational Transformation. In *International Conference on Innovations in Intelligent Computing and Communications* (pp. 47-61). Springer. 10.1007/978-3-031-23233-6_4

Aldaas, A. (2021). A study on electronic payments and economic growth: Global evidences. *Accounting*, *7*(2), 409–414. doi:10.5267/j.ac.2020.11.010

Aldholay, A., Isaac, O., Abdullah, Z., Abdulsalam, R., & Al-Shibami, A. H. (2018). *An extension of Delone and McLean IS success model with self-efficacy*. Academic Press.

Alfauzan, A. H., & Hussain, A. G. (2017). Attitude towards and Perception of Literature in EFL Setting: A Case Study on QU Male Undergraduate Students. *English Language Teaching*, *10*(1), 1–17. doi:10.5539/elt.v10n1p1

Ali, R., Barrdear, J., Clews, R., & Southgate, J. (2014, Q3). Innovations in payment technologies and the emergence of digital currencies. *Bank of England Quarterly Bulletin*.

Ali, B. J., & Anwar, G. (2021). Factors Influencing the Citizens' Acceptance of Electronic Government. *Development*, *5*, 1.

Alkhowaiter, W. A. (2020). Digital payment and banking adoption research in Gulf countries: A systematic literature review. *International Journal of Information Management*, *53*, 102102. doi:10.1016/J.IJINFOMGT.2020.102102

Allen, R., Elks, P., Outhred, R., & Varly, P. (2016). *Uganda's assessment system: A road-map for enhancing assessment in education*. Health & Education Advance & Resource Team. https://www.heart-resources.org/wp-content/uploads/2016/10/Final-report-Enhancing- Uganda's-Assessment-System-September-2016.pdf

Allen, F., Demirguc-Kunt, A., Klapper, L., & Martinez Peria, M. S. (2016). The foundations of financial inclusion: Understanding ownership and use of formal accounts. *Journal of Financial Intermediation*, *27*, 1–30. doi:10.1016/J.JFI.2015.12.003

Almajid, W. M. (2010). Can Electronic Agents Be Granted Legal Personality under Islamic Law? A Conceptual Rethink Is Imperative. *Arab Law Quarterly*, *24*(4), 393–416. doi:10.1163/157302510X526733

Al-Okaily, M., Lutfi, A., Alsaad, A., Taamneh, A., & Alsyouf, A. (2020). The Determinants of Digital Payment Systems' Acceptance under Cultural Orientation Differences: The Case of Uncertainty Avoidance. *Technology in Society*, *63*. Advance online publication. doi:10.1016/J.TECHSOC.2020.101367

Alonso, S., Toye, P. G., Msalya, G., Grace, D., & Unger, F. (2014). *Smallholder dairy farming in Tanzania: Farming practices, animal health and public health challenges and opportunities*. Academic Press.

Alpha, K., Onsoti, N., & Kituyi, A. (2021). The Project Planning and Implementation in Rwanda National Union of Deaf Project Kicukiro District. *Journal of Advance Research in Business Management and Accounting*, *7*(4), 1–15. doi:10.53555/nnbma.v7i4.976

Alqurashi, E. (2019). *Technology tools for teaching and learning in real time*. https://www.igi-global.com/chapter/technology-tools-for-teaching-and-learning-in-real-time/225755

AlSadrani, B., Alzyoudi, M., Alsheikh, N., & Elshazly, E. E. (2020). The digital divide in inclusive classrooms. *International Journal of Learning, Teaching and Educational Research*, *19*(3), 69–85. doi:10.26803/ijlter.19.3.5

Al-Sarayrah, W., Al-Aiad, A., Habes, M., Elareshi, M., & Salloum, S. A. (2021). Improving the deaf and hard of hearing internet accessibility: JSL, text-into-sign language translator for Arabic. In *International Conference on Advanced Machine Learning Technologies and Applications* (pp. 456-468). Springer. 10.1007/978-3-030-69717-4_43

Ameen, N., Tarhini, A., Reppel, A., & Anand, A. (2021). Customer experiences in the age of artificial intelligence. *Computers in Human Behavior*, *114*, 106548. doi:10.1016/j.chb.2020.106548 PMID:32905175

Amiram, D., Bozanic, Z., Cox, J. D., Dupont, Q., Karpoff, J. M., & Sloan, R. (2018). Financial reporting fraud and other forms of misconduct: A multidisciplinary review of the literature. *Review of Accounting Studies*, *23*(2), 732–783. doi:10.1007/S11142-017-9435-X

And, R. S. (2018). *Mapping Hyperlocal Health Data Flows. The Case of Kyela District, Tanzania*. Dar es Salaam. DataZetu.

Angel, J. J. (2017). The Evolution of Money. By David Orrell and Roman Chlupatý. New York: Columbia University Press, 2016. x + 309 pp. Figures, notes, bibliography, index. Cloth, $35.00. ISBN: 978-0-231-17372-8. *Business History Review*, *91*(2), 397–399. doi:10.1017/S0007680517000800

Arakeri, M. P., Vijaya Kumar, B. P., Barsaiya, S., & Sairam, H. V. (2017). Computer vision based robotic weed control system for precision agriculture. *2017 International Conference on Advances in Computing, Communications and Informatics (ICACCI)*, 1201–1205. 10.1109/ICACCI.2017.8126005

Ariom, T. O., Dimon, E., Nambeye, E., Diouf, N. S., Adelusi, O. O., & Boudalia, S. (2022). Climate-Smart Agriculture in African Countries: A Review of Strategies and Impacts on Smallholder Farmers. *Sustainability (Basel)*, *14*(18), 11370. doi:10.3390u141811370

Aristovnik, A., Keržič, D., Ravšelj, D., Tomaževič, N., & Umek, L. (2020). Impacts of the COVID-19 Pandemic on Life of Higher Education Students: A Global Perspective. *Sustainability*, *12*(20), 8438. doi:10.3390/su12208438

Armed Services Vocational Aptitude Battery. (2022). *The Armed Services Vocational Aptitude Battery*. https://www.officialasvab.com/

Arner, D. W., Buckley, R. P., Zetzsche, D. A., & Veidt, R. (2020). Sustainability, FinTech and Financial Inclusion. *European Business Organization Law Review*, *21*(1), 7–35. doi:10.1007/S40804-020-00183-Y

Asia Development Bank and World Tourism Organization. (2021). *Big Data for Better Tourism Policy, Management, and Sustainable Recovery from COVID-19*. https://www.adb.org/sites/default/files/publication/750966/big-data-tourism-policy-management-recovery-covid-19.pdf

Atuhaire, A. M., Mugerwa, S., Kabirizi, J., Okello, S., & Kabi, F. (2014). Production characteristics of smallholder dairy farming in the Lake Victoria agro-ecological zone, Uganda. *Frontiers in Science*, *4*(1), 12–19.

Aurazo, J., & Vega, M. (2021). Why people use digital payments: Evidence from micro data in Peru. *Latin American Journal of Central Banking*, *2*(4), 100044. doi:10.1016/J.LATCB.2021.100044

Ayaz, M., Ammad-Uddin, M., Sharif, Z., Mansour, A., & Aggoune, E.-H. M. (2019). Internet-of-Things (IoT)-Based Smart Agriculture: Toward Making the Fields Talk. *IEEE Access : Practical Innovations, Open Solutions*, *7*, 129551–129583. doi:10.1109/ACCESS.2019.2932609

Aymerich-Franch, L., & Ferrer, I. (2021). Socially assistive robots' deployment in healthcare settings: a global perspective. arXiv preprint arXiv:2110.07404.

Bachas, P., Gertler, P., Higgins, S., & Seira, E. (2018). Digital financial services go a long way: Transaction costs and financial inclusion. *AEA Papers and Proceedings. American Economic Association*, *108*, 444–448. doi:10.1257/pandp.20181013

Bakare Dr, O. D., & Bakare Dr, B. M. (2021). *Global Technological Trend in Academic Libraries. Information & Media Studies*. FIMS.

Bakare, O. D. (2018). *The use of social media technologies (SMTs) in the provision of library and information services in academic libraries of South-West, Nigeria* [Doctoral dissertation].

Bakare, O. D., & Ademakinwa, A. O. (2020). The Impact of Covid-19 on Mentorship of Graduate Students in Nigerian Universities. *Journal of Nigerian Association of Pastoral Counsellors*, *1*(1), 50–65.

Bakare, O. D., & Okuonghae, N. (2022). Information Managers as Change Agents in Achieving Sustainable Development in the 21st Century. *Journal of Environmental Science and Economic*, *1*(2), 68–78.

Bakari, J. B. (2021). Challenges Facing Domestic Tourism Promotion – A Case of Serengeti National Park – Tanzania. *Journal of Tourism & Hospitality (Los Angeles, Calif.)*.

Balakrishnan, V., & Shuib, N. L. M. (2021). Drivers and inhibitors for digital payment adoption using the Cashless Society Readiness-Adoption model in Malaysia. *Technology in Society*, *65*, 101554. doi:10.1016/J.TECHSOC.2021.101554

Balehegn, M., Duncan, A., Tolera, A., Ayantunde, A. A., Issa, S., Karimou, M., Zampaligré, N., André, K., Gnanda, I., Varijakshapanicker, P., Kebreab, E., Dubeux, J., Boote, K., Minta, M., Feyissa, F., & Adesogan, A. T. (2020). Improving adoption of technologies and interventions for increasing supply of quality livestock feed in low-and middle-income countries. *Global Food Security*, *26*, 100372. doi:10.1016/j.gfs.2020.100372 PMID:33324534

Bartneck, C., & Keijsers, M. (2020). The morality of abusing a robot. *Paladyn : Journal of Behavioral Robotics*, *11*(1), 271–283. doi:10.1515/pjbr-2020-0017

Bartneck, C., Kulić, D., Croft, E., & Zoghbi, S. (2009). Measurement instruments for the anthropomorphism, animacy, likeability, perceived intelligence, and perceived safety of robots. *International Journal of Social Robotics*, *1*(1), 71–81. doi:10.100712369-008-0001-3

Bayham, J., & Fenichel, E. P. (2020). Impact of school closures for COVID-19 on the US health-care workforce and net mortality: A modelling study. *The Lancet. Public Health*, *5*(5), e271–e278. doi:10.1016/S2468-2667(20)30082-7 PMID:32251626

Beine, M., Lodigiani, E., & Vermeulen, R. (2012). Remittances and financial openness. *Regional Science and Urban Economics*, *42*(5), 844–857. doi:10.1016/J.REGSCIURBECO.2011.12.005

Bélanger, F., & Carter, L. (2008). Trust and risk in e-government adoption. *The Journal of Strategic Information Systems*, *17*(2), 165–176. doi:10.1016/j.jsis.2007.12.002

Bélanger, F., & Carter, L. (2009). The impact of the digital divide on e-government use. *Communications of the ACM*, *52*(4), 132–135. doi:10.1145/1498765.1498801

Benbya, H., Pachidi, S., & Jarvenpaa, S. (2021). Special issue editorial: Artificial intelligence in organizations: Implications for information systems research. *Journal of the Association for Information Systems*, *22*(2), 10. doi:10.17705/1jais.00662

Benhamou, Y., & Ferland, J. (2020). (Forthcoming). Artificial Intelligence & Damages: Assessing Liability and Calculating the Damages. *Leading Legal Disruption: Artificial Intelligence and a Toolkit for Lawyers and the Law*.

Benhamou, Y., & Ferland, J. (2020). *Artificial intelligence & damages: assessing liability and calculating the damages. Academic Press.*

Benlian, A., Klumpe, J., & Hinz, O. (2020). Mitigating the intrusive effects of smart home assistants by using anthropomorphic design features: A multimethod investigation. *Information Systems Journal*, *30*(6), 1010–1042. doi:10.1111/isj.12243

Berglof, E., & Bolton, P. (2002). The great divide and beyond: Financial architecture in transition. *The Journal of Economic Perspectives*, *16*(1), 77–100. doi:10.1257/0895330027120

Berry, D., Friggens, N., Lucy, M., & Roche, J. (2016). Milk production and fertility in cattle. *Annual Review of Animal Biosciences*, *4*(1), 269–290. doi:10.1146/annurev-animal-021815-111406 PMID:26526546

Bertot, J. C., McClure, C. R., & Jaeger, P. T. (2011). *Public Libraries and the Internet: Roles, Perspectives, and Implications*. Google Books. https://books.google.com.gh/books?hl=en&lr=&id=NZ0zH-jF8tcC&oi=fnd&pg=PP2&dq=Bertot,+J.C.,+Jaeger,+P.T.+and+McClure,+C.R
.+(2011),+Public+Libraries+and+the+Internet:+Roles,+Perspect
ives,+and+Implications,+ABC-CLIO,+Santa+Barbara,+CA.&ots=0EC
U4QQpH0&sig=H1N

Bethany Christian Institute. (2018). *ICT in assessment*. BCI. https://sites.google.com/site/bethanycollegeofteacheredn/ict-in-assessment

Bipasha Biswas, S., & Tariq Iqbal, M. (2018). Solar Water Pumping System Control Using a Low Cost ESP32 Microcontroller. *2018 IEEE Canadian Conference on Electrical & Computer Engineering (CCECE)*, 1–5. 10.1109/CCECE.2018.8447749

Bisanda, E. T. (2016). Empowering learners for effective open and distance learning. In *Third Open and Distance Learning Conference in Namibia* (p. 8). Academic Press.

Bisma, R., Puspita, Y., & Sulistiyani, E. (2020). Technology Compatibility Factors in the Implementation of the Ovo Digital Payment Application. *International Joint Conference on Science and Engineering (IJCSE 2020)*, 146–151.

Bjelčić, N., & Švelec, D. (2019). New perspectives for people with special needs according the development of new generation ICT technologies. In *2019 42nd International Convention on Information and Communication Technology, Electronics and Microelectronics (MIPRO)* (pp. 392-397). IEEE.

Blackman, S., & Maynard, D. M. (2009). In Their Own Words: Exploring the Phenomenological Field of a Sample of Employed Persons Who Are Deaf in Barbados. *International Journal of Disability Management Research*, *4*(1), 12–18. doi:10.1375/jdmr.4.1.12

Blackston, M. (1993). Beyond brand personality: building brand relationships. *Brand equity and advertising: Advertising's role in building strong brands*, 113-124.

Blazer, C. (2010). *Computer-Based Assessments*. Information Capsule. 0918. Research Services, Miami-Dade County Public Schools. https://files.eric.ed.gov/fulltext/ED544707.pdf

Blut, M., Wang, C., Wünderlich, N. V., & Brock, C. (2021). Understanding anthropomorphism in service provision: A meta-analysis of physical robots, chatbots, and other AI. *Journal of the Academy of Marketing Science*, *49*(4), 632–658. doi:10.100711747-020-00762-y

Bonfiglio, A., Coderoni, S., Esposti, R., & Baldoni, E. (2021). The role of rurality in determining the economy-wide impacts of a natural disaster. *Economic Systems Research*, *33*(4), 446–469. doi:10.1080/09535314.2020.1814206

Borg, J., Larsson, S., & Östergren, P.-O. (2011). The right to assistive technology: For whom, for what, and by whom? *Disability & Society*, *26*(2), 151–167. doi:10.1080/09687599.2011.543862

Bosse, D., Thompson, S., & Ekman, P. (2023). In consilium apparatus: Artificial intelligence, stakeholder reciprocity, and firm performance. *Journal of Business Research*, *155*, 113402. doi:10.1016/j.jbusres.2022.113402

BOT. (2019). *Public notice on cryptocurrencies*. https://www.bot.go.tz/Adverts/PressRelease/sw/2020031307240424208.pdf

Bozoglan, B., Demirer, V., & Sahin, I. (2013). Loneliness, self-esteem, and life satisfaction as predictors of Internet addiction: A cross-sectional study among Turkish university students. *Scandinavian Journal of Psychology*, *54*(4), 313–319. doi:10.1111jop.12049 PMID:23577670

Bradić-Martinović, A., & Miletić, B. (2017, June). ICT readiness as a factor of competitiveness of Serbian tourism. In *Tourism International Scientific Conference Vrnjačka Banja-TISC* (*Vol. 2*, No. 1, pp. 448-469). Academic Press.

Braithwaite, B. (2015). Deaf perspectives on deaf education: An ethnographic study from Trinidad and Tobago. *Caribbean Educ. Res. J.*, *3*(1), 18–26.

Bresciani, S., Ferraris, A., Romano, M., & Santoro, G. (2021). *Building a Digital Transformation Strategy. In Digital Transformation Management for Agile Organizations: A Compass to sail the Digital World.* Emerald Publishing Limited. doi:10.1108/978-1-80043-171-320211002

Brett, C. I. (2019). *A new way to boost smallholder dairy productivity in Tanzania.* https://blogs.worldbank.org/voices/new-way-boost-smallholder-dairy-productivity-tanzania

Brett, C. I. (2019). *A new way to boost smallholder dairy productivity in Tanzania.* World Bank. https://blogs.worldbank.org/voices/new-way-boost-smallholder-dairy-productivity-tanzania

Broadband Commission. (2018). *Working Group on Digital Health.* Retrieved from https://broadbandcommission.org/Documents/publications/DigitalHealthReport2018.pdf

Brühl, V. (2020). Libra—A differentiated view on facebook's virtual currency project. *Inter Economics*, *55*(1), 54–61.

Bryant, J. A., Sanders-Jackson, A., & Smallwood, A. (2006). IMing, text messaging, and adolescent social networks. *Journal of Computer-Mediated Communication*, *11*(2), 577–592. doi:10.1111/j.1083-6101.2006.00028.x

Bukht, R., & Heeks, R. (2017). Defining, conceptualising and measuring the digital economy. *Development Informatics Working Paper*, (68).

Burnett, C. (2011). Shifting and Multiple Spaces in Classrooms: An Argument for Investigating Learners' Boundary-Making around Digital Networked Texts. *The Journal of Literacy and Technology*, *12*(3).

Cain, J. (2018). It's Time to Confront Student Mental Health Issues Associated with Smartphones and social media. *Am. J. Pharm. Educ.*, *82*, 6862.

Cai, W., & McKenna, B. (2023). Power and resistance: Digital-free tourism in a connected world. *Journal of Travel Research*, *62*(2), 290–304. doi:10.1177/00472875211061208

Calderaro, A. (2017). Social Media and recruitable. *International Journal of Digital Technologies, Research , Knowledge and Education*, *4*(6), 169–180.

Cambra, C., Díaz, J. R., & Lloret, J. (2015). Deployment and Performance Study of an Ad Hoc Network Protocol for Intelligent Video Sensing in Precision Agriculture. In M. Garcia Pineda, J. Lloret, S. Papavassiliou, S. Ruehrup, & C. B. Westphall (Eds.), *Ad-hoc Networks and Wireless* (Vol. 8629, pp. 165–175). Springer Berlin Heidelberg. doi:10.1007/978-3-662-46338-3_14

Cambra, C., Sendra, S., Lloret, J., & Garcia, L. (2017). An IoT service-oriented system for agriculture monitoring. *2017 IEEE International Conference on Communications (ICC)*, 1–6. 10.1109/ICC.2017.7996640

Carboni, I., & Bester, H. (2020). *When Digital Payment Goes Viral: Lessons from COVID-19s Impact on Mobile Money in Rwanda.* Academic Press.

Castelli, F., Frith, C., Happé, F., & Frith, U. (2002). Autism, Asperger syndrome and brain mechanisms for the attribution of mental states to animated shapes. *Brain, 125*(8), 1839–1849. doi:10.1093/brain/awf189 PMID:12135974

Cebo, P. (2020). Artificial Intelligence In Humanoid Robots. *Conference Paper: Online International Conference on Humanoids.*

Cerulus, L., & Contiguglia, C. (2018, August 14). *Central bankers warn of chaos in a cashless society.* https://www.politico.eu/article/central-bankers-fear-cybersecurity-chaos-in-a-cashless-society/

Chaffey, D., & Ellis-Chadwick, F. (2019). Digital marketing. Academic Press.

Chambers Harrap. (2009). *Chambers Concise Dictionary* (2nd ed.). Author.

Chand, A. A., Prasad, K. A., Mar, E., Dakai, S., Mamun, K. A., Islam, F. R., Mehta, U., & Kumar, N. M. (2021). Design and Analysis of Photovoltaic Powered Battery-Operated Computer Vision-Based Multi-Purpose Smart Farming Robot. *Agronomy (Basel), 11*(3), 530. doi:10.3390/agronomy11030530

Chandler, J., & Schwarz, N. (2010). Use does not wear ragged the fabric of friendship: Thinking of objects as alive makes people less willing to replace them. *Journal of Consumer Psychology, 20*(2), 138–145. doi:10.1016/j.jcps.2009.12.008

Chang, V., Doan, L. M. T., di Stefano, A., Sun, Z., & Fortino, G. (2022). Digital payment fraud detection methods in digital ages and Industry 4.0. *Computers & Electrical Engineering, 100*, 107734. doi:10.1016/J.COMPELECENG.2022.107734

Chaudhuri, R., Carolyne, G., Tayar, G., & Williams, E. (2022). *Sustaining digital payments growth: Winning models in emerging markets.* Academic Press.

Chaveesuk, S., Khalid, B., & Chaiyasoonthorn, W. (2021). Digital payment system innovations: A marketing perspective on intention and actual use in the retail sector. *Innovative Marketing, 17*(3), 109.

Chawala, A., Banos, G., Peters, A., & Chagunda, M. (2019). Farmer-preferred traits in smallholder dairy farming systems in Tanzania. *Tropical Animal Health and Production, 51*(6), 1337–1344. doi:10.100711250-018-01796-9 PMID:30715656

Cheng, X., Zhang, X., Cohen, J., & Mou, J. (2022). Human vs. AI: Understanding the impact of anthropomorphism on consumer response to chatbots from the perspective of trust and relationship norms. *Information Processing & Management, 59*(3), 102940. doi:10.1016/j.ipm.2022.102940

Chen, R., Yamaka, W., & Osathanunkul, R. (2019). Determinants of non-cash payments in Asian countries. *Journal of Physics: Conference Series, 1324*(1), 012103.

Chiu, J., & Wong, T.-N. (2021). Payments on digital platforms: Resiliency, interoperability and welfare. *Journal of Economic Dynamics & Control, 104173.* Advance online publication. doi:10.1016/J.JEDC.2021.104173

Chuma, K. G., & Ngoepe, M. (2021). Security of electronic personal health information in a public hospital in South Africa. *Information Security Journal: A Global Perspective*, 1-17.

Claeys, G., Demertzis, M., & Efstathiou, K. (2018). *Cryptocurrencies and monetary policy.* Bruegel Policy Contribution.

Coccoli, M., Guercio, A., Maresca, P., & Stanganelli, L. (2014). Smarter universities: A vision for the fast-changing digital era. *Journal of Visual Languages and Computing, 25*(6), 1003–1011. doi:10.1016/j.jvlc.2014.09.007

Cockburn, M. (2020). Application and prospective discussion of machine learning for the management of dairy farms. *Animals (Basel), 10*(9), 1690. doi:10.3390/ani10091690 PMID:32962078

Consultancy.uk. (2020). *Global market size of digital payments industry soares*. https://www.consultancy.uk/news/25975/global-market-size-of-digital-payments-industry-soares

Corrales, M. (2018). Robotics, AI and the Future of Law, Perspectives in Law, Business and Innovation. Springer Nature Singapore Pte Ltd.

Crolic, C., Thomaz, F., Hadi, R., & Stephen, A. T. (2022). Blame the bot: Anthropomorphism and anger in customer–chatbot interactions. *Journal of Marketing*, *86*(1), 132–148. doi:10.1177/00222429211045687

Crow, R. (2002a). *Case for Institutional Repositories: A SPARC Position Paper*. Washington, DC: The Scholarly Publishing and Academic Resources Coalition. Retrieved from http://www.arl.org/sparc/bm~doc/ir_final_release_102.pdf

Croxson, K., Frost, J., Gambacorta, L., & Valletti, T. (2022). *Platform-based business models and financial inclusion*. BIS Papers.

Czymmek, V., Schramm, R., & Hussmann, S. (2020). Vision Based Crop Row Detection for Low Cost UAV Imagery in Organic Agriculture. *2020 IEEE International Instrumentation and Measurement Technology Conference (I2MTC)*, 1–6. 10.1109/I2MTC43012.2020.9128695

Dabholkar, A., Kakarla, S., & Saha, D. (2021). Looney tunes: Exposing the lack of DRM protection in indian music streaming services. arXiv preprint arXiv:2103.16360.

Darby, R. M., Jones, C. M., Gilbert, L. D., & Lambert, S. C. (2009). Increasing the productivity of interactions between subject and institutional repositories. *New Review of InformationNetworking*, *14*(2), 117–135. doi:10.1080/13614570903359381

Dash, S. R. (2020). *Systems thinking: The key to process improvements*. UX Collections. https://uxdesign.cc/systems-thinking-the-key-to-process-improvements-ec8a0f71f628

Dash, R., McMurtrey, M., Rebman, C., & Kar, U. K. (2019). Application of artificial intelligence in automation of supply chain management. *Journal of Strategic Innovation and Sustainability*, *14*(3), 43–53.

Das, K. (2021). Digital Technologies on Mathematics Education at the Covid-19 Lockdown Situation in India. *Indonesian Journal of Innovation and Applied Sciences*, *1*(2), 95–104. doi:10.47540/ijias.v1i2.197

Dębski, M., Borkowska-Niszczota, M., & Andrzejczyk, R. (2021). Tourist Accommodation Establishments during the Pandemic – Consequences and Aid Report on a Survey among Polish Micro-enterprises Offering Accommodation Services. *Journal of Intercultural Management*, *13*(1), 1–25. doi:10.2478/joim-2021-0001

Deloitte. (2016). *High-value health care - Innovative approaches to global challenges*. Retrieved from https://www2.deloitte.com/content/dam/Deloitte/global/Documents/Life-Sciences-Health-Care/gx-lshc-high-value-health-care
.pdf

Delone, W. H., & Mclean, E. R. (2003). The DeLone and McLean Model of Information Systems Success: A Ten-Year Update. *Journal of Management Information Systems*, *19*(4), 9–30. Advance online publication. doi:10.1080/07421222.2003.11045748

Dempsey, J. X. (2020). *Artificial Intelligence: An Introduction to the Legal, Policy and Ethical Issues*. Berkeley Center for Law & Technology.

Dempsey, P. S. (2014). *The law of products liability*. McGill University.

Department of Basic Education. (2021). *NSC Examinations*. https://www.education.gov.za/Curriculum/NationalSeniorCertificate(NSC)Examinations.aspx

Devex. (2022). *Malawi National Examinations Board (MANEB)*. https://www.devex.com/organizations/malawi-national-examinations-board-maneb-133621

Dewson, S., Ritchie, H., & Meager, N. (2005). *New Deal for Disabled People: Survey of employers*. Department for Work and Pensions Research Report No.301. DWP.

Dhull, I., & Sakshi, M. S. (2017). Online Learning. *International Education and Research Journal*, *3*(8), 32–34.

Di. Gregorio, D., Kassicieh, S. K., & de Gouvea Neto, R. (2005). Drivers of e-business activity in developed and emerging markets. *IEEE Transactions on Engineering Management*, *52*(2), 155–166. doi:10.1109/TEM.2005.844464

Didham, R. J., & Ofei-Manu, P. (2015). *The role of education in the sustainable development agenda: Empowering a learning society for sustainability through quality education.* ResearchGate. Available online at: https://www.researchgate.net/publication/280458119

DiSalvo, C., Gemperle, F., & Forlizzi, J. (2005). *Imitating the human form: Four kinds of anthropomorphic form.* Unpublished manuscript.

Dobrica, L. (2022). Robotic process automation platform UiPath. *Communications of the ACM*, *65*(4), 42–43. doi:10.1145/3511667

Dossa, L. H., Abdulkadir, A., Amadou, H., Sangare, S., & Schlecht, E. (2011). Exploring the diversity of urban and peri-urban agricultural systems in Sudano-Sahelian West Africa: An attempt towards a regional typology. *Landscape and Urban Planning*, *102*(3), 197–206. doi:10.1016/j.landurbplan.2011.04.005

Drugarin, C., Draghici, S., & Raduca, E. (2016). *Team Viewer Technology for Remote Control of a Computer*. https://www.researchgate.net/profile/Cornelia-Victoria-Anghel-Drugarin/publication/311057172_Team_Viewer_Technology_for_Remote_Control_of_a_Computer/links/583c5d4408ae3cb636556e7a/Team-Viewer-Technology-for-Remote-Control-of-a-Computer.pdf

Du, M., Chen, Q., Xiao, J., Yang, H., & Ma, X. (2020). Supply Chain Finance Innovation Using Blockchain. *IEEE Transactions on Engineering Management*, *67*(4), 1045–1058. doi:10.1109/TEM.2020.2971858

Dunn, R. J., Mead, N. E., Willett, K. M., & Parker, D. E. (2014). Analysis of heat stress in UK dairy cattle and impact on milk yields. *Environmental Research Letters*, *9*(6), 064006. doi:10.1088/1748-9326/9/6/064006

Dziatkovskii, A., Hryneuski, U., Dudov, A., & Krylova, A. (2021). The economic impact of digitalization and the creation of digital products on the development of the state. *Economic Annals-XXI*, *193*(9–10), 4–14. doi:10.21003/EA.V193-01

Eaton, S. E. (2018). The Impact of Technology on how instructors Teach and how students Learn. In R. J. Harnish, K. R. Bridges, D. N. Sattler, M. L. Signorella, & M. Munson (Eds.), *The Use of Technology in Teaching and Learning*. Retrieved from the Society for the Teaching of Psychology website: http://teachpsych.org/ebooks/

Edwards, D., Rentschler, R., Fujimoto, Y., & Le, H. (2010). Why has the rising economic tide failed to float the disability employment boat? A call to action: Business, community, government and people power. *The International Journal of Diversity in Organisations, Communities and Nations*, *10*(1), 117–127. doi:10.18848/1447-9532/CGP/v10i01/39810

Effah, J. (2016). Institutional effects on e-payment entrepreneurship in a developing country: Enablers and constraints. *Information Technology for Development*, *22*(2), 205–219.

Egger, I., Lei, S. I., & Wassler, P. (2020). Digital free tourism–An exploratory study of tourist motivations. *Tourism Management, 79*, 104098. doi:10.1016/j.tourman.2020.104098

Eldeleklioglu, J. & Vural, M. (2013). Predictive effects of academic achievement, internet use duration, loneliness and shyness on internet addiction. *Hacettepe Universitesi Egitim Fakultesi Dergisi, 28*(1), 141-151.

Enang, W. (2021). *5 Functions of West African Examinations Council*. Pro guide. https://proguide.ng/functions-west-african-examinations-council/

Enkhtsogt, T. A., & Kim, Y. (2018). Major Principles of ICT Policy for Improving ICT Integration in Education for Students with Disabilities in Mongolia. *Asia-Pacific Collaborative Education Journal, 14*(2), 21–32.

Epley, N., Waytz, A., & Cacioppo, J. T. (2007). On seeing human: A three-factor theory of anthropomorphism. *Psychological Review, 114*(4), 864–886. doi:10.1037/0033-295X.114.4.864 PMID:17907867

European Agency for Development in Special Needs Education. (2002). Transition from School to Employment: Main problems, issues and options faced by students with special educational needs in 16 European countries. Summary Report October 2002. Brussels: EADSNE.

Examinations Council of Lesotho. (2022). *Background*. https://www.examscouncil.org.ls/web/aboutUs

Fabris, N. (2019). Cashless Society - The Future of Money or a Utopia? *Journal of Central Banking Theory and Practice, 8*(1), 53–66. doi:10.2478/jcbtp-2019-0003

Faiçal, B. S., Freitas, H., Gomes, P. H., Mano, L. Y., Pessin, G., de Carvalho, A. C. P. L. F., Krishnamachari, B., & Ueyama, J. (2017). An adaptive approach for UAV-based pesticide spraying in dynamic environments. *Computers and Electronics in Agriculture, 138*, 210–223. doi:10.1016/j.compag.2017.04.011

Fakunle, S. M., Bakare, O. D., & Adeyeye, S. V. (2022). Digital Literacy Skills as Determinants of Library Use by Undergraduate Students of Private Universities in Oyo State, Nigeria. *Library Philosophy and Practice, 7054*. https://digitalcommons.unl.edu/libphilprac/7054

Fall, I. S., Rajatonirina, S., Yahaya, A. A., Zabulon, Y., Nsubuga, P., Nanyunja, M., ... Talisuna, A. O. (2019). *Integrated Disease Surveillance and Response (IDSR) strategy : Current status, challenges and perspectives for the future in Africa*. doi:10.1136/bmjgh-2019-001427

Fama, M., Fumagalli, A., & Lucarelli, S. (2019). Cryptocurrencies, monetary policy, and new forms of monetary sovereignty. *International Journal of Political Economy, 48*(2), 174–194. doi:10.1080/08911916.2019.1624318

Fan, A., Wu, L. L., & Mattila, A. S. (2016). Does anthropomorphism influence customers' switching intentions in the self-service technology failure context? *Journal of Services Marketing, 30*(7), 713–723. doi:10.1108/JSM-07-2015-0225

Fatima, M., & Pasha, M. (2017). Survey of machine learning algorithms for disease diagnostic. *Journal of Intelligent Learning Systems and Applications, 9*(01), 1–16. doi:10.4236/jilsa.2017.91001

Fatuma Mavura, Mkoba, & Nyambo. (2022). Rule-Based Engine for Automatic Allocation of Smallholder Dairy Producers in Pre-Identified Production Clusters. *The Scientific World Journal*.

Faysse, N., Sraïri, M. T., & Errahj, M. (2012). Local farmers' organisations: A space for peer-to-peer learning? The case of milk collection cooperatives in Morocco. *Journal of Agricultural Education and Extension, 18*(3), 285–299. doi:10.1080/1389224X.2012.670053

Ferrari, M. V. (2022). The platformisation of digital payments: The fabrication of consumer interest in the EU FinTech agenda. *Computer Law & Security Review*, *45*, 105687. doi:10.1016/J.CLSR.2022.105687

Ferrell, L., & Ferrell, O. C. (2012). Redirecting direct selling: High-touch embraces high-tech. *Business Horizons*, *55*(3), 273–281. doi:10.1016/J.BUSHOR.2012.01.004

Festerling, J., & Siraj, I. (2021). Anthropomorphizing Technology: A Conceptual Review of Anthropomorphism Research and How it Relates to Children's Engagements with Digital Voice Assistants. *Integrative Psychological & Behavioral Science*, 1–30. PMID:34811705

Finlay, L. (2009). Debating phenomenological research. *Phenomenology & Practice*, *3*(1), 6–25. doi:10.29173/pandpr19818

Foehr, J., & Germelmann, C. C. (2020). Alexa, can I trust you? Exploring consumer paths to trust in smart voice-interaction technologies. *Journal of the Association for Consumer Research*, *5*(2), 181–205. doi:10.1086/707731

Fondation Pierre Fabre. (2019). *Field survey report AfyaData Project : Promoting Proper Management of Zoonotic Diseases through e-based One Health Training of Frontline Health Worker Global South eHealth Observatory*. Author.

Force, M. H. T. (2016). *Maternal and Child Survival Program (MCSP)*. Retrieved from https://www.mhtf.org/organization/maternal-and-child-survival-program-mcsp/

Foundation, N. (2016). *Ghana Telemedicine: Digital Health Ghana*. Retrieved from https://www.novartisfoundation.org/past-programs/digital-health/ghana-telemedicine

Frączek, B., & Urbanek, A. (2021). Financial inclusion as an important factor influencing digital payments in passenger transport: A case study of EU countries. *Research in Transportation Business & Management*, *41*, 100691. doi:10.1016/J.RTBM.2021.100691

Francis, F., Ishengoma, D. S., Mmbando, B. P., Rutta, A. S. M., Malecela, M. N., Mayala, B., Lemnge, M. M., & Michael, E. (2017). Deployment and use of mobile phone technology for real - time reporting of fever cases and malaria treatment failure in areas of declining malaria transmission in Muheza district north - eastern Tanzania. *Malaria Journal*, *16*(308), 1–14. doi:10.118612936-017-1956-z PMID:28764792

Francois. (2021). *Mapping health data flows and use in rural Tanzania*. Retrieved from https://medium.com/data-zetu/learning-about-hyperlocal-data-f78084136cf

Freedman, D. H. (2008). *Improving skills and productivity of disadvantaged youth*. ILO Working Paper.

Freitas, P.M. (2014). *Criminal Liability of Autonomous Agents: From the unthinkable to the plausible*. Academic Press.

Friha, O., Ferrag, M. A., Shu, L., Maglaras, L., & Wang, X. (2021). Internet of Things for the Future of Smart Agriculture: A Comprehensive Survey of Emerging Technologies. *IEEE/CAA Journal of Automatica Sinica*, *8*(4), 718–752. doi:10.1109/JAS.2021.1003925

Frolova, E. V., Ryabova, T. M., & Rogach, O. V. (2019). Digital Technologies in Education: Problems and Prospects for" Moscow Electronic School" Project Implementation. *European Journal of Contemporary Education*, *8*(4), 779–789.

Fuchs, C. (2009). The role of income inequality in a multivariate cross-national analysis of the digital divide. *Social Science Computer Review*, *27*(1), 41–58. doi:10.1177/0894439308321628

G, L., C, R., & P, G. (2020). An automated low cost IoT based Fertilizer Intimation System for smart agriculture. *Sustainable Computing: Informatics and Systems, 28*, 100300. doi:10.1016/j.suscom.2019.01.002

Gainsbury, S. M., & Blaszczynski, A. (2020). Digital gambling payment methods: Harm minimization policy considerations. *Gaming Law Review*, *24*(7), 466–472. doi:10.1089/GLR2.2020.0015

Gal, D. (2019). *Perspectives and approaches in AI ethics: East Asia. Oxford Handbook of Ethics of Artificial Intelligence*. Oxford University Press.

Gallardo-Rincón, H., Montoya, A., Saucedo-Martínez, R., Mújica-Rosales, R., Suárez-Idueta, L., Martínez-Juárez, L. A., Razo, C., Lozano, R., & Tapia-Conyer, R. (2021). Integrated Measurement for Early Detection (MIDO) as a digital strategy for timely assessment of non-communicable disease profiles and factors associated with unawareness and control: A retrospective observational study in primary healthcare facilities in Mexico. *BMJ Open*, *11*(9), e049836. doi:10.1136/bmjopen-2021-049836 PMID:34475175

Galluzzo, N. (2015). Technical and economic efficiency analysis on Italian smallholder family farms using Farm Accountancy Data Network dataset. *Studies in Agricultural Economics (Budapest)*, *117*(1), 35–42. doi:10.7896/j.1501

García, L., Parra, L., Jimenez, J. M., Lloret, J., & Lorenz, P. (2020). IoT-Based Smart Irrigation Systems: An Overview on the Recent Trends on Sensors and IoT Systems for Irrigation in Precision Agriculture. *Sensors (Basel)*, *20*(4), 1042. doi:10.339020041042 PMID:32075172

Gardecki, A., & Podpora, M. (2017). Experience from the operation of the Pepper humanoid robots. In 2017 Progress in Applied Electrical Engineering (PAEE) (pp. 1-6). IEEE. doi:10.1109/PAEE.2017.8008994

Gathitu, L. N. (2010). *Examination representation using adaptive testing: application in interview process* [Doctoral dissertation]. University of Nairobi. http://erepository.uonbi.ac.ke/bitstream/handle/11295/13095/Gathitu_Examination?sequence=3

Gelbard, R., Goldman, O., & Spiegler, I. (2007). Investigating diversity of clustering methods: An empirical comparison. *Data & Knowledge Engineering*, *63*(1), 155–166. doi:10.1016/j.datak.2007.01.002

Genin, K., & Grote, T. (2021). Randomized controlled trials in medical AI: A methodological critique. *Philosophy of Medicine*, *2*(1), 1–15. doi:10.5195/pom.2021.27

George, M. L. (2020). Effective Teaching and Examination Strategies for Undergraduate Learning During COVID-19 School Restrictions. *Journal of Educational Technology Systems*, *49*(1), 23–48. doi:10.1177/0047239520934017

Ghavifekr, S., & Rosdy, W. A. W. (2015). Teaching and learning with technology: Effectiveness of ICT integration in schools. *International Journal of Research in Education and Science*, *1*(2), 175–191. doi:10.21890/ijres.23596

Ghosh, G. (2021). Adoption of digital payment system by consumer: A review of literature. *International Journal of Creative Research Thoughts*, *9*(2), 2320–2882.

Ghuman, A. (2018). Elements of Crime. *International Journal of Law Management & Humanities, 1*(4).

Gitau, K. J. (2013). *Factors influencing milk production among small scale dairy farmers in Mirangine in Nyandarua county and Mauche in Nakuru county*. University of Nairobi.

Githiru, T. (2018). *How Technology Can Improve Africa*. Techweez. Available online at: https://techweez.com/2018/05/15/technology-can-improve-africa/

Go, E., & Sundar, S. S. (2019). Humanizing chatbots: The effects of visual, identity and conversational cues on human ness perceptions. *Computers in Human Behavior*, *97*, 304–316. doi:10.1016/j.chb.2019.01.020

Goswami, R., Chatterjee, S., & Prasad, B. (2014). Farm types and their economic characterization in complex agro-ecosystems for informed extension intervention: Study from coastal West Bengal, India. *Agricultural and Food Economics*, *2*(1), 1–24. doi:10.118640100-014-0005-2

Graduate Management Admission Council. (2022). *GMAT Exam Structure: An Assessment of the Skills That Matter Most in Business*. https://www.mba.com/exams/gmat/about-the-gmat- exam/GMAT-exa m-structure

Great Schools Partnership. (2015). *Glossary Of Education Reform: Standardized Test Definition*. Great Schools Partnership. https://www.edglossary.org/standardized-test/

Greenhow, C., & Askari, E. (2017). E. Learning and teaching with social network sites: A decade of research in K-12 related education. *Education and Information Technologies*, *22*(2), 623–645. doi:10.100710639-015-9446-9

Greenhow, C., & Chapman, A. (2020). Social distancing meets social media: Digital tools for connecting students, teachers, and citizens in an emergency. *Inf. Learn. Sci.*, *121*(5/6), 341–352. doi:10.1108/ILS-04-2020-0134

Gruszczynska, A., Merchant, G., & Pountney, R. (2013). Digital Futures in Teacher Education": Exploring Open Approaches towards Digital Literacy. *Electronic Journal of e-Learning*, *11*(3), 193–206.

GSMA. (2019). *CASALUD: A suite of digital health services for the prevention and management of NCDs. Delivered in partnership with the Mexico Ministry of Health and Carlos Slim Foundation*. Retrieved from www.gsma.com/mobilefordevelopment/

GSMA. (2023). *Tanzania's Digitalisation Journey: Opportunities for value creation*. GSMA.

GSMA_MobileEconomy2021_3 (1). (2021).

Guerra, J., Acharya, P., & Barnadas, C. (2019). Community-based surveillance : A scoping review. *PLoS One*, 1–25. https://doi.org/https://doi.org/ 10.1371/journal.pone.021527 8 PMID:30978224

Guner, H. R., Hasanoglu, I., & Aktas, F. (2020). COVID-19: Prevention and control measures in the community. *Turkish Journal of Medical Sciences*, *50*(9), 571–577. doi:10.3906ag-2004-146 PMID:32293835

Gupta, S., Kiran, R., & Sharma, R. K. (2022). Validating the role of digital payment mode as a new driver of online shopping: A modified UTAUT2 model. *Journal of Public Affairs*, *22*(2), e2434.

Gursoy, D., Chi, O. H., Lu, L., & Nunkoo, R. (2019). Consumers acceptance of artificially intelligent (AI) device use in service delivery. *International Journal of Information Management*, *49*, 157–169. doi:10.1016/j.ijinfomgt.2019.03.008

Hall, M. L., Hall, W. C., & Caselli, N. K. (2019). Deaf children need language, not (just) speech. *First Language*, *39*(4), 367–395. doi:10.1177/0142723719834102

Han, H. (2021). Consumer behavior and environmental sustainability in tourism and hospitality: A review of theories, concepts, and latest research. *Journal of Sustainable Tourism*, *29*(7), 1021–1042. doi:10.1080/09669582.2021.1903019

Hanif, A. S., Han, X., & Yu, S.-H. (2022). Independent Control Spraying System for UAV-Based Precise Variable Sprayer: A Review. *Drones (Basel)*, *6*(12), 383. doi:10.3390/drones6120383

Harlen, W., & Deakin, C. R. (2003). A systematic review of the impact on students and teachers of the use of ICT for assessment of creative and critical thinking skills. In *Research Evidence in Education Library.* EPPI-Centre, Social Science Research Unit, Institute of Education, University of London. https://eppi.ioe.ac.uk/cms/Default.aspx?tabid=109

Harwood, S. A. (2019). Systems thinking and sustainable development. Encyclopedia of Sustainability in Higher Education, 1892-1897. doi:10.1007/978-3-030-11352-0_399

Hasan, M., Uddin, K. N. W., Sayeed, A., & Tasneem, T. (2021). Smart Agriculture Robotic System Based on Internet of Things to Boost Crop Production. *2021 2nd International Conference on Robotics, Electrical and Signal Processing Techniques (ICREST)*, 157–162. 10.1109/ICREST51555.2021.9331091

Hendal, B. A. (2020). Kuwait University Faculty's Use of Electronic Resources During the Covid-19 Pandemic. *Digital Library Perspectives*, *36*(4), 429–439. doi:10.1108/DLP-04-2020-0023

Hennig-Thurau, T., Gwinner, K. P., Walsh, G., & Gremler, D. D. (2004). Electronic word-of-mouth via consumer-opinion platforms: What motivates consumers to articulate themselves on the Internet? *Journal of Interactive Marketing*, *18*(1), 38–52. doi:10.1002/dir.10073

Heyer, K. (2008). Rights or quotas? The ADA as a model for disability rights. In L. B. Neilsen & R. L. Nelson (Eds.), *Handbook of employment discrimination research III* (pp. 237–257). Springer.

Hidayanto, A. N., Hidayat, L. S., Sandhyaduhita, P. I., & Handayani, P. W. (2015). Examining the relationship of payment system characteristics and behavioural intention in e-payment adoption: A case of Indonesia. *International Journal of Business Information Systems*, *19*(1), 58–86.

Hindman, D. B. (2000). *The Rural-Urban Digital Divide*. Academic Press.

Hinrichs, G., & Bundtzen, H. (2021). Impact of COVID-19 on personal insurance sales – Evidence from Germany. *Financial Markets. Institutions and Risks*, *5*(1), 80–86. doi:10.21272/fmir.5(1).80-86.2021

Hodder Education. (n.d.). *RS Assessment*. www.hoddereducation.co.uk/rsassessment

Howcroft, J. B., & Lavis, J. (1987). Evolution of the payment systems of London clearing banks. *Service Industries Journal*, *7*(2), 176–194.

Hsieh, J. J. P. A., Rai, A., & Keil, M. (2008). Understanding digital inequality: Comparing continued use behavioral models of the socio-economically advantaged and disadvantaged. *Management Information Systems Quarterly*, *32*(1), 97–126. doi:10.2307/25148830

Hult, G. T. M., Ketchen, D. J., Griffith, D. A., Chabowski, B. R., Hamman, M. K., Dykes, B. J., Pollitte, W. A., & Cavusgil, S. T. (2008). An assessment of the measurement of performance in international business research. *Journal of International Business Studies, 39*(6), 1064–1080. https://doi.org/ doi:10.1057/PALGRAVE.JIBS.8400398

Humphrey, D. B., & Hunt, R. (2013). Cost savings from check 21 electronic payment legislation. *Journal of Money, Credit and Banking*, *45*(7), 1415–1429. doi:10.1111/JMCB.12057

Hussein, N., Alashqur, A., & Sowan, B. (2015). Using the interestingness measure lift to generate association rules. *Journal of Advanced Computer Science & Technology*, *4*(1), 156. doi:10.14419/jacst.v4i1.4398

Hyytinen, A., & Takalo, T. (2009). Consumer awareness and the use of payment media: Evidence from young Finnish consumers. *Review of Network Economics*, *8*(2). Advance online publication. doi:10.2202/1446-9022.1175

Idrees, S. M., Nowostawski, M., Jameel, R., & Mourya, A. K. (2021). Security aspects of blockchain technology intended for industrial applications. *Electronics (Basel)*, *10*(8), 951. doi:10.3390/electronics10080951

Iftakhar, S. (2016). *Google classroom: What works and how*. https://jesoc.com/wp-content/uploads/2016/03/KC3_35.pdf

Iivari, N., Sharma, S., & Ventä-Olkkonen, L. (2020). Digital transformation of everyday life – How COVID-19 pandemic transformed the basic education of the young generation and why information management research should care? *International Journal of Information Management*, *55*, 102183. Advance online publication. doi:10.1016/j.ijinfomgt.2020.102183 PMID:32836640

Ikram, N. H. S., & Kepli, M. Y. (2018). Establishing legal rights and liabilities for Artificial Intelligence. IIUM Law Journal, 26(1).

ILO. (2004). *URT: Employment of People with Disabilities-The Impact of Legislation in East Africa*. ILO.

Intel. (2018). *Intel and Partners Come Together to Solve Healthcare*. Retrieved from https://newsroom.intel.com/editorials/intel-partners-come-together-solve-healthcare/

Intelligence, G. S. M. A. (2014). *GSMA: Digital inclusion Report*. Retrieved from https://www.ncbi.nlm.nih.gov/pubmed/19547787

Intelligence, G. S. M. A. (2017). *Scaling digital health in developing markets*. Retrieved from https://www.gsmaintelligence.com/research/?file=c581aa43bdb7b7d236bb937698c2d6fd&download

IQVIA Institute. (2017). *The Growing Value of Digital Health*. Retrieved from https://www.iqvia.com/insights/the-iqvia-institute/reports/the-growing-value-of-digital-health

ISI. (2022). *Developing Countries*. Retrieved 9 August, 2022 from https://www.isi-web.org/resources/developing-countries

Ismail, L., & Materwala, H. (2019). A review of blockchain architecture and consensus protocols: Use cases, challenges, and solutions. *Symmetry*, *11*(10), 1198. doi:10.3390ym11101198

ITU. (2017). Measuring the Information Society Report 2017 (Vol. 1). doi:10.1787/9789264244047-37-en

Ivanov, S., & Webster, C. (2021). Willingness-to-pay for robot-delivered tourism and hospitality services–an exploratory study. *International Journal of Contemporary Hospitality Management*, *33*(11), 3926–3955. doi:10.1108/IJCHM-09-2020-1078

J. R. (2018). Voodoo software and boundary objects in game development: How developers collaborate and conflict with game engines and art tools. *New Media & Society, 20*(7), 2315-2332.

Jain, S. (2022). *Harnessing digital financial inclusion under the G20 Digital Economy Agenda 2023*. ORF. https://www.orfonline.org/expert-speak/g20-digital-economy-agenda-2023/

Javaid, H., Hu, C., & Brebner, G. (2019). *Optimizing validation phase of hyperledger fabric*. Paper presented at the 2019 IEEE 27th International Symposium on Modeling, Analysis, and Simulation of Computer and Telecommunication Systems (MASCOTS). 10.1109/MASCOTS.2019.00038

Javed, M. U., Rehman, M., Javaid, N., Aldegheishem, A., Alrajeh, N., & Tahir, M. (2020). Blockchain-based secure data storage for distributed vehicular networks. *Applied Sciences (Basel, Switzerland)*, *10*(6), 2011. doi:10.3390/app10062011

Jenkins, P. (2018, May 10). *We don't take cash': is this the future of money?* Financial Times. https://www.ft.com/content/9fc55dda-5316-11e8-b24e-cad6aa67e23e

JJoachim, Yassin, Cosmas, & Darcy. (2018). Electronic Integrated Disease Surveillance and Response eIDSR implementation in Tanzania. In *Electronic Integrated Disease Surveillance and Response eIDSR implementation in Tanzania: The 5th Annual Global Digital Health Forum.* Ministry of Health Community Development Gender, Elderly and Children. doi:10.13140/RG.2.2.24365.03049

Jobirovich, Y. M. (2021). The Role Of Digital Technologies In Reform Of The Education System. *The American Journal of Social Science and Education Innovations*, *3*(04), 461–465. doi:10.37547/tajssei/Volume03Issue04-73

John, S. N., Anele, C., Kennedy, O. O., Olajide, F., & Kennedy, C. G. (2016). Realtime fraud detection in the banking sector using data mining techniques/algorithm. *2016 International Conference on Computational Science and Computational Intelligence (CSCI).*

Jones, R., Andrew, T., & MacColl, J. J. (2006). The Institutional Repository. Chandos Publishing (Oxford) Limited.

Jones, K., Nowak, A., Berglund, E., Grinnell, W., Temu, E., Paul, B., Renwick, L. L. R., Steward, P., Rosenstock, T. S., & Kimaro, A. A. (2023). Evidence supports the potential for climate-smart agriculture in Tanzania. *Global Food Security*, *36*, 100666. doi:10.1016/j.gfs.2022.100666

Jukes, I., & Dosaj, A. (2005). *Understanding Digital Kids (DKs): Teaching & learning in the new digital landscape.* The Info Savvy Group.

Jurado-Caraballo, M. Á., Quintana-García, C., & Rodríguez-Fernández, M. (2022). Trends and opportunities in research on disability and work: An interdisciplinary perspective. *Business Research Quarterly*, *25*(4), 366–388. doi:10.1177/2340944420972715

Kadar, B., & Reicher, R. Z. (2020). Innovations in Health Care Management: The Effect of the Pandemic on the Labour Market Change. *Marketing and Management of Innovations*, *4*, 120–130. doi:10.21272/mmi.2020.4-09

Kafle, N. P. (2011). Hermeneutic phenomenological research method simplified. *Bodhi: An Interdisciplinary Journal*, *5*(1), 181–200.

Kajirunga, A., & Kalegele, K. (2015). *Analysis of activities and operations in the current E-Health landscape in Tanzania: focus on interoperability and collaboration.* arXiv preprint arXiv:1507.00176.

Kala Kamdjoug, J. R., Wamba-Taguimdje, S. L., Wamba, S. F., & Kake, I. B. e. (2021). Determining factors and impacts of the intention to adopt mobile banking app in Cameroon: Case of SARA by afriland First Bank. *Journal of Retailing and Consumer Services*, *61*. Advance online publication. doi:10.1016/J.JRETCONSER.2021.102509

Karau, S. (2021). Monetary policy and cryptocurrencies. *Proceedings of Paris December 2021 Finance Meeting EUROFIDAI-ESSEC.*

Kasesera, J. (2012). Assessing the impact of mainstream vocational training in developing capabilities of people with and without disabilities. A case of Danhiko Training Institution in Harare, Zimbabwe. Institute of Social Studies.

Kashyap, P. K., Kumar, S., Jaiswal, A., Prasad, M., & Gandomi, A. H. (2021). Towards Precision Agriculture: IoT-Enabled Intelligent Irrigation Systems Using Deep Learning Neural Network. *IEEE Sensors Journal*, *21*(16), 17479–17491. doi:10.1109/JSEN.2021.3069266

Kastner, M., Makarski, J., Hayden, L., Hamid, J. S., Holroyd-Leduc, J., Twohig, M., ... Sklar, B. (2021). Effectiveness of an eHealth self-management tool for older adults with multimorbidity (KeepWell): Protocol for a hybrid effectiveness–implementation randomised controlled trial. *BMJ Open*, *11*(2), e048350. doi:10.1136/bmjopen-2020-048350 PMID:33597147

Kazuzuru, B. (2014). History, Performance and Challenges of Tourism Industry in Tanzania. *International Journal of Business and Social Science*, *5*(11).

Kett, M. (2012). *Skills development for youth living with disabilities in four developing countries. Paper commissioned for the EFA Global Monitoring Report 2012, Youth and skills: Putting education to work.* UNESCO.

Khando, K., Islam, M. S., & Gao, S. (2022). The Emerging Technologies of Digital Payments and Associated Challenges: A Systematic Literature Review. *Future Internet*, *15*(1), 21. doi:10.3390/fi15010021

Khan, N., Ray, R. L., Sargani, G. R., Ihtisham, M., Khayyam, M., & Ismail, S. (2021). Current Progress and Future Prospects of Agriculture Technology: Gateway to Sustainable Agriculture. *Sustainability (Basel)*, *13*(9), 4883. doi:10.3390u13094883

Khatoon, A. (2020). A blockchain-based smart contract system for healthcare management. *Electronics (Basel)*, *9*(1), 94. doi:10.3390/electronics9010094

Khin, S., & Ho, T. C. (2018). Digital technology, digital capability and organizational performance: A mediating role of digital innovation. *International Journal of Innovation Science*. Advance online publication. doi:10.1108/IJIS-08-2018-0083

Khoa, T. A., Man, M. M., Nguyen, T.-Y., Nguyen, V., & Nam, N. H. (2019). Smart Agriculture Using IoT Multi-Sensors: A Novel Watering Management System. *Journal of Sensor and Actuator Networks*, *8*(3), 45. doi:10.3390/jsan8030045

Kholiavko, N., Popelo, O., & Tulchynska, S. (2021). Priority directions of increasing the adaptivity of universities to the conditions of the digital economy. *Revista Tempos e Espaços Em Educação*, *14*(33), e16383–e16383. doi:10.20952/REVTEE.V14I33.16383

Kholis, A. (2021). Elsa speak app: automatic speech recognition (ASR) for supplementing English pronunciation skills. *Pedagogy: Journal of English Language Teaching*, *9*(1), 1-14.

Kiberu, V. M., Matovu, J. K. B., Makumbi, F., Kyozira, C., Mukooyo, E., & Wanyenze, R. K. (2014). Strengthening district-based health reporting through the district health management information software system : The Ugandan experience. *BMC Medical Informatics and Decision Making*, *14*(40), 1–9. doi:10.1186/1472-6947-14-40 PMID:24886567

Kim, M.-K., Jeong, S.-G., Oh, M.-H., Kim, D.-H., Son, Y.-S., & Ham, J.-S. (2011). Guide to Good Dairy Farming Practice. *Journal of Dairy Science and Biotechnology*, *29*(2), 75–80.

Kim, S., & So, J. (2018). How message fatigue toward health messages leads to ineffective persuasive outcomes: Examining the mediating roles of reactance and inattention. *Journal of Health Communication*, *23*(1), 109–116. doi:10.1080/10810730.2017.1414900 PMID:29272208

Kingu, D., & Ndiege, B. O. (2018). Empowering Small Scale Dairy Farmers Through The Cooperatives Model. *Journal of Co-operative and Business Studies*, *2*(1), 1–12.

Kirina, T., Groot, A., Shilomboleni, H., Ludwig, F., & Demissie, T. (2022). Scaling Climate Smart Agriculture in East Africa: Experiences and Lessons. *Agronomy (Basel)*, *12*(4), 820. doi:10.3390/agronomy12040820

Kitta, S., & Afeli, S. (2017). *Examinations and Competitive Exams in Tanzania.* Regional Workshop on National Learning Assessment Systems in sub-Saharan Africa: Knowledge sharing and needs assessment, Dakar, Senegal. http://education2030-africa.org/images/talent/atelier061217/PPT_Tanzania.pdf

Kiwanuka, B. P. (n.d.). *The East African Examinations Council.* https://www.thecommonwealth-ilibrary.org/index.php/comsec/catalog/view/262/259/1971

Klapper, L., & Singer, D. (2017). The opportunities and challenges of digitizing government-to- person payments. *The World Bank Research Observer*, *32*(2), 211–226. doi:10.1093/WBRO/LKX003

Kolosok, S., & Jakubowska, A. (2020). COVID-19 And Public Health Administration: Trends And Prospects. *Health Economics and Management Review*, *1*(1), 69–75. doi:10.21272/hem.2020.1-06

Kombe, C., Dida, M., & Sam, A. (2018). *A review on healthcare information systems and consensus protocols in blockchain technology*. Academic Press.

Kombe, C. (2020). *A secure and interoperable blockchain-based information sharing system for healthcare providers in developing countries*. NM-AIST.

Krishna, B., Krishnan, S., & Sebastian, M. P. (2022). Examining the relationship between national cybersecurity commitment, culture, and digital payment usage: An institutional trust theory perspective. *Information Systems Frontiers*, 1–29. doi:10.100710796-022-10280-7

Krohn, R., Metcalf, D., & Salber, P. (2017). *Connected health: improving care, safety, and efficiency with wearables and IoT solution*. Productivity Press.

Krumsvik, R. (2006). *ICT-initiated school development in lower secondary school* [Doctoral dissertation]. The University of Bergen.

Kuivanen, K., Alvarez, S., Michalscheck, M., Adjei-Nsiah, S., Descheemaeker, K., Mellon-Bedi, S., & Groot, J. C. (2016). Characterising the diversity of smallholder farming systems and their constraints and opportunities for innovation: A case study from the Northern Region, Ghana. *NJAS Wageningen Journal of Life Sciences*, *78*(1), 153–166. doi:10.1016/j.njas.2016.04.003

Kuivanen, K., Michalscheck, M., Descheemaeker, K., Adjei-Nsiah, S., Mellon-Bedi, S., Groot, J. C., & Alvarez, S. (2016). A comparison of statistical and participatory clustering of smallholder farming systems–A case study in Northern Ghana. *Journal of Rural Studies*, *45*, 184–198. doi:10.1016/j.jrurstud.2016.03.015

Kumalija, C. J. (2017). *The United Republic of Tanzania*. Academic Press.

Kumar, R., Shrestha, M., & Badir, Y. (2021). *Digital transformation of financial institutions and its impact on their profitability.* Korea Advanced Institute of Science and Technology.

Kumar, P., & Chaubey, D. S. (2017). Demonetization and its impact on adoption of digital payment: Opportunities, issues and challenges. *Abhinav National Monthly Refereed Journal of Research in Commerce & Management*, *6*(6), 15.

Kumar, S., & Shekhar. (2020). Digitalization: A strategic approach for development of tourism industry in India. *Paradigm*, *24*(1), 93–108. doi:10.1177/0971890720914111

Kurgat, B. K., Lamanna, C., Kimaro, A., Namoi, N., Manda, L., & Rosenstock, T. S. (2020). Adoption of Climate-Smart Agriculture Technologies in Tanzania. *Frontiers in Sustainable Food Systems*, *4*, 55. doi:10.3389/fsufs.2020.00055

Kurwijila, L. R., Omore, A., & Delia, G. (2012). *The Tanzania Dairy Industry*. Academic Press.

Kushwaha, B. P. (2020). Search engine marketing a new way of marketing in digital age. *PalArch's Journal of Archaeology of Egypt/Egyptology, 17*(6), 2053-2065.

Kweka, I. (2010). *Employment of people with disabilities in Dar es Salaam Tanzania: An assessment of the proportion of people with disabilities in the workplace*. Retrieved on August 1, 2022 from: http://www.radardevelopment.com/fileadmin/downloads/CCBRT_Disability_Employment_Survey.pdf

Laksmidewi, D., Susianto, H., & Afiff, A. Z. (2017). Anthropomorphism in Advertising: The Effect of Anthropomorphic Product Demonstration on Consumer Purchase Intention. Asian Academy of Management Journal, 22(1).

Lei, J. (2009). Digital natives as preservice teachers: What technology preparation is needed? *Journal of Computing in Teacher Education*, *25*(3), 87–97.

Leong, C. M., Tan, K. L., Puah, C. H., & Chong, S. M. (2021). Predicting mobile network operators users m-payment intention. *European Business Review*, *33*(1). Advance online publication. doi:10.1108/EBR-10-2019-0263

Letheren, K., Jetten, J., Roberts, J., & Donovan, J. (2021). Robots should be seen and not heard… sometimes: Anthropomorphism and AI service robot interactions. *Psychology and Marketing*, *38*(12), 2393–2406. doi:10.1002/mar.21575

Lieser, P., Taff, S. D., & Murphy-Hagan, A. (2018). The Webinar Integration Tool: A Framework for Promoting Active Learning in Blended Environments. *Journal of Interactive Media in Education*, *2018*(1), 1–8. doi:10.5334/jime.453

Li, J., Pearce, P. L., & Oktadiana, H. (2020). Can digital-free tourism build character strengths? *Annals of Tourism Research*, *85*, 103037. doi:10.1016/j.annals.2020.103037 PMID:32905012

Liu, T., Pan, B., & Yin, Z. (2020). *Pandemic, Mobile Payment, and Household Consumption: Micro-Evidence from China*. https://doi.org/ doi:10.1080/1540496X.2020.1788539

Liu, K., & Tao, D. (2022). The roles of trust, personalization, loss of privacy, and anthropomorphism in public acceptance of smart healthcare services. *Computers in Human Behavior*, *127*, 107026. doi:10.1016/j.chb.2021.107026

Liu, N., Xu, Z., & Skare, M. (2021). The research on COVID-19 and economy from 2019 to 2020: Analysis from the perspective of bibliometrics. *Oeconomia Copernicana*, *12*(2), 217–268.

Liverpool-Tasie, L. S. O., Wineman, A., Young, S., Tambo, J., Vargas, C., Reardon, T., Adjognon, G. S., Porciello, J., Gathoni, N., Bizikova, L., Galiè, A., & Celestin, A. (2020). A scoping review of market links between value chain actors and small-scale producers in developing regions. *Nature Sustainability*, *3*(10), 799–808. doi:10.103841893-020-00621-2

Lo Prete, A. (2022). Digital and financial literacy as determinants of digital payments and personal finance. *Economics Letters*, *213*, 110378. doi:10.1016/J.ECONLET.2022.110378

Lockey, S., Gillespie, N., Holm, D., & Someh, I. A. (2021). *A review of trust in artificial intelligence: Challenges, vulnerabilities and future directions*. Academic Press.

Lou, C., & Yuan, S. (2019). Influencer Marketing: How Message Value and Credibility Affect Consumer Trust of Branded Content on Social Media. *Journal of Interactive Advertising*, *19*(1), 58–73. doi:10.1080/15252019.2018.1533501

Loyilane, P. (2008). *We should be given a chance: Identifying barriers and enablers from disabled people's employment in the office of the Premier of the Eastern Cape Provincial Government, South Africa* [Unpublished Masters Thesis]. University of Cape Town.

Lu, L. (2018). *How A Little Ant Challenges Giant Banks? The Rise of Ant Financial (Alipay)'s Fintech Empire and Relevant Regulatory Concerns*. Academic Press.

Lukuyu, M. N., Njehu, A., Mwilawa, A., Lukuyu, B. A., Omore, A. O., & Rao, E. (2017). *The role of fodder markets in meeting the year-round forage requirements of smallholder dairy farmers in Tanzania*. Livestock Brief.

Lund, B. D., & Wang, T. (2019). Effect of virtual reality on learning motivation and academic performance. *Kansas Library Association College Proceedings*, *9*(1), 1–7.

Lushasi, K., Steenson, R., Bernard, J., Changalucha, J. J., Govella, N. J., Haydon, D. T., Hoffu, H., Lankester, F., Magoti, F., Mpolya, E. A., Mtema, Z., Nonga, H., & Hampson, K. (2020). One Health in Practice: Using Integrated Bite Case Management to Increase Detection of Rabid Animals in Tanzania. *Frontiers in Public Health*, *8*(February), 1–10. doi:10.3389/fpubh.2020.00013 PMID:32117850

MacInnis, D. J., & Folkes, V. S. (2017). Humanizing brands: When brands seem to be like me, part of me, and in a relationship with me. *Journal of Consumer Psychology*, *27*(3), 355–374. doi:10.1016/j.jcps.2016.12.003

MacKinnon, D. P. (2011). Integrating Mediators and Moderators in Research Design. *Research on Social Work Practice*, *21*(6), 675–681. doi:10.1177/1049731511414148 PMID:22675239

Mader, P. (2016). Card crusaders, cash infidels and the holy grails of digital financial inclusion. *Behemoth-A Journal on Civilisation*, *9*(2), 59–81.

Maebara, K., Yamaguchi, A., Suzuki, T., & Imai, A. (2022). A Qualitative Study on The Function of Information and Communication Technology Utilization in Teaching Students with Intellectual Disabilities: Implications for Techniques of Teaching/Job Coaching. *Journal of Intellectual Disability-Diagnosis and Treatment*, *10*(1), 13–20. doi:10.6000/2292-2598.2022.10.01.2

Mahore, V., Aggarwal, P., Andola, N., & Venkatesan, S. (2019). *Secure and Privacy Focused Electronic Health Record Management System using Permissioned Blockchain.* Paper presented at the 2019 IEEE Conference on Information and Communication Technology. 10.1109/CICT48419.2019.9066204

Majchrzak, A., Markus, M. L., & Wareham, J. (2016). Designing for digital transformation: Lessons for information systems research from the study of ICT and societal challenges. *Management Information Systems Quarterly*, *40*(2), 267–278. doi:10.25300/MISQ/2016/40:2.03

Majid, I. (2019). ICT in Assessment: A Backbone for Teaching and Learning Process. *United International Journal for Research & Technology, 1*(3), 38-40. https://uijrt.com/articles/v1/i3/UIJRTV1I30006.pdf

Majid, I., & Lakshmi, Y. V. (2022). An Analysis of Artificial Intelligence Initiatives and Programmes in India. In *Convergence of Deep Learning and Artificial Intelligence in Internet of Things* (pp. 281–292). CRC Press. doi:10.1201/9781003355960-19

Makeshine, S., Viriyavejak, C., & Sovajassatakul, T. (2021). The impact of Distance Learning for Deaf and Hard of Hearing students during the COVID-19 pandemic in Thailand. In T. Bastiaens (Ed.), Proceedings of EdMedia + Innovate Learning (pp. 7-14). Association for the Advancement of Computing in Education (AACE).

Malusare, L. (2019). Digital payments methods in India: A study of problems and prospects. *International Journal of Scientific Research in Engineering and Management*, *3*(8), 1–7.

Manevich, Y., Barger, A., & Tock, Y. (2018). Service discovery for hyperledger fabric. *Proceedings of the 12th ACM International Conference on Distributed and Event-Based Systems.* 10.1145/3210284.3219766

Manne, R., & Kanthet, S. C. (2021). *Application of Artificial Intelligence in Healthcare: Chances and Challenges.* Current Journal of Applied Science and Technology.

Manyika, J., Chui, M., Bughin, J., Dobbs, R., Bisson, P., & Marrs, A. (2018). *Disruptive Technologies: Advances that will Transform Life, Business, and the Global Economy.* McKinsey Global Institute.

Maracha, V. (2018). Systems thinking and collective problem-solving practices. System analysis in economics. In *Proceedings of the V International research and practice conference–biennale*. Prometheus Publishing House. 10.33278/SAE-2018.eng.269-272

Marda, V. (2018). Artificial intelligence policy in India: A framework for engaging the limits of data-driven decision-making. *Philosophical Transactions - Royal Society. Mathematical, Physical, and Engineering Sciences*, *376*(2133), 20180087. doi:10.1098/rsta.2018.0087 PMID:30323001

Markus, D. G. (2020). Is the online learning, good in the Midst of Covid -19 Pandemic? The case of ETL Learners. *Journal of Sinestesia*, *10*(1), 1–10.

Martin, D. W., Sloan, M. L., Gleason, B. L., Wit, L. De, Vandi, M. A., Kargbo, D. K., … Singh, T. (2020). Implementing Nationwide Facility-based Lessons Learned. *Health Security*, *18*(S1), 1–9. doi:10.1089/hs.2019.0081

Martin, C., DeStefano, K., Haran, H., Zink, S., Dai, J., Ahmed, D., Razzak, A., Lin, K., Kogler, A., Waller, J., Kazmi, K., & Umair, M. (2022). The ethical considerations including inclusion and biases, data protection, and proper implementation among AI in radiology and potential implications. *Intelligence-Based Medicine*, *6*, 100073. doi:10.1016/j.ibmed.2022.100073

Masamila, B. (2014). State of mobile banking in Tanzania and security issues. *International Journal of Network Security & its Applications*, *6*(4), 53–64. doi:10.5121/ijnsa.2014.6405

Maternal and Child Survival Program. (2019). *Disease Surveillance MCSP Tanzania Program Brief*. Author.

Mathrani, A., Sarvesh, T., & Umer, R. (2021). Digital divide framework: Online learning in developing countries during the COVID-19 lockdown. *Globalisation, Societies and Education*, *0*(0), 1–16. doi:10.1080/14767724.2021.1981253

Mato, M., & Mosoma, D. (2022). Factors Influencing Domestic Tourism in Tanzania: A Case of Arusha City. *International Journal of Engineering Business Management*, *6*(4), 1–11. doi:10.22161/ijebm.6.4.1

Matthew, K. (2018). The digital divide – Where are we now? *IIT News Africa*. https://www.itnewsafrica.com/2018/08/the-digital-divide-where-are-we-now/

Mavrou, K., Meletiou-Mavrotheris, M., Kärki, A., Sallinen, M., & Hoogerwerf, E. J. (2017). Opportunities and challenges related to ICT and ICT-AT use by people with disabilities: An explorative study into factors that impact on the digital divide. *Technology and Disability*, *29*(1-2), 63–75. doi:10.3233/TAD-170174

Mavura, F., Pandhare, S. M., Mkoba, E., & Nyambo, D. G. (2022). Rule-Based Engine for Automatic Allocation of Smallholder Dairy Producers in Preidentified Production Clusters. *TheScientificWorldJournal*, *2022*, 2022. doi:10.1155/2022/6944151 PMID:35874847

Mawejje, J., & Lakuma, P. (2019). Macroeconomic effects of Mobile money: Evidence from Uganda. *Financial Innovation*, *5*(1), 1–20. doi:10.118640854-019-0141-5

Mbilu, A. P. (2015). *Smallholder dairy farmers' technical efficiency in milk production: case of EPINAV dairy project in Njombe District*. Sokoine University of Agriculture.

Mboera, L. E. G., Sindato, C., Mremi, I. R., Rumisha, S. F., George, J., Ngolongolo, R., Misinzo, G., Karimuribo, E. D., Rweyemamu, M. M., Haider, N., Hamid, M. A., & Kock, R. (2021). Socio-Ecological Systems Analysis and Health System Readiness in Responding to Dengue Epidemics in Ilala and Kinondoni Districts, Tanzania. *Frontiers in Tropical Diseases*, *2*(September), 1–11. doi:10.3389/fitd.2021.738758

McBride, N. J., & Bagshaw, R. (2018). *Tort Law* (6th ed.). Pearson Education Limited.

McDuie-Ra, D., & Gulson, K. (2020). The backroads of AI: The uneven geographies of artificial intelligence and development. *Area, 52*(3), 626–633. doi:10.1111/area.12602

Meghani, K. (2020). Use of artificial intelligence and Blockchain in banking sector: A study of scheduled commercial banks in India. Use of Artificial Intelligence and Blockchain in Banking Sector: A Study of Scheduled Commercial Banks in India, Kishore Meghani. *Indian Journal of Applied Research*, 10.

Mehta, S., Clarke, F., & Fleming, P. S. (2016). An assessment of student experiences and learning based on a novel undergraduate e-learning resource. *British Dental Journal, 221*(3), 131–136. doi:10.1038/sj.bdj.2016.563

Melnyk, L., Dehtyarova, I., Kubatko, O., Karintseva, O., & Derykolenko, A. (2019). Disruptive technologies for the transition of digital economies towards sustainability. *Економічний часопис-XXI*, (9-10), 22-30.

Mensah, C., Sakyi, R., & Forson, M. A. (2022). *Destination Distribution Systems and Travel Disintermediation in Emerging Economies. In Palgrave Studies of Marketing in Emerging Economies*. Springer.

Mghamba, J., Mboera, L., Krekamoo, W., Senkoro, K., Rumisha, S., Shayo, E., & Mmbuji, P. (2008). Challenges of implementing an Integrated Disease Surveillance and Response strategy using the current Health Management Information System in Tanzania. *Tanzania Health Research Bulletin, 6*(2), 57–63. doi:10.4314/thrb.v6i2.14243

Miethlich, B., & Oldenburg, A. G. (2019). The employment of persons with disabilities as a strategic asset: A resource-based-view using the value-rarity-imitability-organization (VRIO) framework. *Journal of Eastern Europe Research in Business and Economics, 1*, 1–13. doi:10.5171/2019.667087

Milian, E. Z., Spinola, M. de M., & de Carvalho, M. M. (2019). Fintechs: A literature review and research agenda. *Electronic Commerce Research and Applications, 34*. Advance online publication. doi:10.1016/J.ELERAP.2019.100833

Mills, G. M. (2022, January 15). *Exploring The Growing List Of Countries That Indicate…*. https://www.koparunescape2gold.com/exploring-the-growing-list-of-countries-that-indicate/

Milton, K. (2020). Anthropomorphism or egomorphism? The perception of non-human persons by human ones. In *Animals in person* (pp. 255–271). Routledge. doi:10.4324/9781003135883-13

Ministry of Health and Social Welfare Zanzibar. (2016). *National Guidelines for Malaria Surveillance and Response in Zanzibar*. Ministry of Health and Social Welfare Zanzibar.

Ministry of Health and Social Welfare. (2013). *Tanzania eHealth Strategy. Tanzania National eHealth Strategy June, 2013 – July, 2018*. Author.

Mishenina, H., Kirichenko, D., & Puzemsky, V. (2021). COVID-19 impact on the company's development: A case of UNIT.City. *Health Economics and Management Review*, 2(2), 58–70. doi:10.21272/hem.2021.2-06

Mishra, L., Gupta, T., & Shree, A. (2020). Online teaching-learning in higher education during lockdown period of COVID-19 pandemic. *International Journal of Educational Research Open, 1*, 100012. doi:10.1016/j.ijedro.2020.100012 PMID:35059663

Misra, N. N., Dixit, Y., Al-Mallahi, A., Bhullar, M. S., Upadhyay, R., & Martynenko, A. (2020). IoT, big data and artificial intelligence in agriculture and food industry. *IEEE Internet of Things Journal*, 1–1. doi:10.1109/JIOT.2020.2998584

Mittal, D., & Agrawal, S. R. (2022). Determining banking service attributes from online reviews: Text mining and sentiment analysis. *International Journal of Bank Marketing, 40*(3), 558–577. doi:10.1108/IJBM-08-2021-0380

Mizik, T. (2021). Climate-Smart Agriculture on Small-Scale Farms: A Systematic Literature Review. *Agronomy (Basel), 11*(6), 1096. doi:10.3390/agronomy11061096

Mkumbo, K. (2008). *Do children with disabilities have equal access to education? A research report on accessibility to education for children with disabilities in Tanzanian schools.* Retrieved on November 1, 2013 from: http://www.hakielimu.org/hakielimu/documents/document131Children_disabilities.pdf

Mnyanyi, C. B. (2014). Changing Teachers' Practices in Regular Schools Enrolling Children with Visual Impairment: An Action Research Project in Tanzania. Abo Akademi University Press.

Mnyanyi, C. B. F., Bakari, J., & Mbwette, T. S. A. (2010). *Implementing E-learning in Higher Open and Distance Learning Institutions in Developing Countries: The Experience of the Open University of Tanzania.* Paper presented at the 5th MIT LINC 2010 Conference, Boston, MA.

Mnyawi, R., Kombe, C., Sam, A., & Nyambo, D. (2022). Blockchain-based Data Storage Security Architecture for e-Health Care Systems: A Case of Government of Tanzania Hospital Management Information System. *IJCSNS, 22*(3), 364.

MoEST. (2022). *The National Science, Technology and Innovation Policy, 2022.* Academic Press.

Mogas, J., Palau, R., Fuentes, M., & Cebrián, G. (2022). Smart schools on the way: How school principals from Catalonia approach the future of education within the fourth industrial revolution. *Learning Environments Research, 25*(3), 875–893. doi:10.100710984-021-09398-3

MoHCDGEC. (2017). *DHIS 2 Functions and data use for health information system.* MOHCDGEC.

MOHCDGEC. (2019). Data systems, data generation and data use, Technical report. Ministry of Health, Community Development, Gender, Elderly and Children. *Mid Term Review of the Health Sector Strategic Plan, 4*, 2015–2020.

Mons, N. (2009). Theoretical and real effects of standardised assessment. *Eurydice Network.* https://citeseerx.ist.psu.edu/viewdoc/download?doi=10.1.1.174.4813&rep=rep1&type=pdf

Montgomery, L., Hartley, J., Neylon, C., Gillies, M., Gray, E., Herrmann-Pillath, C., Huang, C., Leach, J., Potts, J., Ren, X., Skinner, K., Sugimoto, C., & Wilson, K. (2019). Universities. *Works.*

Mori, M. (1970). The uncanny valley: The original essay by Masahiro Mori. *IEEE Spectrum.*

Morwane, R. E., Dada, S., & Bornman, J. (2021). Barriers to and facilitators of employment of persons with disabilities in low-and middle-income countries: A scoping review. *African Journal of Disability, 10*, 10. doi:10.4102/ajod.v10i0.833 PMID:34230882

Mourdoukoutas, E. (2019). *Digital revolution holds bright promises for Africa.* United Nations Africa Renewal. https://www.un.org/africarenewal/magazine/december-2017-march- 2018/digital-revolution-holds-bright-promises-Africa

Mourelatos, E., Tzagarakis, M., & Dimara, E. (2016). A review of online crowdsourcing platforms. *South-Eastern Europe Journal of Economics, 14*(1).

Mtebe, J., & Nakaka, R. (2018). Assessing electronic medical record system implementation at Kilimanjaro Christian Medical Center. Academic Press.

Mtey, M., & Dida, M. (2019). *Towards interoperable e-Health system in Tanzania: analysis and evaluation of the current security trends and big data sharing dynamics.* Academic Press.

Mureithi, C. (2022, April 4). *Why Africa's digital payment landscape is still highly fragmented*. Quartz. https://qz.com/africa/2149097/why-africas-digital-payment-landscape-is-still-highly-fragmented

Mutisya, T. M. (2020). *Adoption Of Computer Adaptive Testing In Educational Assessment In Kenya* [Doctoral dissertation]. University of Nairobi. http://erepository.uonbi.ac.ke/bitstream/handle/11295/153171/TITUS%20MUTIE%20MUTISYA%20FINAL%20PROJECT%20.pdf?sequence=1&isAllowed=y

Mützel, S. (2021). Unlocking the payment experience: Future imaginaries in the case of digital payments. *New Media & Society*, *23*(2), 284–301. doi:10.1177/1461444820929317

Muza, O., & Debnath, R. (2021). Disruptive innovation for inclusive renewable policy in sub-Saharan Africa: A social shaping of technology analysis of appliance uptake in Rwanda. *Renewable Energy*, *168*, 896–912. doi:10.1016/j.renene.2020.12.091 PMID:33942003

Mwabukusi, M., Karimuribo, E. D., Rweyemamu, M. M., & Beda, E. (2014). Mobile technologies for disease surveillance in humans and animals. *The Onderstepoort Journal of Veterinary Research*, *81*(2), 1–5. doi:10.4102/ojvr.v81i2.737 PMID:25005126

Mwamnyange, M., Luhanga, E., & Thodge, S. R. (2021). Big Data Analytics Framework for Childhood Infectious Disease Surveillance and Response System using Modified MapReduce Algorithm A Case Study of Tanzania. *International Journal of Advanced Computer Science and Applications*, *12*(3), 373–385. doi:10.14569/IJACSA.2021.0120345

Mzingula, E. P. (2019). Socio-economic impacts of smallholder dairy cattle farming on livelihood in Sunga Ward of Lushoto District, Tanzania. *International Journal of Economics and Management*, *1*(2), 41–49.

Nagasubramanian, G., Sakthivel, R. K., Patan, R., Gandomi, A. H., Sankayya, M., & Balusamy, B. (2020). Securing e-health records using keyless signature infrastructure blockchain technology in the cloud. *Neural Computing & Applications*, *32*(3), 639–647. doi:10.100700521-018-3915-1

Nagaty, K. A. (2023). IoT Commercial and Industrial Applications and AI-Powered IoT. In *Frontiers of Quality Electronic Design (QED) AI, IoT and Hardware Security* (pp. 465–500). Springer International Publishing. doi:10.1007/978-3-031-16344-9_12

Nair, P. (2022). Health Technologies and Innovations to Effectively Respond to the Covid-19 Pandemic. *Frontiers in Digital Health*, *4*, 15. doi:10.3389/fdgth.2022.849652 PMID:35237764

Natile, S. (2020). Digital Finance Inclusion and the Mobile Money "Social" Enterprise. *Historical Social Research. Historische Sozialforschung*, *45*(3), 74–94.

National Bureau of Statistics. (2008). *Tanzania disability survey*. Dar es Salaam: NBS.

Natocheeva, N., Shayakhmetova, L., Bekkhozhaeva, A., Khamikhan, N., & Pshembayeva, D. (2020). Digital technologies as a driver for the development of the tourism industry. In *E3S Web of Conferences* (Vol. 159, p. 04002). EDP Sciences. doi:10.1051/e3sconf/202015904002

Navarro, E., Costa, N., & Pereira, A. (2020). A Systematic Review of IoT Solutions for Smart Farming. *Sensors (Basel)*, *20*(15), 4231. doi:10.339020154231 PMID:32751366

Nciizah, A. D., & Wakindiki, I. I. C. (2015). Climate Smart Agriculture: Achievements and Prospects in Africa. *Journal of Geoscience and Environment Protection*, *03*(06), 99–105. doi:10.4236/gep.2015.36016

Ndagijimana, U., & Gomera, M. (2022). *Rwanda's Home-grown Solutions are key to Economic Recovery*. United Nations Development Programme. https://www.undp.org/rwanda/rwanda%E2%80%99s-home-grown-solutions-are-key-economic-recovery-dr-Uzziel-ndagijimana-and-maxwell-gomera

Nehemiah, L. (2014). *Towards EHR interoperability in Tanzania hospitals: issues, challenges and opportunities*. arXiv preprint arXiv:1410.2205.

Ngamije, J. (2021). The impact of Internet use during COVID-19 lockdown in Rwanda: a potential public health threat. Journal of Addictive Diseases, 39(3), 417–420. https://doi.org/ doi:10.1080/10550887.2021.1882649

Ngonyani, J., & Mnyanyi, C. (2021). Assessing the relevance of assistive technologies for people with disabilities in higher learning institutions: A case of university of Dar es salaam in Tanzania. *European Journal of Special Education Research*, *7*(2). Advance online publication. doi:10.46827/ejse.v7i2.3712

Nguyen, T. S. L., Jourjon, G., Potop-Butucaru, M., & Thai, K. L. (2019). *Impact of network delays on Hyperledger Fabric*. Paper presented at the IEEE INFOCOM 2019-IEEE Conference on Computer Communications Workshops (INFOCOM WKSHPS). 10.1109/INFCOMW.2019.8845168

Njeru, I., Kareko, D., Kisangau, N., Langat, D., Liku, N., Owiso, G., Dolan, S., Rabinowitz, P., Macharia, D., Ekechi, C., & Widdowson, M. (2020). Use of technology for public health surveillance reporting : Opportunities, challenges and lessons learnt from Kenya. *BMC Public Health*, *20*(1101), 1–11. doi:10.118612889-020-09222-2 PMID:32660509

Njuguna, C. (2021). *Upgrading Tanzania's dairy value chain to unlock its productivity potential*. https://www.ilri.org/news/upgrading-tanzania%E2%80%99s-dairy-value-chain-unlock-its-productivity-potential

Nkowane, B. M. (2019). *Streamlining and Strengthening the Disease Surveillance System in Tanzania, Disease Surveillance System Review, Asset Mapping, Gap Analysis, and Proposal of Strategies for Streamlining and Strengthening Disease Surveillance*. Maternal and Child Survival Program.

Noor, R., Singh, D., Agarwal, A., Mansoori, S., & Ansari, M. I. (2022). Perception of dental students towards the online method of dental education during the COVID-19 pandemic. *Journal of Oral Biology and Craniofacial Research*, *12*(2), 223–227. doi:10.1016/j.jobcr.2022.02.002 PMID:35186671

Noyes, J. M., & Garland, K. J. (2008). Computer-vs. paper-based tasks: Are they equivalent? *Ergonomics*, *51*(9), 1352–1375. doi:10.1080/00140130802170387 PMID:18802819

Nsubuga, P., Eseko, N., Wuhib, T., Ndayimirije, N., Chungong, S., & McNabb, S. (2002). Structure and performance of infectious disease surveillance and response, United Republic of Tanzania, 1998. *Bulletin of the World Health Organization*, *80*(3), 196–203. PMID:11984605

Nyambo, D. G. (2020). *Use of agent–based models in characterizing farm types and evolvement in smallholder dairy systems*. NM-AIST.

Nyambo, D. G., Luhanga, E. T., & Yonah, Z. O. (2019). Characteristics of smallholder dairy farms by association rules mining based on apriori algorithm. *International Journal of Society Systems Science*, *11*(2), 100–116. doi:10.1504/IJSSS.2019.100101

Nyambo, D. G., Luhanga, E. T., Yonah, Z. O., & Mujibi, F. D. (2019). Application of multiple unsupervised models to validate clusters robustness in characterizing smallholder dairy farmers. *TheScientificWorldJournal*, *2019*, 2019. doi:10.1155/2019/1020521 PMID:30718979

Nyambo, D. G., Luhanga, E. T., Yonah, Z. O., Mujibi, F. D. N., & Clemen, T. (2020). Leveraging peer-to-peer farmer-learning to facilitate better strategies in smallholder dairy husbandry. *Adaptive Behavior*, 1–11.

Obiakor, T., & Adeniran, A. (2020). *Covid-19. Impending Situation threatens to Deepens Nigeria's Education crisis.* Centre for the Study of the Economic Africa. Available at https://media.africaportal.org/documents/covid-19-impendingsituation-threatens-to-Deepens-Nigerias-Education-pdf

Odei-Appiah, S., Wiredu, G., & Adjei, J. K. (2022). Fintech use, digital divide and financial inclusion. *Digital Policy. Regulation & Governance*, *24*(5), 435–448. doi:10.1108/DPRG-09-2021-0111

Office, N. A. (2021). *Ripoti ya mdhibiti na mkaguzi mkuu wa hesabu za serikali kwa mwaka wa fedha 2019/2020.* The National Audit Office.

Ogunjimi, M. O., Ayanwale, M. A., Oladele, J. I., Daramola, D. S., Jimoh, I. M., & Owolabi, H. O. (2021). Simulated Evidence of Computer Adaptive Test Length: Implications for High Stakes Assessment in Nigeria. *Journal of Higher Education Theory and Practice*, *21*(2), 202–212. businesspress.com/JHETP/JHETP21-2/16_OladeleFinal.pdf

Ojha, T., Misra, S., & Raghuwanshi, N. S. (2021). Internet of Things for Agricultural Applications: The State of the Art. *IEEE Internet of Things Journal*, *8*(14), 10973–10997. doi:10.1109/JIOT.2021.3051418

Okolie, C. C., Danso-Abbeam, G., Groupson-Paul, O., & Ogundeji, A. A. (2022). Climate-Smart Agriculture Amidst Climate Change to Enhance Agricultural Production: A Bibliometric Analysis. *Land (Basel)*, *12*(1), 50. doi:10.3390/land12010050

Okoye, R. O., & Nwafor, V. C. (2009). A Comparison of SSCE Questions Set by the West African Examinations Council and the National Examinations Council, Nigeria. *African Research Review*, *3*(5). Advance online publication. doi:10.4314/afrrev.v3i5.51159

Oladele, J. I. (2022). Review of FastTest for Electronic Item Banking for Standardised Assessments: Implications for the Fourth Industrial Revolution and Covid-19 interjections. *Journal of Research and Reviews in Social sciences Pakistan*, *5*(1). https://journal.kinnaird.edu.pk/online-first/

Oladele, J. I., Ndlovu, M., & Spangenberg, E. D. (2022). Simulated computer adaptive testing Method Choices for ability estimation with empirical evidence. *The International Journal of Evaluation and Research in Education*, *11*(3). https://ijere.iaescore.com/index.php/IJERE/issue/view/565

Oladele, J. I. (2022). Estimating Measurement Error in University Students' Work Experience Programme (SWEP) Assessment using Generalizability Theory: Implications for Transdisciplinarity in Engineering Training. *Transdisciplinary Journal of Engineering & Science*, *13*. Advance online publication. doi:10.22545/2022/00185

Oladele, J. I., Ayanwale, M. A., & Owolabi, H. O. (2020). Paradigm Shifts in Computer Adaptive Testing in Nigeria in Terms of Simulated Evidence. *Journal of Social Sciences*, *63*(1-3), 9–20. doi:10.31901/24566756.2020/63.1-3.2264

Oladele, J. I., Bamidele, S.T., Ndlovu, M., & Owolabi, H.O. (2022). Adoption of Computer Adaptive Testing for Standardized Educational Assessment: Case Studies from West and South Africa. *Qualitative Report.*

Oladele, J. I., Koledafe, O. S., & Daramola, D. S. (2021). Prospects for Online Instructional Delivery Using Google Classrooms: Implications for Higher Education in Sub-Sahara Africa. *Journal of Digital Learning and Education*, *1*(3), 92–108. doi:10.52562/jdle.v1i3.227

Oladele, J. I., & Ndlovu, M. (2021). A Review of Standardised Assessment Development Procedure and Algorithms for Computer Adaptive Testing: Applications and Relevance for Fourth Industrial Revolution. *International Journal of Learning, Teaching and Educational Research*, *20*(5), 1–17. Advance online publication. doi:10.26803/ijlter.20.5.1

Olaniyi, E. T., & Akinyoola, O. G. (2021). Implication of digital Innovations for Academic Libraries amidst the covid-19 Pandemic. *Lagos Journal of Library & Information Science., 10*(1/2), 62–79.

Olifirov, A., Makoveichuk, K. A., & Petrenko, S. (2021). *Cybersecurity Measures of the Digital Payment Ecosystem.* Academic Press.

Oloyede, A. A., Faruk, N., & Raji, W. O. (2022). COVID-19 lockdown and remote attendance teaching in developing countries: A review of some online pedagogical resources. *African Journal of Science, Technology, Innovation and Development, 14*(3), 678–696. doi:10.1080/20421338.2021.1889768

Oloyode assumes office at JAMB, commends Ojerinde for adopting CBT. (2016). *The Government Business Journal.* https://govbusinessjournal.ng/2016/08/08/oloyode-assumes-office-at-jamb-commends- ojerinde-for-adopting-cbt/

Omar, M. K., Puad, M. H. M., Yaakub, M., & Muslim, M. (2022). Employability Skills Requirement for People with Disability (PWD) Job Success. *Specialusis Ugdymas, 2*(43), 367–385.

Omary, Z., Lupiana, D., Mtenzi, F., & Wu, B. (2009). Challenges to E-healthcare adoption in developing countries: A case study of Tanzania. In *2009 First International Conference on Networked Digital Technologies* (pp. 201-209). IEEE. 10.1109/NDT.2009.5272067

Ondego, B., & Moturi, C. (2016). Evaluation of the Implementation of the e-Citizen in Kenya. *International Journal of Applied Information Systems, 10*(4), 13–21. doi:10.5120/ijais2016451486

Ong, H. B., & Chong, L. L. (2022). The effect of cashless payments on the internet and mobile banking. *Journal of Financial Services Marketing.* Advance online publication. doi:10.1057/S41264-022-00145-0

Opitz, P. (2019). *Civil Liability and Autonomous Robotic Machines: Approaches in the EU and US.* TTLF Working Papers No. 43.

Oppl, S., Reisinger, F., Eckmaier, A., & Helm, C. (2017). A flexible online platform for computerised adaptive testing. *International Journal of Educational Technology in Higher Education, 14*(1), 1–21. doi:10.118641239-017-0039-0

Owusu, A. (2020). The impact of audio–visual technologies on university teaching and learning in a developing economy. *South African Journal of Information Management, 22*(1), 1–9. doi:10.4102ajim.v22i1.1235

Oyelaran-Oyeyinka, B., & Lal, K. (2005). Internet diffusion in sub-Saharan Africa: A cross-country analysis. *Telecommunications Policy.* https://www.sciencedirect.com/science/article/pii/S0308596105000479

Özekinci, E. (2018). *Anadolu Ajansı, Adım atan robot 'Akıncı-4' görücüye çıktı.* Retrieved on 12.04.2023 from https://www.aa.com.tr/tr/bilim-teknoloji/adim-atan-robot-akinci-4-gorucuye-cikti/1276507

Ozili, P. K. (2018). Impact of digital finance on financial inclusion and stability. *Borsa Istanbul Review, 18*(4), 329–340. doi:10.1016/j.bir.2017.12.003

Paas, W., & Groot, J. C. (2017). Creating adaptive farm typologies using Naive Bayesian classification. *Information Processing in Agriculture, 4*(3), 220–227. doi:10.1016/j.inpa.2017.05.005

Paik, H.-Y., Xu, X., Bandara, H. D., Lee, S. U., & Lo, S. K. (2019). Analysis of Data Management in Blockchain-Based Systems: From Architecture to Governance. *IEEE Access : Practical Innovations, Open Solutions, 7*, 186091–186107. doi:10.1109/ACCESS.2019.2961404

Pairoa, I., & Arunrangsiwed, P. (2016). The effect of brand mascots on consumers' purchasing behaviors. *International Journal of Economics and Management Engineering*, *10*(5), 1702–1705.

Pak, R., McLaughlin, A. C., & Bass, B. (2014). A multi-level analysis of the effects of age and gender stereotypes on trust in anthropomorphic technology by younger and older adults. *Ergonomics*, *57*(9), 1277–1289. doi:10.1080/00140139.2014.928750 PMID:24935771

Palanivelu, V.R., & Vasanthi, B. (2020). Article. *International Journal of Advanced Science and Technology, 29*(4).

Pardal, P., Dias, R., Šuleř, P., Teixeira, N., & Krulický, T. (2020). Integration in Central European capital markets in the context of the global COVID-19 pandemic. *Equilibrium: Quarterly Journal of Economics and Economic Policy*, *15*(4), 627–650.

Parmar, R. R., Roy, S., Bhattacharyya, D., Bandyopadhyay, S. K., & Kim, T.-H. (2017). Large-scale encryption in the Hadoop environment: Challenges and solutions. *IEEE Access : Practical Innovations, Open Solutions*, *5*, 7156–7163. doi:10.1109/ACCESS.2017.2700228

Parmenter, T. R. (2011). *Promoting training and employment opportunities for people with intellectual disabilities: international experience*. ILO.

Pascoe, L. (2016). *Electronic information capturing, processing and reporting of routine health data using smartphone-based application*. The Nelson Mandela African Institution of Science and Technology NM-AIST.

Pascoe, L., Lungo, J., Kaasbøll, J., & Koleleni, I. (2012). Collecting Integrated Disease Surveillance and Response Data through Mobile Phones. *IST-Africa*, 1–6.

Patel, D. N., Lambert, E. V., da Silva, R., Greyling, M., Nossel, C., Noach, A., Derman, W., & Gaziano, T. (2010). The association between medical costs and participation in the vitality health promotion program among 948,974 members of a South African health insurance company. *American Journal of Health Promotion*, *24*(3), 199–204. doi:10.4278/090217-QUAN-68R2.1 PMID:20073387

Patii, U., Saxena, P., & Sidnal, N. (2017). Peer-to-peer knowledge sharing platform for farmers with auto-recommendation feature. *2017 International Conference On Smart Technologies For Smart Nation (SmartTechCon)*.

Patterson, A., Khogeer, Y., & Hodgson, J. (2013). How to create an influential anthropomorphic mascot: Literary musings on marketing, make-believe, and meerkats. *Journal of Marketing Management*, *29*(1-2), 69–85. doi:10.1080/0267257X.2012.759992

Patwardhan, A. (2018). Financial inclusion in the digital age. In Handbook of Blockchain, Digital Finance, and Inclusion (vol. 1, pp. 57–89). Elsevier. doi:10.1016/B978-0-12-810441-5.00004-X

Paul, Y., Hickok, E., Sinha, A., Tiwari, U., Mohandas, S., Ray, S., & Bidare, P. M. (2018). *Artificial intelligence in the healthcare industry in India*. The Centre for Internet and Society.

Pazarbasioglu, C., & Mora, A. G. (2020). *Expanding digital financial services can help developing economies cope with crisis now and boost growth later. World BankVoices* Blog.

Pelau, C., Dabija, D. C., & Ene, I. (2021). What makes an AI device human-like? The role of interaction quality, empathy and perceived psychological anthropomorphic characteristics in the acceptance of artificial intelligence in the service industry. *Computers in Human Behavior*, *122*, 106855. doi:10.1016/j.chb.2021.106855

Pelgrum, W. J. (2001). Obstacles to the integration of ICT in education: Results from a worldwide educational assessment. *Computers & Education*, *37*(2), 163–178. doi:10.1016/S0360-1315(01)00045-8

Pérez-Ortiz, M., Peña, J. M., Gutiérrez, P. A., Torres-Sánchez, J., Hervás-Martínez, C., & López-Granados, F. (2016). Selecting patterns and features for between- and within- crop-row weed mapping using UAV-imagery. *Expert Systems with Applications*, *47*, 85–94. doi:10.1016/j.eswa.2015.10.043

Pfeuffer, N., Benlian, A., Gimpel, H., & Hinz, O. (2019). Anthropomorphic information systems. *Business & Information Systems Engineering*, *61*(4), 523–533. doi:10.100712599-019-00599-y

Phillips, B., & Lee, W. N. (2005). Interactive animation: Exploring spokes-characters on the internet. *Journal of Current Issues and Research in Advertising*, *27*(1), 1–17. doi:10.1080/10641734.2005.10505170

Pietrzykowski, T., & Kurki, V. A. J. (2017). *Legal Personhood: Animals, Artificial Intelligence and the Unborn*. Springer International Publishing AG.

Pitardi, V., & Marriott, H. R. (2021). Alexa, she's not human but… Unveiling the drivers of consumers' trust in voice-based artificial intelligence. *Psychology and Marketing*, *38*(4), 626–642. doi:10.1002/mar.21457

Pittman, J., Severino, L., DeCarlo-Tecce, M. J., & Kiosoglous, C. (2021). An action research case study: Digital equity and educational inclusion during an emergent COVID-19 divide. *Journal for Multicultural Education*, *15*(1), 68–84. doi:10.1108/JME-09-2020-0099

Plummer, J. T. (2000). How personality makes a difference. *Journal of Advertising Research*, *40*(6), 79–83. doi:10.2501/JAR-40-6-79-83

Powell, J., & Buchan, I. (2005). Electronic health records should support clinical research. *Journal of Medical Internet Research*, *7*(1). Advance online publication. doi:10.2196/JMIR.7.1.E4

Pozo, J. I., Pérez Echeverría, M. P., Cabellos, B., & Sánchez, D. L. (2021). Teaching and Learning in Times of COVID-19: Uses of Digital Technologies During School Lockdowns. *Frontiers in Psychology*, *12*, 1511. doi:10.3389/fpsyg.2021.656776 PMID:33995217

Prensky, M. (2001). Digital natives, digital immigrants part 1. *On the Horizon*, *9*(5), 1–6. doi:10.1108/10748120110424816

President's Office – Regional Administration and Local Government. (2017). *Government of Tanzania-Hospital Management Information System (GoT-HOMIS version 3.0) User Manual v1*. President's Office – Regional Administration and Local Government.

Prince, R. (2017). The relationship between school-leaving examinations and university entrance assessments: The case of the South African system. *Journal of Education (University of KwaZulu-Natal)*, (70), 133-160. http://www.scielo.org.za/scielo.php?script=sci_arttext&pid=S2520-98682017000300007

Prior, S., & Conway, M. (2008). 'All the Doors are Closing': National Deaf Services Users' Thoughts and Views on Deafness, Mental Health and Employment. *British Journal of Occupational Therapy*, *71*(3), 95–102. doi:10.1177/030802260807100304

Punch. (2021). *Hitches in the conduct of UTME, inexcusable*. Punch. https://punchng.com/hitches- in-the-conduct-of-utme-inexcusable/

Purwanti, P., Susilo, E., & Indrayani, E. (2020). Business empowerment program and household economic welfare: Lesson from Indonesia. *Journal of Asian Finance. Economics and Business*, *7*(1), 313–320. doi:10.13106/JAFEB.2020.VOL7.NO1.313

Putra, R. L., Setiawan, M., Hussein, A. S., & Yuniarinto, A. (2022). Perceived Digital Value Toward Continuous Intention to Use Among Mobile Payment Users During Pandemic Outbreak. *Frontiers in Psychology*, *0*, 1995. doi:10.3389/FPSYG.2022.892821

Quibria, M. G., Ahmed, S. N., Tschang, T., & Reyes-Macasaquit, M. L. (2002). Digital divide: Determinants and policies with special reference to Asia. *ERD Working Paper Series, 27*, 1–16.

Qureshi, M. R. N. M., Almuflih, A. S., Sharma, J., Tyagi, M., Singh, S., & Almakayeel, N. (2022). Assessment of the Climate-Smart Agriculture Interventions towards the Avenues of Sustainable Production–Consumption. *Sustainability (Basel)*, *14*(14), 8410. doi:10.3390u14148410

RadcliffeD.VoorhiesR. (2012). A digital pathway to financial inclusion. Available at SSRN 2186926.

Rahman, A. (2015). Toward a Comprehensive Conceptualization of Digital Divide and its Impact on E- Government System Success. In *Advances in Business Marketing and Purchasing* (Vol. 23). https://www.scopus.com/inward/record.url?eid=2-s2.0-84943382451&partnerID=tZOtx3y1

Raja, D. S. (2016). *Bridging the disability divide through digital technologies. Background paper for the World Development report*. The World Bank.

Rana, R. L., Giungato, P., Tarabella, A., & Tricase, C. (2019). Blockchain applications and sustainability issues. *Amfiteatru Economic, 21*(13), 669. https://doi.org/ doi:10.24818/EA/2019/S13/861

Rathnayaka, P., Mills, N., Burnett, D., De Silva, D., Alahakoon, D., & Gray, R. (2022). A mental health chatbot with cognitive skills for personalised behavioural activation and remote health monitoring. *Sensors (Basel)*, *22*(10), 3653. doi:10.339022103653 PMID:35632061

Red Cross. (2020, April 21). *What social distancing means*. https://www.redcross.org/about- us/news-and-events/news/2020/coronavirus-what-social-distancing-means.html

Reinly, J. C. (2020). *Look out Alexa, Southfield-based IT firm bets future on 'Sophie'*. Retrieved on 12.04.2023 from https://www.freep.com/story/money/business/2020/02/15/southfield-stefanini-michigan-sophie/4759791002/

Remuzzi, A., & Remuzzi, G. (2020). COVID-19 and Italy: What next? *Lancet*, *395*(10231), 1225–1228. doi:10.1016/S0140-6736(20)30627-9 PMID:32178769

Rennock, M. J., Cohn, A., & Butcher, J. R. (2018). Blockchain technology and regulatory investigations. *Practical Law Litigation*, 35-44.

Reserve Bank of India. (2020). *Annual Report 2020*. Author.

Reynolds, E. (2022). Implementation of DHIS2 for Disease Surveillance in Guinea : 2015 – 2020. *Frontiers in Public Health, 9*, 2015–2020. doi:10.3389/fpubh.2021.761196

Reynolds, M., Blackmore, C., Ison, R., Shah, R., & Wedlock, E. (2018). The role of systems thinking in the practice of implementing sustainable development goals. In *Handbook of sustainability science and research* (pp. 677–698). Springer. doi:10.1007/978-3-319-63007-6_42

Ribeiro, R. (2020, April 14). How university faculty embraced the remote learning shift. *EdTechMagazine*. https://edtechmagazine.com/higher/article/2020/04/how-university-faculty-embraced-remote-learning-shif

Riches, V., Gadow, F., & MacDonald, J. (2018). Transition from university to employment. In *People with intellectual disability experiencing university life* (pp. 255–266). Brill.

Rizki Habibulah, R. (2020). *The Criminal Liability of Artificial Intelligence: Is It Plausible to Hitherto Indonesian Criminal System?* Academic Press.

Robertson, J. (2020). *Zoom Guide*. Google Search. https://www.google.com/search?q=Robertson%2C+Julia.+2020.+Zoom+Guide.pdf&rlz=1C1CHWL_enGH964GH965&oq=Robertson%2C+Julia.+2020.+Zoom+Guide.pdf&aqs=chrome.69i57j69i60.1010j0j4&sourceid=chrome&ie=UTF-8

Rodríguez-Abitia, G., Martínez-Pérez, S., Ramirez-Montoya, M. S., & Lopez-Caudana, E. (2020). Digital gap in universities and challenges for quality education: A diagnostic study in Mexico and Spain. *Sustainability (Basel)*, *12*(21), 9069. doi:10.3390u12219069

Rodriguez-Carrion, A., Rebollo-Monedero, D., Forné, J., Campo, C., Garcia-Rubio, C., Parra-Arnau, J., & Das, S. K. (2015). Entropy-based privacy against profiling of user mobility. *Entropy (Basel, Switzerland)*, *17*(6), 3913–3946. doi:10.3390/E17063913

Rossum, C. V. (2018). *Liability of robots: Legal responsibility in cases of errors or malfunctioning, LLM Paper*. Ghent University.

Rumisha, S. F., Lyimo, E. P., Mremi, I. R., Tungu, P. K., Mwingira, V. S., Mbata, D., Malekia, S. E., Joachim, C., & Mboera, L. E. G. (2020). Data quality of the routine health management information system at the primary healthcare facility and district levels in Tanzania. *BMC Medical Informatics and Decision Making*, *20*(1), 1–22. doi:10.118612911-020-01366-w PMID:33334323

Rumisha, S. F., Mboera, L. E., Senkoro, K. P., Gueye, D., & Mmbuji, P. K. (2007). Monitoring and evaluation of integrated disease surveillance and response in selected districts in Tanzania. *Tanzania Health Research Bulletin*, *9*(1), 1–11. doi:10.4314/thrb.v9i1.14285 PMID:17547094

Rutatola, E. P., Yonah, Z. O., Nyambo, D. G., Mchau, G. J., & Musabila, A. K. (2018). A Framework for Timely and More Informative Epidemic Diseases Surveillance: The Case of Tanzania. *Journal of Health Informatics in Developing Countries*, *12*(2).

Saad, M., Spaulding, J., Njilla, L., Kamhoua, C., Shetty, S., Nyang, D., & Mohaisen, A. (2019). *Exploring the attack surface of blockchain: A systematic overview*. arXiv preprint arXiv:1904.03487.

Sahara Ventures. (2019). *Artificial Intelligence in Tanzania, What's happening? Latest Information on Artificial Intelligence Startups and projects in Tanzania*. Author.

Sahi, A. M., Khalid, H., & Abbas, A. F. (2021). Digital payment adoption: A review (2015-2020). *Journal of Management Information & Decision Sciences*, *24*(7).

Sahu, G. P., & Singh, N. K. (2018). Identifying Critical Success Factor (CSFs) for the adoption of digital payment systems: A study of Indian national banks. *Emerging Markets from a Multidisciplinary Perspective: Challenges, Opportunities and Research Agenda*, 61–73.

Said, M. (2023, March 15). *Samia forms council to oversee food, agriculture—Daily News*. https://dailynews.co.tz/samia-forms-council-to-oversee-food-agriculture/, https://dailynews.co.tz/samia-forms-council-to-oversee-food-agriculture/

Saini. (2018). Understanding the role of institutional repository in digital preservation in Academic libraries: A Review of Literature. *Library Philosophy & Practice, 1904.*

Salasya, B., & Stoorvogel, J. (2010). Fuzzy classification for farm household characterization. *Outlook on Agriculture, 39*(1), 57–63.

Saleh, F., Kitau, J., Konradsen, F., Mboera, L. E. G., & Schiøler, K. L. (2021). Assessment of the core and support functions of the integrated disease surveillance and response system in Zanzibar, Tanzania. *BMC Public Health, 21*(1), 1–12. doi:10.118612889-021-10758-0 PMID:33865347

Salles, A., Evers, K., & Farisco, M. (2020). Anthropomorphism in AI. *AJOB Neuroscience, 11*(2), 88–95. doi:10.1080/21507740.2020.1740350 PMID:32228388

Sampene, A. K., Agyeman, F. O., Robert, B., & Wiredu, J. (2022). Artificial Intelligence as a Path Way to Africa's TransformationS. *Artificial Intelligence, 9*(1).

Saner, R., Yiu, L., & Filadoro, M. (2019). Tourism development in least developed countries: Challenges and opportunities. *Sustainable Tourism: Breakthroughs in Research and Practice*, 94-120.

Sankar, L. S., Sindhu, M., & Sethumadhavan, M. (2017). *Survey of consensus protocols on blockchain applications.* Paper presented at the 2017 4th International Conference on Advanced Computing and Communication Systems (ICACCS). 10.1109/ICACCS.2017.8014672

Sardana, V., & Singhania, S. (2018). Digital technology in the realm of banking: A review of literature. *International Journal of Research in Finance and Management, 1*(2), 28–32.

Schill, R. (2011). *Social networking teens are more likely to drink, and use drugs, study finds.* Retrieved on March 01, 202e from the website: https://jjie.org/teens-on-facebook-more-likely-drink-or-use-drugs-study-finds/

Seattle, W. A. (2018). *Financing global health 2017: funding universal health coverage and the unfinished HIV.* AIDS Agenda.

Selbonne, S., Guindé, L., Causeret, F., Chopin, P., Sierra, J., Tournebize, R., & Blazy, J.-M. (2023). How to Measure the Performance of Farms with Regard to Climate-Smart Agriculture Goals? A Set of Indicators and Its Application in Guadeloupe. *Agriculture, 13*(2), 297. doi:10.3390/agriculture13020297

Seo, S. (2022). When Female (Male) Robot Is Talking To Me: Effect of service robots' gender and anthropomorphism on customer satisfaction. *International Journal of Hospitality Management, 102*, 103166. doi:10.1016/j.ijhm.2022.103166

Serrate, J. S., Lopez, C., Unver, H., Drobyshovsky, S., & Trunin, P. (2020). Digital money is here: G20 (Thinking) must go digital. A systemic agenda is necessary to steer the risky transition process and reap long-term benefits. *G20 Insights.* https://www.g20-insights.org/policy_briefs/digital-money-is-here-g20-thinking-must-go-digital-a-systemic-agenda-is-neces
sary-to-steer-the-risky-transition-process-and-reap-long-ter
m-benefits/

Setor, T. K., Senyo, P. K., & Addo, A. (2021a. Do digital payment transactions reduce corruption? Evidence from developing countries. *Telematics and Informatics, 60*, 101577. doi:10.1016/J.TELE.2021.101577

Severson, R. L., & Woodard, S. R. (2018). Imagining others' minds: The positive relation between children's role play and anthropomorphism. *Frontiers in Psychology, 9*, 2140. doi:10.3389/fpsyg.2018.02140 PMID:30483176

Shahnaz, A., Qamar, U., & Khalid, A. (2019). Using blockchain for electronic health records. *IEEE Access : Practical Innovations, Open Solutions*, *7*, 147782–147795. doi:10.1109/ACCESS.2019.2946373

Shahul Ikram, N. A. H., & Zul Kepli, M.Y. (2018). Establishing Legal Rights and Liabilities for Artificial. IIUM Law Journal, 26(1).

Shahzad, S. J. H., Anas, M., & Bouri, E. (2022). Price explosiveness in cryptocurrencies and Elon Musk's tweets. *Finance Research Letters*, *47*, 102695. doi:10.1016/J.FRL.2022.102695

Shapiro, J. S. (1999). Loneliness: Paradox or artifacts? *The American Psychologist*, *54*(9), 782–783. doi:10.1037/0003-066X.54.9.782

Shum, H. Y., He, X. D., & Li, D. (2018). From Eliza to XiaoIce: Challenges and opportunities with social chatbots. *Frontiers of Information Technology & Electronic Engineering*, *19*(1), 10–26. doi:10.1631/FITEE.1700826

Sindato, C., Mboera, L. E. G., Beda, E., Mwabukusi, M., & Karimuribo, E. D. (2021). Community health workers and disease surveillance in Tanzania: Promoting the use of mobile technologies in detecting and reporting health events. *Health Security*, *19*(1), 116–129. doi:10.1089/hs.2019.0096 PMID:33217238

Sineviciene, L., Hens, L., Kubatko, O., Melnyk, L., Dehtyarova, I., & Fedyna, S. (2021). Socio-economic and cultural effects of disruptive industrial technologies for sustainable development. *International Journal of Global Energy Issues*, *43*(2-3), 284–305. doi:10.1504/IJGEI.2021.115150

Singh, D., Bajpai, N., & Kulshreshtha, K. (2021). The effect of brand anthropomorphism on customers' behaviour towards the indian hypermarket brands. *Journal of Creative Communications*, *16*(3), 266–284. doi:10.1177/09732586211002104

Singh, P., & Rajput, R. S. (2019). Cybersecurity analysis in the context of digital wallets. *International Journal of Advanced Studies of Scientific Research*, *4*(3).

Singh, S. K., & Bhattacharya, K. (2017). Does easy availability of cash affect corruption? Evidence from a panel of countries. *Economic Systems*, *41*(2), 236–247. doi:10.1016/J.ECOSYS.2016.06.002

Singh, U. S., Singh, N., Gulati, K., Bhasin, N. K., & Sreejith, P. M. (2022). A study on the revolution of consumer relationships as a combination of human interactions and digital transformations. *Materials Today: Proceedings*, *51*, 460–464. doi:10.1016/j.matpr.2021.05.578

Sipior, J., & Ward, B. (2011). *The digital divide and t-government in the United States: using the technology acceptance model to understand usage.* Taylor & Francis. doi:10.1057/ejis.2010.64

Sirbikyte, G. (2015). Liability for damages caused by artificial intelligence. *Computer Law & Security Review.*

Sırt, T. (2023). *Meet Cere: Türkiye's first AI-powered mobile chatbot.* Retrieved on 12.04.2023 from https://www.dailysabah.com/business/tech/meet-cere-turkiyes-first-ai-powered-mobile-chatbot

Sitorus, T., & Yustisia, M. (2018). The influence of service quality and customer trust toward customer loyalty: The role of customer satisfaction. *International Journal of Qualitative Research*, *12*(3), 639.

Sivathanu, B. (2019). Adoption of digital payment systems in the era of demonetization in India: An empirical study. *Journal of Science and Technology Policy Management*, *10*(1), 143–171.

Slimani, T., & Lazzez, A. (2014). *Efficient analysis of pattern and association rule mining approaches.* arXiv preprint arXiv:1402.2892.

Slycan Trust. (2021). *Issue Paper: Challenges and Opportunities for a Just Transition.* ReliefWeb. https://www.slycantrust.org/knowledge-resources/issues-paper-challenges-and-opportunities-for-a-just-transition

Sobaih, A. E. E., Palla, I. A., & Baquee, A. (2022). A Social Media Use in E-Learning amid Covid-19 Pandemic: Indian Students Perspective. *International Journal of Environmental Research and Public Health, 19*(9), 5380. doi:10.3390/ijerph19095380 PMID:35564771

Song, X., Xu, B., & Zhao, Z. (2022). Can people experience romantic love for artificial intelligence? An empirical study of intelligent assistants. *Information & Management, 59*(2), 103595. doi:10.1016/j.im.2022.103595

Sousa, J., Bessani, A., & Vukolic, M. (2018). *A byzantine fault-tolerant ordering service for the hyperledger fabric blockchain platform.* Paper presented at the 2018 48th annual IEEE/IFIP international conference on dependable systems and networks (DSN). 10.1109/DSN.2018.00018

Sowmiya, S., Ramachandran, M., Chinnasamy, S., Prasanth, V., & Sriram, S. (2022). A Study on Humanoid Robots and Its Psychological Evaluation. *Design. Modelling and Fabrication of Advanced Robots, 1*(1), 48–54. doi:10.46632/dmfar/1/1/8

Srivastava, N. (2019). Digital Financial Services: Challenges and Prospects for Liberalized and Globalized Indian Economy. *Proceedings of 10th International Conference on Digital Strategies for Organizational Success.* 10.2139srn.3309294

Statista. (2021). *Tanzania voice telecom and internet penetration 2020.* Statista.

Statista. (n.d.). *Mobile POS Payments—Tanzania | Statista Market Forecast.* Statista. Retrieved 1 April 2023, from https://www.statista.com/outlook/dmo/fintech/digital-payments/mobile-pos-payments/tanzania

Stefan, G., Coca, O., Creanga, D. E., Mursa, G. C., & Mihai, C. (2020). The impact of the crisis generated by covid-19 on the population concerns. A comparative study at the level of the European Union. *Transformations in Business & Economics*, 19.

Stofkova, K. R., Laitkep, D., & Stofkova, Z. (2022). Shopping Behavior in the Context of the Digital Economy. *Journal of Risk and Financial Management, 15*(2). Advance online publication. doi:10.3390/JRFM15020039

Sukums, F., Mzurikwao, D., Sabas, D., Chaula, R., Mbuke, J., Kabika, T., Kaswija, J., Ngowi, B., Noll, J., Winkler, A. S., & Andersson, S. W. (2023). The use of artificial intelligence-based innovations in the health sector in Tanzania: A scoping review. *Health Policy and Technology, 12*(1), 100728. doi:10.1016/j.hlpt.2023.100728

Sukums, F., Simba, D., Kumalija, C., Asiimwe, S., Pothepragada, S., & Githendu, P. (2021). Avoiding pitfalls: Key insights and lessons learnt from customizing and rolling out a national web-based system in Tanzania. *The Electronic Journal on Information Systems in Developing Countries, 87*(6), 1–16. doi:10.1002/isd2.12193

Sullivan, H. R., & Schweikart, S. J. (2019). Are Current Tort Liability Doctrines Adequate for Addressing Injury Caused by AI? *AMA Journal of Ethics, 21*(2). PMID:30794126

Sun, T., Spiess, K., & Kulakoglu, A. (2016). *G20 High-Level Principles for digital Financial inclusion.* https://www.gpfi.org/sites/gpfi/files/G20%20High%20Level%20Principles%20for%20Digital%20Financial%20Inclusion.pdf

Sun, J., & Liu, Z. (2019). Analysis of public satisfaction on the webcast in Taiyuan city, Shanxi Province. *2019 International Conference on Management, Finance and Social Sciences Research (MFSSR 2019) Analysis.* https://doi.org/10.25236/mfssr.2019.157

Sun, Y., Zhang, L., Feng, G., Yang, B., Cao, B., & Imran, M. A. (2019). Blockchain-enabled wireless Internet of Things: Performance analysis and optimal communication node deployment. *IEEE Internet of Things Journal*, *6*(3), 5791–5802. doi:10.1109/JIOT.2019.2905743

Suri, T. (2017). Mobile money. *Annual Review of Economics*, *9*, 497–520. doi:10.1146/ANNUREV-ECONOMICS-063016-103638

Surpass. (2019). *Computer Adaptive Testing: Background, benefits and case study of a large-scale national testing programme*. Surpass. https://surpass.com/news/2019/computer- adaptive-testing-background-benefits-and-case- study-of-a-large-scale-national-testing-programme/

Suyunchaliyeva, M. M., Nautiyal, R., Shaikh, A. A., & Sharma, R. (2021). *The Use of Mobile Payment Systems in Post-COVID-19 Economic Recovery: Primary Research on an Emerging Market for Experience Goods*. https://doi.org/doi:10.3390/su132413511

Swamy, M. (2022). Speech Enhancement, Databases, Features and Classifiers in Automatic Speech Recognition. *RE:view*.

Symulevich, A., & Hamilton, M. (2022). Using Open Access Institutional Repositories to Save the Student Symposium during the COVID-19 Pandemic. *Information Technology and Libraries*, *41*(1). Advance online publication. doi:10.6017/ital.v41i1.14175

Takwa, E. (2022, December 30). *How digitalisation accelerates Tanzania's economic growth—Daily News*. https://dailynews.co.tz/how-digitalisation-accelerates-tanzanias-economic-growth/, https://dailynews.co.tz/how-digitalisation-accelerates-tanzanias-economic-growth/

Taneja, M., Jalodia, N., Malone, P., Byabazaire, J., Davy, A., & Olariu, C. (2019). Connected cows: Utilizing fog and cloud analytics toward data-driven decisions for smart dairy farming. *IEEE Internet of Things Magazine*, *2*(4), 32–37. doi:10.1109/IOTM.0001.1900045

Tătar, C. F., Herman, G. V., & Gozner, M. (2018). Tourist guides' contribution to sustainability in Romania. *Geo Journal of Tourism and Geosites*, *21*(1), 282–287. doi:10.30892/gtg.21122-287

Taylor, E. (2016). Mobile payment technologies in retail: A review of potential benefits and risks. *International Journal of Retail & Distribution Management*, *44*(2), 159–177. doi:10.1108/IJRDM-05-2015-0065

Team, T. C. E. R. (2019-2021). *Tanzania Computer Emergency Response Team-Honeypots weekly report*. Dar-es-Salaam: Tanzania Communication Regulatory Authority.

Thakur, D., & Chander, M. (2018). Use of social media in agricultural extension: Some evidences from India. *International Journal of Science, Environment and Technology*, *7*(4), 1334–1346.

The World Bank. (2021). *The Global Findex Database 2021*. Author.

Thiam, S. M. b., & Matofari, J. W. (2018). The Role of Information and Communication Sharing Pathway in Improving Peri-Urban Dairy System of Bamako, Mali. *American Journal of Science. Engineering and Technology*, *3*(1), 21.

Thomas, S. (2016). *Future Ready Learning: Reimagining the Role of Technology in Education*. 2016 National Education Technology Plan. Office of Educational Technology, US Department of Education. https://eric.ed.gov/?id=ED571884

Thompson, N. A. (2019). *What Is Computerized Adaptive Testing?* Assessment System Corporation. https://assess.com/what-is-computerized-adaptive-testing/

Thompson, S. (2018). Mobile Technology and Inclusion of Persons with Disabilities. K4D Emerging Issues Report. Brighton, UK: Institute of Development Studies.

Thompson, K. M., & Afzal, W. (2011). A look at information access through physical, intellectual, and socio-cultural lenses. *OMNES: The Journal of Multicultural Society*, *2*(2), 22–42. doi:10.15685/omnes.2011.12.2.2.22

Thompson, N. A., & Weiss, D. A. (2011). A Framework for the Development of Computerised Adaptive Tests. *Practical Assessment, Research & Evaluation*, *16*(1). Advance online publication. doi:10.7275/wqzt-9427

Tiutiunyk, I., Humenna, Y., & Flaumer, A. (2021). COVID-19 Impact on Business Sector Activity in the EU Countries: Digital Issues. *Health Economics and Management Review*, *1*, 54–66. doi:10.21272/hem.2021.1

Toledo, I. (2018). Are Cows Comfortable in Modern Dairy Facilities? AN349, 12/2018. *EDIS, 2018*(6).

Tomcikova, L., Svetozarovova, N., & Coculova, J. (2021). Challenges and priorities in talent management during the global pandemic caused by COVID-19. *Marketing and Management of Innovations*, *5*(2), 94–103. doi:10.21272/mmi.2021.2-08

Tororei, K. (2009). The right to work: A strategy for addressing the invisibility of people with disability. *Disability Studies Quarterly*, *29*(4). Advance online publication. doi:10.18061/dsq.v29i4.973

Torres, N. M. S. (2022). *Awareness of new payment technologies in the digital banking transformation-Accelerated by the COVID 19 pandemia* [PhD Thesis].

Towers, A., Field, J., Stokes, C., Maddock, S., & Martin, N. (2019). A scoping review of the use and application of virtual reality in pre-clinical dental education. *British Dental Journal, 226*(5), 358–366. doi:10.1038/s41415-019-0041-0

Tran, V. D. (2013). Theoretical Perspectives Underlying the Application of Cooperative Learning in Classrooms. *International Journal of Higher Education*, *2*(4), 101–115. doi:10.5430/ijhe.v2n4p101

Tricco, A. C., Lillie, E., Zarin, W., O'Brien, K. K., Colquhoun, H., Levac, D., Moher, D., Peters, M. D. J., Horsley, T., Weeks, L., Hempel, S., Akl, E. A., Chang, C., McGowan, J., Stewart, L., Hartling, L., Aldcroft, A., Wilson, M. G., Garritty, C., ... Straus, S. E. (2018). PRISMA extension for scoping reviews (PRISMA-ScR): Checklist and explanation. *Annals of Internal Medicine*, *169*(7), 467–473. doi:10.7326/M18-0850 PMID:30178033

Tripathi, P., & Saxena, P. (2020). Are robots criminally liable? *International Journal of Creative Research Thoughts*, *8*(12).

Tripney, J., Hogrebe, N., Schmidt, E., Vigurs, C., & Stewart, R. (2019). Employment supports for adults with disabilities in low-and middle-income countries: A Campbell systematic review. *Research on Social Work Practice*, *29*(3), 243–255. doi:10.1177/1049731517715316

Tronnier, F., Harborth, D., & Hamm, P. (2022). Investigating privacy concerns and trust in the digital Euro in Germany. *Electronic Commerce Research and Applications*, *53*, 101158. doi:10.1016/J.ELERAP.2022.101158

Tsoulias, K., Palaiokrassas, G., Fragkos, G., Litke, A., & Varvarigou, T. A. (2020). A Graph Model Based Blockchain Implementation for Increasing Performance and Security in Decentralized Ledger Systems. *IEEE Access : Practical Innovations, Open Solutions*, *8*, 130952–130965. doi:10.1109/ACCESS.2020.3006383

Turiansky, E. J. Q. A. (2021). *Unlocking the Dairy Sector's Potential for Smallholder Farmers*. Mathematica. https://www.mathematica.org/blogs/unlocking-the-dairy-sectors-potential-for-smallholder-farmers

Turmusani, M. (2012). The employability of people with disabilities and groups at risk in enterprises of skills development: International Perspective of Convention on the Rights of People with Disabilities (CRDP). *Revue Développement humain, handicap et changement social, 20*(3), 7-24.

Twaig, O. (2020). *Whose robot is it anyway? Liability for artificial-intelligence-based robots. Academic Press.*

Ugwuegbe, U., Iloh, E. & Urama, N.E. (2018). *Meeting the 2030 SDG in Nigeria: The Role Of Entrepreneurship Development.* AfriHeritage Policy Brief No. 16.

Ukwoma, S. C., & Okafor, V. N. (2017). Institutional Repository in Nigerian Universities: Trends and Development. *Library Collections, Acquisitions & Technical Services, 40*(1-2), 46–57. doi:10.1080/14649055.2017.1331653

Ullmann, H., Jones, F., Williams, R. C., & Williams, D. (2018). *Information and communications technologies for the inclusion and empowerment of people with disabilities in Latin America and the Caribbean.* Academic Press.

UNCTAD. (2020). United Republic of Tanzania Rapid eTrade Readiness Assessment. United Nations.

UNDESA. (2012). *Building a better tomorrow: the voices of young people with disabilities.* Department of Economic and Social Affairs.

UNESCO-Institute of Statistics. (2015). *Uganda National Examinations Board – Government.* http://nada.uis.unesco.org/nada/en/index.php/catalogue/105

University of Cape Town. (2022). *Centre for Educational Assessment (CEA).* http://www.ched.uct.ac.za/ched/cetap

Urassa, J., & Raphael, E. (2017). *The contribution of small scale dairy farming to community welfare: A case study of Morogoro Municipality.* Academic Press.

URT. (2019). *Digital health strategy: July 2019-June 2024.* URT.

USAID. (2019). *Health Information Systems Interoperability Maturity Toolkit.* USAID.

Utrecht University. (2022). *Why transdisciplinary research?* https://www.uu.nl/en/research/transdisciplinary-field-guide/get-started/why-transdisciplinary-research

van Deursen, A. J. A. M., & van Dijk, J. A. G. M. (2018). *The first-level digital divide shifts from inequalities in physical access to inequalities in material access.* doi:10.1177/1461444818797082

van Dijk, J., & Hacker, K. (2011). *The Digital Divide as a Complex and Dynamic Phenomenon.* https://doi.org/doi:10.1080/01972240309487

van Dijk, J. A. G. M. (2005). The Deepening Divide: Inequality in the Information Society. Thousand Oaks, CA: Sage, 2005, 240 pp., ISBN 141290403X (paperback). *Mass Communication & Society, 11*(2), 221–224. doi:10.1080/15205430701528655

Van Schalkwyk, F. (2018). *Connecting Flows and Places: Making data Useful to Hyperlocal Communities in Tanzania.* Retrieved from https://www.academia.edu/38423614/Connecting_Flows_and_Places_Making_Data_Useful_to_Hyperlocal_Communities_in_Tanzania

van Schalkwyk, F. S. R. W. (2018). Connecting Flows and Places. Dar es Salaam: DataZetu.

Varshney, D., Kumar, A., Mishra, A. K., Rashid, S., & Joshi, P. K. (2021). India's COVID-19 social assistance package and its impact on the agriculture sector. *Agricultural Systems, 189*, 103049. doi:10.1016/J.AGSY.2021.103049

Vericash, C. I. T. (2023, January 19). Digital Payments in Africa. *CIT Vericash.* https://citvericash.com/digital-payments-in-africa/

Verkijika, S. F. (2018). Factors influencing the adoption of mobile commerce applications in Cameroon. *Telematics and Informatics, 35*(6), 1665–1674. doi:10.1016/J.TELE.2018.04.012

Verma, S., Sharma, J., Kaushik, K., & Vyas, V. (2023). Mounting Cases of Cyber-Attacks and Digital Payment. In Cybersecurity Issues, Challenges, and Solutions in the Business World (pp. 59–80). IGI Global.

Viner, R., Russell, S., & Croker, H. (n.d.). *School closure and management practices during coronavirus outbreaks including COVID-19: A rapid systematic review.* Elsevier. Retrieved June 30, 2022, from https://www.sciencedirect.com/science/article/pii/S235246422030095X

Vinitha, K., & Vasantha, S. (2017). Influence of demographic variables on usage of e-payment system. *Int J Mech Eng Technol*, *8*, 265–276.

W.H.O. (2020). *Coronavirus disease (COVID-19) pandemic.* World Health Organization. https://www.who.int/emergencies/diseases/novel-coronavirus-2019

Wachira, A. C. (2023, March 3). Global Finance Magazine - Africa: Digital Payments Progress. *Global Finance Magazine.* https://www.gfmag.com/magazine/march-2023/africa-digital-payments-progress

Wakarima. (2022, May 13). *Africa accounts for 70% of the World's $ 1 trillion Mobile Money Market—Kenyan Wallstreet.* https://kenyanwallstreet.com/africa-accounts-70-of-the-worlds-mobile-money/

Wang, C., & Chu, X. (2020). *Performance characterization and bottleneck analysis of hyperledger fabric.* Paper presented at the 2020 IEEE 40th International Conference on Distributed Computing Systems (ICDCS). 10.1109/ICDCS47774.2020.00165

Wang, H., & Zhang, J. (2019). Blockchain Based Data Integrity Verification for Large-Scale IoT Data. *IEEE Access : Practical Innovations, Open Solutions*, *7*, 164996–165006. doi:10.1109/ACCESS.2019.2952635

Wardel, I.A. (2022). Product Liability Applied to Automated Decisions, Law school student scholarship. Seton Hall University.

Waytz, A., Cacioppo, J., & Epley, N. (2010). Who sees human? The stability and importance of individual differences in anthropomorphism. *Perspectives on Psychological Science*, *5*(3), 219–232. doi:10.1177/1745691610369336 PMID:24839457

WB. (2014, September 8). *The opportunities of digitizing payments: How digitization of payments, transfers, and remittances contributes to the G20 goals of broad-based economic growth, financial inclusion, and women's economic empowerment - GSDRC.* https://gsdrc.org/document-library/the-opportunities-of-digitizing-payments-how-digitization-of-payments-transfers-and-remittances-contributes-to-the-g20-goals-of-broad-based-economic-growth-financial-inclusion-and-womens/, https://gsdrc.org/document-library/the-opportunities-of-digitizing-payments-how-digitization-of-payments-transfers-and-remittances-contributes-to-the-g20-goals-of-broad-based-economic-growth-financial-inclusion-and-womens/

Webex, C. (2014). *How would you like to work together? Cisco Webex Events Cisco Webex Training Offer courses and training.* Luettavissa. Http://Www.Webex.Com/Products/Webconferencing.Html

Weisman, W. D., & Peña, J. F. (2021). Face the uncanny: The effects of doppelganger talking head avatars on affect-based trust toward artificial intelligence technology are mediated by uncanny valley perceptions. *Cyberpsychology, Behavior, and Social Networking*, *24*(3), 182–187. doi:10.1089/cyber.2020.0175 PMID:33646048

Wellcom.com. (2018). *WellDoc Validates Potential of Its Digital Therapeutic, BlueStar®, to Significantly Reduce Healthcare Costs*. Author.

Wernick, D. (2016). Innovation in Africa: A view from the peaks and hilltops of a spiky continent. *Innovation in Emerging Markets*, 121-139.

White, H. (2023). *PROFITENCE 2022 E-commerce Report: Banking & Online Payment Gateways*. Academic Press.

White, L.F., & Chopra, S. (2014). *A Legal Theory for Autonomous Artificial Agents*. The University of Michigan Press.

WHO Regional Office for Africa. (2019). *Integrated Disease Surveillance and Response Technical Guidelines, Booklet One: Introduction Section*. WHO Regional Office for Africa.

WHO. (2016a). *Framework on integrated people-centred health services. Report by the Secretariat. World Health Organization.*

WHO. (2016b). *Global Health Estimates*. Retrieved from https://www.who.int/data/gho/data/themes/mortality-and-global-health-estimates

WHO. (2018). *Non Communicable Diseases*. Retrieved from https://www.who.int/news-room/fact-sheets/detail/noncommunicable-diseases

WHO. (n.d.-a). Retrieved from https://www.afro.who.int/

WHO. (n.d.-b). Retrieved from https://www.afro.who.int

Williamson, O. E. (1975). *Markets and hierarchies: analysis and antitrust implications: a study in the economics of internal organization*. University of Illinois at Urbana-Champaign's Academy for Entrepreneurial Leadership Historical Research Reference in Entrepreneurship.

Wirtz, J., Patterson, P. G., Kunz, W. H., Gruber, T., Lu, V. N., Paluch, S., & Martins, A. (2018). Brave new world: Service robots in the frontline. *Journal of Service Management*, *29*(5), 907–931. doi:10.1108/JOSM-04-2018-0119

World Bank. (2021). *Project Appraisal Document on a Proposed Credit in the Amount of SDR 105.9 Million (US$150 Million Equivalent) to the United Republic of Tanzania for the Digital Tanzania Project*. https://documents1.worldbank.org/curated/en/485771622426544909/pdf/Tanzania-Digital-Tanzania-Project.pdf

World Bank. (2021). *Remote Learning During Covid-19 Lockdown is Preventing Learning Loss in Nigeria*. https://www.worldbank.org/en/news/feature/2021/12/08/remote-learning-during-covid-19-lockdown-is-preventing-learning-loss-in-nigeria

World Bank's World Development Report. (2016). *Digital Dividends*. Washington DC: International Bank for Reconstruction and Development/The World Bank.

World Economic Forum. (2015). *Future of Economic Progress: Why education is the key to sustainable development*. https://www.weforum.org/agenda/2015/05/why-education-is- the-key-to-sustainable-development/

World Economic Forum. (2017). *The Travel & Tourism Competitiveness Report 2017: Paving the Way for a More Sustainable and Inclusive Future*. https://www3.weforum.org/docs/WEF_TTCR_2017_web_0401.pdf

World Economic Forum. (2020). *Latin America and Caribbean Travel & Tourism Competitiveness Landscape Report: Assessing Regional Opportunities and Challenges in the Context of COVID-19*. https://www3.weforum.org/docs/ WEF_LAC_Tourism_Compet_Report_2020.pdf

World Economic Forum. (2022). *The Travel & Tourism Development Index 2021: Rebuilding for a Sustainable and Resilient Future*. https://www3.weforum.org/docs/WEF_Travel_Tourism_Development_2021.pdf

World Health Organization & World Bank. (2011). *World report on disability 2011*. World Health Organization.

World Health Organization. (2016). *Monitoring and evaluating digital health interventions. A practical guide to conducting research and assessment*. WHO. Retrieved from https://www.who.int/reproductivehealth/publications/mhealth/digital-health-interventions/en/%0Ahttp://www.who.int/reprod uctivehealth/publications/mhealth/digital-health-interventio ns/en/

World Health Organization. (2018). *Deafness and hearing loss*. WHO.

World Health Organization. (2018). *WHO Water, Sanitation and Hygiene strategy 2018-2025*. World Health Organization. Retrieved from https://apps.who.int/iris/bitstream/handle/10665/274273/WHO-CED-PHE-WSH-18.03-eng.pdf

World Health Organization. (2021). *World Report on hearing*. WHO.

Wright, J. (2019). Robots vs migrants? Reconfiguring the future of Japanese institutional eldercare. *Critical Asian Studies*, *51*(3), 331–354. doi:10.1080/14672715.2019.1612765

Yadav, P., Bisoyi, D., & Chakrabati, D. (2015). Anthropomorphic Brand Mascot Serve as the vehicle: To quickly remind customers who you are and what you stand for in Indian Cultural context. *International Scientific Research and Experimental Development*, 1814-1818.

Yang, S., Lu, Y., Gupta, S., Cao, Y., & Zhang, R. (2012). Mobile payment services adoption across time: An empirical study of the effects of behavioral beliefs, social influences, and personal traits. *Computers in Human Behavior*, *28*(1), 129–142. doi:10.1016/J.CHB.2011.08.019

Yao, M. Z., & Zhong, Z. (2014). Loneliness, social contacts, and Internet addiction: A cross-lagged panel study. *Computers in Human Behavior*, *30*, 164–170. doi:10.1016/j.chb.2013.08.007

Yeasmin, S. (2019). Benefits of artificial intelligence in medicine. In *2019 2nd International Conference on Computer Applications & Information Security (ICCAIS)* (pp. 1-6). IEEE. 10.1109/CAIS.2019.8769557

Yeratziotis, G., & Van Greunen, D. (2013). *Making ICT accessible for the deaf. In 2013 IST-Africa Conference & Exhibition*. IEEE.

Yuan, L., & Dennis, A. R. (2019). Acting like humans? Anthropomorphism and consumer's willingness to pay in electronic commerce. *Journal of Management Information Systems*, *36*(2), 450–477. doi:10.1080/07421222.2019.1598691

Yu, B., Ndumu, A., Mon, L. M., & Fan, Z. (2018). E-inclusion or digital divide: An integrated model of digital inequality. *The Journal of Documentation*, *74*(3), 552–574. doi:10.1108/JD-10-2017-0148

Yu, C. E., & Ngan, H. F. B. (2019). The power of head tilts: Gender and cultural differences of perceived human vs human-like robot smile in service. *Tourism Review*, *74*(3), 428–442. doi:10.1108/TR-07-2018-0097

Zacharia, J. M. (2013). *Integrated Disease Surveillance and Response Systems in Resource - Limited Settings* [Doctoral thesis]. University of Glasgow.

Zamfir, A.-M., Raccanello, D., Balbontín-Alvarado, R., Bezerra, D. da S., Burro, R., Cheraghi, M., Dobrowolska, B., Fagbamigbe, A. F., Faris, M. E., França, T., González-Fernández, B., Hall, R., Inasius, F., Kar, S. K., Keržič, D., Lazányi, K., Lazăr, F., Machin-Mastromatteo, J. D., Marôco, J., ... Aristovnik, A. (2022). Higher education students' achievement emotions and their antecedents in e-learning amid COVID-19 pandemic: A multi-country survey. *Learning and Instruction*, *80*(May), 101629. doi:10.1016/j.learninstruc.2022.101629 PMID:35578734

Zandi, M., Koropeckyj, S., Singh, V., & Matsiras, P. (2016). *The Impact of Electronic Payments on Economic Growth*. Academic Press.

Zech, H. (2021). *Liability for AI: Public policy considerations*. ERA Forum.

Zhao, J., Liu, D., & Huang, R. (2023). A Review of Climate-Smart Agriculture: Recent Advancements, Challenges, and Future Directions. *Sustainability (Basel)*, *15*(4), 3404. doi:10.3390u15043404

Zheng, X., Mukkamala, R. R., Vatrapu, R., & Ordieres-Mere, J. (2018). *Blockchain-based personal health data sharing system using cloud storage*. Paper presented at the 2018 IEEE 20th International Conference on e-Health Networking, Applications and Services (Healthcom). 10.1109/HealthCom.2018.8531125

Zhou, Z.-H. (2021). *Machine learning*. Springer Nature. doi:10.1007/978-981-15-1967-3

Zhuang, Y., Sheets, L. R., Chen, Y.-W., Shae, Z.-Y., Tsai, J. J., & Shyu, C.-R. (2020). A patient-centric health information exchange framework using blockchain technology. *IEEE Journal of Biomedical and Health Informatics*, *24*(8), 2169–2176. doi:10.1109/JBHI.2020.2993072 PMID:32396110

Zoumenou, V., Sigman-Grant, M., Coleman, G., Malekian, F., Zee, J. M. K., Fountain, B. J., & Marsh, A. (2015). Identifying Best Practices for an Interactive Webinar. *Journal of Family and Consumer Sciences*, *107*(2), 62–69.

About the Contributors

Fredrick Japhet Mtenzi's research interests include designing secure mobile micropayment transactions in low-end mobile devices, design of robust protocols for gathering online evidence and investigations, cyber security, security auditing, techniques for improving predictive protection in cyber security, and security metrics development. Recently the editor has been working on developing de-identification strategies which will increase the utility and privacy of sensitive information in the era of big data. Specifically, these de-identification strategies are used in increasing the sharing of electronic healthcare records.

George S. Oreku is a highly skilled Information Technology professional, with more than 14 years of experience in Research, Information Communication Technology, Information Security and IT Consultancies. Knowledge in development of culturally sensitive educational models (South Africa, Finland, China and Tanzania), able to function optimally in multilingual and its integrations to R&D. Highly motivated skilled trainer and researcher in computer science, cyber security, cyber power and national security, the editor possesses specialised knowledge in eCommerce and DBMS solutions and have experience across the full system development lifecycle in particular banking systems.

Dennis M. Lupiana is a researcher, consultant and a lecturer at the Institute of Finance Management (IFM), Tanzania with experience of over 16 years in ICT. He taught in the Dublin Institute of Technology and the Griffith College in Dublin, Ireland for over four years. He is very familiar with the ICT landscape of Tanzania. He has led and completed many consulting assignments in areas such as assessment of ICT infrastructures, software development, IT governance and digital marketing in the country. His research interests include Smart system and their applications, digital payments and digital capacity building.

* * *

Oluwabunmi Bakare is an Information Professional/Researcher in the Department of Information Management, Faculty of Communication & Information Sciences, Lead City University. Her research interest covers emerging technologies, digital & virtual libraries, information use and user communities, bullying and mobile bullying, etc. She is passionate about emphasizing the significant roles of Librarians in solving different societal issues with the arsenal of information at their disposal. She is a fellow of the Council for the Development of Social Science Research in Africa and a Queen Elizabeth Scholar in the Advanced Scholars West Africa (QES-AS-WA) program, Carleton University, Canada.

Ranjan Kumar, with 12 years of expertise in software development and management, is a Vice President in Digital Banking at Siam Commercial Bank Thailand. Ranjan holds 2 master's degrees in Computer science and Business Administration. Currently, he is a Ph.D. candidate at the School of Management, Asian Institute of Technology, Thailand and doing research in the field of Business Analytics and firm performance. He likes to read books and listen to Indian music and ghazals in his free time.

Glory C. Malamsha is a researcher at Nelson Mandela African Institution of Science and Technology (NM-AIST). She received a bachelor degree of Science in Business Information and Communication Technology at Moshi Co-operative University (MoCU) in 2020 in Kilimanjaro, Tanzania. She is interested in data mining specifically using unsupervised machine learning techniques and realising new patterns in datasets. Her current research project is on "Mobile Based Recommender System for Smallholder Dairy Farmers to Increase their Production in Tanzania". Her goal is to become an international data scientist and participate in developing new ideas world-wide using data mining techniques and other technologies.

Bossi A. Masamila is an Information Technology professional with over a decade of experience in higher education. During the past 15 years, he has been responsible for network operations at the Institute of Finance Management (IFM). He received his B.Sc & MSc in Electrical Engineering from The University of Dar es Salaam in Tanzania in 1998 and 2002 and his MSc in Computing (IT) from Dublin Institute of Technology (DIT) in 2008. He has been a faculty member since 2003 and has taught courses: Data Communications, Computer Networking, Computer Network Security, Computer Network Design, Network Management Systems, Information System Management, and Research Methodologies. His main research interests include Cyber Security, Payment Technologies, and Recommender Systems. He is also a member of the Engineering Registration Board (ERB), Institute of Engineers Tanzania (IET), IEEE and a Member of the Society for Digital Informatics and Wireless Communications (SIDWC). Outside of academia, he has acted as a consultant for private and public sectors. He has achieved several certifications from Cisco and CompTIA.

Fatuma Mavura is a young researcher at The Nelson Mandela African Institution of Science and Technology (NM-AIST). Her concentration is on enhancing the outputs of small-scale farming as part of the advancement of agriculture. With research titled "Mobile-based Peer-to-peer Learning Prototype for Smallholder Dairy Producers," she is currently focusing on increasing milk yields for smallholder dairy farmers. This research implements machine learning output for automatic allocation of smallholder dairy farmers into the pre-identified production Clusters.

Cosmas Mnyanyi is a Senior Lecturer in Special and Inclusive Education in the Department of Psychology and Special Education in the Faculty of Education at the Open University of Tanzania. His research interest is on ICT Skills Training for persons with disabilities, digital inclusion, inclusive education, action research, inclusive vocational education training, special needs education, distance learning and access to lifelong learning to persons with disabilities.

Richard W. Mnyawi is a graduate from the Nelson Mandela African Institution of Science and Technology (NM-AIST) and works at the Mwenge Catholic University as an Assistant Lecturer. He received his master's degree in Wireless and Mobile Computing in 2022, Postgraduate Diploma in Computing in 2013, Advanced Diploma in Information Technology in 2010, and Diploma in Education (Chemistry and

Biology) in 2005. His research interest is on information system security and blockchain technology as one of the disruptive technologies. "Blockchain based data storage architecture" is one of his research work output in application of blockchain technology.

Ummul-khair Mustafa is a PhD student in health and biomedical sciences at Nelson Mandela African Institution of Science and Technology (NM-AIST) -Arusha, Tanzania. Also, Ms. Ummul-khair is Assistant lecturer in the department of biological sciences at Dar es salaam University College of Education (DUCE)-Tanzania. Her research interest are: parasitology, medical entomology, arboviral diseases and digital health.

Lilian C. Mutalemwa is a Telecoms Engineer and Lecturer at the Open University of Tanzania. Her current research interests include 5G networks, 4th Industrial Revolution technologies, and the application of Internet of Things (IoT) smart systems. She is well published in International Journals, Conferences, and in the IEEE Xplore Digital Library. She has been involved in various ICT related projects funded by International organizations such as the Swedish International Development Cooperation Agency, Commonwealth of Learning in Canada, and the Brain Korea 21. Due to her participation in various projects, she has had opportunities to attend trainings, workshops, and conferences in various countries including Japan, Sweden, Switzerland, Malaysia, Taiwan, South Korea, Cambodia, Mauritius, Kenya, Benin, and Rwanda. She holds a BEng. degree in Telecommunications Engineering from the University of Essex, United Kingdom. MSc. degree in Mobile and Satellite Communications from the University of Surrey, United Kingdom. PhD. degree in Computer Engineering from Chosun University, South Korea.

Mdutshekelwa Ndlovu is an NRF-rated Professor of Mathematics Education at the University of Johannesburg. He was awarded several research grants to investigate mathematics pre-service teachers' beliefs about technology integration in the teaching of mathematics. During this time, he was appointed Vice-Dean, Research and Postgraduate Studies in the Faculty of Education, a post he still holds. Overall, he completed 17 years of teaching and educational leadership in basic education and has now completed 19 years of lecturing and management experience in higher education. He has accumulated more than 45 publications in mathematics and science education and graduated with 7 PhDs, 8 Masters and 18 Honors students. To date, he has examined 26 doctoral theses and 27 Masters dissertations and peer-reviewed over 150 pieces of work. He has also delivered several keynote addresses, invited lectures, and panel discussions.

Edephonce Nfuka is a lecturer and ICT/Computer Science expert mainly in area of Systems analysis, design, monitoring and evaluation; IT governance; e-Government; and e-Learning in which over 15 years he has acquired ODeL based teaching experience, developed and supervised a number of related projects, and researched and published in conferences, journals and books outlets. Academically Dr. Nfuka has a PhD in Computer and systems science from Stockholm University, Master Degree in Software Engineering from Universitat Polytecnic de Catalunya in Barcelona and a Bachelor degree in Automatic Control and Computer Engineering (BSc) from CUJAE in Havana. Additionally he has a Diploma in management and Leadership from Damelin School of management in Cape Town & e-learning related short training in USA, Sweden and Tanzania. Till recently Dr Nfuka was a Director, Institute of educational and management Technologies at the Open University of Tanzania (OUT). He is now a coordinator of UNESCO Chair activities in Africa on Teacher Education and Curriculum at OUT and also a coordinator of EPICA project.

Devotha G. Nyambo is a researcher and lecturer at the Nelson Mandela African Institution of Science and Technology, Tanzania. Her research focus has been on Artificial Intelligence (AI) and modelling of agricultural systems, especially the livestock systems. She leads the Artificial Intelligence and Complexity Sciences research group at the institution, and also lead of the Agriculture and Environmental Conservation group at the Africa's Anglophone Artificial Intelligence for Development (AI4D) Multidisciplinary Research Lab. Her current project is on Leveraging Multi-Agent Models for Learning Recommendations and Improvement of Farmer-to-Farmer Interactions in Small Scale Dairy. Her research interests are extended to the application of AI in health and education sectors.

Nosakhare Okuonghae is the Head of Law Library, Glorious Vision University, Ogwa, Edo State, Nigeria. He holds a Bachelor of Laws (LL.B) degree from University of Benin, a Qualifying Certificate from the Council of Legal Education and has in view a Master degree in Library and Information Science (MLIS) from Lead City University, Ibadan. He is a Legal Information Professional, a Blogger, and a Researcher. He is well published in international and local Journals. Nosakhare Okuonghae is a member of different professional bodies including the Nigerian Bar Association; British Project Management Association and the Nigerian Library Association. He is also a volunteer content contributor for Wikimedia Foundation projects particularly Wikipedia. In 2022, he was ranked among the top 10 Wikipedia Editor during the 3rd edition of African Library Week.

Jumoke I. Oladele holds a permanent teaching position with the University of Ilorin, Nigeria, and is on her Postdoctoral research fellowship with the University of Johannesburg, South Africa. Her specialization is in educational evaluation and psychometrics. Her research interests are in item response theory-based psychometrics in educational assessments with computer adaptive testing, applicable to a wide range of subjects focusing on improving standardized assessment in Africa, educational evaluation, and innovation studies. So far, her research has generated a good number of publications in national/international journals. She is the initiator of the Association of Computer Adaptive Testing in Africa, of which she is a member and serves as the research/membership director. She is also a member of other learned societies such as the Teacher's Registration Council of Nigeria, the Association of Educational Researchers and Evaluators of Nigeria, and the International Association for Computerized Adaptive Testing. For her, transdisciplinarity is an evolving area of research interest driven by the need for a more holistic view of problem-solving as applicable to pedagogical and assessment practices in higher education.

Ece Özer Çizer is a Ph.D. candidate and Research Assistant at the Department of Business Administration, Faculty of Economics and Administrative Sciences, Yildiz Technical University. Her research interests are digital marketing and sharing economy.

Elingarami Sauli holds a PhD from Southeast University (China) and a Master's Degree in Biomedicine from Linkoping University (Sweden). He also holds a Bachelor Degree in Medicine from St. Petersburg State Pavlov Medical University (Russia). Dr. Sauli is currently working at NM-AIST as a Senior Lecturer at School of Life Science and Bioengineering, teaching Non-Communicable Diseases and Special topics in Global Health. He also worked as Acting Head of Global Health and Biomedical

Sciences' Department at school of Life Science and Bioengineering. He is also a member of Medical Council of Tanganyika. Dr. Sauli's research interest is mainly on molecular epidemiology of cancer and other NCDs, focusing also on biomarker diagnostics. Dr. Sauli has authored and co-authored more than 40 articles in the peer reviewed International Journals, as can be accessed in the herein.

Maheshwor Shrestha, with eight years of expertise in Data Analytics and Business Intelligence, is a Data Architect in Analytics Team at Siam Makro Public Company Limited Thailand. Maheshwor holds a master's degrees in Business Administration with specialization in Digital Transformation. Currently, he is a Ph.D. candidate at the School of Management, Asian Institute of Technology, Thailand and doing research in the field of Digital Transformation. He likes to read books and listen to Indian music and ghazals in his free time.

Index

Recommended Reference Books

IGI Global's reference books are available in three unique pricing formats: Print Only, E-Book Only, or Print + E-Book.

Order direct through IGI Global's Online Bookstore at **www.igi-global.com** or through your preferred provider.

ISBN: 9781799846796
EISBN: 9781799846802
© 2022; 271 pp.
List Price: US$ **215**

ISBN: 9781799876144
EISBN: 9781799876168
© 2022; 167 pp.
List Price: US$ **195**

ISBN: 9781668450970
EISBN: 9781668450987
© 2023; 472 pp.
List Price: US$ **245**

ISBN: 9781668446201
EISBN: 9781668446225
© 2022; 327 pp.
List Price: US$ **215**

ISBN: 9781799885320
EISBN: 9781799885344
© 2022; 284 pp.
List Price: US$ **215**

ISBN: 9781668436745
EISBN: 9781668436752
© 2022; 696 pp.
List Price: US$ **325**

Do you want to stay current on the latest research trends, product announcements, news, and special offers?
Join IGI Global's mailing list to receive customized recommendations, exclusive discounts, and more.
Sign up at: **www.igi-global.com/newsletters.**

Publisher of Timely, Peer-Reviewed Inclusive Research Since 1988

IGI Global
PUBLISHER of TIMELY KNOWLEDGE

www.igi-global.com Sign up at www.igi-global.com/newsletters facebook.com/igiglobal twitter.com/igiglobal linkedin.com/igiglobal

www.ingramcontent.com/pod-product-compliance
Lightning Source LLC
LaVergne TN
LVHW062154300926
849161LV00010B/2660